FUNDAMENTALS OF
MATH

for Christian Schools®

FUNDAMENTALS OF MATH

for Christian Schools®

Hal C. Oberholzer II

Bob Jones University Press
Greenville, South Carolina 29614

NOTE:
The fact that materials produced by other publishers are referred to in this volume does not constitute an endorsement by Bob Jones University Press of the content or theological position of materials produced by such publishers. The position of Bob Jones University Press, and the University itself, is well known. Any references and ancillary materials are listed as an aid to the student or the teacher and in an attempt to maintain the accepted academic standards of the publishing industry.

FUNDAMENTALS OF MATH for Christian Schools®

Hal C. Oberholzer II, M.A.

Produced in cooperation with the Bob Jones University Department of Mathematics of the College of Arts and Science, and Bob Jones Academy.

for Christian Schools is a registered trademark of Bob Jones University Press.

ISBN 0-89084-842-4

15   14   13   12   11   10   9   8   7   6   5   4   3   2   1

1 CHAPTER

2 CHAPTER

3 CHAPTER

Adding and Subtracting Decimals 69

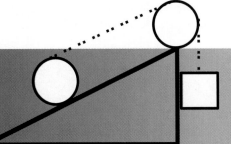

4 CHAPTER

Multiplying and Dividing Decimals 95

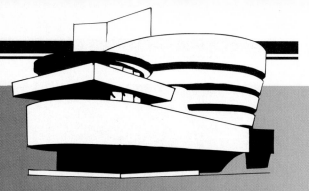

5 CHAPTER

12

6 CHAPTER

11

7 CHAPTER

8 CHAPTER

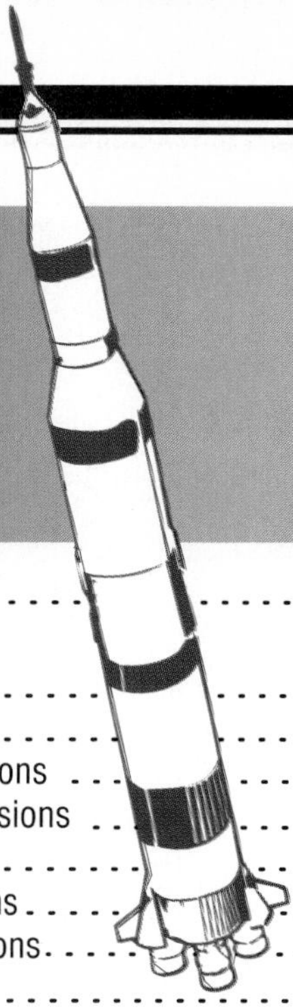

9 CHAPTER

11

10 CHAPTER

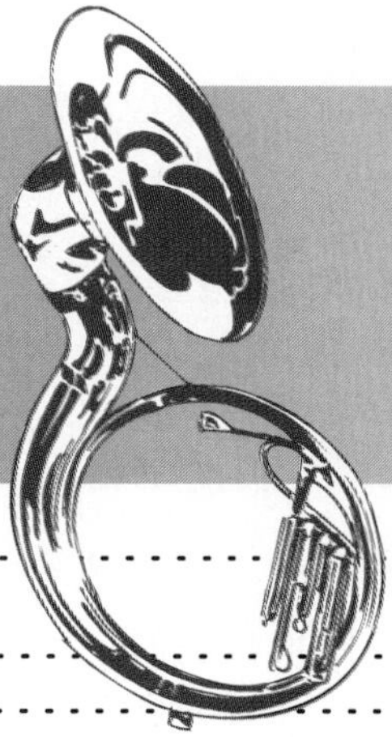

9

11 CHAPTER

12 CHAPTER

13 CHAPTER

14 CHAPTER

15 CHAPTER

CHARLES LINDBERGH
AVIATION/NAVIGATION

From an early age, Charles Lindbergh displayed an amazing mechanical ability. Growing up on the family farm in Minnesota, he was constantly fiddling with mechanical objects—taking things apart and putting them back together again. Despite his mechanical brilliance, Charles struggled in school. He treated his academic studies with indifference, barely putting forth enough effort to pass. Although he was accepted into the mechanical engineering program at the University of Wisconsin, poor grades during his sophomore year, including an *F* in math, forced him to drop out.

It was then that Charles convinced his parents to allow him to enroll in a flight school in Lincoln, Nebraska. Although Charles was interested in flying during his high school years, his parents viewed aviation as a dangerous and second-rate profession. For Charles, flying symbolized freedom and adventure. In the spring of 1923, he completed his first solo flight in a reconditioned World War I plane which he had purchased just minutes before taking off.

In 1924 Charles joined the army as a cadet in one of the military's flying schools. During his year at Brooks Field in San Antonio, Texas, Charles perfected his flying technique. Though struggling once again in the classroom, Charles was determined to succeed. If he wanted to become a world-class pilot, he could no longer be apathetic about his studies. In order to navigate his plane, he needed to master the mathematical concepts which had frustrated him so in college. Determined to succeed, he graduated number one in his class of 104 cadets.

After graduating in 1925, Charles helped to establish the first airmail route between St. Louis and Chicago. It was during this time that he first heard of the Ortieg Prize, an offer of $25,000 to the first pilot to fly nonstop from New York to Paris. Intrigued by this contest, Charles secured the backing of several St. Louis businessmen and threw himself into the preparations for the flight. He designed his plane, the *Spirit of St. Louis,* and mapped out his route. On May 20, 1927, Charles's dream came true as he was greeted with a hero's welcome upon landing in Paris. The young airmail pilot had become an international celebrity overnight.

1902-1974

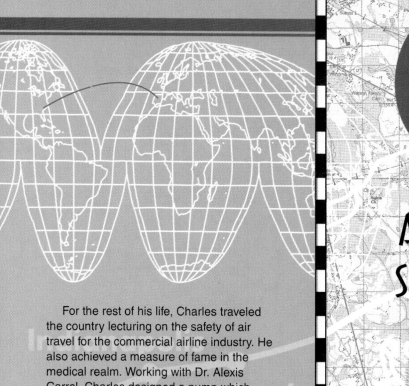

For the rest of his life, Charles traveled the country lecturing on the safety of air travel for the commercial airline industry. He also achieved a measure of fame in the medical realm. Working with Dr. Alexis Carrel, Charles designed a pump which enabled organs designated for transplant to live longer outside of the human body. When the Lindbergh pump became operational after five years of fine tuning, it revolutionized the process of organ transplants. In fact, a modified version of this pump is still in use today, serving as a lasting tribute to a man whose perseverance and courage helped him to overcome a lifetime of obstacles.

1 CHAPTER

ADDING AND SUBTRACTING WHOLE NUMBERS

1.1 PLACE VALUE

Our decimal numeration system is based upon *place value.* The value of each digit in a numeral depends upon its place in the numeral. Commas are used to separate the digits into groups of three called *periods.*

A place value chart is helpful for reading a number written in *standard form.* Study the example below.

	Billions			Millions			Thousands			Ones		
Period names												
Place value names	Hundreds	Tens	Ones	Hundreds	Tens	Ones	Hundreds	Tens	Ones	Hundreds	Tens	Ones
Numeral			4,	2	0	5,	0	0	9,	3	6	0

Standard form: 4,205,009,360

Word name: four billion, two hundred five million, nine thousand, three hundred sixty

You can write 4,205,009,360 in *expanded form* to show the value of each digit.

Long form: $(4 \times 1{,}000{,}000{,}000) + (2 \times 100{,}000{,}000) + (5 \times 1{,}000{,}000) + (9 \times 1{,}000) + (3 \times 100) + (6 \times 10)$

Short form: $4{,}000{,}000{,}000 + 200{,}000{,}000 + 5{,}000{,}000 + 9{,}000 + 300 + 60$

Additional Example

Write the word name for 18,700,030; then write the number in short expanded form.

Word name: eighteen million, seven hundred thousand, thirty

Short form: $18{,}000{,}000 + 700{,}000 + 30$

☑SKILL CHECK

Read each number. Write the value of the digit 5; then write the number in short expanded form.

1. 740,500   2. 5,020,000   3. 13,004,500,020

Exercises

Write the value of the underlined digit.

1. 6,4<u>7</u>5   2. 38,<u>2</u>92   3. 4<u>9</u>2,321

4. <u>8</u>,927,000   5. <u>6</u>98,275   6. <u>7</u>5,462,950

For the number 8,236,547,129, write the digit that is in the named place.

7. thousands   8. hundreds   9. ten thousands

10. millions   11. hundred thousands   12. billions

Write in standard form.

13. two thousand, three hundred sixty-five
14. seven hundred forty thousand, fifty-seven
15. thirteen thousand, thirteen
16. fifty-one million, two thousand, thirty
17. six million, fifty-five thousand, eight hundred seventy-two
18. two billion, seventy million, eight thousand

Write in short expanded form.

19. 369   20. 2,670

21. 804,000   22. 2,700,050

Write in standard form.

23. $5,000 + 400 + 60 + 8$ 24. $60,000 + 300 + 7$

25. $12,000,000 + 30,000 + 600$ 26. $400,000 + 7,000 + 200 + 9$

27. $9,000,000 + 30 + 5,000 + 70,000$ 28. $200 + 500,000 + 70,000 + 6$

Adding and Subtracting Whole Numbers

Application

29. The attendance at Bible Conference last year totaled thirty-two thousand, eighty-five people. Write this number in standard form.

30. The offering at Bible Conference last year was $209,073. Write this number in short expanded form.

1.2 Comparing and Ordering Whole Numbers

On two occasions in the Old Testament, God directed that a census be taken of every male Israelite of twenty years old and upward.

Which reference lists the greater number of men?

To compare two whole numbers, follow the steps below.

Census Figures in the Old Testament	
Reference	Number of Men
Exodus 38:26	603,550
Numbers 26:51	601,730

STEP 1	STEP 2	STEP 3
Start at the left and compare digits of the same place value.	Find the first place value where the digits are different.	The numbers compare the same way that these digits compare.
603,550	603,550	3 > 1
601,730	601,730	603,550 > 601,730

Exodus 38:26 lists the greater number of men, since 603,550 > 601,730.

In Numbers chapter 1, Moses numbered the tribes in the wilderness of Sinai. List the numbers of the tribes below in order from least to greatest. Follow the steps below.

Ordering Numbers
1. Identify the least and greatest numbers.
2. Compare the remaining numbers.

Reuben: 46,500   ◄ greatest

Asher: 41,500

Ephraim: 40,500   ◄ least

Gad: 45,650

The numbers in order are 40,500; 41,500; 45,650; and 46,500.

☑ SKILL CHECK

Compare. Write >, <, or = for each ☐.

1. 5,293 ☐ 5,239

2. 75,010 ☐ 75,100

3. 674,821 ☐ 67,483

List in order from least to greatest.

4. 72,030; 72,300; 73,020; 73,002

5. 8,742; 8,472; 8,274; 8,724

Adding and Subtracting Whole Numbers

Exercises

Compare. Write >, <, or = for each ☐.

1. 4,375 ☐ 4,357
2. 5,893 ☐ 53,981
3. 72,365 ☐ 72,365

4. 35,758 ☐ 35,746
5. 93,406 ☐ 94,703
6. 36,973 ☐ 241,835

7. 437,126 ☐ 437,216
8. 175,038 ☐ 175,029
9. 943,001 ☐ 942,010

10. 4,238,009 ☐ 4,238,090
11. 84,007,135 ☐ 8,407,135

12. 83,147,643 ☐ 83,147,643
13. 500,349,172 ☐ 500,439,172

List in order from least to greatest.

14. 807; 780; 870
15. 1,987; 1,978; 1,897; 1,879

16. 26,517; 25,671; 26,751; 26,157
17. 432,821; 423,821; 432,218; 423,218

List in order from greatest to least.

18. 237; 273; 327
19. 2,053; 2,530; 2,350; 2,035

20. 83,475; 84,375; 83,745; 84,753
21. 500,050; 505,000; 500,500; 500,005

Application

Use the data in the table below to answer the questions.

Mountains in Palestine	
Name	Height in Feet
Mt. Meron	3,963
Mt. Tabor	1,929
Mt. Gilboa	1,640
Mt. Ebal	3,083

22. Which mountain is the highest?

23. Which mountain is higher, Mt. Tabor or Mt. Ebal?

24. Which mountain is lower than Mt. Tabor?

25. List the heights of the mountains in order from least to greatest.

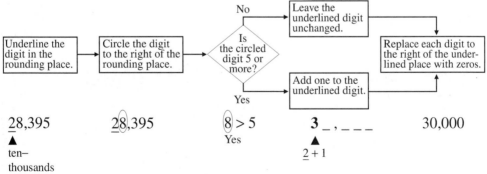

1.3 Rounding Whole Numbers

Dr. Keesee is raising money for a special project to send Bibles and tracts to Poland. He calculated the cost of the literature to be $28,395. To the nearest ten thousand dollars, how much money does he need to raise?

To round whole numbers, you can follow the steps in this flowchart.

```
                                    No    ┌─────────────────┐
                                ┌────────▶│ Leave the       │
                                │         │ underlined digit│──────┐
┌────────────┐  ┌────────────┐  ◇         │ unchanged.      │      ▼
│ Underline  │  │ Circle the │ Is         └─────────────────┘ ┌──────────────┐
│ the digit  │─▶│ digit to   │ the circled                    │ Replace each │
│ in the     │  │ right of   │ digit 5 or                     │ digit to the │
│ rounding   │  │ the        │ more?                          │ right of the │
│ place.     │  │ rounding   │  │                             │ underlined   │
└────────────┘  │ place.     │  │         ┌─────────────────┐ │ place with   │
                └────────────┘  ▼  Yes    │ Add one to the  │ │ zeros.       │
                                └────────▶│ underlined digit│─┘              
                                          └─────────────────┘ └──────────────┘
```

28,395   2⑧,395   ⑧ > 5   **3** _ , _ _ _   30,000
▲   Yes   ▲
ten–   2 + 1
thousands

Dr. Keesee will need to raise about $30,000.

Adding and Subtracting Whole Numbers

Additional Examples

Round to the specified place.

a. Round 738 to the nearest hundred. 738 rounds to 700.
b. Round 29,643 to the nearest thousand. 29,643 rounds to 30,000.
c. Round 2,075,328 to the nearest hundred thousand. 2,075,328 rounds to 2,100,000.
d. Round 47,286,935 to the nearest million. 47,286,935 rounds to 47,000,000.

☑ **SKILL CHECK**

Round each number to the specified place.

1. 408,219 (nearest ten thousand)   2. 78,419 (nearest thousand)

Round 7,506,481 to the specified place.

3. nearest thousand   4. nearest hundred thousand

Exercises

Round to the nearest hundred.

1. 827   2. 3,651   3. 42,083   4. 137,745

Round to the nearest thousand.

5. 6,842   6. 30,298   7. 385,620   8. 3,422,087

Round to the nearest ten thousand.

9. 54,732   10. 835,200   11. 207,689   12. 1,761,008

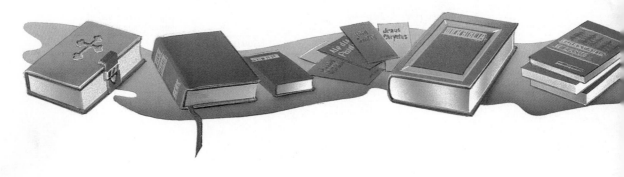

Round to the nearest hundred thousand.

13. 654,831   **14.** 3,457,285   **15.** 908,687   **16.** 4,981,313

Round to the nearest million.

17. 1,723,105   **18.** 3,284,614   **19.** 19,499,890   **20.** 507,378

Write the rounding place for each. Example: 94 → 90; ten.

21. 36 → 40   **22.** 365 → 370

23. 681 → 700   **24.** 3,492 → 3,500

25. 18,242 → 18,000   **26.** 763,234 → 800,000

Find the least and greatest possible original number.

	Rounding Place	Rounded Number	Least Number	Greatest Number
	Hundreds	400	350	449
27.	Thousands	2,000		
28.	Hundred Thousands	800,000		

Application

29. A missionary has 20,914 Bibles ready for shipment to Poland. What is the number of Bibles rounded to the nearest thousand?

30. The same missionary also has 157,545 tracts to be included in this shipment. When rounded to the nearest hundred, is the number of tracts 158,000 or 157,500?

Adding and Subtracting Whole Numbers

1.4 Properties of Addition

Study the properties of addition listed below. Notice that when parentheses are used, the operation inside the parentheses is done first.

Commutative Property	
Changing the order of the addends does not change the sum. $a + b = b + a$	Example: $4 + 7 = 7 + 4$ $11 = 11$
Associative Property	
Changing the grouping of the addends does not change the sum. $(a + b) + c = a + (b + c)$	Example: $(5 + 4) + 6 = 5 + (4 + 6)$ $9 + 6 = 5 + 10$ $15 = 15$
Identity Property	
The sum of any number and zero is that number. $a + 0 = a$ and $0 + a = a$	Example: $7 + 0 = 7$ and $0 + 7 = 7$

To find sums mentally, you can use the properties of addition to group addends that add to multiples of 10.

$$(18 + 3) + 12 = 12 + (18 + 3) \quad \blacktriangleleft \text{Commutative Property}$$
$$= (12 + 18) + 3 \quad \blacktriangleleft \text{Associative Property}$$
$$= 30 + 3$$
$$= 33$$

Additional Example

Find the sum mentally. Use the properties of addition.

$$17 + 31 + 23 + 19 = (17 + 23) + (31 + 19) \quad \blacktriangleleft \text{Rearrange and reorder}$$
$$= 40 + 50 \qquad \qquad \text{the addends.}$$
$$= 90$$

☑SKILL CHECK

Find each missing addend. Name the property illustrated.

1. $(58 + 23) + 17 = 58 + (23 + \square)$
2. $37 + 0 = \square$
3. $14 + 29 = 29 + \square$
4. $23 + (31 + 17) = (23 + \square) + 31$

Exercises

Name the property illustrated.

1. $4 + 9 = 9 + 4$
2. $(6 + 2) + 8 = 6 + (2 + 8)$
3. $13 + 0 = 13$
4. $2 + (7 + 8) = 2 + (8 + 7)$
5. $7 + (13 + 9) = (7 + 13) + 9$
6. $13 + (9 + 7) = (13 + 7) + 9$

Find each missing addend.

7. $34 + (26 + 18) = (34 + \square) + 18$
8. $23 + 15 = 15 + \square$
9. $28 + (\square + 12) = 28 + (12 + 9)$
10. $\square + 0 = 18$
11. $(37 + 11) + 13 = \square + (37 + 13)$
12. $(17 + 8) + \square = 4 + (17 + 8)$

Find the sum mentally. Use the properties of addition.

13. $41 + 10 + 9$ **14.** $0 + 37 + 8$ **15.** $23 + 14 + 7$

16. $4 + 12 + 3 + 8$ **17.** $3 + 14 + 27 + 6$ **18.** $15 + 29 + 11 + 10$

19. $12 + 6 + 18 + 34$ **20.** $17 + 20 + 13 + 7$ **21.** $16 + 23 + 17 + 14$

22. $164 + 20 + 6$ **23.** $123 + 41 + 7$ **24.** $112 + 18 + 53$

Application

Solve. Use mental math.

25. In four football games, Andrew gained 75 yd., 90 yd., 125 yd., and 60 yd. What is the total gain for the four games?

1.5 Estimating Sums and Differences

The Pacific, Atlantic, Indian, and Arctic Oceans are the four major bodies of water recognized by geographers and mapmakers.

Oceans	Area (mi.^{2})	Average Depth (ft.)
Pacific	64,186,300	12,925
Atlantic	33,420,000	11,730
Indian	28,350,500	12,598
Arctic	5,105,700	3,407

Estimate the combined area of the Atlantic and Indian Oceans.

Atlantic Ocean: 33,420,000 mi.^{2}

Indian Ocean: 28,350,500 mi.^{2}

To estimate a sum or difference, follow these steps.

Estimating Sums and Differences
1. Round each number to the greatest place of the largest number.
2. Add or subtract.

1. Round each number to the nearest ten million.

$$33,420,000 \xrightarrow{\text{rounds to}} 30,000,000$$
$$+ 28,350,000 \xrightarrow{\text{rounds to}} 30,000,000$$

2. Add.

$$\begin{array}{r} 30,000,000 \\ + 30,000,000 \\ \hline 60,000,000 \end{array}$$

The combined area of the Atlantic and Indian Oceans is about 60,000,000 mi.^{2}.

To obtain a more accurate estimate, you round each number to the next place on the right. Consider the following example.

Adding and Subtracting Whole Numbers

Additional Example

Estimate 684,517 − 49,217.

Estimate:
Round each number to the
nearest hundred thousand.

$$700,000$$
$$- \quad\quad 0$$
$$700,000$$

This estimate is not meaningful.

More accurate estimate:
Round each number to the
nearest ten thousand.

$$680,000$$
$$- \quad 50,000$$
$$630,000$$

This estimate is more accurate.

☑SKILL CHECK

Estimate each sum or difference.

1.	389	2.	9,326	3.	$7,629	4.	5,243
	+ 732		− 2,857		+ 2,858		− 1,682

Find the estimate and a more accurate estimate.

5. $16,285 + 5,647$

6. $6,815 - 495$

7. $2,663 + 3,496 + 8,069$

8. $18,426 - 15,839$

The F-4 Phantom, a mainstay of the Vietnam War, holds the record for the longest production run of any modern military aircraft. It is one of the most popular fighters ever built and has served in air forces all over the world.

Although the A-10 Thunderbolt, a U.S. Air Force ground attack aircraft, definitely belongs to the jet age, many aspects of its design, such as the straight wing and twin tails, hark back to Lindbergh's time.

Exercises

Estimate each sum or difference by rounding.

1. $933 + 576$

2. $1,387 + 2,635$

3. $316 + 498 + 225$

4. $738 - 285$

5. $8,225 - 1,895$

6. $38,696 - 17,787$

7. $83,675 + 36,218$

8. $74,257 + 6,158$

9. $83,209 + 27,275 + 23,692$

10. $92,358 - 19,259$

11. $389,612 - 234,623$

12. $578,258 - 43,915$

Find the estimate and a more accurate estimate.

13. $9,727 + 3,562$

14. $269,315 + 84,795$

15. $97,108 + 13,565$

16. $69,316 - 48,307$

Adding and Subtracting Whole Numbers

17. $198,813 - 142,724$ **18.** $142,752 - 75,398$

Choose the letter of the best estimate for each sum.

19. $36,279 + 13,593 + 29,601$ A. 40,000

20. $12,158 + 8,426 + 17,854$ B. 50,000

21. $22,738 + 15,574 + 3,448 + 27,238$ C. 60,000

22. $31,415 + 17,490 + 952 + 14,975$ D. 70,000

23. $8,796 + 14,292 + 19,415 + 11,987$ E. 80,000

Application

Solve. Use the table on page 13.

24. Round to get a more accurate estimate for how much less the average depth of the Arctic Ocean is than that of the Pacific Ocean.

25. Round to get a more accurate estimate for the combined area of the Atlantic, Indian, and Arctic Oceans.

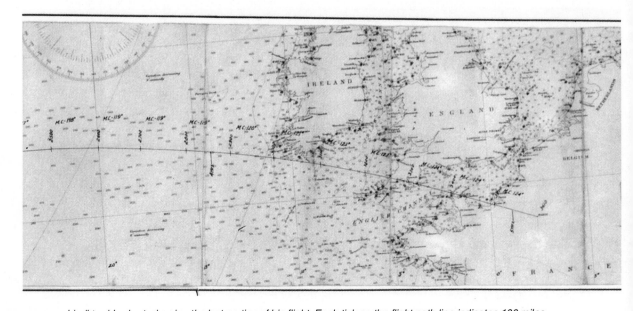

Lindbergh's chart, showing the last portion of his flight. Each tick on the flight path line indicates 100 miles.

1.6 Adding Whole Numbers

Aluminum Can Drive	
Week 1	1,425
Week 2	966
Week 3	1,703

Calvary Christian School conducted a three-week drive to collect aluminum cans for recycling. What is the total number of cans collected?

You add $1,425 + 966 + 1,703$ to find the total number of cans.

To add whole numbers, follow these steps. Regroup if necessary.

STEP 1	STEP 2	STEP 3	STEP 4
Add the ones.	Add the tens.	Add the hundreds.	Add the thousands.

$$\begin{array}{r} 1 \\ 1,425 \\ 966 \\ +1,703 \\ \hline 4 \end{array} \qquad \begin{array}{r} 1 \\ 1,425 \\ 966 \\ +1,703 \\ \hline 94 \end{array} \qquad \begin{array}{r} 2 \\ 1,425 \\ 966 \\ +1,703 \\ \hline 094 \end{array} \qquad \begin{array}{r} 2 \\ 1,425 \\ 966 \\ +1,703 \\ \hline 4,094 \end{array}$$

Calvary Christian School collected 4,094 cans in all.

You can estimate to check whether the answer is reasonable.

$$\begin{array}{r} 1,425 \longrightarrow 1,000 \\ 966 \longrightarrow 1,000 \\ +1,703 \longrightarrow 2,000 \\ \hline 4,000 \end{array}$$

The answer is reasonable.

You can also add in reverse order to check the answer.

$$\begin{array}{r} 1,425 \quad 1,703 \\ 966 \quad 966 \\ +1,703 \quad 1,425 \\ \hline 4,094 \end{array}$$

The answer is correct.

Additional Examples

Add.

a.
```
   2,541
 + 4,308
   6,849
```

b.
```
    1 2
   2,936
     627
 + 3,408
   6,971
```

c.
```
  1 11   1
  40,256,307
   1,489,502
 +   600,143
  42,345,952
```

☑ **SKILL CHECK**

Add.

1.
```
   2,865
 + 6,397
```

2.
```
   71,425
   92,806
 + 43,177
```

3.
```
   12,854
    7,602
 +    974
```

4.
```
  59,417,243
     285,402
 + 4,749,018
```

Exercises

Add.

1.
```
   43
 + 58
```

2.
```
   728
 + 463
```

3.
```
   2,107
 + 7,329
```

4.
```
   12,437
 + 78,496
```

5.
```
   4,325
   9,284
 + 2,976
```

6.
```
   10,743
   15,482
 + 16,915
```

7.
```
   22,536
    1,887
 + 33,975
```

8.
```
   98,382
    2,735
 +    641
```

9.
```
   287,503
   638,015
 + 759,102
```

10.
```
   326,291
     2,974
 +  75,598
```

11. 2,693,480
     5,178,302
   + 4,857,016

12. 63,786,530
        893,106
    + 9,524,283

Find the sums.

13. 358 + 237 + 649

14. 285 + 96 + 3,854

15. 8,250 + 7,446 + 3,890

16. 694 + 18,316 + 4,205

17. 2,973 + 56 + 37,468 + 784

18. 19 + 73,048 + 314 + 5,080

19. 1,733,642 + 18,082 + 43,605

20. 46,525 + 273,199 + 5,636,024

Find the missing addend.

21.   3,4 7 2
    + □,□□□
      5,9 7 6

22.   □,□□□
     + 9,8 5 4
      1 4,5 8 6

23.   7 4,9 3 8
    + □□,□□□
     1 0 5,5 9 2

24.   □□□,□□□
    + 3 2 8,7 2 6
      7 6 8,0 5 0

Application

25. Mrs. Smith's class collected 198 more cans than Mr. Robbins's class. Mr. Robbins's class collected 265 cans. What is the total number of cans collected by the 2 classes?

Adding and Subtracting Whole Numbers

1.7 Subtracting Whole Numbers

Mr. Johnson gave $3,857 in tithes and offerings to his church last year. This year he gave $5,349. What is the difference of these amounts?

To find the difference, you subtract $5,349 − $3,857. Study the following steps.

STEP 1	STEP 2	STEP 3	STEP 4
Subtract the ones.	Rename. Subtract the tens.	Rename. Subtract the hundreds.	Subtract the thousands.

	2 14	12 4 2 14	12 4 2 14
$5,349	$5,349	$5,349	$5,349
− 3,857	− 3,857	− 3,857	− 3,857
2	92	492	1,492

Mr. Johnson gave $1,492 more this year.

You can estimate to check whether the answer is reasonable.

$$5,349 \rightarrow 5,000$$
$$- 3,857 \rightarrow 4,000$$
$$\overline{\,1,000}$$

The answer is reasonable.

You can check subtraction by adding.

$$
\begin{array}{cc}
5,349 & 1,492 \\
- 3,857 & + 3,857 \\
\hline
1,492 & 5,349
\end{array}
$$

The answer is correct.

Additional Examples

Subtract.

a.
$$
\begin{array}{r}
9 \\
7\,10\,10 \\
8\,0\,0 \\
- 256 \\
\hline
544
\end{array}
$$

b.
$$
\begin{array}{r}
8\ 12\ 14 \\
9{,}3\,4\,5 \\
- 683 \\
\hline
8{,}662
\end{array}
$$

c.
$$
\begin{array}{r}
9 \quad 9 \\
6\,10\,10\ 3\,10\,13 \\
7\,0\,0{,}4\,0\,3 \\
- 278{,}167 \\
\hline
422{,}236
\end{array}
$$

✓SKILL CHECK

Subtract.

1. 8,259
  − 5,674

2. 700
  − 486

3. 5,083
  − 749

4. 300,504
  − 162,847

Exercises

Subtract.

1. 84
  − 39

2. 947
  − 685

3. 7,308
  − 2,519

4. 6,800
  − 3,457

5. 46,085
  − 1,790

6. 35,000
  − 12,627

7. 738,221
  − 419,325

8. 1,867,508
  − 1,591,427

9. 900 − 567

10. 7,005 − 4,829

11. 8,496 − 6,338

12. 37,205 − 19,804

13. 861,519 − 179,321

14. 4,000,000 − 832,971

Add or subtract. Perform the operations inside the parentheses first.

15. (736 − 565) + 189

16. 894 + (1,036 − 478)

17. 600 − (718 − 453)

18. 2,457 − (986 + 759)

19. (3,264 − 1,628) + 4,356

20. (61,432 − 38,617) − 15,674

Find the missing number.

21.   □,□□□
   − 2,5 9 3
   ‾‾‾‾‾‾‾‾
    1,2 0 5

22.   8 2,5 3 7
   − □□,□□□
   ‾‾‾‾‾‾‾‾
    3 4,5 7 9

23.   □□□,□□□
   − 2 5 8,1 7 3
   ‾‾‾‾‾‾‾‾‾‾
    3 4 1,8 2 7

Adding and Subtracting Whole Numbers

Application

24. The Johnsons' annual food expense is $4,386. Their expenses for debts, savings, and medical costs are $1,094, $1,973, and $731 respectively. How much more is their food expense than their combined expenses for debts, savings, and medical costs?

25. The Johnsons have $31,000 in net spendable income. Their total household expenses are $29,758. How much less are their annual expenses than their net spendable income?

1.8 Adding and Subtracting Units of Time

Consider the table which shows the flight schedules for two plane trips.

The time which passes between the departure and arrival of each flight is called the *elapsed time.*

To find the elapsed time for flight 748, you subtract the departure time from the arrival time.

Flight Number	Departure	Arrival
748	6:45 A.M.	11:10 A.M.
857	10:40 A.M.	4:45 P.M.

STEP 1	STEP 2	STEP 3
Write the problem in hours and minutes.	Rename 1 hour as 60 minutes.	Subtract the minutes and the hours.

STEP 1
11 h. 10 min.
− 6 h. 45 min.

STEP 2
10   70
1̸1̸ h. 1̸0 min.
− 6 h. 45 min.

STEP 3
10   70
1̸1̸ h. 1̸0 min.
− 6 h. 45 min.
4 h. 25 min.

The elapsed time for flight 748 is 4 hours and 25 minutes.

You can compute the elapsed time for flight 857 in 2 steps.

Step 1: Find the time from 10:40 A.M. to noon by subtracting.

$$\begin{array}{r} \overset{11}{\cancel{12}}\text{ h.} \quad \overset{60}{\cancel{0}}\text{ min.} \\ -\ 10\text{ h. }40\text{ min.} \\ \hline 1\text{ h. }20\text{ min.} \end{array}$$

◄ Rename 1h. as 60 min.

Step 2: The time from noon to 4:45 P.M. is 4 h. 45 min. Find the total elapsed time by adding.

$$\begin{array}{r} 1\text{ h. }20\text{ min.} \\ +\ 4\text{ h. }45\text{ min.} \\ \hline 5\text{ h. }65\text{ min.} = 6\text{ h. }5\text{ min.} \end{array}$$

◄ 65 min. = 1 h. 5 min.

The elapsed time for flight 857 is 6 hours and 5 minutes.

Additional Examples

a. Find the time that is 2 h. 35 min. after 5:45 A.M.

$$\begin{array}{r} 5\text{ h. }45\text{ min.} \\ +\ 2\text{ h. }35\text{ min.} \\ \hline 7\text{ h. }80\text{ min.} = 8\text{ h. }20\text{ min.} \end{array}$$

The time is 8:20 A.M.

b. Find the time that is 4 h. 40 min. before 9:00 P.M.

$$\begin{array}{r} \overset{8}{\cancel{9}}\text{ h.} \quad \overset{60}{\cancel{0}}\text{ min.} \\ -\ 4\text{ h. }40\text{ min.} \\ \hline 4\text{ h. }20\text{ min.} \end{array}$$

◄ 9 h. = 8 h. 60 min.

The time is 4:20 P.M.

In 1910, Louis Poulhan made a record flight to 4,600 feet, almost a mile into the air. Seventeen years later, Lindbergh flew as high as 10,500 feet on his historic flight.

This Ford Trimotor 3AT is a variant of the famous "Tin Lizzie," which was the first successful U.S. transport aircraft and one of the first all-metal aircraft.

Adding and Subtracting Whole Numbers

National Air and Space Museum, Smithsonian Institution, Photo No. A336

Charles Lindbergh, standing by the nose of his airplane, the Spirit of St. Louis.

☑**SKILL CHECK**

Add or subtract.

1.　2 h. 10 min.
　+ 4 h. 50 min.

2.　1 h. 40 min.
　+ 2 h. 55 min.

3.　5 h.
　− 1 h. 10 min.

4.　6 h. 20 min.
　− 4 h. 40 min.

Write the time.

5. 4 h. 35 min. before 7:00 P.M.　　6. 4h. 15 min. after 8:55 A.M.

Find the elapsed time.

7. From 3:45 P.M. to 7:10 P.M.　　8. From 10:20 P.M. to 3:50 A.M.

Exercises

Add or subtract.

1.　1 h. 45 min.
　+ 3 h. 15 min.

2.　4 h. 23 min.
　+ 2 h. 57 min.

3.　5 h. 49 min.
　+ 3 h. 43 min.

4.　2 h. 41 min.
　1 h. 28 min.
　+ 5 h. 21 min.

5.　7 h. 49 min.
　3 h. 32 min.
　+ 1 h. 39 min.

6.　5 h. 43 min.
　− 2 h. 17 min.

7. 10 h.
  − 4 h. 37 min.

8. 8 h. 20 min.
  − 3 h. 50 min.

9. 7 h. 26 min.
  − 1 h. 58 min.

Write the specified time.

10. 3 h. before 6:45 P.M.

11. 5 h. after 9:07 A.M.

12. 2 h. 50 min. before 11 P.M.

13. 3 h. 25 min. after 7:50 A.M.

14. 5 h. 35 min. before 9:05 A.M.

15. 4 h. 20 min. after 10:00 P.M.

Find the elapsed time.

16. From 7:40 A.M. to 10:20 A.M.

17. From 1:52 P.M. to 7:48 P.M.

18. From midnight to 7:39 A.M.

19. From 11:09 A.M. to 9:03 P.M.

20. From 8:47 P.M. to 3:15 A.M.

21. From 2:20 A.M. to 11:18 P.M.

22. From 8:00 A.M. to 7:00 A.M.

23. From 11:15 P.M. to noon

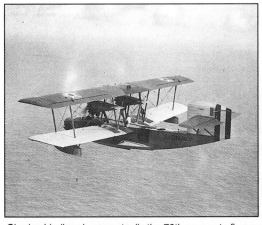 

Charles Lindbergh was actually the 79th person to fly across the Atlantic, although he was the first to fly nonstop from New York to Paris. Some earlier flights were made in amphibious aircraft, similar to this navy patrol plane. While Lindbergh's flight took $33\frac{1}{2}$ hours, today the same distance can be covered in $3\frac{1}{2}$ hours by passengers on the supersonic Concorde.

Adding and Subtracting Whole Numbers

Application

  24. A plane departs at 7:10 A.M. and arrives at 1:55 P.M. How long was the plane in the air?

  25. A plane arrived at 8:10 P.M. The flight was 5 h. 40 min. long. At what time did the flight begin?

Problem Solving: Select the Operation

You can use the four-point check list as a guide to help you solve word problems in an organized way.

In Step 2 of the check list, a common strategy for solving problems is called "Select the Operation."

Read the following problem. Plan what to do to solve the problem by selecting the correct operation.

The Hamiltons traveled 1,386 miles on a two-week vacation. During the first week they drove 498 miles. How far did they travel during the second week?

✓ Four-Point Check List

1 READ to understand the question and identify the needed data.

2 PLAN what to do to solve the problem.

3 SOLVE the problem by carrying out the plan.

4 CHECK to make sure the solution is reasonable.

  1. READ: Understand the question.
       ■ How far did the Hamiltons travel during the second week of their vacation?
      Identify the needed data.
       ■ 1,386 total miles for 2 weeks
       ■ 498 miles for the first week

  2. PLAN: Use the strategy "Select the Operation."

       ■ Subtract $1,386 - 498$.

  3. SOLVE: $1,386 - 498 = 888$ miles

  4. CHECK: $498 + 888 = 1,386$

☑SKILL CHECK

Select the letter which indicates the correct operation for solving each problem.

1. Mr. Rogers tithed $276 each month to his local church. How much does he give in 7 months?

   a. Add $276 + 7$ **b.** Subtract $276 - 1$

   c. Multiply 276×7 **d.** Divide $276 \div 7$

2. Jack went fishing and caught 28 fish altogether. He threw 19 fish back because they were too small. How many fish did he keep?

   a. Add $28 + 16$ **b.** Subtract $28 - 19$

   c. Multiply 28×19 **d.** Divide $28 \div 19$

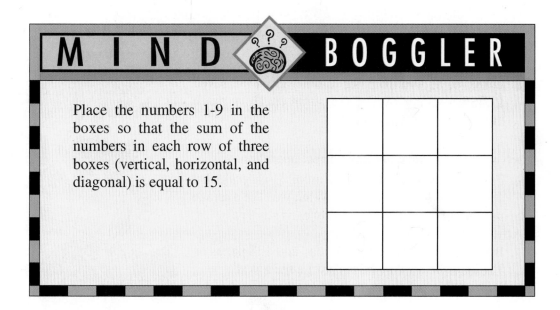

M I N D ❓ B O G G L E R

Place the numbers 1-9 in the boxes so that the sum of the numbers in each row of three boxes (vertical, horizontal, and diagonal) is equal to 15.

Adding and Subtracting Whole Numbers

Exercises

Write the correct operation needed to solve each problem.

1. Sandy wants to buy a new outfit to wear to church. The blouse costs $26 and the skirt costs $35. How much money does she need to buy the clothes?

2. Jeff has $55 and wants to buy a bicycle that costs $137. How much more money does he need?

3. The Turner family is planning a 14-day vacation. They expect to spend $95 each day for food and gas. How much money will they need for food and gas on the vacation?

4. David traveled 312 miles on a weekend trip. His car averages 24 miles per gallon. How many gallons of gas did he use?

5. Jan saved $1,896 from her summer job. Matt saved $2,459 working during the summer. How much more did Matt save than Jan?

Solve each problem using the correct operation.

6. The 157 students at Grace Junior High collected 6,123 pounds of newspaper. What was the average number of pounds collected by each student?

7. Brian read 163 pages on Monday and 138 pages on Tuesday. How many pages did he read in all?

8. Each of the 157 students at Grace Junior High gave $3 to the mission project. How much money was given all together?

9. Expenses for the Leedy family vacation included $387 for lodging, $295 for meals, and $176 for transportation. What was the total amount of these expenses?

10. There are 4,750 soup labels in the school office. The school secretary will put the labels in bundles of 250 labels. How many bundles will there be when she completes the job?

Chapter 1 Review

1.1 Write the place value of the underlined digit.

1. 5<u>6</u>3,975

2. 7<u>4</u>,381,950

Write in standard form.

3. Two million, forty thousand, five

Write in short expanded form.

4. 73,508

Write in standard form.

5. $400,000 + 70,000 + 40 + 9$

1.2 Compare. Use >, <, or = for each ☐.

6. 68,943 ☐ 68,934

7. 27,560 ☐ 275,412

List in order from least to greatest.

8. 1,045; 1,540; 1,450

9. 36,542; 36,452; 35,692; 36,254

1.3 Round 506,849 to the indicated place.

10. hundreds

11. thousands

12. ten thousands

Adding and Subtracting Whole Numbers

1.4 Find each missing addend. Name the property or properties of addition illustrated.

13. $8 + 7 = 7 + \square$ 　　　　**14.** $3 + (4 + 9) = (3 + \square) + 9$

15. $\square + 0 = 16$ 　　　　**16.** $(5 + 14) + \square = 14 + (5 + 9)$

1.5 Estimate each sum or difference by rounding.

17. $9,386 - 2,831$ 　　　　**18.** $38,536 + 54,329 + 65,371$

Find the estimate and a more accurate estimate.

19. $479,163 - 146,738$ 　　　　**20.** $173,572 + 94,628$

1.6 Add.

21. $57,624 + 365,288 + 8,737,035$ 　　**22.** $9,163 + 7,335 + 5,890$

1.7 Add or subtract. Perform the operations inside the parentheses first.

23. $48,009 - 29,146$ 　　　　**24.** $752,638 - 264,519$

25. $800 - (439 + 275)$ 　　　　**26.** $793 + (1,032 - 576)$

1.8 Add or subtract.

27. 　5 h. 34 min.
　　$+ 2$ h. 46 min.

28. 　7 h. 25 min.
　　$- 1$ h. 52 min.

Write the time.

29. 4 h. 50 min. after 6:15 A. M.

30. From 9:53 A. M. to 4:13 P. M.

Chapter 1 Cumulative Review

1. What is the standard form for three million, two hundred thousand, nineteen?
  a. 3,020,019   **b.** 3,002,019
  c. 3,200,019   **d.** not given

2. What is the standard form for 300,000 + 7,000 + 100 + 8?
  a. 307,108   **b.** 307,180
  c. 370,108   **d.** not given

3. What is the value of the underlined digit in 724,319?
  a. 200,000   **b.** 2,000
  c. 20,000   **d.** not given

4. Which is correct?
  a. 3,659 < 3,695   **b.** 17,065 > 17,650
  c. 82,409 < 82,049   **d.** not given

5. Round 483,629 to the nearest thousand.
  a. 483,000   **b.** 500,000
  c. 480,000   **d.** not given

6. Round 1,506,293 to the nearest ten thousand.
  a. 1,500,000   **b.** 1,510,000
  c. 1,506,000   **d.** not given

7. Estimate the sum 47 + 94.
  a. 140   **b.** 150
  c. 130   **d.** not given

8. Estimate the difference 723 − 285.
  a. 300   **b.** 400
  c. 420   **d.** not given

9. Name the property illustrated by
  3 + (5 + 9) = (3 + 5) + 9.
  a. associative   **b.** commutative
  c. identity   **d.** not given

10. Name the property illustrated by
  3 + (5 − 5) = 3
  a. associative   **b.** commutative
  c. identity   **d.** not given

11. Add.   9,375
        6,418
      + 7,206
  a. 22,989   **b.** 22,999
  c. 23,099   **d.** not given

12. Subtract.   27,602
        −   8,754
  a. 18,858   **b.** 18,848
  c. 19,848   **d.** not given

13. Perform the indicated operations.
  873 + (2,049 − 681)
  a. 2,241   **b.** 2,321
  c. 2,141   **d.** not given

14. Subtract.   5 h. 24 min.
        − 2 h. 56 min.
  a. 3 h. 8 min.   **b.** 3 h. 32 min.
  c. 2 h. 28 min.   **d.** not given

15. Find the elapsed time from 10:42 A.M. to 3:19 P.M.
  a. 4 h. 37 min.   **b.** 5 h. 1 min.
  c. 7 h. 23 min.   **d.** not given

Adding and Subtracting Whole Numbers

Fanny Farmer
STANDARD MEASUREMENTS/COOKING

American cuisine owes a huge debt to the illness which prevented Fanny Farmer from attending college. Confined to her house by doctor's orders, Fanny turned to cooking to relieve her boredom. She soon became a very talented cook. When her health improved, her parents insisted that she attend the Boston Cooking School. Two years after graduating in 1889, she was appointed director of the school.

Fanny's pet peeve was the haphazard way in which cookbooks listed recipe ingredients—a pinch of this, a dash of that. As a result, a recipe seldom tasted the same when prepared by two different cooks. Determined to alleviate this problem, Fanny introduced standardized measurements in the classrooms of the Boston Cooking School. She insisted that her teachers always use measuring cups and continually drilled into her students' minds that "a cupful is measured level."

In 1896, her new system of measurement was introduced to the American public with the release of *The Boston Cooking School Cookbook.* This enormously popular cookbook went through a total of twenty-one editions during Fanny's lifetime. It was through reading this book that American women first learned about measurements such as the tablespoon, the teaspoon, and the measuring cup.

Fanny left the Boston Cooking School in 1902 to establish her own school, Miss Farmer's School of Cookery. Her goal was to educate the average American housewife in the art of cookery. She taught her students to follow recipes closely and to implement her standard level measurements in their cooking. Fanny also developed a set of principles for preparing food for the sick. Her

1857–1915

one 5

2 ta

3 tab

1 1/4 tea

1/4 teaspoon gr

experience as an invalid had taught her the importance, physically and emotionally, of food that was both nutritious and delicious.

As a result of being an authority in her field, Fanny had many opportunities to share her philosophy with the students and nurses of Harvard Medical School. Because she believed that patients must be made to feel special, Fanny taught that hospitals and other caregivers should always prepare food for individuals. She warned them to "never serve a patient custard scooped from a large pudding dish." She emphasized that the patient "wants to feel that he is being particularly looked out for."

Fanny truly initiated a revolution in American cooking. Most cooks of our day cannot imagine preparing even the simplest of recipes without using their measuring cups and spoons. These necessities, found in kitchens everywhere, serve as tokens of the innovation and wisdom of Fanny Farmer.

2 CHAPTER

MULTIPLYING AND DIVIDING WHOLE NUMBERS

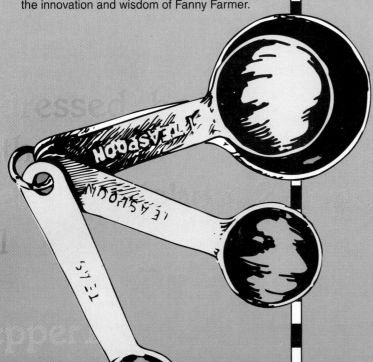

2.1 Properties of Multiplication

Study the properties of multiplication listed below. Observe that when parentheses are used, you perform the operation inside the parentheses first.

Commutative Property	Associative Property
Changing the order of the factors does not change the product. $$a \times b = b \times a$$ Example: $3 \times 13 = 13 \times 3$ $39 = 39$	Changing the grouping of the factors does not change the product. $$(a \times b) \times c = a \times (b \times c)$$ Example: $(8 \times 6) \times 3 = 8 \times (6 \times 3)$ $48 \times 3 = 8 \times 18$ $144 = 144$
Identity Property	Zero Property
The product of one and any number is that number. $$a \times 1 = a \quad 1 \times a = a$$ Example: $9 \times 1 = 9 \quad 1 \times 9 = 9$	The product of zero and any number is zero. $$a \times 0 = 0 \quad 0 \times a = 0$$ Example: $3 \times 0 = 0 \quad 0 \times 3 = 0$

Distributive Property
The product of a factor and a sum is equal to the sum of the products. $$a \times (b + c) = (a \times b) + (a \times c)$$ Example: $3 \times (5 + 8) = (3 \times 5) + (3 \times 8)$ $3 \times 13 = 15 + 24$ $39 = 39$

You can use the properties of multiplication to help you compute mentally. Study the following examples. Note the properties used.

Additional Examples

Name the property used to find each of the following products.

a. $(19 \times 5) \times 2 = 19 \times (5 \times 2)$ ◀ Associative Property
$= 19 \times 10$
$= 190$

b. $5 \times 38 = 5 \times (30 + 8)$
$\qquad = (5 \times 30) + (5 \times 8)$ ◀ Distributive Property
$\qquad = 150 + 40$
$\qquad = 190$

c. $25 \times (7 \times 4) = 25 \times (4 \times 7)$ ◀ Commutative Property
$\qquad\qquad\quad = (25 \times 4) \times 7$ ◀ Associative Property
$\qquad\qquad\quad = 100 \times 7$
$\qquad\qquad\quad = 700$

☑SKILL CHECK

Find each missing factor. Name the property illustrated.

1. $8 \times 1 = \square$

2. $(2 \times 7) \times 5 = 2 \times (7 \times \square)$

3. $2 \times (4 + 9) = (2 \times \square) + (2 \times 9)$

4. $6 \times 24 = 24 \times \square$

Use the properties of multiplication to find each product mentally.

5. $4 \times 13 \times 25$

6. 5×49

Exercises

Name the property of multiplication illustrated.

1. $18 \times 35 = 35 \times 18$

2. $3 \times (10 + 8) = (3 \times 10) + (3 \times 8)$

3. $29 \times 1 = 29$

4. $(9 \times 8) \times 15 = 9 \times (8 \times 15)$

5. $0 \times 4 = 0$

6. $(6 \times 4) + (6 \times 11) = 6 \times (4 + 11)$

Find each missing factor.

7. $8 \times 2 = 2 \times \square$

8. $27 \times 1 = \square$

9. $4 \times (9 + 25) = (4 \times \square) + (4 \times 25)$

10. $(7 \times 9) \times 2 = 7 \times (9 \times \square)$

11. $\square \times 18 = 0$

12. $\square \times 26 = 26 \times 43$

Today you can still find the Fannie Farmer cookbook in bookstores and libraries.

Multiplying and Dividing Whole Numbers

13. $15 \times (\square + 2) = (15 \times 10) + (15 \times 2)$

14. $(10 \times \square) \times 15 = 15 \times (10 \times 4)$

Find the product mentally.

15. $5 \times (2 \times 8)$ **16.** $4 \times 6 \times 5$ **17.** $(17 \times 5) \times 2$

18. $25 \times 7 \times 4$ **19.** 6×54 **20.** $37 \times (5 \times 0)$

21. 4×43 **22.** $5 \times 9 \times 20$ **23.** $5 \times (3 \times 20)$

Application

24. Mr. Jaworski's car gets 27 miles per gallon in highway driving. His gas tank has a capacity of 13 gallons. How many miles can he travel on the highway with a full tank of gas?

25. Mr. Halstead drives 7 miles to meet his car pool and then rides 13 miles to work. How far does he travel round trip each five-day work week?

2.2 Multiplication Patterns: Mental Math

You can use mental math to multiply by powers of 10. Study the patterns below, which show multiplication of numbers by 10, 100, and 1,000.

$3 \times 10 = 30$ $45 \times 10 = 450$ $128 \times 10 = 1,280$

$3 \times 100 = 300$ $45 \times 100 = 4,500$ $128 \times 100 = 12,800$

$3 \times 1,000 = 3,000$ $45 \times 1,000 = 45,000$ $128 \times 1,000 = 128,000$

To multiply by a power of 10, follow these steps.

Multiplying by a Power of 10
1. Multiply the first factor by 1.
2. Write as many zeros as there are in the power of 10.

Study the patterns below, which show multiplying when the factors are multiples of 10, 100, and 1,000.

$40 \times 2 = 80$ $30 \times 2 = 60$ $900 \times 7 = 6,300$

$40 \times 20 = 800$ $300 \times 2 = 600$ $900 \times 70 = 63,000$

$40 \times 200 = 8,000$ $3,000 \times 2 = 6,000$ $900 \times 700 = 630,000$

To multiply by multiples of powers of 10, follow these steps.

Multiplying by a Multiple of a Power of 10
1. Multiply the nonzero numbers.
2. Write as many zeros as there are in all of the factors.

Additional Examples

Find the products mentally.

a. $3,000 \times 500 = 1,500,000$ ◀ $3 \times 5 = 15$

b. $20 \times 100 \times 8 = 16,000$ ◀ $2 \times 1 \times 8 = 16$

Multiplying and Dividing Whole Numbers

☑SKILL CHECK

Find the products mentally.

1. 10×17	100×17	$1,000 \times 17$
2. 3×20	3×200	$3 \times 2,000$
3. 30×15	300×15	300×150
4. 35×100	**5.** $8 \times 3,000$	**6.** $400 \times 6,000$

Exercises

Complete the table.

	Number	× 10	× 100	× 1,000
1.	7			
2.	20			
3.	34			
4.	450			

Find the products mentally.

5. 38×10 **6.** 70×100 **7.** $1,000 \times 15$

8. 725×100 **9.** 6×50 **10.** 30×90

11. 800×7 **12.** 40×200 **13.** 700×900

14. $8,000 \times 3$ **15.** $5,000 \times 50$ **16.** $600 \times 1,000$

17. 80×500 **18.** 330×20 **19.** $4,000 \times 25$

20. $7 \times 10 \times 5$ **21.** $30 \times 100 \times 2$

22. $50 \times 40 \times 10$ **23.** $9 \times 1,000 \times 4$

24. $3,000 \times 2 \times 10$ **25.** $5 \times 30 \times 200 \times 60$

Application

26. In a recent year, a midwestern state collected $2,000 in taxes from each person in the state. How much state tax was collected in a city of 7,000 people?

27. In a recent year, the federal government spent $900 on projects for each resident of a New England city. How much money was spent on projects in a city of 300,000 people?

2.3 Estimating Products

If Robert's heart beats 3,840 times in one hour, about how many times does his heart beat in 24 hours? You must estimate $24 \times 3,840$ to find the answer.

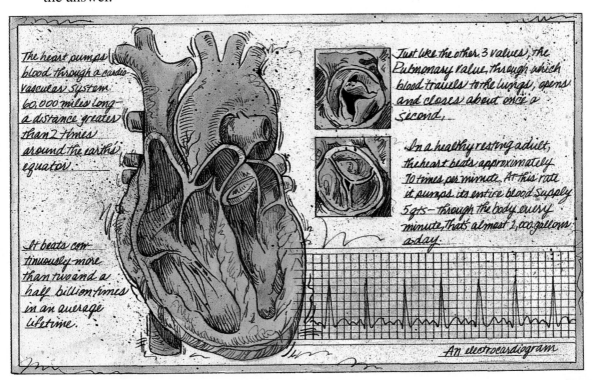

The heart pumps blood through a cardiovascular system 60,000 miles long—a distance greater than 2 times around the earth's equator.

It beats continuously more than two and a half billion times in an average lifetime.

Just like the other 3 valves, the Pulmonary valve, through which blood travels to the lungs, opens and closes about once a second.

In a healthy resting adult, the heart beats approximately 70 times per minute. At this rate it pumps its entire blood supply 5 qts— through the body every minute. That's almost 2,000 gallons a day.

An electrocardiogram

To estimate a product, follow these steps:

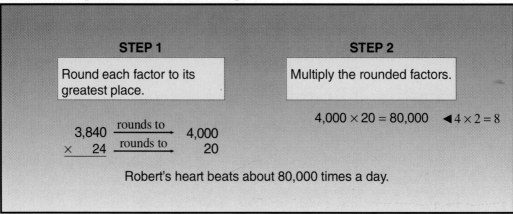

STEP 1

Round each factor to its greatest place.

$$3,840 \xrightarrow{\text{rounds to}} 4,000$$
$$\times \quad 24 \xrightarrow{\text{rounds to}} 20$$

STEP 2

Multiply the rounded factors.

$$4,000 \times 20 = 80,000 \quad \blacktriangleleft 4 \times 2 = 8$$

Robert's heart beats about 80,000 times a day.

To find the range for a product, follow these steps:

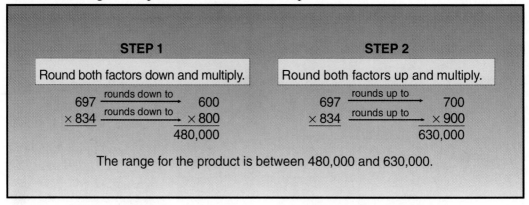

STEP 1

Round both factors down and multiply.

$$697 \xrightarrow{\text{rounds down to}} 600$$
$$\times 834 \xrightarrow{\text{rounds down to}} \times 800$$
$$480,000$$

STEP 2

Round both factors up and multiply.

$$697 \xrightarrow{\text{rounds up to}} 700$$
$$\times 834 \xrightarrow{\text{rounds up to}} \times 900$$
$$630,000$$

The range for the product is between 480,000 and 630,000.

Additional Examples

Estimate the products.

a. $\quad 6,287 \rightarrow \quad 6,000$
$\quad \underline{\times \quad 43} \rightarrow \underline{\times \quad 40}$
$\qquad\qquad\qquad 240,000$

b. $18 \times 35 \times 53$
$\quad \downarrow \quad\; \downarrow \quad\;\; \downarrow$
$20 \times 40 \times 50 = 40,000$

☑**SKILL CHECK**

Estimate the products.

1. 572
    × 36

2. 714
    ×281

3. 5,387
    ×   16

4. 3,586
    × 434

Find the range.

5. 319×27

Estimate. Use the properties of multiplication.

6. $18 \times 39 \times 53$

Exercises

Round each factor to its greatest place. Choose the correct letter.

1. 38×72 becomes—

   a. 40×80

   b. 30×70

   c. 40×70

   d. 40×100

M I N D ❓ B O G G L E R

A marksman was taking target practice on the target on the right. Suppose that he took 6 shots and made a score of exactly 100. Where did his shots land?

16
17
23
24
39

Multiplying and Dividing Whole Numbers

2. 192×65 becomes—

   a. 190×70 **b.** 200×70

   c. 200×60 **d.** 200×100

3. 642×835 becomes—

   a. 600×840 **b.** 700×800

   c. 640×840 **d.** 600×800

Estimate the products.

4. $\begin{array}{r} 47 \\ \times 12 \\ \hline \end{array}$ **5.** $\begin{array}{r} 43 \\ \times 57 \\ \hline \end{array}$ **6.** $\begin{array}{r} 308 \\ \times 25 \\ \hline \end{array}$

7. $\begin{array}{r} 895 \\ \times 43 \\ \hline \end{array}$ **8.** $\begin{array}{r} 423 \\ \times 618 \\ \hline \end{array}$ **9.** $\begin{array}{r} 6{,}478 \\ \times 27 \\ \hline \end{array}$

10. $\begin{array}{r} 2{,}504 \\ \times 49 \\ \hline \end{array}$ **11.** $\begin{array}{r} 7{,}463 \\ \times 315 \\ \hline \end{array}$ **12.** $\begin{array}{r} 3{,}119 \\ \times 2{,}765 \\ \hline \end{array}$

13. $\begin{array}{r} 65{,}082 \\ \times 16 \\ \hline \end{array}$ **14.** $\begin{array}{r} 13{,}226 \\ \times 65 \\ \hline \end{array}$ **15.** $\begin{array}{r} 52{,}350 \\ \times 736 \\ \hline \end{array}$

16. 94×27 **17.** 36×469 **18.** 683×247

19. $547 \times 6{,}381$ **20.** $2{,}413 \times 1{,}986$ **21.** $85 \times 17{,}304$

Find the range for the products.

22. 21×44 **23.** 657×46 **24.** $2{,}567 \times 215$

Estimate. Use the properties of multiplication.

25. $84 \times 62 \times 48$ **26.** $19 \times 87 \times 54$

27. $39 \times 57 \times 45$ **28.** $189 \times 675 \times 524$

Application

29. Jan jogs 28 miles per week. About how many miles does she jog in a year?

30. Juan's resting heart rate is 67 beats per minute. About how many times does his heart beat during a two-hour nap?

2.4 Multiplying Whole Numbers

According to the table, a slice of cheese pizza contains 145 calories.

If a cheese pizza has a total of 8 slices, how many calories are contained in the pizza?

To find the number of calories, you multiply 145 × 8. Study the following steps.

Food	Calories
Apple pie, 1 slice	345
Bread, 1 slice	65
Peanut butter sandwich	225
Pizza (cheese), 1 slice	145
Roast beef, 3 oz.	165
Milk (skim), 1 cup	85
Cola, 12 fl. oz.	145

STEP 1	STEP 2	STEP 3
Multiply the ones.	Multiply the tens.	Multiply the hundreds.
$\begin{array}{r} 4 \\ 145 \\ \times\ \ 8 \\ \hline 0 \end{array}$	$\begin{array}{r} 34 \\ 145 \\ \times\ \ 8 \\ \hline 60 \end{array}$	$\begin{array}{r} 34 \\ 145 \\ \times\ \ 8 \\ \hline 1{,}160 \end{array}$

A cheese pizza contains 1,160 calories.

Multiplying and Dividing Whole Numbers

How many calories are contained in 14 slices of apple pie?

To find the number of calories, you multiply 345 × 14.

To check your answer, estimate the product.

$$
\begin{array}{r}
345 \\
\times\ 14 \\
\hline
1{,}380 \\
3{,}450 \\
\hline
4{,}830
\end{array}
$$

◀ 4 × 345
◀ 10 × 345
◀ 14 × 345

$$
\begin{array}{r}
345 \\
\times\ 14 \\
\hline
4{,}830
\end{array}
\quad\rightarrow\quad
\begin{array}{r}
300 \\
\times\ 10 \\
\hline
3{,}000
\end{array}
$$

└ compare ┘

Fourteen slices of apple pie
contain 4,830 calories.

The answer is reasonable.

Additional Examples

Multiply.

a.
$$
\begin{array}{r}
647 \\
\times\ 80 \\
\hline
51{,}760
\end{array}
$$

b.
$$
\begin{array}{r}
5{,}036 \\
\times\ 49 \\
\hline
45{,}324 \\
201{,}440 \\
\hline
246{,}764
\end{array}
$$

c. Compare. Use >, <, or =.

$25 \times 4 \times 13 \ \square\ 5 \times 12 \times 20$
$(25 \times 4) \times 13 \ \square\ (5 \times 20) \times 12$
$100 \times 13 \ \square\ 100 \times 12$
$1{,}300 > 1{,}200$

☑ **SKILL CHECK**

Write the letter of the correct answer.

1. 87×34

   a. 609   b. 2,958

   c. 2,938   d. 2,978

2. 609×83

   a. 6,699   b. 49,547

   c. 50,467   d. 50,547

Multiply.

3.	627	4.	5,409	5.	754	6.	5,682
	$\times\ \ \ 9$		$\times\ \ \ 6$		$\times\ \ 25$		$\times\ \ \ 47$

Exercises

Multiply.

1.	326	2.	5,346	3.	7,308
	$\times\ \ \ 9$		$\times\ \ \ 5$		$\times\ \ \ 5$

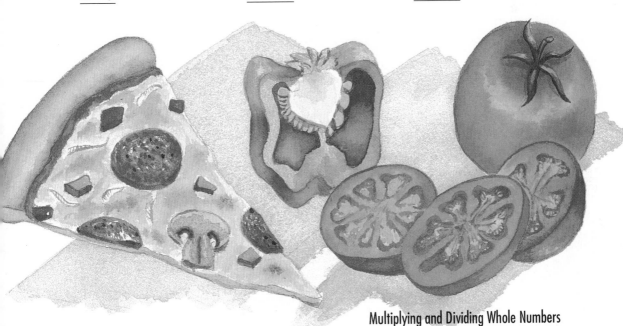

Multiplying and Dividing Whole Numbers

4. 24,386
   ×   6

5. 20,734
   ×   7

6.   652
   × 13

7.   581
   × 60

8. 6,793
   ×   58

9. 3,009
   ×   37

10. 42,970
    ×   92

11. 60,385
    ×   40

12. 356,418
    ×   26

13. $7 \times 34,008$

14. $18 \times 10,073$

15. $39 \times 425,000$

16. $52 \times 43 \times 86$

17. $302 \times 86 \times 4$

18. $247 \times 34 \times 10$

Compare. Use >, <, or =.

19. $297 \times 45 \square 45 \times 297$

20. $43 \times 98 \square 89 \times 34$

21. $16 \times 34 \times 15 \square 357 \times 24$

22. $8 \times 54 \square (8 \times 50) + (8 \times 4)$

23. $8 \times 125 \times 38 \square 4 \times 37 \times 250$

24. $25 \times 4 \times 79 \square 256 \times 0 \times 31$

Application

Use the table on page 43 for exercises 25-26.

25. How many calories are contained in a roast beef sandwich made with 2 slices of bread and 3 oz. of roast beef?

26. Terri packed 2 slices of pizza, a slice of apple pie, and a can of cola in her lunch. Anna's lunch consisted of two peanut butter sandwiches and two cups of skim milk. Whose lunch contained more calories? How many more?

2.5 Multiplying Larger Numbers

The state of Hawaii has a land area of about 6,425 square miles. If the population density is 169 people per square mile, what is the total population of Hawaii?

To find the total population, you multiply $6,425 \times 169$.

STEP 1	STEP 2	STEP 3	STEP 4
Multiply the ones.	Multiply the tens.	Multiply the hundreds.	Add the partial products.

<table>
<tr><td>

6,425
× 169
57 825

</td><td>

6,425
× 169
57 825
385 50

</td><td>

6,425
× 169
57 825
385 50
642 5

</td><td>

6,425
× 169
57 825
385 50
642 5
1,085,825

</td></tr>
</table>

To check the answer, you can estimate the product. Round each factor to its greatest place value.

$$\begin{array}{r} 6,425 \\ \times\ \ 169 \\ \hline 1,085,825 \end{array} \quad \xrightarrow{\text{Round to the nearest thousand.}} \quad \begin{array}{r} 6,000 \\ \times\ \ 200 \\ \hline 1,200,000 \end{array}$$

Round to the nearest hundred.

Compare. The answer is reasonable.

The total population of Hawaii is 1,085,825 people.

Multiplying and Dividing Whole Numbers

Additional Examples

Multiply.

a.
$$\begin{array}{r} 734 \\ \times\ 207 \\ \hline 5\ 138 \\ 146\ 80 \\ \hline 151{,}938 \end{array}$$

b.
$$\begin{array}{r} {}^{3}\ {}^{1} \\ 1{,}823 \\ \times\ \ 400 \\ \hline 729{,}200 \end{array}$$

c.
$$\begin{array}{r} 2{,}007 \\ \times\ \ 530 \\ \hline 60\ 210 \\ 1\ 003\ 5 \\ \hline 1{,}063{,}710 \end{array}$$

☑ SKILL CHECK

Multiply.

1.
$$\begin{array}{r} 845 \\ \times\ 307 \\ \hline \end{array}$$

2.
$$\begin{array}{r} 475 \\ \times\ 260 \\ \hline \end{array}$$

3.
$$\begin{array}{r} 5{,}008 \\ \times\ \ 451 \\ \hline \end{array}$$

4.
$$\begin{array}{r} 5{,}826 \\ \times\ \ 379 \\ \hline \end{array}$$

5. $405 \times 1{,}050$

6. $131 \times 122 \times 232$

Exercises

Multiply.

1.
$$\begin{array}{r} 843 \\ \times\ 295 \\ \hline \end{array}$$

2.
$$\begin{array}{r} 921 \\ \times\ 408 \\ \hline \end{array}$$

3.
$$\begin{array}{r} 670 \\ \times\ 493 \\ \hline \end{array}$$

4.
$$\begin{array}{r} 409 \\ \times\ 320 \\ \hline \end{array}$$

5.
$$\begin{array}{r} 6{,}815 \\ \times\ \ 903 \\ \hline \end{array}$$

6.
$$\begin{array}{r} 4{,}937 \\ \times\ \ 158 \\ \hline \end{array}$$

7. 7,002
× 643

8. 3,217
× 560

9. 8,407
× 903

10. 56,790
× 800

11. 32,008
× 442

12. 68,921
× 527

13. 187×980

14. $263 \times 4,502$

15. $307 \times 1,060$

16. $113 \times 221 \times 332$

17. $132 \times 315 \times 124$

18. $107 \times 3,004 \times 121$

Estimate to choose the correct product for each.

19. 184×525 **a.** 96,600   **b.** 116,600   **c.** 136,600

20. 398×203 **a.** 75,794   **b.** 80,794   **c.** 85,794

Multiplying and Dividing Whole Numbers

21. $114 \times 28 \times 501$ **a.** 999,192   **b.** 1,299,192   **c.** 1,599,192

22. $35 \times 19 \times 22 \times 11$

               a. 160,930   **b.** 165,930   **c.** 170,930

Application

23. Charlotte, North Carolina, has a land area of 138 square miles. In a recent year, the population density was 2,869 people per square mile. What was the population of the city?

24. Phoenix, Arizona, has a land area of 324 square miles. In a recent year, the population density was 3,036 people per square mile. How many less than 1 million was the population of the city?

2.6 Exponents

The expression 3^4 is written in **_exponential form._** The 3 is the **_base_** and the 4 is the **_exponent._** Observe below that the exponent tells how many times the base is repeated as a factor.

$$3^4 = \underbrace{3 \times 3 \times 3 \times 3}_{\text{repeated factors}} = 81 \blacktriangleleft \text{read "three to the fourth power"}$$

exponent

base

Study the examples in the table below.

Exponential Form	Read	Factor Form	Standard Form
4^2	Four to the second power, or four _squared_	4×4	16
2^3	Two to the third power, or two _cubed_	$2 \times 2 \times 2$	8
1^5	One to the fifth power	$1 \times 1 \times 1 \times 1 \times 1$	1

Study the pattern below.

$10^3 = 10 \cdot 10 \cdot 10 = 1,000$

$10^2 = 10 \cdot 10 = 100$

$10^1 = 10$

$10^0 = 1$

A number with an exponent of 1 is equal to the number itself.

$3^1 = 3 \quad 27^1 = 27 \quad 865^1 = 865$

A nonzero number with an exponent of 0 is equal to 1.

$8^0 = 1 \quad 42^0 = 1 \quad 342^0 = 1$

Sometimes a raised dot is used to indicate multiplication.

Additional Examples

Complete.

a. $3^4 = \square$
$3^4 = 3 \cdot 3 \cdot 3 \cdot 3$
$\quad = 81$

b. $2^\square = 32$
$2^5 = 2 \cdot 2 \cdot 2 \cdot 2 \cdot 2$
$\quad = 32$

c. $6 \cdot 10^3 = \square$
$6 \cdot 10^3 = 6 \cdot (10 \cdot 10 \cdot 10)$
$\quad = 6,000$

Multiplying and Dividing Whole Numbers

☑**SKILL CHECK**

Write in exponential form.

1. 5 squared   **2.** $6 \cdot 6 \cdot 6 \cdot 6$ **3.** 9 cubed   **4.** $3 \cdot 3 \cdot 3 \cdot 3 \cdot 3$

Write each number in standard form.

5. 7^2 **6.** 2^4 **7.** 10^3 **8.** $2 \cdot 5^3$

Exercises

Write in exponential form.

1. $7 \times 7 \times 7 \times 7$ **2.** 12×12 **3.** $1 \times 1 \times 1 \times 1 \times 1 \times 1$

Write each in factor form.

4. 10^3 **5.** 2^5 **6.** 8^2

Write each in standard form.

7. 7^2 **8.** 2^4 **9.** 7^1 **10.** 5^3

11. 1^6 **12.** 3^5 **13.** 14^2 **14.** 10^4

15. 4^0 **16.** 8^3 **17.** 2^7 **18.** 7^2

Find the products.

19. $7 \cdot 5^2$ **20.** $4 \cdot 10^3$ **21.** $3 \cdot 2^6$ **22.** $9 \cdot 10^5$

Make each sentence true.

23. $13^\square = 169$ **24.** $5^\square = 625$ **25.** $\square^3 = 1{,}000$ **26.** $2^\square = 64$

Application

27. A number is 6 more than 7^2. What is the number?

28. A number is greater than 3^3 and less than 3^4. It is a power of 4. What is the number?

2.7 Estimating Quotients

The total attendance at Bible Conference was 31,928 people. If the conference lasted 6 days, about how many people were in attendance each day?

You must estimate 31,928 ÷ 6 to find the average daily attendance. To estimate a quotient, follow these steps.

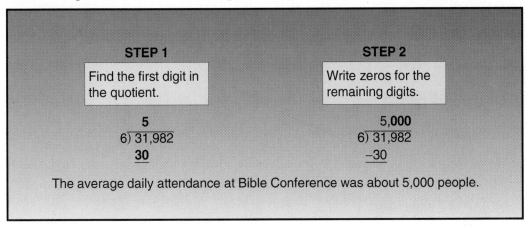

STEP 1

Find the first digit in the quotient.

$$\begin{array}{r} 5 \\ 6\overline{)\,31{,}982} \\ 30 \end{array}$$

STEP 2

Write zeros for the remaining digits.

$$\begin{array}{r} 5{,}000 \\ 6\overline{)\,31{,}982} \\ -30 \end{array}$$

The average daily attendance at Bible Conference was about 5,000 people.

In the problem 13,562 ÷ 43, the divisor has more than 1 digit. To estimate quotients when the divisor has more than 1 digit, follow the steps below.

STEP 1

Round the divisor to its greatest place.

$$43\overline{)\,13{,}562} \rightarrow 40\overline{)\,13{,}562}$$

43 ──rounds to──▶ 40

STEP 2

Find the first digit in the quotient.

$$\begin{array}{r} 3 \\ 40\overline{)\,13{,}562} \\ 12\,0 \end{array}$$

STEP 3

Write zeros for the remaining digits.

$$\begin{array}{r} 300 \\ 40\overline{)\,13{,}562} \\ -12\,0 \end{array}$$

Multiplying and Dividing Whole Numbers

During the turn of the nineteenth century, evangelists held citywide campaigns in which many Bible-believing churches participated. Often, the sponsors of the campaign built a special temporary building, called a tabernacle (as in the picture above), in which the evangelist held his services.

Additional Examples

Estimate.

a. $6,629 \div 78$

$$78 \overline{)6,629} \rightarrow 80 \overline{)6,629} \atop {-6\ 40}}$$ with quotient 80

b. $289,351 \div 329$

$$329 \overline{)289,351} \rightarrow 300 \overline{)289,351} \atop {-270\ 0}}$$ with quotient 900

☑ SKILL CHECK

Estimate.

1. $8 \overline{)5,137}$ **2.** $73 \overline{)38,295}$ **3.** $687 \overline{)725,168}$

4. $1,968 \div 32$ **5.** $75,006 \div 87$ **6.** $152,718 \div 349$

Exercises

Estimate. Choose the most reasonable estimate.

1. $6\overline{)428}$
   a. 7
   b. 70
   c. 700

2. $32\overline{)25,419}$
   a. 8
   b. 80
   c. 800

3. $456\overline{)313,264}$
   a. 60
   b. 600
   c. 6,000

Estimate.

4. $4\overline{)3,896}$

5. $75\overline{)6,529}$

6. $9\overline{)28,431}$

7. $81\overline{)5,003}$

8. $6\overline{)368,246}$

9. $32\overline{)1,639}$

10. $35\overline{)12,467}$

11. $478\overline{)21,432}$

12. $19\overline{)200,487}$

13. $384\overline{)809,625}$

14. $24\overline{)615,708}$

15. $714\overline{)4,371,523}$

16. $3,192 \div 6$

17. $28,321 \div 9$

18. $1,895 \div 34$

19. $165,231 \div 78$

20. $23,652 \div 519$

21. $633,279 \div 877$

During the Second Great Awakening, shortly after the American Revolution, camp meetings became a major means of evangelizing the lost on the western frontier. The artist of this lithograph, however, took some liberties in dressing his frontiersmen in the garb of the eastern cities.

Multiplying and Dividing Whole Numbers

Choose the appropriate division for each estimate.

22. Estimate is 40.
  a. 6) 253
  b. 6) 225
  c. 6) 325

23. Estimate is 700.
  a. 219) 15,280
  b. 219) 152,800
  c. 219) 1,528,000

24. Estimate is 3,000.
  a. 78) 2,697
  b. 78) 26,970
  c. 78) 269,700

Application

25. On Friday, those attending the Bible Conference gave $27,842 in the offering. There were 5,492 people in attendance. About how much did each person give to the offering?

26. The auditorium has 6,127 seats in 18 sections. If each section has the same number of seats, about how many seats are in each of the sections?

In the latter part of the nineteenth century, many Methodists tried to revive the camp meeting, as shown in this scene from the motion picture Sheffey *(Unusual Films).*

2.8 Dividing Whole Numbers

When dividing whole numbers, you repeat the following steps as needed:

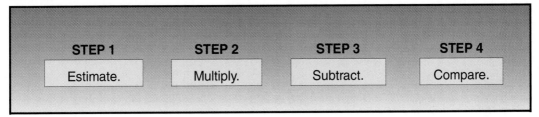

Divide $2,857 \div 8$.

1. Estimate. →
$$\begin{array}{r} 3 \\ 8\overline{)28} \end{array} \qquad \begin{array}{r} 5 \\ 8\overline{)45} \end{array} \qquad \begin{array}{r} 7 \\ 8\overline{)57} \end{array}$$

2. Multiply. →
$$\begin{array}{r} 3 \\ 8\overline{)2{,}857} \end{array} \qquad \begin{array}{r} 35 \\ 8\overline{)2{,}857} \end{array} \qquad \begin{array}{r} 357\ r\,1 \\ 8\overline{)2{,}857} \end{array}$$

3. Subtract. →

4. Compare. →
$$\begin{array}{r} -24 \\ \hline 4 \end{array} \blacktriangleleft 4 < 8$$

The estimate is correct.

$$\begin{array}{r} -24 \\ \hline 45 \\ -40 \\ \hline 5 \end{array} \blacktriangleleft 5 < 8$$

The estimate is correct.

$$\begin{array}{r} -24 \\ \hline 45 \\ -40 \\ \hline 57 \\ -56 \\ \hline 1 \end{array} \blacktriangleleft 1 < 8$$

The estimate is correct.

So, $2,857 \div 8 = 357\ r\,1$.

Check: $(357 \times 8) + 1 = 2,856 + 1 = 2,857$ ◄ The answer is correct.

When the divisor has more than one digit, round the divisor before estimating. If the estimate is too large or too small, adjust it down or up accordingly.

Divide 2,765 ÷ 18.

1. Estimate.→

$$\begin{array}{r} 1 \\ 20\overline{)27} \end{array}$$
$$\begin{array}{r} 4 \\ 20\overline{)96} \end{array}$$
$$\begin{array}{r} 3 \\ 20\overline{)65} \end{array}$$

2. Multiply.→

$$\begin{array}{r} \mathbf{1} \\ 18\overline{)2{,}765} \end{array}$$
$$\begin{array}{r} 14 \\ 18\overline{)2{,}765} \end{array}$$
$$\begin{array}{r} 15 \\ 18\overline{)2{,}765} \end{array}$$
$$\begin{array}{r} 15\mathbf{3\ r\ 11} \\ 18\overline{)2{,}765} \end{array}$$

3. Subtract.→
4. Compare.→

$$\begin{array}{r} -\mathbf{18} \\ \hline \mathbf{9} \end{array}$$ ◄ 9 < 18

The estimate is correct.

$$\begin{array}{r} -18 \\ \hline 96 \\ -72 \\ \hline 24 \end{array}$$ ◄ 24 > 18

Increase the estimate.

$$\begin{array}{r} -18 \\ \hline 96 \\ -90 \\ \hline 6 \end{array}$$ ◄ 6 < 18

The estimate is correct.

$$\begin{array}{r} -18 \\ \hline 96 \\ -90 \\ \hline 65 \\ -54 \\ \hline 11 \end{array}$$ ◄ 11 < 18

The estimate is correct.

So, 2,765 ÷ 18 = 153 r 11

Additional Examples

Divide.

a.
$$\begin{array}{r} 308 \\ 7\overline{)2{,}156} \\ 2\ 1 \\ \hline 05 \\ 0 \\ \hline 056 \\ 56 \end{array}$$

b.
$$\begin{array}{r} 370\ r\ 5 \\ 22\overline{)8{,}145} \\ 6\ 6 \\ \hline 1\ 54 \\ 1\ 54 \\ \hline 05 \end{array}$$

c.
$$\begin{array}{r} 503\ r\ 57 \\ 58\overline{)29{,}231} \\ 29\ 0 \\ \hline 23 \\ 0 \\ \hline 231 \\ 174 \\ \hline 57 \end{array}$$

☑ SKILL CHECK

Divide.

1. $6\overline{)918}$
2. $8\overline{)3{,}040}$
3. $5\overline{)2{,}494}$
4. $2\overline{)6{,}141}$
5. $24\overline{)906}$
6. $73\overline{)3{,}687}$
7. $19\overline{)6{,}213}$
8. $38\overline{)19{,}342}$

Exercises

Divide.

1. $5\overline{)322}$
2. $6\overline{)903}$
3. $4\overline{)7{,}912}$
4. $3\overline{)1{,}826}$
5. $9\overline{)4{,}750}$
6. $2\overline{)8{,}141}$

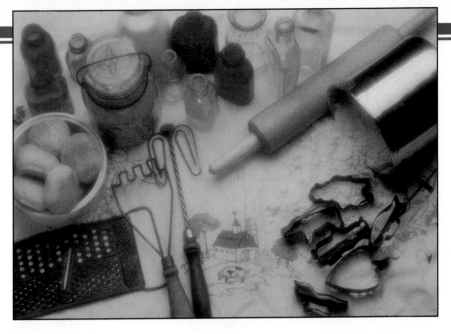

7. $5\overline{)14{,}245}$ **8.** $7\overline{)23{,}869}$ **9.** $31\overline{)899}$

10. $46\overline{)708}$ **11.** $49\overline{)2{,}819}$ **12.** $24\overline{)7{,}826}$

13. $34\overline{)9{,}400}$ **14.** $60\overline{)38{,}049}$ **15.** $72\overline{)43{,}800}$

16. $824 \div 30$ **17.** $7{,}255 \div 15$ **18.** $98{,}450 \div 24$

Find the missing dividend.

        3 1 5   1 4 3 r 5   2 8 r 15

19. $7\overline{)\square{,}\square\square\square}$ **20.** $9\overline{)\square{,}\square\square\square}$ **21.** $67\overline{)\square{,}\square\square\square}$

Application

22. Calvary Christian School sold magazine subscriptions as a fund-raising project. The total profit of $894 was divided evenly among grades 5, 6, and 7. How much money did each grade receive?

23. Calvary Christian School has 351 students and 13 teachers. If the students are assigned equally to the teachers, how many students will be in each teacher's class?

Multiplying and Dividing Whole Numbers

2.9 Dividing by Larger Numbers

The Swales family traveled 5,904 miles during their summer vacation. If they drove for a total of 123 hours, how many miles per hour did they average?

To find the average number of miles per hour, you divide 5,904 ÷ 123. Study the steps below.

Getting Started	Dividing Tens	Dividing Ones
1. Round the divisor to its greatest place. 2. Determine the location of the first digit.	1. Estimate. 2. Multiply. 3. Subtract. 4. Compare.	1. Estimate. 2. Multiply. 3. Subtract. 4. Compare.

$$
\begin{array}{r}
100 \\
123\overline{)\,5{,}904}
\end{array}
\qquad
\begin{array}{r}
100 \quad 5 \\
123\overline{)\,5{,}904} \\
-6\,15 \\
\end{array}
\qquad
\begin{array}{r}
100 \quad 4 \\
123\overline{)\,5{,}904} \\
-4\,92 \\
\hline
98
\end{array}
\qquad
\begin{array}{r}
100 \quad 48 \\
123\overline{)\,5{,}904} \\
-4\,92 \\
\hline
984 \\
984 \\
\hline
0
\end{array}
$$

The estimate is too large; so decrease it by 1.

Check: 123 × 48 = 5,904 ◄ The answer is correct.

The Swales family averaged 48 miles per hour.

Additional Examples

Divide.

a. $\overset{\overset{\scriptstyle 200 \quad\quad 36}{}}{189\overline{)6{,}804}}$
$-5\,67$
$\overline{1\,134}$
$1\,134$
$\overline{0}$

b. $\overset{\overset{\scriptstyle 300 \quad\quad\quad 70\text{ r }85}{}}{306\overline{)21{,}505}}$
$-21\,42$
$\overline{85}$
0
$\overline{85}$

c. $\overset{\overset{\scriptstyle 500 \quad\quad\quad 109\text{ r }490}{}}{491\overline{)54{,}009}}$
$49\,1$
$\overline{4\,90}$
0
$\overline{4\,909}$
$4\,419$
$\overline{490}$

☑SKILL CHECK

Divide.

1. $217\overline{)5{,}692}$

2. $163\overline{)4{,}953}$

3. $308\overline{)8{,}167}$

Exercises

Divide.

1. $300\overline{)14{,}075}$

2. $618\overline{)14{,}832}$

3. $439\overline{)13{,}714}$

4. $563\overline{)27{,}213}$

5. $285\overline{)23{,}534}$

6. $197\overline{)70{,}132}$

7. $547\overline{)15{,}416}$

8. $356\overline{)36{,}312}$

9. $128\overline{)53{,}921}$

10. $264\overline{)75{,}300}$

11. $729\overline{)247{,}860}$

12. $312\overline{)158{,}370}$

13. $35{,}020 \div 412$

14. $7{,}075 \div 295$

15. $309{,}504 \div 806$

16. $137{,}870 \div 196$

Solve.

17. $\overset{1\,2\,4}{38\overline{)\square{,}\square\square\square}}$

18. $\overset{1\,7\text{ r }59}{626\overline{)\square\square{,}\square\square\square}}$

19. $\overset{1\,2\,5}{\square\square\overline{)4{,}625}}$

20. $\overset{8\,4}{\square\square\square\overline{)53{,}088}}$

Multiplying and Dividing Whole Numbers

Estimate. Choose the exact quotient for each.

21. $29\overline{)92{,}075}$
    a. 2,175
    b. 3,175
    c. 4,175

22. $317\overline{)127{,}434}$
    a. 42
    b. 302
    c. 402

23. $192\overline{)81{,}600}$
    a. 425
    b. 525
    c. 625

Application

24. One month an amateur roller skater completed 7,426 laps in 158 hours. What was his average number of laps per hour?
25. Another skater completed 8,106 laps over a period of several months. If she had an average of 42 laps per hour, how many hours did she skate?

Problem Solving: Find the Solution

To solve word problems, you follow the steps of the four-point check list. In step 3, you solve the problem by carrying out the plan.

Read the following problem. Plan what to do to solve the problem; then carry out the plan to find the solution.

Bill bought a wool sportscoat for $79. If he paid for his purchase with a $100 bill, how much change did Bill receive?

> ✓ **Four-Point Check List**
>
> 1 **READ** to understand the question and identify the needed data.
>
> 2 **PLAN** what to do to solve the problem.
>
> 3 **SOLVE** the problem by carrying out the plan.
>
> 4 **CHECK** to make sure the solution is reasonable.

1. READ: Understand the question.
   ■ How much change did Bill receive?
   Identify the needed data.
   ■ The sportscoat cost $79.
   ■ Bill paid with a $100 bill.

2. PLAN: Subtract $100 − $79.

3. SOLVE: $100 − $79 = $21
   Bill received $21 in change.

4. CHECK: $21 + $79 = $100

☑**SKILL CHECK**

Solve.

1. The Hartz family traveled 1,445 miles during the first week of their vacation. During the second week, they drove a total of 1,389 miles. How far did they travel altogether?

2. During the first 6 months of the year, Mr. Mahajan gave a total of $1,050 in tithes and offerings to his local church. On the average, how much did he give each month?

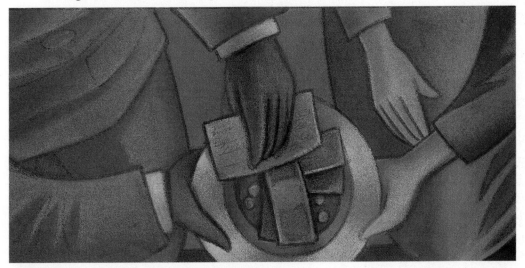

Exercises

Solve.

1. Esther collected 48 aluminum cans this week. Last week she collected 3 times this amount. How many cans did she collect last week?

2. Mr. Roy bought his wife a bottle of perfume for $27. She bought him a bottle of cologne for $19. How much did they spend altogether?

Multiplying and Dividing Whole Numbers

3. The Cates family is planning a 7-day vacation. They have saved $833 to use for food and transportation expenses. How much should they allocate each day for these expenses?

4. Mt. McKinley has an elevation of 20,320 feet. This is 5,826 feet higher than Mt. Whitney. How high is Mount Whitney?

5. The Adamses' car averages 27 miles per gallon. Their fuel tank has a capacity of 16 gallons. How many miles can they travel on a full tank of gas?

6. Rod has saved $78 to be used to go to camp with his youth group. The total expense for a week at camp is $195. How much more money does Rod need to save?

7. On a tankful of gas, the Edwards family drove a total of 406 miles. If their fuel tank has a capacity of 14 gallons, how many miles per gallon did they average?

8. On the average, each of the 143 students at Grace Junior High donated 17 pounds of canned goods for the food drive. What was the total number of pounds collected?

9. Betty has 173 pages left to read in a 391-page classic. How many pages has she read?

10. There are 25 bundles of soup labels in the school office. Each bundle contains 175 soup labels. What is the total number of soup labels?

Chapter 2 Review

2.1 Name the property of multiplication illustrated.

1. $3 \times (7 \times 12) = (3 \times 7) \times 12$ 2. $16 \times 28 = 28 \times 16$

3. $5 \times (10 + 7) = (5 \times 10) + (5 \times 7)$ 4. $5 \times 0 = 0$

Write the missing number.

5. $13 \times \square = 27 \times 13$ 6. $3 \times (2 \times 9) = (3 \times \square) \times 9$

2.2 Find the products mentally.

7. $80 \times 1,000$ 8. 900×700 9. $4,000 \times 250$

2.3 Estimate the products.

10. 948×3 11. 785×62 12. $8,431 \times 295$

2.4 - 2.5 Multiply.

13. $\begin{array}{r} 8,035 \\ \times \quad 7 \\ \hline \end{array}$ 14. $\begin{array}{r} 763 \\ \times \quad 92 \\ \hline \end{array}$ 15. $\begin{array}{r} 4,685 \\ \times \quad 36 \\ \hline \end{array}$

16. $\begin{array}{r} 732 \\ \times 184 \\ \hline \end{array}$ 17. $\begin{array}{r} 4,518 \\ \times \quad 620 \\ \hline \end{array}$ 18. $\begin{array}{r} 57,832 \\ \times \quad 395 \\ \hline \end{array}$

2.6 Write in standard form.

19. 13^2 20. 7^3 21. 2^5

2.7 Estimate the quotients.

22. $5)\overline{3,297}$ 23. $28)\overline{918,365}$ 24. $439)\overline{2,872,419}$

2.8 - 2.9 Divide.

25. $4)\overline{2,039}$ 26. $36)\overline{6,264}$ 27. $18)\overline{57,852}$

28. $517)\overline{19,646}$ 29. $638)\overline{159,580}$ 30. $172)\overline{70,376}$

Chapter 2 Cumulative Review

1. Identify the standard form for seven hundred thousand, seventy.
   - **a.** 707,000
   - **b.** 700,700
   - **c.** 700,070
   - **d.** not given

2. Identify the short expanded form for 850,090.
   - **a.** 800,000 + 50,000 + 900
   - **b.** 800,000 + 50,000 + 90
   - **c.** 800,000 + 5,000 + 90
   - **d.** not given

3. Write the numbers in order from greatest to least.
   - **a.** 2,403; 2,430; 2,340; 2,304
   - **b.** 2,430; 2,403; 2,340; 2,304
   - **c.** 2,304; 2,340; 2,403; 2,430
   - **d.** not given

4. Identify the rounding place for 8,276 → 8,300.
   - **a.** thousands
   - **b.** hundreds
   - **c.** tens
   - **d.** not given

5. Identify the missing addend.
   $17 + (\square + 9) = (17 + 3) + 9$
   - **a.** 3
   - **b.** 9
   - **c.** 17
   - **d.** not given

6. Compute 23 + 4 + 7 + 1 mentally.
   - **a.** 30
   - **b.** 35
   - **c.** 40
   - **d.** not given

7. Identify the more accurate estimate for 147,365 − 89,213.
   - **a.** 0
   - **b.** 10,000
   - **c.** 60,000
   - **d.** not given

8. Find the sum. 2,874 + 53 + 697
   - **a.** 4,101
   - **b.** 3,624
   - **c.** 3,634
   - **d.** not given

9. Identify the property illustrated.
   $4 \times (12 + 5) = (4 \times 12) + (4 \times 5)$
   - **a.** associative
   - **b.** commutative
   - **c.** distributive
   - **d.** not given

10. Compute mentally. $7,000 \times 40$
    - **a.** 2,800
    - **b.** 28,000
    - **c.** 280,000
    - **d.** not given

11. Estimate the product. 418×36
    - **a.** 12,000
    - **b.** 16,000
    - **c.** 20,000
    - **d.** not given

12. Multiply $8,406 \times 7$.
    - **a.** 59,842
    - **b.** 58,842
    - **c.** 57,842
    - **d.** not given

13. Multiply 724×385.
    - **a.** 277,740
    - **b.** 278,640
    - **c.** 278,740
    - **d.** not given

14. Write 3^4 in standard form.
    - **a.** 12
    - **b.** 27
    - **c.** 64
    - **d.** not given

15. Estimate $43\overline{)38,291}$. Choose the most reasonable estimate.
    - **a.** 9
    - **b.** 90
    - **c.** 900
    - **d.** not given

Multiplying and Dividing Whole Numbers

LEONARDO DA VINCI
ART/INVENTION/SCIENCE/ENGINEERING

1452-1519

One of the most prominent artists of the Italian Renaissance, Leonardo da Vinci has fascinated historians and artists for centuries. A man of many talents, Leonardo was skilled in painting, sculpture, engineering, and mechanical design.

Leonardo's father arranged for his fifteen-year-old son to become an apprentice of the renowned Florentine artist Andrea del Verrocchio. For ten years, Leonardo studied under his mentor. He developed an impressive foundation of knowledge in painting, sculpture, and mechanical arts. In 1482 Leonardo set up his own studio in the city of Milan, where he worked as a court painter, architect, and engineer for the Duke of Milan.

Only seventeen of Leonardo's paintings have survived the four centuries since his death. The most famous of these is the *Mona Lisa,* which now hangs in the Louvre museum of Paris. Leonardo's paintings display his special talent for capturing human emotions on canvas. His works also testify to his meticulous attention to detail, a habit developed through his mathematical and scientific studies.

Despite a lifelong interest in science and math, Leonardo considered himself first and foremost an artist. His other studies were merely avenues for him to further his artistic development. Leonardo desired to use his artistic abilities to analyze every object he could find and record its form and structure. This desire led him to plan several essays on subjects such as anatomy, architecture, and mechanics. Although these books were not published during Leonardo's lifetime, his research has been preserved in thirty-one notebooks which detail his artistic exploration of numerous scientific subjects.

It was Leonardo's work as an architect and engineer that first caused him to become fascinated with the application of mathematics. As a result, he plunged him-

self into the study of math, often neglecting his art in favor of arithmetic and geometry. Intrigued by the practical use of mathematical concepts, Leonardo filled his notebooks with intricate sketches of inventions which operated on the principles of friction and resistance.

These notebooks, Leonardo's greatest legacy to mankind, contain thousands of anatomical, architectural, and mechanical sketches. Each sketch is accompanied by a detailed explanation of the illustration. It was in these books that scholars discovered Leonardo's plans for gears, screw threads, and many other modern mechanical devices such as the helicopter. These elaborate diagrams are beautiful illustrations of one man's fascination with the way machines work.

Hundreds of years after Leonardo's death, other men would actually produce the inventions of which he only dreamed. However, his sketches remain as timeless reminders of a man whose vision and ingenuity far surpassed the age in which he lived.

3 CHAPTER

ADDING AND SUBTRACTING DECIMALS

3.1 Decimal Place Value

If a whole unit is divided into ten equal parts, each part is called a ***tenth.*** Each part of a whole unit divided into one hundred equal parts is called a ***hundredth.*** Consider the examples on the right.

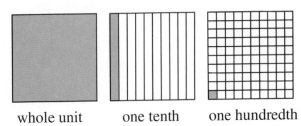

whole unit   one tenth   one hundredth

The place value chart can be extended to show the value of places to the right of the ones place. Each place has a value that is $\frac{1}{10}$ the value of the place to its left. Consider the number in the place value chart below.

Ten thousands 10,000	Thousands 1,000	Hundreds 100	Tens 10	Ones 1	Tenths 0.1	Hundredths 0.01	Thousandths 0.001	Ten-thousandths 0.0001	Hundred-thousandths 0.00001	Millionths 0.000001
				5 .	0	0	0	2	6	9

Standard Form: 5.000269

Word Form: five and two hundred sixty-nine millionths

To show the value of each digit in 5.000269, you can write the decimal in either long or short ***expanded form.*** Consider the examples below:

Long Form: $(5 \times 1) + (2 \times 0.0001) + (6 \times 0.00001) + (9 \times 0.000001)$

Short Form: $5 + 0.0002 + 0.00006 + 0.000009$

Zeros written after the last digit of a decimal do not change the value of the decimal. For example, $0.4 = 0.40 = 0.400$. Decimals like these, which name the same number, are called ***equivalent decimals.***

☑**SKILL CHECK**

Write the value of the underlined digit.

1. 5.3<u>7</u>   2. 7.01<u>3</u>5   3. 0.698<u>7</u>8

Complete.

4. $0.285 = 0.2 + \square + 0.005$ 5. $\square = 4 + 0.01 + 0.003 + 0.0002$

Exercises

Write the value of the underlined digit.

1. 0.<u>8</u>25   2. 0.29<u>6</u>4   3. <u>4</u>5.16   4. 0.002<u>9</u>5

Write in standard form.

5. fifty-nine hundredths

6. three and eight-thousandths

7. two hundred seventy-five millionths

8. sixty-three hundred-thousandths

9. $8 + 0.5 + 0.07$

10. $0.03 + 0.006$

11. $0.2 + 0.004 + 0.0001$

12. $6 + 0.003 + 0.0001$

13. $0.003 + 0.8 + 0.0002 + 0.04$

14. $0.005 + 9 + 0.6 + 0.0001$

Among Leonardo's mechanical ideas was a design for a submarine. This is the U.S.S. Aspro, a modern nuclear-powered submarine.

Adding and Subtracting Decimals

Complete.

15. $0.79 = 0.7 + \square$

16. $4.38 = 4 + \square + 0.08$

17. $6.204 = 6 + 0.2 + \square$

18. $9.8002 = 9 + 0.8 + \square$

Write the decimal in short expanded form.

19. 7.514

20. 0.093

21. 3.1072

22. 0.20806

Match each word form with the appropriate standard form.

23. forty-seven hundredths

a. 4.7

24. forty and seven-thousandths

b. 0.047

25. four and seven-tenths

c. 0.47

26. forty-seven thousandths

d. 47.47

27. four and seven-hundredths

e. 40.007

28. forty-seven and forty-seven hundredths

f. 4.07

Write the two equivalent decimals.

29. $0.24, 0.240, 0.024$

30. $8.4, 8.040, 8.400$

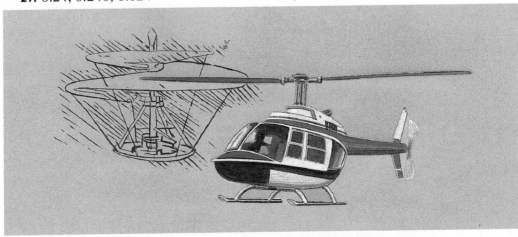

The helical airscrew, or helicopter, as Leonardo envisioned it and as it eventually came to be.

3.2 Comparing and Ordering Decimals

In the championship basketball game, the Patriots made 0.563 of their shots. The Crusaders made 0.567 of their shots. Which team made the greater part of their shots?

To compare decimals, follow the steps below.

Step 1	Step 2	Step 3
Starting from the left, compare the digits in the same place.	Identify the first place where the digits are different.	Compare the decimals in the same order these digits compare.
0.56**3** 0.56**7**	0.56**3** 0.56**7**	0.56**3** < 0.56**7** **3** < **7**

The Crusaders made the greater part of their shots.

Additional Examples

a. Compare. $7.423 \square 7.4235$ ⟶ **7.423** $\square$ **7.423**5

$7.423\mathbf{0} \square 7.4235$ ◀ $0 < 5$

$7.423 < 7.4235$

b. List the decimals in order from least to greatest: 2.367, 2.29, 2.5, 2.376

Step 1	Step 2	Step 3
Annex zeros as needed.	Compare to find the least and greatest decimals.	Compare and order the remaining decimals.
2.367	2.367	2.290 < 2.367
2.290	2.290 ◀ least	2.367 < 2.376
2.500	2.500 ◀ greatest	2.376 < 2.500
2.376	2.376	

So, the correct order is 2.29, 2.367, 2.376, 2.5.

☑**SKILL CHECK**

Compare. Use >, <, or =.

1. $0.6734 \square 0.6743$
2. $5.34 \square 5.259$
3. $0.07 \square 0.073$
4. $17.48 \square 17.480$
5. $0.867 \square 0.876$
6. $9.007 \square 9.070$

List in order from least to greatest.

7. 0.317, 0.33, 0.3172, 0.308
8. 4.5, 4.501, 4.05, 4.051, 4.510

Exercises

Compare. Use >, <, or =.

1. 0.43 ☐ 0.34

2. 6.468 ☐ 6.472

3. 0.602 ☐ 0.6020

4. 107.08 ☐ 107.008

5. 0.5349 ☐ 0.5354

6. 6.39 ☐ 6.3748

7. 0.0538 ☐ 0.5380

8. 7.809 ☐ 7.888

9. 0.278 ☐ 0.1978

10. 0.3589 ☐ 0.3589

11. 4.5674 ☐ 3.6574

12. 0.201243 ☐ 0.201342

Write the greatest decimal.

13. 0.075, 0.057, 0.475

14. 4.158, 4.15, 4.149

15. 0.0803, 0.0083, 0.3080

16. 8.407, 8.4, 8.47

Write in order from least to greatest.

17. 0.562, 0.526, 0.565

18. 0.3546, 0.3534, 0.3528

19. 0.825, 0.082, 0.8251

20. 0.253, 0.2027, 0.23

21. 2.04, 2.045, 2.005

22. 7.304, 7.034, 7.340, 7.043

23. 2.93, 2.9, 2.39, 2.5

24. 6.3341, 6.0333, 6.433, 6.3033

Application

25. Rogers of the Panthers made 0.876 of his free throws. Creason of the Lions made 0.867 of his free throws. Which player made the greater part of his free throws?

26. For the Patriots, Johnson made 0.466 of his field goal attempts. Taylor made 0.46, and Guntle made 0.5. Which player made the greatest part of his field goal attempts?

Adding and Subtracting Decimals

3.3 Rounding Decimals

The Sears Tower in Chicago, Illinois, is 443.1792 meters high. What is the height of the Sears Tower rounded to the nearest tenth?

To round decimals, follow the steps in the flowchart below.

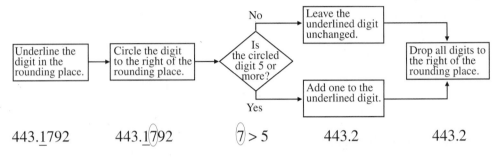

| Underline the digit in the rounding place. | Circle the digit to the right of the rounding place. | Is the circled digit 5 or more? | | Drop all digits to the right of the rounding place. |

443.1792   443.1792   7 > 5   443.2   443.2

Rounded to the nearest tenth, the height of the Sears Tower is 443.2 meters.

Grant H. Kessler

You can round the same decimal to several different places. Study the examples in the chart below.

Decimal	Nearest Tenth	Nearest Hundredth	Nearest Thousandth	Nearest Whole Number
3.5284	3.5	3.53	3.528	4
0.78529	0.8	0.79	0.785	1
0.4604	0.5	0.46	0.460	0

Additional Examples

a. Round 0.8049 to the nearest hundredth.
0.8049 rounds to 0.80.

b. Round 6.2395 to the nearest thousandth.
6.2395 rounds to 6.240.

☑ **SKILL CHECK**

Round to the nearest tenth.

1. 18.743

2. 0.9512

Round to the nearest hundredth.

3. 0.0263

4. 5.3962

Round to the nearest thousandth.

5. 0.4521

6. 4.8995

Round to the nearest whole number.

7. 7.143

8. 261.6658

Exercises

Round to the nearest tenth.

1. 7.34

2. 35.782

3. 2.18773

4. 0.2863

5. 3.9958

6. 0.0734

Round to the nearest hundredth.

7. 0.134

8. 4.0372

9. 63.331

Adding and Subtracting Decimals

10. 80.008   **11.** 149.7575   **12.** 0.09561

Round to the nearest thousandth.

13. 0.28835   **14.** 1.6836   **15.** 0.0092

16. 7.9634   **17.** 0.00058   **18.** 3.9997

Round to the nearest whole number.

19. 74.65   **20.** 506.3   **21.** 2.891

22. 412.035   **23.** 0.569   **24.** 0.43871

Round 347.15093 to the specified place.

25. nearest tenth   **26.** nearest ten   **27.** nearest thousandth

28. nearest whole number   **29.** nearest ten-thousandth   **30.** nearest hundred

Application

31. The atomic weight of silicon is 28.086. Round this number to the nearest tenth.

32. Chromium has an atomic weight of 51.996. Round this number to the nearest hundredth.

3.4 Estimating Sums and Differences

Tom decided to buy a pair of gloves, a helmet, and a patch kit for his racing bicycle. He listed the prices from a catalog and then estimated the total cost. What was Tom's estimate?

Helmet	$36.95
Gloves	12.95
Patch Kit	2.59

To estimate a sum or difference, round each number to the greatest place of the largest number.

Round to the nearest ten dollars.

$36.95 → $40
 12.95 →   10
+ 2.59 → +   0
               $50

Tom's estimate was $50.

To get a more accurate estimate, round each number to the next place on the right.

Round to the nearest dollar.

$36.95 → $37
 12.95 →   13
+ 2.59 → +   3
               $53

Tom's more accurate estimate was $53.

Adding and Subtracting Decimals

Sometimes you estimate by rounding to a specified place.

Additional Examples

a. Estimate $273.49 - 28.36$.
Round to the nearest ten.

$$273.49 \rightarrow \quad 270$$
$$\underline{+ \quad 28.36 \rightarrow + \quad 30}$$
$$\qquad\qquad\qquad 300$$

The estimate is 300.

b. Estimate $119.213 - 87.657$.
Round to the nearest whole number.

$$119.213 \rightarrow \quad 119$$
$$\underline{- \quad 87.657 \rightarrow - \quad 88}$$
$$\qquad\qquad\qquad 31$$

The estimate is 31.

☑**SKILL CHECK**

Estimate each sum or difference by rounding to the nearest—

1. whole number.

$$\begin{array}{r} 2.87 \\ 5.16 \\ + 1.75 \\ \hline \end{array}$$

2. ten.

$$\begin{array}{r} 181.45 \\ - \quad 56.50 \\ \hline \end{array}$$

3. hundred dollars.

$$\begin{array}{r} \$3,205.99 \\ + \quad 473.24 \\ \hline \end{array}$$

Estimate. Round to the greatest place of the greatest number; then find a more accurate estimate.

4. $86.512 - 4.983$ **5.** $347.36 + 58.79$ **6.** $25.72 - 8.94$

Exercises

Estimate each sum or difference by rounding to the nearest whole number or the nearest dollar.

1.
$$\begin{array}{r} 3.152 \\ + 1.063 \\ \hline \end{array}$$

2.
$$\begin{array}{r} 13.874 \\ - \quad 4.265 \\ \hline \end{array}$$

3.
$$\begin{array}{r} \$8.60 \\ 3.45 \\ + \quad 7.81 \\ \hline \end{array}$$

4.
$$\begin{array}{r} 30.75 \\ - 19.83 \\ \hline \end{array}$$

Estimate each sum or difference by rounding to the nearest ten or the nearest ten dollars.

5.
$$\begin{array}{r} 34.15 \\ + 68.92 \\ \hline \end{array}$$

6.
$$\begin{array}{r} \$92.65 \\ - \quad 34.99 \\ \hline \end{array}$$

7.
$$\begin{array}{r} 73.15 \\ 27.98 \\ + 55.14 \\ \hline \end{array}$$

8.
$$\begin{array}{r} 473.15 \\ - \quad 19.85 \\ \hline \end{array}$$

Estimate by rounding to the nearest hundred or to the nearest hundred dollars.

9. $789.63
 − 328.17

10.   109.17
      251.23
    + 385.14

11.   805.29
    − 418.73

12.   718.63
      296.05
    + 89.45

Estimate. Round to the greatest place of the greatest number; then find a more accurate estimate.

13. $58.14
 −   3.19

14.   31.68
    + 8.62

15. 6,390.17
   +   375.01

16.   79.817
    − 4.765

17. 218.28 − 94.63

18. 11.645 + 1.71 + 18.75 + 7.98

Estimate; then compare, using < or > for each ☐.

19. 39.627 + 58.762 ☐ 90

20. 8.27 − 3.981 ☐ 5

21. 9.85 + 68.73 + 13.24 ☐ 100

22. 53.8 − 18.7 ☐ 20

Application

23. James planned to buy some bicycle accessories that cost $19.75, $6.19, $34.49, and $8.50. He estimated the total by rounding to the nearest dollar. What was his estimate?

24. Adena purchased some miscellaneous bicycle parts that cost $1.98, $5.19, $8.15, and $3.49. She paid with a $20 bill. To the nearest dollar, estimate how much change she should get back.

Adding and Subtracting Decimals

3.5 Adding Decimals

The four runners of a 400-meter relay team had individual times of 56.76 sec., 60.63 sec., 55.45 sec., and 59.27 sec. What was the team's total time for the race?

You add to find the relay team's total time. To add decimals, follow the steps below.

Step 1	Step 2	Step 3
Line up the decimal points.	Add as with whole numbers.	Place the decimal point in the sum.
56.76 60.63 55.45 + 59.27	2 2 2 56.76 60.63 55.45 + 59.27 232 11	56.76 60.63 55.45 + 59.27 232.11

The total time for the team was 232.11 seconds.

If necessary, you can write zeros to help you line up the decimal places before adding. Study the examples below.

Additional Examples

a. Add 25.08 + 6.523 + 239.4.
Round to the nearest ten.

$$
\begin{array}{rcl}
\overset{2\,1\ \ 1}{25.08\mathbf{0}} & \rightarrow & 30 \\
6.523 & \rightarrow & 10 \\
+\,239.4\mathbf{00} & \rightarrow & +\,240 \\
\hline
271.003 & \text{Estimate:} & 280
\end{array}
$$

b. Add \$35 + \$17.85 + \$9.65.
Round to the nearest ten.

$$
\begin{array}{rcl}
\overset{2\,1\ \ 1}{\$35.\mathbf{00}} & \rightarrow & \$40 \\
17.85 & \rightarrow & 20 \\
+\ \ \ 9.65 & \rightarrow & +\ \ 10 \\
\hline
\$62.50 & \text{Estimate:} & \$70
\end{array}
$$

☑**SKILL CHECK**

Add. Estimate to be sure your answer is reasonable.

1. 1.496
    + 2.875

2. 17.65
    + 8.701

3. $35.64
    + 17.85

4. 0.7359
    + 0.5876

5. 0.8 + 0.59 + 0.673

6. $65 + $8.97 + $0.34

Exercises

Add.

1. 6.94
    + 5.97

2. 5.073
    + 0.908

3. $57.49
    + 8.53

4. 0.8746
    + 0.0549

5. $215.93
    +   17.85

6. 84.272
    + 39.75

7. 59.378
    + 75.468

8. 4.3286
    + 8.7675

9. 68.2
    84.7
    + 52.3

10. 0.932
     5.374
     + 0.085

11. $12.83
     5.09
     + 14.50

12. 54.173
     8.9175
     + 32.718

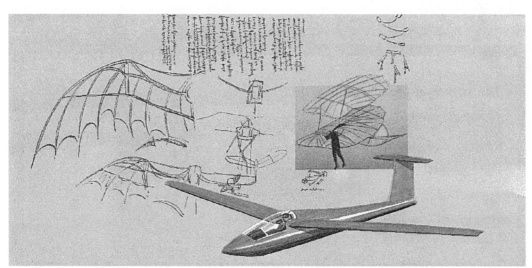

A page from Leonardo's sketchbook showing his concept of a glider alongside an illustration of a modern sailplane.

Adding and Subtracting Decimals

13. $312.15 + $469.27

14. $3.4 + 6 + 8.513$

15. $12.45 + 1.245 + 124.5$

16. $25.93 + $44.29 + $6.75

17. $74.23 + 742.3 + 7,423 + 7.423$

18. $37.2 + 6.5 + 5.83 + 7.09$

Place a decimal point in each addend to make the sentence true.

19. $25 + 635 + 81 = 16.95$

20. $75 + 635 + 82 = 15.3$

21. $625 + 75 + 325 = 11.375$

22. $625 + 1125 + 2625 = 10$

Application

23. Four members of a mile relay team had times of 1.040 min., 1.058 min., 1.092 min., and 1.037 min. What is the total time in minutes for the team?

24. Brent ran the first lap of a mile race in 64.3 sec. and the second lap in 65.1 sec. The last 2 laps were 2.8 sec. longer than his first lap. What was his total time in seconds?

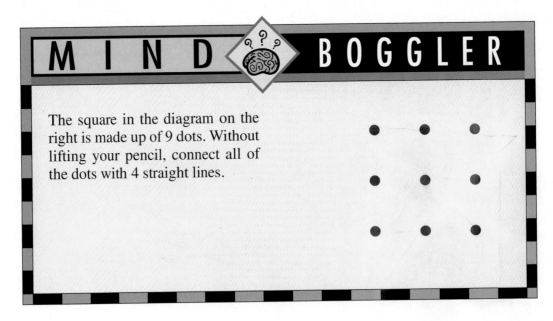

The square in the diagram on the right is made up of 9 dots. Without lifting your pencil, connect all of the dots with 4 straight lines.

3.6 Subtracting Decimals

Andrew's fast ball was timed by an electronic device at 69.284 mph. His curve ball was timed at 57.576 mph. What was the difference in the speed of these two pitches?

You subtract to find the difference in the speed of the two pitches. To subtract decimals, follow these steps.

Step 1	Step 2	Step 3	
Line up the decimal points.	Subtract as with whole numbers.	Place the decimal point in the difference.	You can check subtraction by adding:

$$\begin{array}{r} 69.284 \\ -\ 57.576 \\ \hline \end{array}$$

$$\begin{array}{r} {}^{8}\ {}^{12}\ {}^{7}\ {}^{14} \\ \mathbf{69.284} \\ -\ \mathbf{57.576} \\ \hline \mathbf{11\ 708} \end{array}$$

$$\begin{array}{r} {}^{8}\ {}^{12}\ {}^{7}\ {}^{14} \\ 69.284 \\ -\ 57.576 \\ \hline 11.708 \end{array}$$

$$\begin{array}{r} 11.708 \\ +\ 57.576 \\ \hline 69.284 \end{array}$$

Andrew's fast ball was 11.708 mph faster than his curve ball.

Additional Examples

Subtract. Annex zeros where necessary.

a. $32 - 16.485$

$$\begin{array}{r} 32.\mathbf{000} \\ -\ 16.485 \\ \hline 15.515 \end{array}$$

b. $74.8163 - 6.9$

$$\begin{array}{r} 74.8163 \\ -\ \ 6.\mathbf{9000} \\ \hline 67.9163 \end{array}$$

c. $\$5,400 - \$897.65$

$$\begin{array}{r} \$5,400.\mathbf{00} \\ -\ \ \ \ 897.65 \\ \hline \$4,502.35 \end{array}$$

Adding and Subtracting Decimals

☑**SKILL CHECK**

Subtract.

1. 47.31
 − 38.76

2. 8.39
 − 5.948

3. 0.5361
 − 0.3624

4. $602.00
 − 328.97

5. 26.4 − 8.3596

6. 79.8462 − 8.9

Exercises

Subtract.

1. 97.2
 − 39.5

2. 0.572
 − 0.286

3. 7.148
 − 5.327

4. 70.00
 − 28.73

5. 800.4
 − 257.3

6. 70.55
 − 34.88

7. 0.0728
 − 0.0459

8. 6.9734
 − 3.4872

9. $68.03
 − 25.64

10. $47.00
 − 8.95

11. $749.91
 − 670.50

12. $2,041.29
 − 1,759.65

13. 8.05 − 3.483

14. 3 − 1.765

15. 53.25 − 38.6

16. 0.0142 − 0.00738

17. 408 − 362.55

18. $50,000 − $37,450.50

Perform the indicated operations.

19. 35.42 − (7.47 + 6.25)
20. (2.084 − 0.675) + 3.429
21. 475.3 − (629.7 − 348.2)
22. (16.49 + 37.86) − (15.82 + 29.41)
23. ($100 − $73.48) + $5.87
24. $350 − ($127.42 − $96.51)

Application

25. A baseball had a speed of 94.378 mph. A hockey puck was timed at 79.481 mph. How much slower was the speed of the hockey puck?

26. The average speed for the winner in a 500-mile race was 168.352 mph. The second place car averaged 167.594 mph. How much faster was the speed of the winning car?

Adding and Subtracting Decimals

Problem Solving: Estimating the Solution

To solve word problems, you follow the steps of the four-point check list.

In step 4, you check to make sure that your solution is reasonable.

Solve the following problem. To determine whether the answer is reasonable, estimate the solution by rounding.

Dan bought some new school clothes with his birthday money. He purchased a shirt for $17.39, a pair of pants for $31.85, and a tie for $9.50. How much did Dan spend altogether?

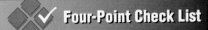

Four-Point Check List

1 READ to understand the question and identify the needed data.

2 PLAN what to do to solve the problem.

3 SOLVE the problem by carrying out the plan.

4 CHECK to make sure the solution is reasonable.

To solve this problem, you add $17.39, $31.85, and $9.50.

$$\begin{array}{r} \$17.39 \\ 31.85 \\ +\quad 9.50 \\ \hline \$58.74 \end{array}$$

Dan spent $58.74 altogether.

To estimate the solution, round each number to the nearest dollar.

$$\begin{array}{r} \$17.39 \rightarrow \quad \$17 \\ 31.85 \rightarrow \quad 32 \\ +\quad 9.50 \rightarrow +\quad 10 \\ \hline \$59 \end{array}$$

The estimate, $59, is close to the solution, $58.74; so the answer is reasonable.

☑ SKILL CHECK

Solve each problem; then estimate the solution by rounding.

1. Grace Elementary School is planning to take 13 members of the safety patrol to an amusement park. Each ticket to the park costs $19.75. How much will the tickets cost?

2. A total of 576 people attended a sacred concert. The seating capacity of the auditorium was 905. How many of the seats were empty?

Exercises

Solve each problem; then estimate the solution using rounding.

1. Faith Elementary School has 28 students in grade 1, 23 students in grade 2, and 31 students in grade 3. How many students are there in grades 1 through 3?

2. A restaurant purchases 195 pounds of potatoes per week. How many pounds of potatoes will they buy in 11 weeks?

3. The boys are setting up 414 chairs for a special assembly. If there are to be 18 rows, how many chairs should be in each row?

Adding and Subtracting Decimals

Leonardo's sketch of a crank-operated paddleboat and an example of a working paddleboat.

4. Denny saved $304 from jobs he had during the summer. Ken saved $581. How much more did Ken save than Denny?

5. Grace Junior High School is purchasing new science books. If each science book costs $23, how much will 85 books cost?

6. Todd and John were passing out tracts. Todd passed out 272 and John passed out 421. How many tracts did they pass out altogether?

7. Richard made a down payment on a car. After the down payment, he had to make 42 payments of $103. How much did Richard pay after the down payment?

8. Last year a store made a profit of $12,116. The 4 owners divided the profit equally among themselves. How much did each receive?

9. Mike worked 49 hours one week on his job. He earned $12 per hour. How much did he earn that week?

10. Mr. Martin traveled at an average speed of 54 miles per hour on a trip. If he went 1,998 miles, how many hours did he drive?

Chapter 3 Review

3.1 Write in standard form.

1. five and one hundred eighty-four thousandths

2. nineteen ten-thousandths

3. $0.04 + 0.008 + 0.0001$

4. $7 + 0.3 + 0.009$

Write the decimal in short expanded form.

5. 4.209

6. 0.0654

3.2 Compare. Use >, <, or =.

7. $0.87 \square 0.78$

8. $0.7619 \square 0.7623$

9. $6.382 \square 6.39$

Write in order from least to greatest.

10. $0.473, 0.437, 0.434$

11. $6.205, 6.025, 6.250, 6.052$

3.3 Round 428.25071 to the specified place.

12. nearest tenth

13. nearest hundredth

14. nearest whole number

15. nearest thousandth

Adding and Subtracting Decimals

3.4 Estimate each sum or difference by rounding to the specified place:

16. nearest dollar   **17.** nearest ten   **18.** nearest hundred

$$\begin{array}{r} \$9.51 \\ +\ 2.37 \\ \hline \end{array}$$
$$\begin{array}{r} 562.19 \\ -\ 31.14 \\ \hline \end{array}$$
$$\begin{array}{r} 438.75 \\ 162.18 \\ +\ 71.36 \\ \hline \end{array}$$

Estimate by rounding to the greatest place of the greatest number; then find a more accurate estimate.

19. $6,481.25 + 273.19 + 1,723.19$ **20.** $\$326.52 - \$194.78$

3.5 Add.

21.
$$\begin{array}{r} 4.068 \\ +0.905 \\ \hline \end{array}$$
22.
$$\begin{array}{r} 6.2748 \\ +7.2693 \\ \hline \end{array}$$
23.
$$\begin{array}{r} 54.28 \\ 9.8241 \\ +73.625 \\ \hline \end{array}$$

24. $7.5 + 4 + 2.423$ **25.** $27.39 + 2.739 + 273.9$

3.6 Subtract.

26.
$$\begin{array}{r} 0.463 \\ -0.178 \\ \hline \end{array}$$
27.
$$\begin{array}{r} 900.3 \\ -369.2 \\ \hline \end{array}$$
28.
$$\begin{array}{r} \$3,052.48 \\ -2,643.72 \\ \hline \end{array}$$

Perform the indicated operations.

29. $48.31 - (6.39 + 7.28)$ **30.** $\$270 - (\$134.25 - \$81.73)$

Cumulative Review

1. What is the place value of the underlined digit in 5$\underline{8}$1,426?

   a. 800,000   **b.** 80,000

   c. 8,000   **d.** not given

2. What is the standard form for
7,000,000 + 4,000 + 500 + 2?

   a. 7,040,502   **b.** 7,004,520

   c. 7,004,502   **d.** not given

3. Round 4,675,209 to the nearest hundred thousand.

   a. 5,000,000   **b.** 4,700,000

   c. 4,680,000   **d.** not given

4. Name the property illustrated by
$3 + (5 + 9) = 3 + (9 + 5)$.

   a. associative   **b.** commutative

   c. distributive   **d.** not given

5. Subtract. $8.002 - 4.639$

   a. 3.463   **b.** 4.363

   c. 3.363   **d.** not given

6. Add.   6 h. 38 min.
       + 2 h. 47 min.

   a. 8 h. 25 min.   **b.** 8 h. 85 min.

   c. 9 h. 25 min.   **d.** not given

7. What time is it 3 h. 20 min. before
10 P.M.?

   a. 7:40 P.M.   **b.** 6:40 P.M.

   c. 6:20 P.M.   **d.** not given

8. Name the property illustrated.
$18 \times 1 = 18$

   a. commutative   **b.** identity

   c. zero   **d.** not given

9. Find the missing multiplicand.
$9 \times 7 = \square \times 9$

   a. 7   **b.** 9

   c. 63   **d.** not given

10. Estimate the product.   8,541
                  ×   329

   a. 2,700,000   **b.** 270,000

   c. 27,000   **d.** not given

11. Multiply.   53,824
           ×   96

   a. 5,067,104   **b.** 5,167,104

   c. 5,267,104   **d.** not given

12. Multiply.   6,005
           ×   531

   a. 2,188,655   **b.** 3,288,655

   c. 3,188,655   **d.** not given

13. Write 2^5 in standard form.

   a. 64   **b.** 16

   c. 32   **d.** not given

14. Estimate. $289 \overline{)\,16,482}$

   a. 5,000   **b.** 500

   c. 50   **d.** not given

15. Divide. $6 \overline{)\,2952}$

   a. 492   **b.** 482

   c. 491   **d.** not given

Adding and Subtracting Decimals

GALILEO GALILEI
ASTRONOMY

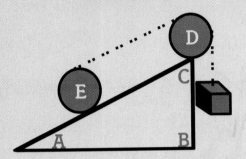

Galileo Galilei was born into a family which clearly recognized the value of a good education. Vincenzo and Giulia Galilei provided their inquisitive son with many opportunities to develop his logical mind.

In 1589 Galileo was appointed professor of mathematics at the University of Pisa. Here the young mathematician began to attack the ancient geocentric view of the universe developed by Aristotle. This view, which held that the earth was the center of the universe, was still advocated by many sixteenth-century scholars. Needless to say, Galileo's beliefs were not very popular with many of his colleagues. In 1592 he left Pisa to become a professor of mathematics at the University of Padua.

It was at Padua that Galileo blossomed both as a mathematician and as a scientist. His work to develop instruments for use in scientific research proved to be quite financially rewarding. An instrument which combined a compass and a quadrant, two devices that enable the user to make mathematical calculations by measuring distances and angles, was his greatest commercial success. In fact, Galileo's proportional compass was widely used by surveyors, navigators, and other mathematicians throughout the world for nearly three centuries until the invention of the slide rule.

In 1609 Galileo improved the instrument that would completely change the direction of his scientific inquiry—the telescope. When asked to evaluate the quality of a telescope for the ruler of Padua, he immediately realized that the instrument was inferior to even his own experimental models. Within months, Galileo had produced a telescope which magnified objects nine times and provided an upright image rather than the usual upside down image produced by the telescopes of his day.

Although he had not been previously interested in astronomy, the telescope fascinated Galileo. As his telescope brought into focus the night sky above him, the inquisitive Galileo began to formulate a mathematical approach to astronomy. He set out to prove mathematically Copernicus's theory that the sun was the center of the universe and that the earth revolved around the sun. This quest threw Galileo into a lifelong conflict with the Roman Catholic church, which had strongly condemned this theory as heretical and contrary to Scripture.

As Galileo experimented with the theory of Copernicus, he began to uncover evidence that the earth did indeed revolve around the sun. He discovered that the earth made one complete turn on its axis every twenty-four hours. When Galileo recorded the findings in his book, *The Dialogue of the Two Great World Systems,* the Roman Catholic church moved quickly to silence him.

Early in 1633 Galileo was summoned to Rome to appear before the Inquisition. For months Galileo was questioned by church officials about his beliefs. Finally, on June 22, 1633, they succeeded in forcing Galileo to publicly deny his belief in the Copernican theory.

Defeated and depressed, Galileo retired to the country. Nevertheless, he soon overcame his depression and wrote his final book, *Discourses and Mathematical Demonstrations Concerning Two New Sciences*. This treatise established the mathematical principles of motion for generations to come. These laws form the backbone of modern-day physics.

1564-1642

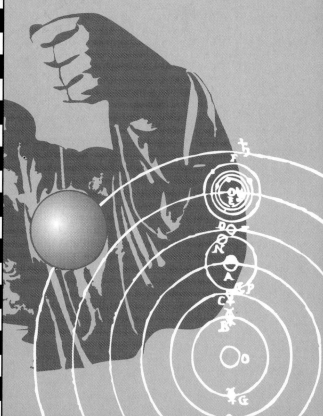

4 CHAPTER

MULTIPLYING AND DIVIDING DECIMALS

4.1 Estimating Products

Tim earns $6.35 per hour working after school as a math tutor. If Tim works for 2.6 hours, about how much will he earn?

You can estimate to find Tim's approximate earnings.

To estimate products with decimals, follow these steps:

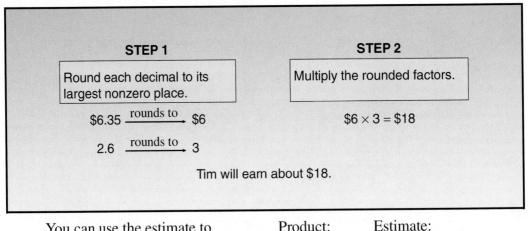

STEP 1	STEP 2
Round each decimal to its largest nonzero place.	Multiply the rounded factors.

$6.35 $\xrightarrow{\text{rounds to}}$ $6

2.6 $\xrightarrow{\text{rounds to}}$ 3

$6 × 3 = $18

Tim will earn about $18.

You can use the estimate to determine the location of the decimal point in the product.

	Product:	Estimate:
	$6.35	$6
	× 2.6	× 3
	$16.510	$18

The product is equal to $16.51, since the estimate is equal to $18.

Additional Examples

Estimate; then use the estimate to place the decimal point in the product.

a. 8×6.742

$$6.742 \rightarrow 7$$
$$\times \quad 8 \rightarrow \times 8$$
$$\overline{53.936} \quad \overline{56}$$

b. 4.8×42.31

$$42.31 \rightarrow 40$$
$$\times \quad 4.8 \rightarrow \times 5$$
$$\overline{203.088} \quad \overline{200}$$

☑SKILL CHECK

Estimate.

1. 8.37×6
2. $\$3.89 \times 5.7$
3. 7.486×59.2
4. 113.4×17.57

Estimate; then use the estimate to place the decimal point in the product.

5. $9.6 \times 4 = 384$
6. $5.43 \times 2.6 = 14118$
7. $18.3 \times 4.1 = 7503$
8. $2.143 \times 10.4 = 222872$

Exercises

Estimate.

1. 5.36×6
2. 4.53×8.2
3. $\$3.47 \times 2.5$
4. 6.48×9.75

5. 14.7×2.59
6. 19.4×5.37
7. 2.683×4.1
8. 1.342×9.6

9. 6.25×100.97
10. 8.597×48.6

11. 278.39×30.57
12. $5.48 \times 19.23 \times 7.6$

13. $6.82 \times 1.71 \times 3.43$
14. $9.345 \times 5.714 \times 13.508$

Multiplying and Dividing Decimals

Estimate. Select the correct answer.

15. 6×7.39
   a. 4.434
   b. 44.34
   c. 443.4

16. $12 \times \$8.05$
   a. $96.60
   b. $966.00
   c. $9,660.00

17. 13.8×6.4
   a. 8.832
   b. 883.2
   c. 88.32

18. 8.95×48.6
   a. 43.497
   b. 434.97
   c. 4,349.7

Estimate; then use the estimate to place the decimal point in the product.

19.
$$\begin{array}{r} 8.3 \\ \times\ 7 \\ \hline 581 \end{array}$$

20.
$$\begin{array}{r} 6.83 \\ \times\ 2.4 \\ \hline 16392 \end{array}$$

21.
$$\begin{array}{r} 4.97 \\ \times\ 4.5 \\ \hline 22365 \end{array}$$

22.
$$\begin{array}{r} 7.38 \\ \times\ 3.75 \\ \hline 276750 \end{array}$$

23.
$$\begin{array}{r} 49.4 \\ \times\ 1.95 \\ \hline 96330 \end{array}$$

24.
$$\begin{array}{r} 19.8 \\ \times\ 5.2 \\ \hline 10296 \end{array}$$

25.
$$\begin{array}{r} 8.746 \\ \times\ 6.5 \\ \hline 568490 \end{array}$$

26.
$$\begin{array}{r} 1.975 \\ \times\ 10.2 \\ \hline 201450 \end{array}$$

Application

27. One nickel weighs about 5.2 g. Estimate the weight of 27 nickels.

28. One quarter weighs about 5.6 g, and one nickel weighs about 5.2 g. Estimate the weight of 5 quarters and 6 nickels.

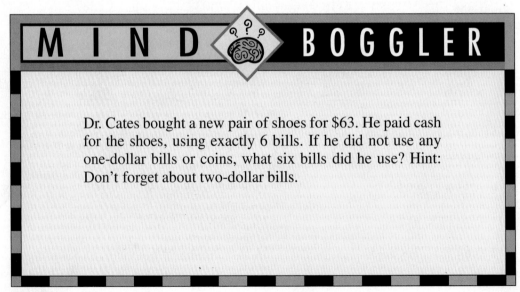

MIND BOGGLER

Dr. Cates bought a new pair of shoes for $63. He paid cash for the shoes, using exactly 6 bills. If he did not use any one-dollar bills or coins, what six bills did he use? Hint: Don't forget about two-dollar bills.

4.2 Multiplying Decimals

Ken's new car gets 34.7 miles per gallon for highway driving. The gas tank has a capacity of 12.5 gallons. How many miles can Ken travel on the highway with a full tank of gas?

You multiply 34.7×12.5 to find the answer.

To multiply decimals, follow these steps.

STEP 1	STEP 2	STEP 3
Multiply as with whole numbers.	Find the total number of decimal places in the factors.	Place the decimal point so that the product has the same number of decimal places as the total.

STEP 1:
```
  34.7
× 12.5
─────
  173
  694
 347
─────
43375
```

STEP 2:
```
  34.7  ◄ 1 decimal place
× 12.5  ◄ 1 decimal place

Total:   2 decimal places
```

STEP 3:
```
   34.7
 × 12.5
 ──────
  17 35
  69 4
 347
 ──────
 433.75  ◄ 2 decimal places
```

Estimate to check the answer: $30 \times 10 = 300$.

Ken's car can travel 433.75 miles on a tank of fuel.

Additional Examples

Multiply.

a.
```
  5.7   ◄ 1 decimal place
×   4   ◄ 0 decimal places
─────
 22.8   ◄ 1 decimal place
```

b.
```
  0.659  ◄ 3 decimal places
×   0.8  ◄ 1 decimal place
───────
 0.5272  ◄ 4 decimal places
```

Multiplying and Dividing Decimals

☑SKILL CHECK

Place the decimal point correctly in each product.

1.	2.	3.	4.
4.65	8.3	7.004	0.3721
× 9	× 0.27	× 3.8	× 6.4
4185	2241	266152	238144

Multiply; then estimate to make sure that the product is reasonable.

5.	6.	7.	8.
6.83	0.47	3.256	2.5132
× 0.2	× 3.9	× 0.41	× 6.5

Exercises

Place the decimal point correctly in each product.

1.	2.	3.	4.
5.7	0.47	5.03	2.917
× 3.4	× 2.1	× 0.68	× 3.14
1938	987	34204	915938

Multiply.

5.	6.	7.	8.
4.8	6.9	34.2	82.5
× 0.7	× 0.27	× 0.06	× 3.9

9.	10.	11.	12.
27.84	42.6	62.9	2.501
× 0.56	× 42.6	× 1.35	× 8.07

Telescopes which use only glass lenses to magnify an image are called refractor telescopes. This refractor telescope built by Galileo could magnify 20 times.

In 1609, Galileo tested his famous improved telescope, which he made for the ruler of Padua. It magnified nine times and was the first telescope of his day to produce an upright image.

13. 0.5×4.87

14. 19×0.65

15. 0.89×7.48

16. 1.07×2.16

17. 6.2×18.74

18. 0.78×900

19. 0.83×4.709

20. 6.15×12.37

21. 58×0.936

22. $0.5 \times 6.2 \times 7$

23. $1.9 \times 0.3 \times 4.25$

24. $4.01 \times 3.7 \times 0.23$

Application

25. A certain subcompact car gets 31.4 mpg for city driving. Its gas tank has a capacity of 12.6 gallons. How many miles can this subcompact car travel in the city on a full tank of gas?

26. A midsize car gets 24.7 mpg for highway driving. Its gas tank has a capacity of 13.9 gallons. How much farther than 325 miles can this car travel on the highway with a full tank of gas?

Multiplying and Dividing Decimals

4.3 Zeros in Products

Dottie purchased a spiral notebook for $1.89. The sales tax rate was 5% (0.05 of the price). To the nearest cent, what was the amount of the sales tax on the notebook?

You multiply $1.89 × 0.05 to find the amount of sales tax.

To place the decimal point correctly in some products, you must annex zeros. Consider the example below.

STEP 1	STEP 2	STEP 3
Multiply as with whole numbers.	Find the total number of decimal places in the factors.	Annex zeros as needed to place the decimal point in the product.

$$\begin{array}{r} \$1.89 \\ \times\ 0.05 \\ \hline 945 \end{array}$$

$$\begin{array}{r} \$1.89 \quad \blacktriangleleft 2\text{ decimal places} \\ \times\ 0.05 \quad \blacktriangleleft 2\text{ decimal places} \\ \hline 945 \end{array}$$

$$\begin{array}{r} \$1.89 \\ \times\ 0.05 \\ \hline 0.0945 \quad \blacktriangleleft 4\text{ decimal places} \end{array}$$

Round the product to the nearest cent: $0.0945 ≈ $0.09

The amount of sales tax on the notebook was $0.09.

Additional Examples

Multiply.

a.
$$0.07 \blacktriangleleft 2 \text{ decimal places}$$
$$\underline{\times \, 0.04} \blacktriangleleft 2 \text{ decimal places}$$
$$0.0028 \blacktriangleleft 4 \text{ decimal places}$$

b.
$$0.016 \blacktriangleleft 3 \text{ decimal places}$$
$$\underline{\times \, 0.28} \blacktriangleleft 2 \text{ decimal places}$$
$$128$$
$$\underline{32}$$
$$0.00448 \blacktriangleleft 5 \text{ decimal places}$$

Multiply. Round to the nearest hundredth.

c.
$$\$1.98 \blacktriangleleft 2 \text{ decimal places}$$
$$\underline{\times \, 0.07} \blacktriangleleft 2 \text{ decimal places}$$
$$0.1386 \blacktriangleleft 4 \text{ decimal places} \qquad 0.1386 \approx \$0.14$$

☑SKILL CHECK

Write zeros and a decimal point to make each product correct.

1.
$$0.5$$
$$\underline{\times 0.7}$$
$$35$$

2.
$$1.6$$
$$\underline{\times 0.009}$$
$$144$$

3.
$$18$$
$$\underline{\times 0.004}$$
$$72$$

4.
$$0.0075$$
$$\underline{\times \quad 0.3}$$
$$225$$

Multiply.

5.
$$0.08$$
$$\underline{\times \, 0.9}$$

6.
$$0.13$$
$$\underline{\times 0.04}$$

7.
$$0.934$$
$$\underline{\times 0.006}$$

8.
$$0.039$$
$$\underline{\times \, 0.25}$$

Exercises

Write zeros and a decimal point to make each product correct.

1.
$$0.158$$
$$\underline{\times \, 0.06}$$
$$948$$

2.
$$0.84$$
$$\underline{\times 0.09}$$
$$756$$

3.
$$1.7$$
$$\underline{\times 0.04}$$
$$68$$

4.
$$0.007$$
$$\underline{\times 0.042}$$
$$294$$

Multiply.

5.
$$0.034$$
$$\underline{\times \, 0.06}$$

6.
$$0.0572$$
$$\underline{\times \quad 0.3}$$

7.
$$97$$
$$\underline{\times 0.0008}$$

8.
$$0.086$$
$$\underline{\times \quad 0.7}$$

9.
$$0.37$$
$$\underline{\times 0.05}$$

10.
$$4.3$$
$$\underline{\times 0.09}$$

11.
$$0.46$$
$$\underline{\times 0.12}$$

12.
$$15.8$$
$$\underline{\times \, .06}$$

Multiplying and Dividing Decimals

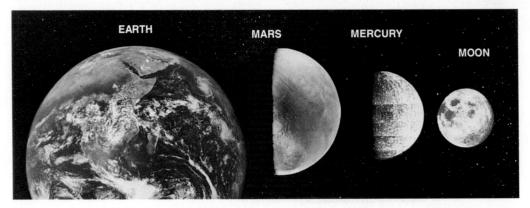

EARTH MARS MERCURY MOON

These planets and Earth's moon are all pictured at the same scale, but not the same magnification. The more distant ones must be magnified more to appear on the same scale.

13. 1.028
    $\times 0.033$

14. 0.037
    $\times 0.051$

15. 429
    $\times 0.0084$

16. 8.36
    $\times 0.0027$

17. 0.07×0.438

18. 0.316×0.21

19. 2.3×0.006

20. $0.42 \times 1.1 \times 0.8$

21. $13.7 \times 0.003 \times 0.2$

22. $12.5 \times 0.02 \times 0.018$

Multiply. Round to the nearest hundredth.

23. $\$2.74$
    $\times \ 0.08$

24. $\$36.85$
    $\times \ \ 0.06$

25. $\$9.89$
    $\times \ 0.35$

26. $\$145.90$
    $\times \ \ 0.13$

Application

27. A ball-point pen costs $1.29. The sales tax is 0.06 of the cost. What is the amount of the sales tax rounded to the nearest cent?

28. A pencil costs $0.29 and an eraser costs $0.35. The sales tax is 0.05 of the cost. What is the total cost of the pencil and eraser (including sales tax)?

4.4 Multiplying and Dividing Decimals by Powers of 10

Rachel used a calculator to multiply 3.896 by 10, 100, and 1,000.
Numbers such as 10, 100, and 1,000 are called *powers* of 10.

Study the resulting pattern below.

Multiplication	Decimal shifts
$3.896 \times 10 = 38.96$	**1** place to the right
$3.896 \times 100 = 389.6$	**2** places to the right
$3.896 \times 1,000 = 3,896.0$	**3** places to the right

When one of the factors is a power of ten, you can use this pattern to
find products mentally. Observe below that a similar pattern exists for
dividing by 10, 100, and 1,000.

Division	Decimal shifts
$84.2 \div 10 = 8.42$	**1** place to the left
$84.2 \div 100 = 0.842$	**2** places to the left
$84.2 \div 1,000 = 0.0842$	**3** places to the left

*Comet West was first seen on September 24, 1975. This was probably both its first and last appearance because
it broke up into four fragments shortly after this photograph was taken.*

Multiplying and Dividing Decimals

You can express powers of 10 in standard form. Study the pattern in the following examples.

$$10^1 = 10$$
(1 zero)

$$10^2 = 10 \cdot 10$$
$$= 100$$
(2 zeros)

$$10^3 = 10 \cdot 10 \cdot 10$$
$$= 1{,}000$$
(3 zeros)

$$10^4 = 10 \cdot 10 \cdot 10 \cdot 10$$
$$= 10{,}000$$
(4 zeros)

Additional Examples

Multiply or divide.

a. $0.095 \times 1{,}000 = 95$

b. $0.6 \div 1{,}000 = 0.0006$

c. $\$3.95 \times 10 = \$39.5 = \$39.50$

d. $7.42 \times 10{,}000 = 74{,}200$

e. $\$0.46 \times 100 = \$46$

f. $59¢ \times 10 = 590¢ = \$5.90$

☑ **SKILL CHECK**

Multiply or divide.

1. 2.745×100

2. $0.0593 \times 1{,}000$

3. 0.61×10

4. $67.82 \div 10$

5. $2{,}583 \div 10{,}000$

6. $1.73 \div 100$

7. $\$0.39 \times 100$

8. $\$6.75 \times 10$

9. $23¢ \times 10$

Exercises

Multiply or divide.

1. 2.83×10

2. $0.074 \times 1{,}000$

3. 46.5×100

4. $76.2 \div 100$

5. $1.83 \div 10$

6. $36.9 \div 1{,}000$

7. 65.31×10

8. $258 \times 1{,}000$

9. $0.765 \div 10$

10. $0.09 \div 100$

11. $5.29 \times 10{,}000$

12. $0.03 \div 100$

13. $2.468 \times 10{,}000$

14. $7{,}050.6 \div 10{,}000$

15. $187 \div 100{,}000$

16. $126.3 \times 10{,}000$

17. $0.0036 \times 1{,}000$

18. $74 \div 10{,}000$

Write each number as a power of 10.

19. 100 **20.** 10,000 **21.** 10 **22.** 100,000

Find the amounts mentally.

23. $0.07 × 100 **24.** $2.89 × 10 **25.** $14.50 × 1,000

26. $1.387 × 10 **27.** $1.62 × 10,000 **28.** 46¢ × 100

Application

29. A school bought 100 graduated cylinders for $375. How much did each graduated cylinder cost?

30. Test tubes are packaged 24 to a box and sold for $6.89 per box. If a school purchased 240 test tubes, how much did the test tubes cost?

4.5 Dividing Decimals by Whole Numbers

For a 13.5-km bicycle race, cyclists must complete 5 laps around a course through the city streets. How long is one lap?

You divide $13.5 ÷ 5$ to find the length of one lap.

To divide a decimal by a whole number, follow these steps.

STEP 1	STEP 2
Place the decimal point in the quotient above the decimal point in the dividend.	Divide as with whole numbers.

$$
\begin{array}{r}
. \\
5\overline{)13.5}
\end{array}
$$

$$
\begin{array}{r}
2.7 \\
5\overline{)13.5} \\
-10 \\
\hline
3\,5 \\
-3\,5 \\
\hline
0
\end{array}
$$

Multiply to check: $5 × 2.7 = 13.5$

The length of one lap is 2.7 km.

Multiplying and Dividing Decimals

Sometimes you must annex zeros (as needed) to the dividend until the quotient terminates. Consider the example at right.

```
   0.42
8) 3.42
  -3 2
     22
   - 16
      6
```

```
   0.4275
8) 3.4200   ◄ Annex zeros.
  -3 2
     22
   - 16
     60
   - 56
     40
   - 40
      0
```

Additional Examples

Divide.

a.
```
   0.038
4) 0.152
   12
   32
   32
    0
```

b.
```
    2.07
26) 53.82
    52
    1 8
      0
    1 82
    1 82
       0
```

c.
```
    $0.69
18) $12.42
    10 8
    1 62
    1 62
       0
```

☑**SKILL CHECK**

Divide.

1. 2) 9.36   **2.** 4) 0.224   **3.** 7) 305.13

4. 42) 159.6   **5.** 19) 1.406   **6.** 32) 65.92

Exercises

Divide.

1. 6) 16.8   **2.** 7) 66.5   **3.** 5) 30.75

4. 2) $3.52   **5.** 8) 0.72   **6.** 9) 72.63

7. 6) 256.02   **8.** 5) 40.45   **9.** 4) 0.268

10. 6) 2.748   **11.** 12) 59.4   **12.** 51) 4.08

Each planet has well-known characteristics that distinguish it from the others. Can you identify these planets and the two other astronomical bodies from the characteristics visible here?

13. $23\overline{)59.8}$

14. $78\overline{)\$252.72}$

15. $37\overline{)1.406}$

16. $16\overline{)30}$

17. $58\overline{)6.322}$

18. $36\overline{)116.82}$

19. $5.000 \div 8$

20. $36.63 \div 9$

21. $2.22 \div 6$

22. $171.6 \div 24$

23. $32.76 \div 42$

24. $1.204 \div 14$

Application

25. Matthias rode his bicycle 109.2 miles in 7 hours. What was his average speed?

26. During one month, Evamarie rode her bicycle a total of 241.2 miles on 18 training rides. How many miles did she average on each training ride?

Multiplying and Dividing Decimals

4.6 Rounding Decimal Quotients

Joel bought a package of 36 tracts for $4.98. To the nearest cent, what was the cost of each tract?

You divide $4.98 ÷ 36 to find the cost of each tract.

To find the price to the nearest cent, round the quotient to the nearest hundredth. Follow these steps:

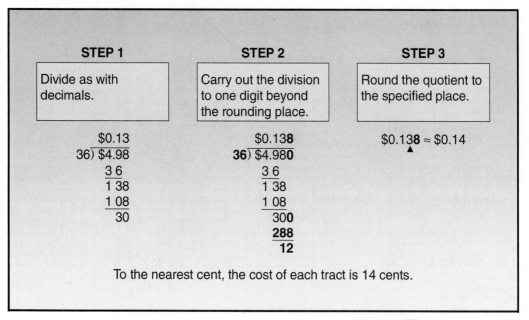

STEP 1	STEP 2	STEP 3
Divide as with decimals.	Carry out the division to one digit beyond the rounding place.	Round the quotient to the specified place.

STEP 1:
```
      $0.13
36) $4.98
     3 6
     1 38
     1 08
        30
```

STEP 2:
```
      $0.138
36) $4.980
     3 6
     1 38
     1 08
        300
        288
         12
```

STEP 3:
$0.138 ≈ $0.14

To the nearest cent, the cost of each tract is 14 cents.

Additional Examples

Divide. Round to the indicated place.

a. nearest tenth:

$$
\begin{array}{r}
6.74 \\
39\overline{)263.00} \\
-234 \\
\hline
29\,0 \\
-27\,3 \\
\hline
1\,70 \\
1\,56 \\
\hline
14
\end{array}
$$

◄ Divide to the hundredths place.

$6.74 \xrightarrow{\text{rounds to}} 6.7$

b. nearest thousandth:

$$
\begin{array}{r}
0.7647 \\
17\overline{)13.000} \\
-11\,9 \\
\hline
1\,10 \\
-1\,02 \\
\hline
80 \\
68 \\
\hline
120 \\
119 \\
\hline
1
\end{array}
$$

◄ Divide to the ten-thousandths place.

$0.7647 \xrightarrow{\text{rounds to}} 0.765$

☑ **SKILL CHECK**

Divide. Round to the indicated place.

1. nearest tenth: $15 \div 32$

2. nearest hundredth: $37.1 \div 13$

3. nearest cent: $\$43.95 \div 28$

4. nearest thousandth: $8.2 \div 3$

Exercises

Divide. Round to the nearest tenth.

1. $6\overline{)10}$
2. $9\overline{)13}$
3. $4\overline{)27}$
4. $7\overline{)19}$
5. $12\overline{)23}$
6. $23\overline{)50}$
7. $35\overline{)47.2}$
8. $49\overline{)74}$

Divide. Round to the nearest hundredth.

9. $6\overline{)8}$
10. $3\overline{)7.1}$
11. $7\overline{)19.2}$
12. $9\overline{)35}$
13. $17\overline{)13}$
14. $28\overline{)29.2}$
15. $43\overline{)45}$
16. $61\overline{)52}$

Divide. Round to the nearest thousandth.

17. $3\overline{)8}$
18. $7\overline{)9.2}$
19. $13\overline{)17}$
20. $49\overline{)28}$

Multiplying and Dividing Decimals

Divide. Round to the nearest cent.

21. 6) $23.90   **22.** 18) $17.60   **23.** 45) $126.10   **24.** 120) $26.15

Application

25. A package of 24 tracts costs $3.98. What is the cost of each tract to the nearest cent?

26. A dozen packages of tracts cost $43. What is the cost of 1 package to the nearest cent?

4.7 Dividing by a Decimal

You can multiply the divisor and the dividend in a division problem by the same power of 10, and the value of the quotient is not changed. Consider the examples below.

$$24 \div 8 = 3 \qquad\qquad 240 \div 80 = 3 \qquad\qquad 2{,}400 \div 800 = 3$$

	↑	↑	
	24×10	8×10	

	↑	↑	
	24×100	8×100	

Using this pattern, you can rename a decimal divisor as a whole number before you divide. To divide by a decimal, follow these steps.

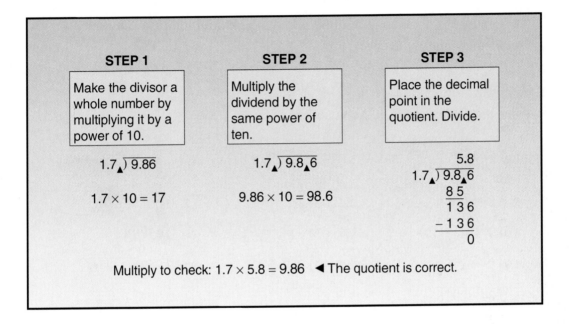

STEP 1	STEP 2	STEP 3
Make the divisor a whole number by multiplying it by a power of 10.	Multiply the dividend by the same power of ten.	Place the decimal point in the quotient. Divide.

$1.7_{\blacktriangle}) \overline{9.86}$

$1.7 \times 10 = 17$

$1.7_{\blacktriangle}) \overline{9.8_{\blacktriangle}6}$

$9.86 \times 10 = 98.6$

$$\begin{array}{r} 5.8 \\ 1.7_{\blacktriangle}) \overline{9.8_{\blacktriangle}6} \\ \underline{8\,5} \\ 1\,3\,6 \\ \underline{-1\,3\,6} \\ 0 \end{array}$$

Multiply to check: $1.7 \times 5.8 = 9.86$ ◄ The quotient is correct.

Additional Examples

Divide; then multiply to check.

a.
$$\begin{array}{r} 16.4 \\ 0.15_{\blacktriangle}) \overline{2.46_{\blacktriangle}0} \\ \underline{-1\,5} \\ 96 \\ \underline{-90} \\ 6\,0 \\ \underline{-6\,0} \\ 0 \end{array}$$

Check:
$$\begin{array}{r} 16.4 \\ \times 0.15 \\ \hline 820 \\ 164 \\ \hline 2.460 \end{array}$$

b.
$$\begin{array}{r} 140. \\ 0.005_{\blacktriangle}) \overline{0.700_{\blacktriangle}} \\ \underline{-5} \\ 20 \\ \underline{-20} \\ 0 \\ \underline{-0} \\ 0 \end{array}$$

Check:
$$\begin{array}{r} 140 \\ \times 0.005 \\ \hline 0.700 \end{array}$$

Multiplying and Dividing Decimals

☑SKILL CHECK

Place the decimal point in each quotient.

$$\begin{array}{r} 28 \\ \textbf{1. } 0.4\overline{)\ 1.12} \end{array} \qquad \begin{array}{r} 35 \\ \textbf{2. } 0.76\overline{)\ 2.660} \end{array} \qquad \begin{array}{r} 412 \\ \textbf{3. } 3.75\overline{)\ 15.450} \end{array} \qquad \begin{array}{r} 12 \\ \textbf{4. } 5.8\overline{)\ 6.96} \end{array}$$

Divide; then multiply to check.

$$\textbf{5. } 0.8\overline{)\ 0.376} \qquad \textbf{6. } 0.06\overline{)\ 0.312} \qquad \textbf{7. } 0.003\overline{)\ 1.47} \qquad \textbf{8. } 4.5\overline{)\ 0.819}$$

Exercises

Place the decimal point in each quotient.

$$\begin{array}{r} 63 \\ \textbf{1. } 0.7\overline{)\ 4.41} \end{array} \qquad \begin{array}{r} 216 \\ \textbf{2. } 3.4\overline{)\ 73.44} \end{array} \qquad \begin{array}{r} 3885 \\ \textbf{3. } 0.08\overline{)\ 3.1080} \end{array} \qquad \begin{array}{r} 437 \\ \textbf{4. } 0.013\overline{)\ 5.681} \end{array}$$

Divide.

$$\textbf{5. } 0.8\overline{)\ 1.056} \qquad\qquad \textbf{6. } 0.03\overline{)\ 7.2} \qquad\qquad \textbf{7. } 0.06\overline{)\ 7.02}$$

$$\textbf{8. } 0.7\overline{)\ 0.413} \qquad\qquad \textbf{9. } 0.02\overline{)\ 6.9} \qquad\qquad \textbf{10. } 0.05\overline{)\ 15}$$

$$\textbf{11. } 0.9\overline{)\ 1.278} \qquad\qquad \textbf{12. } 0.13\overline{)\ 0.455} \qquad\qquad \textbf{13. } 0.062\overline{)\ 0.1116}$$

$$\textbf{14. } 0.34\overline{)\ 0.918} \qquad\qquad \textbf{15. } 1.8\overline{)\ 1.35} \qquad\qquad \textbf{16. } 0.004\overline{)\ 1.4}$$

17. $10.4 \div 0.65$ **18.** $16.12 \div 0.31$ **19.** $72 \div 0.06$

20. $150 \div 0.025$ **21.** $0.672 \div 0.042$ **22.** $1.332 \div 7.4$

Compare. Use >, <, or =.

23. $0.117 \div 0.26 \ \square\ 11.7 \div 2.6$ **24.** $124.2 \div 2.7 \ \square\ 124.2 \div 0.27$

25. $62.9 \div 6.8 \ \square\ 6.29 \div 0.68$ **26.** $79.95 \div 2.6 \ \square\ 7.995 \div 2.6$

Application

27. On a deputation trip, the Adamses traveled 330.6 miles on 14.5 gallons of gasoline. How many miles per gallon did they average on this trip?

28. For the month, Mr. Adams figured that he used a total of 56 gallons of gasoline and averaged 23.9 miles per gallon. How many miles did he travel that month?

4.8 Scientific Notation

Earth's maximum distance from the sun is about 152,000,000 km. You can write this number in *scientific notation.*

Using the product of two factors, you can write 152,000,000 in scientific notation. The first factor is a number between 1 and 10. The second factor is a power of 10. To write a number in scientific notation, follow these steps.

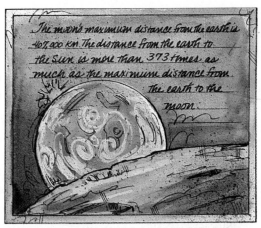

The moon's maximum distance from the earth is 407,000 km. The distance from the earth to the sun is more than 373 times as much as the maximum distance from the earth to the moon.

STEP 1	**STEP 2**
Move the decimal point to the left to form a number between 1 and 10.	Write the number of places the decimal point was moved as the exponent of 10.
1,52,000,000 : 1.52 8 places	1.52×10^8

In scientific notation, $152,000,000 = 1.52 \times 10^8$

Study the examples in the table below.

Standard Form	Number between 1 and 10	Power of 10	Scientific Notation
962,000	9.62000 5 places	10^5	9.62×10^5
394.08	3.94.08 2 places	10^2	3.9408×10^2

To rename a number from scientific notation to standard form, you move the decimal point to the right the number of places indicated by the exponent.

Multiplying and Dividing Decimals

Additional Examples

Write in standard form.

a. $3.075 \times 10^3 \rightarrow 3.075 \rightarrow 3,075$

   3 places

b. $8.04 \times 10^4 \rightarrow 8.0400 \rightarrow 80,400$

   4 places

☑SKILL CHECK

Write the missing number.

1. $5 \times 10^{\square} = 50,000$

2. $\square \times 10^5 = 349,000$

Write in scientific notation.

3. 3,000

4. 5,290,000

5. 15 thousand

Write in standard form.

6. 4×10^4

7. 7.2×10^5

8. 3.14×10^8

Exercises

Write each missing number.

1. $7 \times 10^{\square} = 7,000$

2. $\square \times 10^4 = 25,000$

3. $5.21 \times 10^{\square} = 521,000$

4. $\square \times 10^6 = 7,062,000$

Write in scientific notation.

5. 7,000

6. 5,400

7. 28,000

8. 60,900

9. 130,000

10. 306,900

11. 5,000,000

12. 88,000,000

13. 6,430,000

14. 287 thousand

15. 65 million

16. 4 billion

Choose the letter that shows the number in standard form.

17. 2.75×10^3 a. 27.5   b. 275   c. 2,750

18. 1.8×10^5 a. 18,000   b. 180,000   c. 1,800,000

19. 4.098×10^4 a. 40,980   b. 409,800   c. 4,098,000

Write in standard form.

20. 5×10^3

21. 9.2×10^4

22. 6.98×10^6

23. 3.06×10^5

24. 8.671×10^7

25. 5.071×10^5

26. 4.2×10^6

27. 3.76×10^8

28. 2×10^9

Application

29. Saturn is about 1,600,000,000 km from Earth. Write this number in scientific notation.

30. The diameter of Saturn's largest ring is about 4.8×10^5 km. Write this number in standard form.

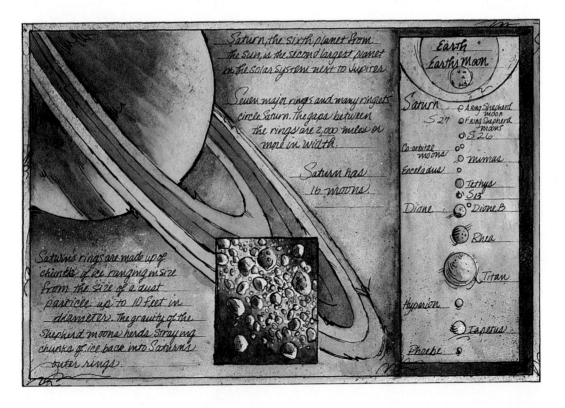

Multiplying and Dividing Decimals

Problem Solving: Solving Multi-Step Problems

You may need to use more than one step to solve some word problems. When a problem has two or more steps, you find the solution by solving one step at a time.

Plan what steps are necessary to solve the following problem; then find the solution.

Greg rented a car for $29 per day plus $0.15 per mile. He kept the car for 3 days and drove a total of 495 miles. What was his total cost of renting the car?

Four-Point Check List

1 READ to understand the question and identify the needed data.

2 PLAN what to do to solve the problem.

3 SOLVE the problem by carrying out the plan.

4 CHECK to make sure the solution is reasonable.

STEP 1	STEP 2	STEP 3
Find the cost for 3 days.	Find the cost for 495 miles.	Find the total cost.

STEP 1	STEP 2	STEP 3
$29	495	$87.00
× 3	× $0.15	+ 74.25
$87	2475	$161.25
	495	
	$74.25	

The total cost of renting the car was $161.25.

Is the answer reasonable? To determine whether the solution is reasonable, estimate the solution by rounding.

STEP 1	STEP 2	STEP 3
$30 × 3 $90	500 × $0.20 $100.00	$90.00 + $100.00 = $190.00 The solution is reasonable.

☑ **SKILL CHECK**

Solve.

1. A bag of bark chips costs $3.98, and an evergreen shrub costs $7.29. How much do 5 bags of bark chips and 3 evergreen shrubs cost?

2. There were 105 students at the school play. Out of every 15 students, 4 were with their parents. How many students were with their parents?

Multiplying and Dividing Decimals

Exercises

Solve.

1. If the price per dozen is $1.29, how much will 156 eggs cost?

2. Pam wants to buy a new formal for the school banquet. She has $20, and her dad has promised to give her $25. The dress costs $63. How much more money does she need to buy the dress?

3. Dudley picks strawberries for a farmer. He is paid $0.30 for each quart he picks. He picked 42 quarts on Monday, 37 on Tuesday,

   and 53 on Wednesday. How much money did he make?

4. A school has decided to pay each of the 8 bus drivers $875 per month. What was the total cost for bus drivers in a 9-month school year?

5. Rob weighs 12 pounds more than Kevin, and Tim weighs 23 pounds more than Kevin. If Tim weighs 112 pounds, how much does Rob weigh?

6. Lupe earns $3.50 per hour doing yard work. He worked 7 hours last week and 12 hours this week. How much did Lupe earn?

7. Tia bought 20 dwarf fruit trees on sale at 2 for $21. The regular price is $11.74 per tree. How much did Tia save by buying the trees on sale?

8. Anna earns $4.10 per hour for the first 40 hours each week. She earns double that rate for overtime above 40 hours. If Anna worked 47 hours in one week, how much would she earn?

9. Derek calculated that it would take 4 hours of equipment rental at $14.50 per hour and $28.67 in materials to landscape a flower garden. If Derek would like to make a $25 profit, how much should he charge?

10. Mr. Lobatos needs 94 feet of edging to landscape his back yard. A heavy grade of edging costs $1.09 per foot. A lighter grade of edging costs $0.82 per foot. How much would he save by choosing the lighter grade of edging?

This picture of Saturn is actually not a single photograph. Three images taken through ultraviolet, violet, and green filters were combined to make this photograph.

Multiplying and Dividing Decimals

Chapter 4 Review

4.1 Estimate.

1. $\begin{array}{r} 6.982 \\ \times \quad 9.5 \\ \hline \end{array}$

2. $\begin{array}{r} 18.7 \\ \times 5.49 \\ \hline \end{array}$

3. $4.73 \times 1.64 \times 3.16$

4.2 Multiply.

4. $\begin{array}{r} 0.58 \\ \times \quad 3.2 \\ \hline \end{array}$

5. $\begin{array}{r} 90.6 \\ \times \quad 6.4 \\ \hline \end{array}$

6. $\begin{array}{r} 51.7 \\ \times 2.48 \\ \hline \end{array}$

4.3 Multiply.

7. $\begin{array}{r} 0.059 \\ \times \quad 0.08 \\ \hline \end{array}$

8. $\begin{array}{r} 0.43 \\ \times 0.15 \\ \hline \end{array}$

9. $\begin{array}{r} 2.039 \\ \times 0.026 \\ \hline \end{array}$

10. $0.6 \times 8.3 \times 5$ 11. $15.9 \times 0.004 \times 0.6$

4.4 Multiply or divide.

12. 3.81×10

13. 237×100

14. $\$1.62 \times 1,000$

15. $2.64 \div 10$

16. $0.09 \div 100$

17. $154 \div 1,000$

4.5 Divide.

18. $5 \overline{)\, 18.5}$

19. $9 \overline{)\, 5.436}$

20. $32 \overline{)\, 50.88}$

4.6 Divide. Round to the specified place.

21. Nearest tenth:

$8 \overline{)\, 15}$

22. Nearest hundredth:

$6 \overline{)\, 16.1}$

23. Nearest thousandth:

$17 \overline{)\, 13}$

4.7 Divide.

24. $0.7 \overline{)\, 1.722}$

25. $0.004 \overline{)\, 3.44}$

26. $0.58 \overline{)\, 2.262}$

4.8 Write in scientific notation.

27. 37,000

28. 8,025,000

Write in standard form.

29. 2×10^5

30. 4.26×10^8

Chapter 4 Cumulative Review

1. Which is correct?
   a. 4,791 < 4,719   **b.** 2,341 > 2,431
   c. 64,265 > 64,256   **d.** not given

2. Find the missing addend.
   $(28 + 5) + 12 = \square + (28 + 12)$.
   a. 5   **b.** 12
   c. 30   **d.** not given

3. Find the missing addend.   3, 5 9 6
   $+ \square, \square\square\square$
   5, 0 7 8

   a. 2,582   **b.** 1,482
   c. 1,582   **d.** not given

4. Calculate $800 - (623 - 157)$.
   a. 20   **b.** 434
   c. 334   **d.** not given

5. Find the elapsed time from 8:45 A.M. to 1:05 P.M.
   a. 3 h. 15 min.   **b.** 3 h. 20 min.
   c. 4 h. 20 min.   **d.** not given

6. Find the missing number in
   $4 \times (8 + 17) = (4 \times \square) + (4 \times 17)$.
   a. 4   **b.** 8
   c. 17   **d.** not given

7. Compare. $20 \times 5 \times 32 \ \square\ 33 \times 0 \times 97$
   a. >   **b.** <
   c. =   **d.** not given

8. Write $5 \times 5 \times 5 \times 5$ in exponential form.
   a. 4^5 **b.** 1,024
   c. 625   **d.** not given

9. Find the product. $3 \cdot 7^2$
   a. 42   **b.** 147
   c. 441   **d.** not given

10. Divide. $48\overline{)8,256}$
    a. 162   **b.** 182
    c. 172   **d.** not given

11. What is the value of the underlined digit in 0.29$\underline{7}$5?
    a. 7 hundredths   **b.** 7 thousandths
    c. 7 ten-thousandths **d.** not given

12. Compare. 0.5268 $\square$ 0.5286
    a. >   **b.** <
    c. =   **d.** not given

13. Round 0.2674 to the nearest thousandth.
    a. 0.267   **b.** 0.268
    c. 0.27   **d.** not given

14. Estimate by rounding to the nearest dollar. $14.95
    $\times$ 6.38

    a. $8   **b.** $90
    c. $10   **d.** not given

15. Add. $4.7 + 8 + 6.94$
    a. 12.44   **b.** 18.64
    c. 19.64   **d.** not given

Multiplying and Dividing Decimals

FRANK LLOYD WRIGHT
ARCHITECTURE

1867-1959

Throughout his childhood, Frank Lloyd Wright's mother believed that her son Frank would one day be an architect. Recognizing Frank's fascination with "making things," she encouraged the toddler to build objects with geometric wooden blocks, strips of brightly colored paper, and small sticks. Convinced that painting was a necessary skill for a future architect, she invested in art lessons for young Frank. To top it off, she decorated his room with pictures of English cathedrals, hoping to instill in him a love of beautiful buildings.

Mrs. Wright's belief soon became Frank's dream. As an engineering student at the University of Wisconsin, Frank witnessed the collapse of a recently built wing of the Wisconsin state capitol building. Later he learned that the contractor who built the new wing had wrongly filled the supporting columns with crushed brick and stone. Unable to support the weight of the building, the weakened columns crumpled, bringing the rest of the structure down with them. As a result of the vivid impact of this tragedy, Frank determined that the buildings he designed would be standing long after his death.

After a course in civil engineering, Frank moved to Chicago to look for work. It was in the Windy City that Frank gained his first foothold in the world of architecture. There he became an employee of the talented architect Louis Sullivan, a pioneer in the design of large commercial buildings. Although Frank later became at odds with Sullivan, he readily admitted that the older man had a great influence on his work.

Throughout his long career, Wright was a revolutionary architect. Focusing primarily on residential architecture, he designed 269 houses throughout the United States. Frank prided himself in designing houses in such a way that they blended in with their natural surroundings. One of his most famous houses, Fallingwater, located in Mill Run, Pennsylvania, juts out dramatically over a waterfall.

Frank was also well known for the use of geometric patterns throughout his designs. He often said that these designs were inspired by the building blocks and colorful paper shapes his mother encouraged him to play with as a child. Many of the windows in his houses contain geometric glass designs, such as the stylized tulip motif found in the playroom of his personal home in Oak Park,

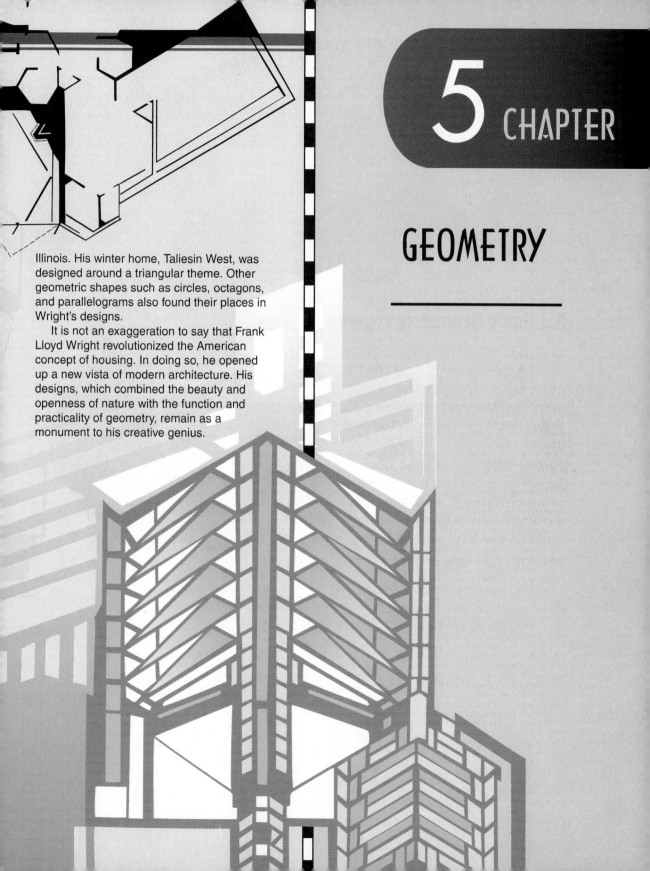

Illinois. His winter home, Taliesin West, was designed around a triangular theme. Other geometric shapes such as circles, octagons, and parallelograms also found their places in Wright's designs.

It is not an exaggeration to say that Frank Lloyd Wright revolutionized the American concept of housing. In doing so, he opened up a new vista of modern architecture. His designs, which combined the beauty and openness of nature with the function and practicality of geometry, remain as a monument to his creative genius.

5 CHAPTER

GEOMETRY

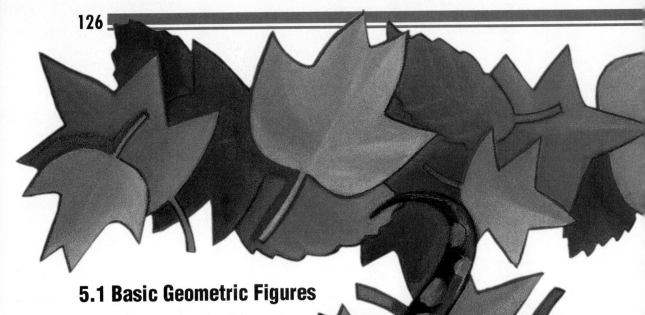

5.1 Basic Geometric Figures

God used many different shapes in creating the universe. Each part of nature is one type of geometric shape or another. The study of points and the shapes that they form is called *geometry.*

Points, lines, and *planes* are basic geometric figures that consist of a set of points. Although these figures cannot be formally defined, you can describe properties of each of them.

Study the following examples:

A *point* is an exact location in space. It has no length, width, or thickness.

• *P*

Symbol: *P*

A *line* is a set of points along a straight path with no endpoints.

Symbols: $\overleftrightarrow{QR}$, $\overleftrightarrow{RQ}$, or line *l*

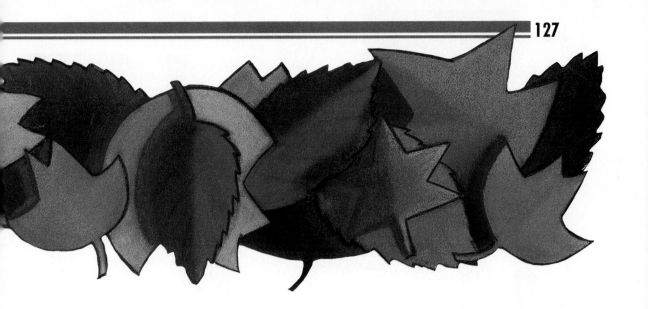

A **_ray_** is part of a line that
has one endpoint. It extends
endlessly in one direction.

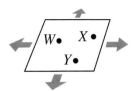

Symbol: $\overrightarrow{ST}$

A **_line segment_** is part of a
line that has two endpoints.

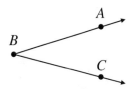

Symbols: $\overline{UV}$, or $\overline{VU}$

A **_plane_** is a flat surface
that extends endlessly in
all directions.

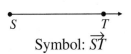

Symbol: plane *WXY*

An **_angle_** is formed by two
rays that have a common
endpoint. The common end-
point is called the **_vertex_**.

Symbols: $\angle ABC$, $\angle CBA$,
or $\angle B$

Geometry

Frank Lloyd Wright often looked to nature for the inspiration for his designs. He believed that a building should grow easily from its site and harmonize with its natural surroundings.

☑SKILL CHECK

Draw a picture of each geometric figure; then write the symbol for the picture.

1. segment *DE*

2. point *X*

3. ray *PQ*

4. line *ST*

5. plane *CBR*

6. angle *JKL*

Exercises

Write the name of each basic geometric figure.

1.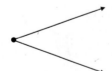

2. ●

3. ●————————●

4.

5. ←————————→

6.

Write the symbol for each figure.

7.
Q P

8.
C D

9.
M N

10.

R
S T

Draw and label each figure.

11. ∠DOT

12. plane *STR*

13. $\overrightarrow{GH}$

14. $\overleftrightarrow{PR}$

15. $\overline{BF}$

16. point *E*

Name three different segments in this figure.

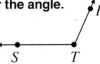

17.

Use the figure on the right for exercises 18-21.

18. Name three lines.
19. Name two rays from point *Y*.
20. On what two lines is point *X*?
21. Name a point on $\overleftrightarrow{XY}$ and $\overleftrightarrow{YZ}$.

Write the three different names for the angle.

22.

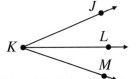

Use the figure on the right for exercises 23-24.

23. Identify the vertex.
24. Write the names of three different angles.

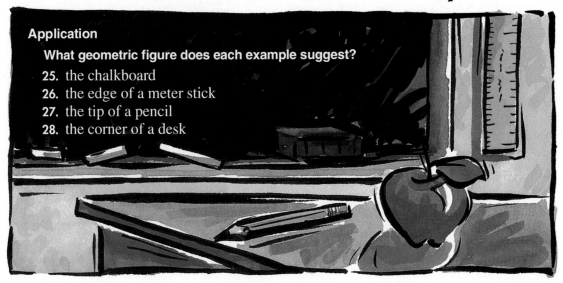

Application

What geometric figure does each example suggest?

25. the chalkboard
26. the edge of a meter stick
27. the tip of a pencil
28. the corner of a desk

Geometry

5.2 Angles

You can use a ***protractor*** to measure angles. The unit of measure is called a ***degree*** (°). Study the examples below.

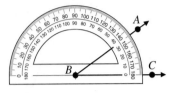

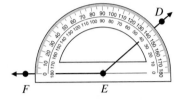

The measure of ∠*ABC* is 35°.

$m \angle ABC = 35°$

The measure of ∠*DEF* is 140°.

$m \angle DEF = 140°$

According to its measure, you can classify an angle as ***acute, right, obtuse,*** or ***straight.***

acute angle:
measures
less than 90°

right angle:
measures 90°

obtuse angle:
measures
greater than
90° and less
than 180°

straight angle:
measures
180°

Two angles are **complementary** if their measures have a sum of 90°.

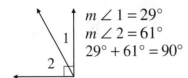

$m \angle 1 = 29°$
$m \angle 2 = 61°$
$29° + 61° = 90°$

∠1 and ∠2 are complementary angles.

Two angles are **supplementary** if their measures have a sum of 180°.

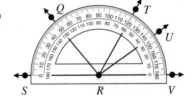

$m \angle G = 115°$
$m \angle H = 65°$
$115° + 65° = 180°$

∠G and ∠H are supplementary angles.

☑ SKILL CHECK

Write the measure of each angle.

1. ∠VRT   2. ∠SRQ

3. ∠URV   4. ∠TRS

Find the measure of the complement of the given angle.

5. 37°

Find the measure of the supplement of the given angle.

6. 114°

Exercises

Write the measure of each angle. Classify the angle as acute, right, obtuse, or straight.

1. ∠BAC   2. ∠BAD

3. ∠BAE   4. ∠BAG

5. ∠HAB   6. ∠HAF

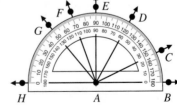

With a protractor, find the measure of each angle.

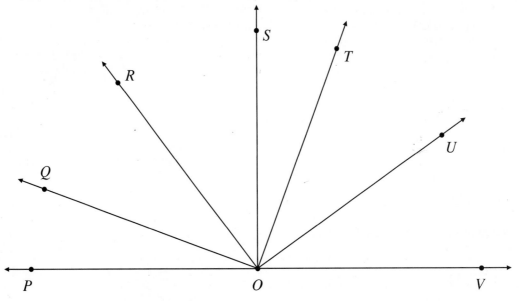

7. ∠UOV	**8.** ∠POT	**9.** ∠ROV	**10.** ∠SOP
11. ∠TOV	**12.** ∠POV	**13.** ∠SOU	**14.** ∠TOQ

Find the measure of the complement of the given angle.

15. $m \angle A = 30°$ **16.** $m \angle B = 65°$ **17.** $m \angle C = 13°$

18. $m \angle D = 28°$ **19.** $m \angle E = 52°$ **20.** $m \angle Z = 67°$

Find the measure of the supplement of the given angle.

21. $m \angle U = 50°$ **22.** $m \angle V = 140°$ **23.** $m \angle W = 90°$

24. $m \angle X = 138°$ **25.** $m \angle Y = 33°$ **26.** $m \angle Z = 167°$

Application

Classify the angle formed by the hands of a clock for the given times as acute, right, or obtuse.

27. 1:00   **28.** 3:00   **29.** 5:00   **30.** 5:15

5.3 Perpendicular and Parallel Lines

Perpendicular lines are lines that intersect to form right angles.

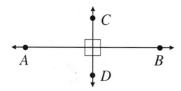

Line *AB* is perpendicular to line *CD*. Write: $\overleftrightarrow{AB} \perp \overleftrightarrow{CD}$

Parallel lines are lines in the same plane that never intersect.

Line *EF* is parallel to line *GH*. Write: $\overleftrightarrow{EF} \parallel \overleftrightarrow{GH}$

A line that intersects two or more lines is called a ***transversal.***

Consider the diagram below. When parallel lines *m* and *n* are intersected by transversal *t*, the following angle relationships are formed.

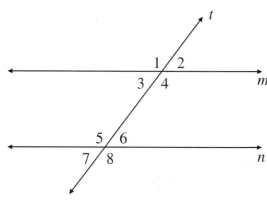

Vertical angles: ∠1 and ∠4, ∠2 and ∠3, ∠5 and ∠8, ∠6 and ∠7.

The ***vertical angles*** have equal measures.

Corresponding angles: ∠2 and ∠6, ∠4 and ∠8, ∠1 and ∠5, ∠3 and ∠7.

The ***corresponding angles*** have equal measures.

Since two angles are supplementary if their measures have a sum of 180°, there are 8 pairs of adjacent supplementary angles in the above diagram.

Supplementary angles: ∠1 and ∠2, ∠2 and ∠4, ∠4 and ∠3, ∠3 and ∠1, ∠5 and ∠6, ∠6 and ∠8, ∠8 and ∠7, ∠7 and ∠5.

☑**SKILL CHECK**

Identify each pair of lines as perpendicular, parallel, or neither.

1.   2.    3.

Identify each pair of angles as vertical angles, corresponding angles, or supplementary angles.

4. $\angle 1$ and $\angle 6$

5. $\angle 3$ and $\angle 7$

6. $\angle 2$ and $\angle 4$

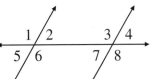

Exercises

Identify each pair of lines as perpendicular, parallel, or neither.

1.    2. 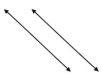   3.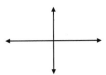

4. 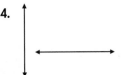   5. 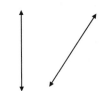   6.

Draw each figure.

7. $\overleftrightarrow{XY} \perp \overleftrightarrow{ZW}$ 8. $\overleftrightarrow{AB} \parallel \overleftrightarrow{CD}$ 9. $\overleftrightarrow{MP} \perp \overleftrightarrow{MN}$

10. $\overline{EF} \parallel \overline{GH}$ 11. $\overline{RS} \perp \overline{ST}$ 12. $\overline{KM} \perp \overleftrightarrow{JK}$

13. $\overleftrightarrow{HI} \parallel \overleftrightarrow{JK}$ with transversal t 14. $\overleftrightarrow{QR} \perp \overleftrightarrow{ST}$ intersecting at point P

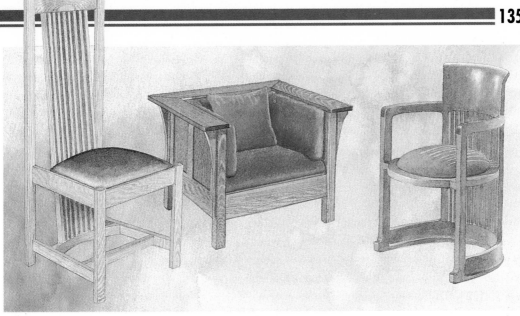

Wright did not stop with designing a structure; he also designed the details of accessories and furniture to harmonize with the building in which they were found. Here are three of his chair designs, from right to left: the prairie dining room chair, the prairie chair, and the barrel chair.

Identify each pair of angles as vertical angles, corresponding angles, or supplementary angles.

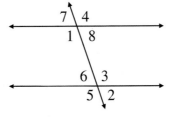

15. ∠7 and ∠8   **16.** ∠1 and ∠5

17. ∠6 and ∠3   **18.** ∠4 and ∠3

19. ∠5 and ∠2   **20.** ∠3 and ∠5

21. ∠4 and ∠8   **22.** ∠1 and ∠4

23. ∠2 and ∠8   **24.** ∠2 and ∠6

Application

Write always, sometimes, or never for each statement.

25. Parallel lines intersect at a point.

26. Transversals form right angles with lines they intersect.

27. Intersecting lines are perpendicular.

28. Two points determine a line.

Geometry

5.4 Polygons

A *polygon* is a closed geometric figure whose sides are segments. You can classify polygons according to the numbers of their sides. Study the examples in the table below.

Polygon		Number of sides
△	triangle	3
▱	quadrilateral	4
⬠	pentagon	5
⬡	hexagon	6

Polygon		Number of sides
⬡	heptagon	7
⯃	octagon	8
◯	nonagon	9
◯	decagon	10

A polygon in which all the sides have the same length and all the angles have the same measure is called *regular.* Consider the examples below.

| regular triangle | regular quadrilateral | regular pentagon | regular hexagon | regular octagon |

In a polygon, the endpoints of the sides are called *vertices.*

A line segment that joins two vertices of a polygon and is not a side of the polygon is called a *diagonal.*

Observe that you can draw two diagonals from vertex *E* in the pentagon on the right.

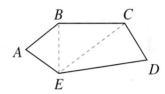

Vertices: *A, B, C, D, E*
Diagonals: *EB, EC*

☑ **SKILL CHECK**

Name each polygon. Identify those that are regular. Write the number of diagonals that you can draw from vertex *A* in each figure.

1.

   A

2.

   A

3.

   A

Exercises

Name each polygon. Identify those that are regular.

1.

2.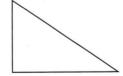

3.

Geometry

4.   **5.**   **6.**

Match.

7. regular triangle

8. nonagon

9. regular hexagon

10. quadrilateral

a.  b.

c.    d.

Write the number of all the diagonals that you can draw from vertex _A_ in each figure.

11.   12.    13.

14.    15.   16.

Application

Write true or false.

17. All hexagons have 6 vertices.
18. Some quadrilaterals have right angles.
19. All octagons are regular.
20. All polygons have a diagonal.

CHAPTER 5

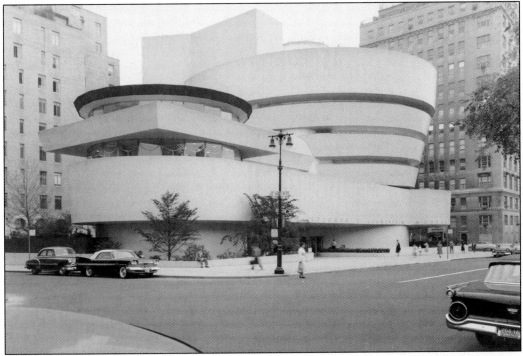

Completed in 1959, the Guggenheim Museum was Frank Lloyd Wright's last great work. It is shaped like a spiral with a hollow center and is lit by a large central skylight. It has been said that it was Wright's monument to himself.

5.5 Triangles

All triangles have three sides, three vertices, and three angles. There are two ways to classify a triangle.

You can classify a triangle according to the measures of its angles.

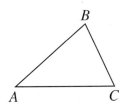

Acute triangle:
three acute angles

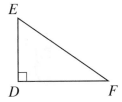

Right triangle:
one right angle

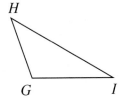

Obtuse triangle:
one obtuse angle

Geometry

You can also classify a triangle according to the lengths of its sides.

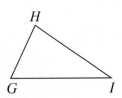

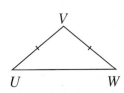

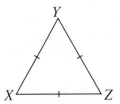

| Scalene triangle: All three sides have different lengths. | Isosceles triangle: At least two sides have the same length. | Equilateral triangle: All three sides have the same length. |

In any triangle, the sum of the measures of the angles is 180°.

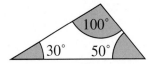

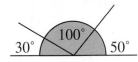

$30° + 100° + 50° = 180°$

If you know the measures of two angles in a triangle, you can find the measure of the third angle.

What is the measure of $\angle A$ in $\triangle ABC$?

$$m\angle A + m\angle B + m\angle C = 180°$$
$$? + 89° + 44° = 180°$$
$$? + 133° = 180°$$
$$? = 47°$$
$$m\angle A = 47°$$

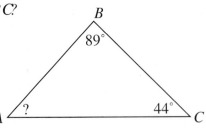

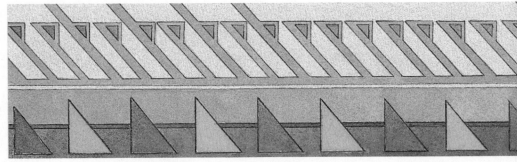

Wright often designed stained glass windows with geometric patterns for his houses. Some of those designs are presented here and on the following pages.

Classify each triangle according to the measures of its angles and the lengths of its sides.

1. 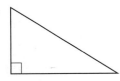   2.   3.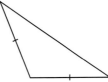

Find the measure of the missing angle in each triangle.

4. 37°, 54°, ☐   5. 118°, 26°, ☐

Exercises

Classify each triangle according to the measures of its angles.

1.    2.    3.

4. 50°, 70°, 60°   5. 19°, 117°, 44°   6. 90°, 25°, 65°

Classify each triangle according to the lengths of its sides.

7. 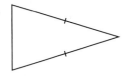   8.   9.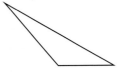

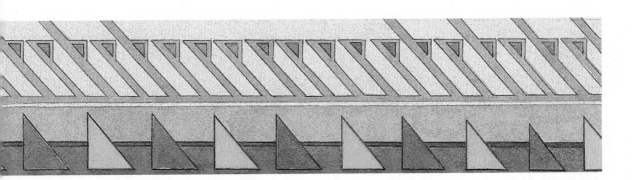

Geometry

10. 23 cm, 18 cm, 20 cm

11. 8 m, 4 m, 8 m

12. 12 cm, 12 cm, 12 cm

Find the missing measure in each triangle.

13.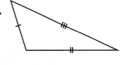

14.

15.

16. 37°, 56°, ☐

17. 129°, 14°, ☐

18. 23°, 67°, ☐

Classify each triangle two ways.

19.

20.

21.

Draw a triangle to fit each description. Mark equal parts alike.

22. obtuse isosceles

23. right scalene

24. acute isosceles

Application

Write true or false.

25. All equilateral triangles are obtuse.

26. All equilateral triangles are isosceles.

27. Some scalene triangles are acute.

28. Some obtuse triangles have one right angle.

5.6 Quadrilaterals

Quadrilaterals have four sides, four vertices, and four angles. Some quadrilaterals have special names. Consider the examples below.

Trapezoid:

a quadrilateral with at least one pair of opposite sides parallel

Parallelogram:

a quadrilateral with both pairs of opposite sides parallel

In a parallelogram, opposite sides have the same length, and opposite angles have the same measure. Some parallelograms have special names. Consider the following examples.

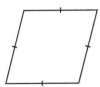

Rhombus:

a parallelogram with all sides the same length

Rectangle:

a parallelogram with four right angles

Square:

a rectangle with all sides the same length

Geometry

Observe that diagonal $\overline{XZ}$ divides quadrilateral *XYZW* into two triangles. Since the sum of the measures of the angles in each triangle is 180°, the sum of the measures of the four angles of a quadrilateral is 2 × 180°, or 360°.

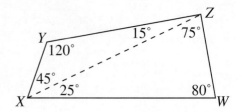

☑SKILL CHECK

Name each quadrilateral.

1.

2.

3.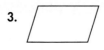

4.

Find the measure of the fourth angle of each quadrilateral.

5. 75°, 34°, 109°, ☐

6. 131°, 67°, 84°, ☐

Exercises

Name each quadrilateral.

1.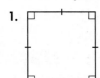

2.

3.

4.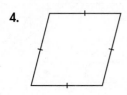

5.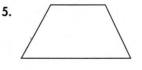

6.

Write true or false.

7. Every trapezoid is a quadrilateral.

8. Every quadrilateral is a trapezoid.

9. Every parallelogram is a rhombus.

10. Every rhombus is a parallelogram.

11. Every square is a rectangle.

12. Every rectangle is a square.

Find the measure of the fourth angle in each quadrilateral.

13.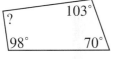

14.

15.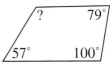

16.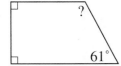

17.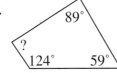

18.

Fallingwater, which became Wright's most famous structure, was built into the side of a hill and over a waterfall.

Geometry

Application

Write the letters of the figures described below.

19. trapezoid   20. parallelogram

21. quadrilateral   22. rectangle

23. square   24. rhombus

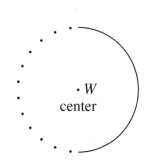

5.7 Circles

A *circle* is the set of all points in a plane that are the same distance from one point called the *center.* In the diagram on the right, point *W* is the center of a circle *W.*

A *radius* is a line segment from the center of the circle to a point on the circle. In circle *A* below, $\overline{AB}$, $\overline{AC}$, and $\overline{AD}$ are radii (plural of radius).

A line segment whose endpoints are on the circle is called a *chord.* $\overline{CB}$ and $\overline{EF}$ are both chords of circle *A.*

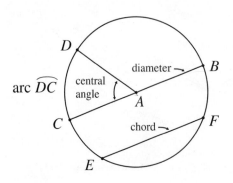

A chord that passes through the center of the circle is called a *diameter.* $\overline{CB}$ is a diameter of circle *A.* The length of the diameter is twice the length of the radius.

A *central angle* is an angle with its vertex at the center of the circle. $\angle DAB$ and $\angle DAC$ are central angles of circle *A.*

An *arc* is part of a circle. The arc with endpoints *D* and *C* is written as $\overset{\frown}{DC}$ or $\overset{\frown}{CD}$.

☑SKILL CHECK

Use circle *G* for exercises 1-8.

1. Name the center of the circle.
2. Name two radii.
3. Name two chords.
4. Name a diameter.
5. Name two arcs.
6. Name one central angle.
7. If the length of $\overline{GL}$ is 3.5 cm, what is the length of *HI?*
8. If the measure of ∠*HGL* is 70°, what is the measure of ∠*LGI?*

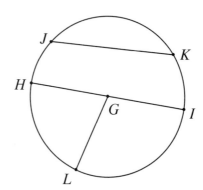

Exercises

Use circle *M* for exercises 1-8.

1. Name the center of the circle.
2. Name three radii.
3. Name a diameter of the circle.
4. Name two chords of the circle.
5. Name three arcs of the circle.
6. Name two central angles of the circle.
7. If the length of $\overline{MN}$ is 5 cm, how long is *NO?*
8. If the length of $\overline{NO}$ is 13 cm, how long is *PM?*

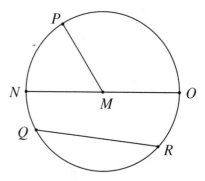

Use circle *S* to identify each as either a center, a radius, a chord, a diameter, an arc, or a central angle.

9. $\overline{YZ}$

10. $\overline{SV}$

11. $\overline{TU}$

12. $\overparen{WX}$

13. ∠*TSV*

14. *S*

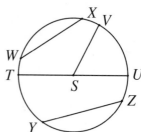

Geometry

In circle *A*, $\overline{AC}$ = 5 cm is 5 cm and *m* ∠*BAC* = 65°. Find the measure of each.

15. $\overline{AB}$

16. $\overline{FC}$

17. ∠*FAB*

18. $\overline{BE}$

19. $\overline{AF}$

20. ∠*FAE*

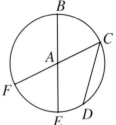

Write true or false.

21. All diameters are chords.
22. Some radii are chords.
23. All chords are diameters.
24. Some central angles are acute.

Application

25. Draw a circle with center *A*. Draw two radii, $\overline{AB}$ and $\overline{AC}$. Draw chord $\overline{BC}$. What kind of triangle is △*ABC*?

26. Draw a circle with center *P*. Draw diameter $\overline{QR}$ and mark point *S* on the circle. Draw $\overline{QS}$ and $\overline{RS}$. What kind of triangle is △*QRS*?

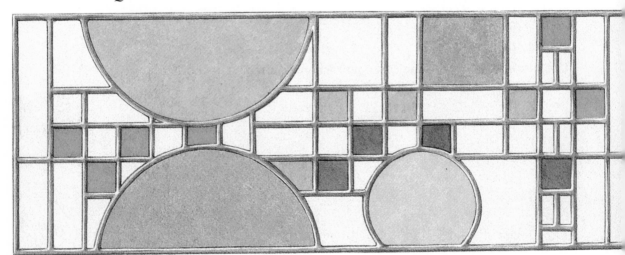

The Ingalls house is an example of Wright's Prairie Style houses.

5.8 Congruent Figures

If two geometric figures have the same size and the same shape, they are *congruent*.

Two segments are congruent if they have the same length.

A •────────────• B

C •────────────• D

$\overline{AB}$ is congruent to $\overline{CD}$.
$$\overline{AB} \cong \overline{CD}$$

Two angles are congruent if they have the same measure.

$\angle E$ is congruent to $\angle F$.
$$\angle E \cong \angle F$$

Two polygons are congruent if their corresponding sides and corresponding angles are congruent.

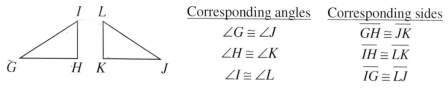

Corresponding angles	Corresponding sides
$\angle G \cong \angle J$	$\overline{GH} \cong \overline{JK}$
$\angle H \cong \angle K$	$\overline{IH} \cong \overline{LK}$
$\angle I \cong \angle L$	$\overline{IG} \cong \overline{LJ}$

$\triangle GHI$ is congruent to $\triangle JKL$.
$$\triangle GHI \cong \triangle JKL$$

If $m \angle G = 30°$, then $m \angle J = 30°$. ◄ Corresponding angles are congruent.

If $m \overline{GH} = 3.5$ cm, then $m \overline{JK} = 3.5$ cm. ◄ Corresponding sides are congruent.

☑**SKILL CHECK**

Triangles *RST* and *XYZ* are congruent. Complete each sentence.

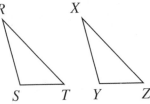

1. $\overline{RS} \cong$ ___
2. $\overline{ST} \cong$ ___
3. $\overline{XZ} \cong$ ___
4. $\angle S \cong$ ___
5. $\angle X \cong$ ___
6. $\angle T \cong$ ___
7. If $m\,\angle Y = 110°$, then $m\,\angle S =$ ___.
8. If $\overline{RS} = 28$ mm, then $XY =$ ___ mm.

Exercises

Write which pair of figures is congruent.

1.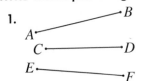

2.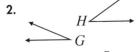

3.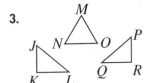

Complete. Triangles *MNO* and *PRQ* are congruent.

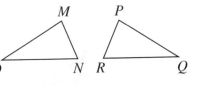

4. $\overline{MN} \cong$ _____
5. $\angle P \cong$ _____
6. $\overline{RQ} \cong$ _____
7. $\angle N \cong$ _____
8. $\overline{OM} \cong$ _____
9. $\angle Q \cong$ _____

Complete. Quadrilaterals *ABCD* and *EFGH* are congruent.

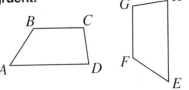

10. $\overline{AB} \cong$ _____
11. $\angle A \cong$ _____
12. $\overline{BC} \cong$ _____
13. $\angle B \cong$ _____
14. $\overline{HE} \cong$ _____
15. $\angle H \cong$ _____
16. $\overline{HG} \cong$ _____
17. $\angle G \cong$ _____

Complete. Triangles *RST* and *YZX* are congruent.

18. If $m\,\angle R = 30°$, then $m\,\angle Y =$ _____.
19. If $m\,\angle S = 90°$, then $m\,\angle$_____ $= 90°$.
20. If $m\,\angle X = 60°$, then $m\,\angle$_____ $= 60°$.
21. If $\overline{ST}$ is 3 cm long, then $\overline{ZX}$ is _____ cm long.
22. If $\overline{XY}$ is 5 cm long, then _____ is 5 cm long.
23. If $\overline{RS}$ is 4 cm long, then _____ is 4 cm long.

Application

Write true or false.

24. If $\triangle GHI$ and $\triangle JKL$ are congruent and $\triangle GHI$ has one obtuse angle, then $\triangle JKL$ has one obtuse angle.

25. If quadrilateral $ABCD$ is a rectangle and quadrilateral $EFGH$ is a rectangle, then $ABCD \cong EFGH$.

5.9 Constructing Segments and Angles

You can construct congruent segments and congruent angles using a compass and straightedge.

To construct a segment congruent to a given segment $\overline{AB}$, follow these steps.

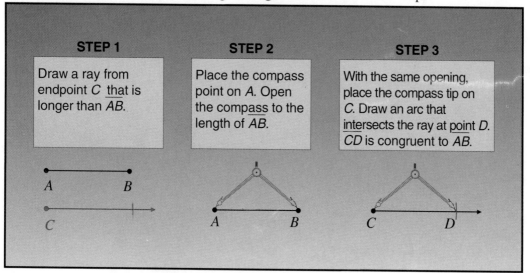

STEP 1	STEP 2	STEP 3
Draw a ray from endpoint C that is longer than $\overline{AB}$.	Place the compass point on A. Open the compass to the length of $\overline{AB}$.	With the same opening, place the compass tip on C. Draw an arc that intersects the ray at point D. $\overline{CD}$ is congruent to $\overline{AB}$.

To construct an angle congruent to a given angle *EFG*, follow these steps.

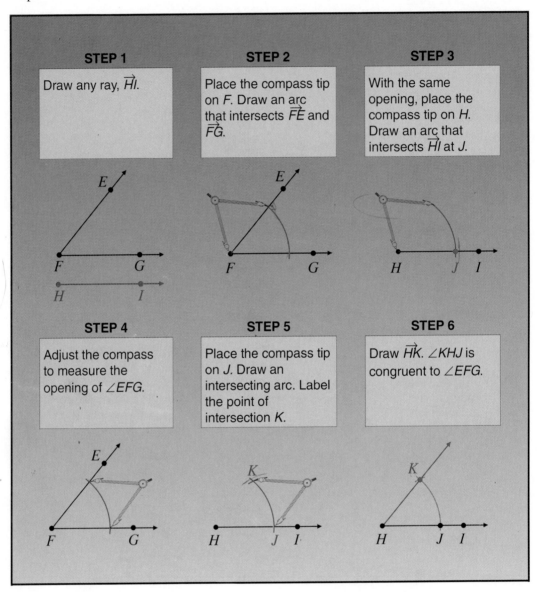

STEP 1

Draw any ray, $\overrightarrow{HI}$.

STEP 2

Place the compass tip on *F*. Draw an arc that intersects $\overrightarrow{FE}$ and $\overrightarrow{FG}$.

STEP 3

With the same opening, place the compass tip on *H*. Draw an arc that intersects $\overrightarrow{HI}$ at *J*.

STEP 4

Adjust the compass to measure the opening of ∠*EFG*.

STEP 5

Place the compass tip on *J*. Draw an intersecting arc. Label the point of intersection *K*.

STEP 6

Draw $\overrightarrow{HK}$. ∠*KHJ* is congruent to ∠*EFG*.

☑SKILL CHECK

Trace each figure; then construct a congruent figure for each.

1.

2.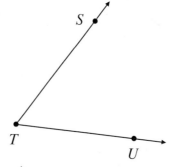

3.

4.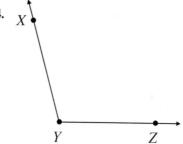

Exercises

Trace each figure; then construct a congruent figure for each.

1.

2.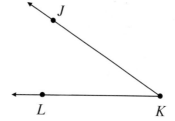

Geometry

3.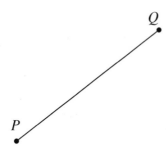

Q

P

4.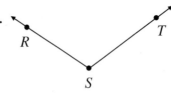

R

S

T

Use a ruler to draw a segment with the given length; then construct a segment congruent to each.

5. 3 cm   **6.** 5 cm   **7.** 8 cm

8. 4.5 cm   **9.** 6.2 cm   **10.** 3.9 cm

Use a protractor to draw an angle with the given measure; then construct an angle congruent to each.

11. 40°   **12.** 130°   **13.** 90°

14. 65°   **15.** 78°   **16.** 113°

Application

Perform the following constructions.

17. Given:

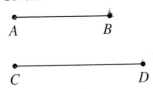

A B

C D

Construct $\overline{RS}$ equal to the sum of $\overline{AB}$ and $\overline{CD}$.

18. Given:

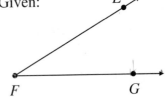

E

F G

Construct $\angle XYZ$ equal to twice the measure of $\angle EFG$.

Problem Solving: Identifying Needed Data

Some word problems contain more information than is needed to find the solution.

To solve problems like these, you must identify the needed data from the given information.

✓ **Four-Point Check List**

1 **READ** to understand the question and identify the needed data.

2 **PLAN** what to do to solve the problem.

3 **SOLVE** the problem by carrying out the plan.

4 **CHECK** to make sure the solution is reasonable.

Solve.

Mr. Bell bought 75 shares of Amtec stock at $9.18 per share and 163 shares of Excel stock at $15.75 per share. He paid a brokerage fee of $48 on these transactions. How many more shares of Excel stock did he buy?

1. READ: Understand the question.
   - How many more shares of Excel stock did he buy?
   To identify the needed data, cross out the extra information.
   - 75 shares of Amtec at ~~$9.18 per share~~
   - 163 shares of Excel at ~~$15.75 per share~~
   - ~~$48 brokerage fee~~

2. PLAN: Subtract $163 - 75$.

3. SOLVE: $163 - 75 = 88$

4. CHECK: $88 + 75 = 163$ ◀ Check the subtraction by adding.

Mr. Bell purchased 88 more shares of Excel stock.

Geometry

☑**SKILL CHECK**

Solve. If any data are missing, tell what additional information is needed to solve the problem.

1. David bought 75 shares of NCL stock at $9 per share. When the price dropped $2 per share, he purchased 45 more shares. How much did he pay for the additional purchase of NCL stock?

2. When the price of CBX stock rose $4 per share, Roger sold all but 65 shares of his CBX stock. If he purchased the stock at $9 per share, how much profit did he make on this transaction?

Exercises

Solve. If any data are missing, tell what additional information is needed to solve the problem.

1. Jed invested $1,900 in Biotech Corporation stock. The following year he bought another 50 shares at $63 per share. How many total shares of Biotech stock does Jed own?

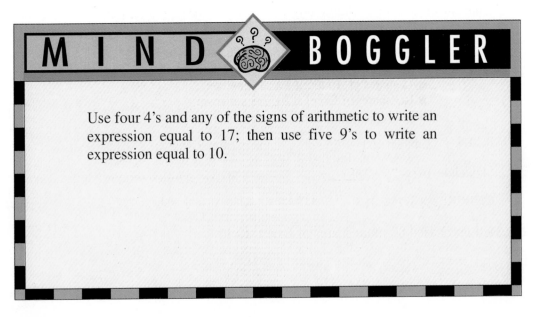

MIND ❓ BOGGLER

Use four 4's and any of the signs of arithmetic to write an expression equal to 17; then use five 9's to write an expression equal to 10.

2. Debbie invested $840 in Acme Toy stock at $24 per share. Three months later she sold all of her shares for $935. How many shares did she own?

3. Fred bought 47 shares of BSC Corporation stock at $34 per share. The stock paid a dividend of $3 per share. How much money from dividends did Fred receive?

4. Janet sold her shares of Food City stock at $27 per share. After she paid a broker's commission of $39, how much money did Janet make on this transaction?

5. During the past year, Westel stock sold as high as $34 per share and as low as $28 per share. Dan bought 75 shares at the lowest price. How much did Dan pay for these shares?

6. Beth purchased 75 shares of ALCAN Oil stock at $19 per share. She later sold 46 of these shares at $28 per share. How much profit did Beth make on this transaction?

7. Shanda bought 18 shares of Ultra Tech Computer stock at $52 per share. She later sold her shares for $780. How much money did Shanda lose on this transaction?

8. Pedro bought 37 shares of XYZ Corporation stock one year and twice that number the next year. He received dividends of $18 per share each year. How many shares of XYZ Corporation stock does Pedro own?

Geometry

9. Don bought 68 shares of IBN stock at $49 per share and 115 shares of the same stock at $52 per share. When the price dropped to $45, he sold 94 shares. How many shares of IBN stock does Don own now?

Chapter 5 Review

5.1 Write the name of each basic geometric figure.

1. •

2.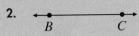
   B   C

3.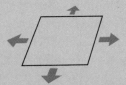

Write the symbol for each figure below.

4. •————→
    G   H

5.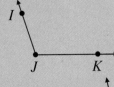
   I
   J   K

6. •————•
   L   M

5.2 Write the measure of each angle.

7. ∠BAC   8. ∠DAE

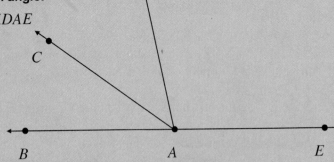

D

C

B   A   E

Find the measure of the complement of the given angle.

9. $m \angle X = 21°$

Find the measure of the supplement of the given angle.

10. $m \angle Y = 147°$

5.3 Identify each pair of lines as perpendicular, parallel, or neither.

11.

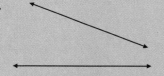

12.

Identify each pair of angles as vertical angles, corresponding angles, or supplementary angles.

13. ∠3 and ∠4
14. ∠8 and ∠6
15. ∠2 and ∠5

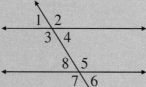

5.4 Name each polygon. Identify those that are regular.

16.

17.

18.

5.5 Classify the triangle according to the measure of its angles.

Classify the triangle according to the lengths of its sides.

19.

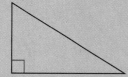

20.

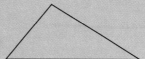

Classify the triangle two ways.

Find the missing angle measure in the triangle.

21.

22.

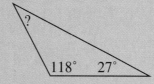

118°   27°

5.6 Name each quadrilateral.

23.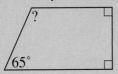

24.

25.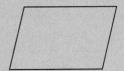

26. Write the measure of the missing angle in exercise 23.

5.7 Use circle Y to identify each as either a center, a radius, a chord, a diameter, an arc, or a central angle.

27. $\overline{WY}$ 28. $\overline{XZ}$ 29. $\overline{UV}$

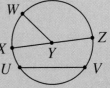

5.8 Triangles ABC and XYZ are congruent. Complete each sentence.

30. $\overline{AB} \cong$ ____   31. $\angle Z \cong \angle$ ____

32. If $\overline{BC}$ is 3 cm long, then ____ is 3 cm long.

33. If $m \angle Y$ is 93°, then $m \angle$ ____ is 93°.

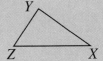

5.9 Construct $\overline{GH}$ so that $\overline{GH}$ is congruent to $\overline{EF}$.

Construct $\angle KLM$ so that $\angle KLM$ is congruent to $\angle HIJ$.

34.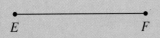

35.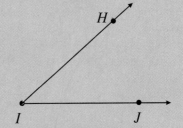

Chapter 5 Cumulative Review

1. Estimate to choose the correct product for 297 × 198.
- **a.** 48,800
- **b.** 58,806
- **c.** 68,806
- **d.** not given

2. Write 2^3 in factored form.
- **a.** $2 \times 2 \times 2$
- **b.** 2×3
- **c.** 3×3
- **d.** not given

3. Choose the appropriate division for an estimate of 40.
- **a.** $7)\overline{192}$
- **b.** $7)\overline{219}$
- **c.** $7)\overline{291}$
- **d.** not given

4. Find the missing dividend.

$$2\ 3\ 9\ r\ 4$$
$$8)\overline{\square,\square\square\square}$$
- **a.** 1,912
- **b.** 1,916
- **c.** 1,908
- **d.** not given

5. Divide. $452)\overline{75,936}$
- **a.** 158
- **b.** 168
- **c.** 178
- **d.** not given

6. What is the standard form for two hundred seven thousandths?
- **a.** 2.107
- **b.** 200.007
- **c.** 0.207
- **d.** not given

7. Choose the greatest decimal: 6.203, 6.21, 6.3.
- **a.** 6.203
- **b.** 6.21
- **c.** 6.3
- **d.** not given

8. Estimate by rounding to the nearest hundred.
$$623.51$$
$$284.29$$
$$+\ \ 45.86$$
- **a.** 900
- **b.** 950
- **c.** 1,000
- **d.** not given

9. Add. 65.78 + 657.8 + 6.578 + 6,578
- **a.** 7,380.158
- **b.** 7,038.158
- **c.** 7,308.158
- **d.** not given

10. Subtract. 9.07 − 4.293
- **a.** 4.787
- **b.** 4.777
- **c.** 4.773
- **d.** not given

11. Use estimation to select the correct answer. 7 × 8.52
- **a.** 5.964
- **b.** 59.64
- **c.** 596.4
- **d.** not given

12. Multiply. 63 × 0.815
- **a.** 51.335
- **b.** 41.345
- **c.** 51.345
- **d.** not given

13. Write zeros and a decimal point to make the product correct.
0.007 × 0.38 = 266
- **a.** 0.266
- **b.** 0.0266
- **c.** 0.00266
- **d.** not given

14. Divide. 48.7 ÷ 1,000
- **a.** 0.00487
- **b.** 0.0487
- **c.** 0.487
- **d.** not given

15. Divide. $7)\overline{2.443}$
- **a.** 0.348
- **b.** 0.359
- **c.** 0.349
- **d.** not given

Geometry

BENJAMIN BANNEKER
MATHEMATICS/ASTRONOMY

Benjamin Banneker, America's first black scientist and mathematician, was born the son of a slave. However, his father purchased his freedom when Benjamin was just a small boy. Along with his freedom, Mr. Banneker purchased one hundred twenty acres of land in the wilderness of Maryland.

In the frontier lands of colonial America, survival was far more important than education. Although Benjamin's parents recognized the intelligence of their young son, they needed Benjamin on the farm to help the family maintain its bare existence. Instruction in reading, writing, and arithmetic would have to wait until more prosperous times.

In 1744 a young Quaker by the name of Peter Heinrich started a school near the Banneker farm. Recognizing the genius of young Benjamin, Heinrich persuaded his parents to allow the boy to attend school in the winter when he wasn't needed on the farm. Benjamin flourished under Heinrich's teaching. He demonstrated an instinctive skill in mathematics. For enjoyment, Benjamin would sit up nights creating and solving his own mathematical puzzles.

Benjamin's fascination with mathematics went hand-in-hand with an extraordinary mechanical genius. In his early twenties, he constructed a clock by carving each part from pieces of wood. The amazing thing about this accomplishment is the fact that Benjamin had never seen a clock. He had once taken a watch apart and studied the movement of its gears. His clock was a larger version of the watch, fashioned from memory. The clock, which took two years to complete, kept accurate time for more than twenty years.

Benjamin later turned his interest in mathematics upward toward the night sky. He had studied astronomy as a boy under the knowledgeable eye of Peter Heinrich. Now he began to study the heavens in an effort to determine the effects of astronomy on farming. Benjamin compiled tables which listed the position of celestial bodies for each day of the year. In 1789 he correctly predicted a solar eclipse.

1731-
1806

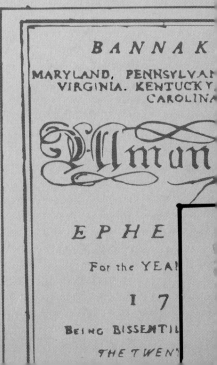

BANNAK

MARYLAND, PENNSYLVAN
VIRGINIA. KENTUCKY.
CAROLINA

Aman

E P H E

For the YEA!

1 7

BEING BISSEXTIL

THE TWEN'

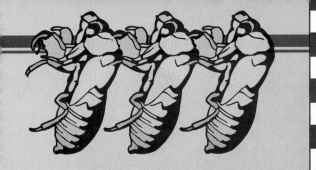

Three years later, he published his calculations in an almanac bearing his name. This book, which contained weather predictions along with snippets of literary works and historical facts, was cherished by farmers in the states of Pennsylvania, Delaware, Maryland, and Virginia. Thomas Jefferson once sent a copy of the popular almanac to the prestigious French Academy of Sciences as an example of the type of scientific inquiry that America was capable of fostering.

In 1791 President Washington asked Benjamin to help with the surveying of the nation's new capital in the Territory of Columbia. Slightly over a year later, Pierre-Charles L'Enfant, the city's designer, abruptly quit, taking the surveyor's maps and blueprints with him. Without these papers, the project came to a grinding halt. However, Benjamin came to the rescue. Working from memory, he redrew all the plans in only three days. This allowed the builders to complete the city of Washington, D.C.

Throughout his life, Benjamin was active in championing the abilities of other members of his race. He strongly believed that if black men and women were given their freedom and access to quality education, they would become vital assets to the intellectual development of America. Benjamin Banneker serves as a brilliant example of what can be accomplished when those conditions are met.

6 CHAPTER

NUMBER THEORY
•
DEVELOPING FRACTIONS

Benjamin Bannaker's
YLVANIA, DELAWARE, MARY-
LAND, AND VIRGINIA
LMANAC

6.1 Divisibility

Roger has 117 tomato plants to plant in a large garden. If he wants the same number of plants in each row, can Roger plant the tomatoes in 3 rows?

To find out, you must divide 117 by 3.

$$\begin{array}{r} 39 \text{ r } 0 \\ 3\overline{)117} \\ \underline{9} \\ 27 \\ \underline{-27} \\ 0 \end{array}$$

The answer is yes, since the remainder is 0.

If the remainder is 0 when a whole number is divided by another whole number, the first number is *divisible* by the second.

You can use divisibility rules to determine whether a whole number is divisible by 2, 3, 4, 5, 6, 9, or 10. Study the rules in the table below.

Divisibility Rules	
A number is divisible by—	If—
2	the ones digit is 0, 2, 4, 6, or 8.
3	the sum of the digits is divisible by 3.
4	the number named by the last 2 digits is divisible by 4.
5	the ones digit is 0 or 5.
6	the number is divisible by both 2 and 3.
9	the sum of the digits is divisible by 9.
10	the ones digit is 0.

Additional Example

Is 384 divisible by the following digits?

2	yes	◄ The ones digit is 4.
3	yes	◄ 3 + 8 + 4 = 15, and 15 is divisible by 3.
4	yes	◄ 84 is divisible by 4.
5	no	◄ The ones digit is not 0 or 5.
6	yes	◄ 384 is divisible by both 2 and 3.
9	no	◄ 3 + 8 + 4 = 15, and 15 is not divisible by 9.
10	no	◄ The ones digit is not 0.

☑ SKILL CHECK

Use the divisibility rules to determine whether each number is divisible by 2, 3, 4, 5, 6, 9, 10, or none of these numbers.

1. 75   2. 216   3. 650   4. 157

5. 2,421   6. 1,460   7. 8,625   8. 73,261

Exercises

State whether each number is divisible by 2, 4, 5, 10, or none of these numbers.

1. 28   2. 75   3. 97   4. 154

5. 724   6. 600   7. 1,325   8. 94,080

State whether each number is divisible by 3, 9, or neither of these numbers.

9. 87   10. 531   11. 296   12. 684

13. 4,773   14. 1,362   15. 34,848   16. 545,246

Number Theory—Developing Fractions

State whether each number is divisible by 6.

17. 96 **18.** 412 **19.** 5,232 **20.** 372,458

State whether each number is divisible by 2, 3, 4, 5, 6, 9, 10, or none of these numbers.

21. 534 **22.** 1,790 **23.** 6,103 **24.** 4,356

25. 5,640 **26.** 9,312 **27.** 93,150 **28.** 823,618

Application

29. Marie must plant 127 pepper plants. Can she divide that number of plants into 9 rows with the same number in each row?

30. Gary must plant a number of rows of green beans that can be divided by 3, 5, and 9. What is the smallest number of rows that he can plant?

6.2 Factors

The *factors* of a number are the whole numbers that when multiplied together give the original number.

Study the factors of 24 and 36 listed in the table below.

Factors of 24	Factors of 36
1 × 24	1 × 36
2 × 12	2 × 18
3 × 8	3 × 12
4 × 6	4 × 9
	6 × 6

24 has 8 factors: 1, 2, 3, 4, 6, 8, 12, and 24.

36 has 9 factors: 1, 2, 3, 4, 6, 9, 12, 18, and 36.

Observe below that the number 24 is divisible by each of its factors.

$24 \div 1 = 24$ $24 \div 2 = 12$ $24 \div 3 = 8$ $24 \div 4 = 6$

$24 \div 6 = 4$ $24 \div 8 = 3$ $24 \div 12 = 2$ $24 \div 24 = 1$

The following pattern demonstrates that every whole number is a factor of 0.

$0 \times 0 = 0$ $\qquad$ $1 \times 0 = 0$ $\qquad$ $2 \times 0 = 0$ $\qquad$ $3 \times 0 = 0$

Zero is not a factor of any whole number except 0. Observe below that 3 is not divisible by 0.

$$\overset{?}{0)\overline{3}} \rightarrow 0 \times ? = 3 \quad \blacktriangleleft \text{There is no number that, multiplied by 0, is equal to 3.}$$

Division by 0 is **undefined** because any number times 0 is equal to 0.

Additional Examples

Is the first number a factor of the second number?

a. 8 and 142

$$\overset{17 \text{ r } 6}{8)\overline{142}} \quad \blacktriangleleft \text{The remainder is not 0.}$$

So, 8 is not a factor of 142.

b. 13 and 351

$$\overset{27 \text{ r } 0}{13)\overline{351}} \quad \blacktriangleleft \text{The remainder is 0.}$$

So, 13 and 27 are factors of 351.

☑ SKILL CHECK

List all the factors of each number in numerical order.

1. 9 $\qquad$ **2.** 22 $\qquad$ **3.** 30

Is the first number a factor of the second number?

4. 4 and 132 $\qquad$ **5.** 12 and 352 $\qquad$ **6.** 160 and 480

Exercises

List all the factors of each number.

1.
20
1×20
2×10
4×5

2.
35
1×35
5×7

3.
48
1×48
2×24
3×16
4×12
6×8

4.
76
1×76
2×38
4×19

5. 15 $\qquad$ **6.** 23 $\qquad$ **7.** 42 $\qquad$ **8.** 50

9. 64 $\qquad$ **10.** 77 $\qquad$ **11.** 81 $\qquad$ **12.** 108

Number Theory—Developing Fractions

Is the first number a factor of the second number? Write yes or no.

13. 7 and 161   **14.** 8 and 274   **15.** 11 and 299   **16.** 15 and 180

17. 18 and 254   **18.** 23 and 368   **19.** 39 and 897   **20.** 42 and 950

Is the first number a factor of both of the next two numbers?
Hint: Use divisibility tests.

21. 2; 124, 125   **22.** 5; 200, 260   **23.** 3; 108, 201   **24.** 6; 174, 189

25. 4; 124, 136   **26.** 9; 117, 159   **27.** 10; 180, 195   **28.** 3; 189, 195

Application

29. What number is a factor of every even number?

30. What is the smallest whole number with exactly 2 different factors?

31. What is the smallest whole number with exactly 3 different factors?

32. What is the smallest whole number with exactly 4 different factors?

MIND ??? BOGGLER

Andrew told his sister Ashley that he would sell her some of the stamps in his collection at a special rate. He agreed to sell the first stamp for 1¢, the second for 2¢, the third for 4¢, the fourth for 8¢, and so on. If Ashley bought 13 stamps, how much did she owe her brother?

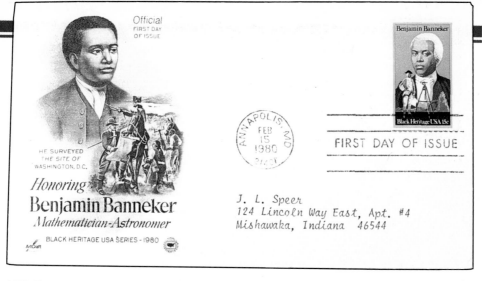

In 1980, Benjamin Banneker was honored with this stamp. In 1791 Banneker assisted Major Andrew Ellicot in making the survey of the planned site of the national capital.

6.3 Prime and Composite Numbers

Study the table on the right which lists the factors of the whole numbers 1 through 8.

A *prime number* is a whole number greater than 1 with exactly two factors (1 and itself). In the table, 2, 3, 5, and 7 are prime.

A *composite number* is a whole number greater than 1 with more than two factors. In the table, 4, 6, and 8 are composite.

The numbers 0 and 1 are neither prime nor composite.

Every composite number can be written as the product of two or more prime numbers. This product is called the *prime factorization* of the number.

Number	Factors
1	1
2	1, 2
3	1, 3
4	1, 2, 4
5	1, 5
6	1, 2, 3, 6
7	1, 7
8	1, 2, 4, 8

You can use a factor tree to help you find prime factorizations.

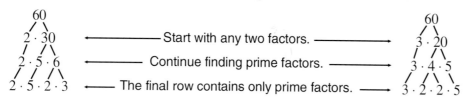

The prime factorization of 60 is $2 \cdot 2 \cdot 3 \cdot 5$.

Number Theory—Developing Fractions

When a factor is repeated, you can write that prime factorization using exponents. For example, $2 \cdot 2 \cdot 3 \cdot 5$ can be written as $2^2 \cdot 3 \cdot 5$.

Additional Examples

Write the prime factorization using exponents.

a.
```
    12
   / \
  4 · 3
 /\   \
2·2 · 3,
or 2² · 3
```

b.
```
    125
    / \
   5 · 25
  /   / \
 5 · 5 · 5,
   or 5³
```

c.

```
     100
     / \
   10 · 10
  /\    /\
 2·5 · 2·5,
  or 2² · 5²
```

☑ **SKILL CHECK**

Write prime, composite, or neither for each number.

1. 16   2. 29   3. 43   4. 57

Write the prime factorization using exponents.

5. 8   6. 18   7. 72   8. 250

Exercises

Write prime, composite, or neither for each number.

1. 17   2. 21   3. 38   4. 49   5. 75
6. 61   7. 53   8. 89   9. 93   10. 100

Find the prime number in each list.

11. 12, 13, 14, 15   12. 63, 65, 67, 69   13. 81, 87, 91, 97

Find the composite number in each list.

14. 31, 41, 51, 61   15. 19, 39, 59, 79   16. 53, 63, 73, 83

Complete each factor tree; then write the prime factorization.

17.

```
    36
   /  \
  4  ·  9
 /\    /\
□·□ · □·□
```

18.

```
    70
   /  \
  □  · 14
 /    /  \
□ · 2 · □
```

19.
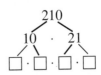
```
      210
     /   \
   10  ·  21
  /\      /\
 □·□  · □·□
```

Write the prime factorization of each number using exponents.

20. 27   **21.** 75   **22.** 48   **23.** 105

24. 78   **25.** 100   **26.** 120   **27.** 300

Name the composite number for each prime factorization.

28. $3^2 \cdot 11$ **29.** $2^2 \cdot 3 \cdot 7$ **30.** $2^3 \cdot 3 \cdot 5^2$

These iron-wheeled bicycles of the 1890s were challenging for the average rider to master.

6.4 Greatest Common Factor (GCF)

If two numbers have factors that are the same, these factors are called *common factors.* Consider the example below.

Factors of 18: ①,②,③,⑥, 9, 18
Factors of 24: ①,②,③, 4,⑥, 8, 12, 24
Common factors: 1, 2, 3, 6

The largest factor of two or more numbers is called the *greatest common factor (GCF).*

The above example illustrates that the GCF of 18 and 24 is 6.

You can also use the prime factorizations to find the GCF of two or more numbers.

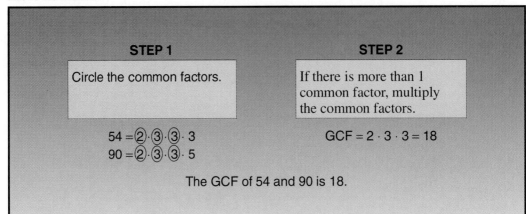

STEP 1

Circle the common factors.

$54 = ②·③·③· 3$
$90 = ②·③·③· 5$

STEP 2

If there is more than 1 common factor, multiply the common factors.

$GCF = 2 · 3 · 3 = 18$

The GCF of 54 and 90 is 18.

If the GCF of two numbers is 1, the numbers are ***relatively prime.***

Factors of 9: ①, 3, 9
Factors of 10: ①, 2, 5, 10
GCF = 1
So, 9 and 10 are relatively prime.

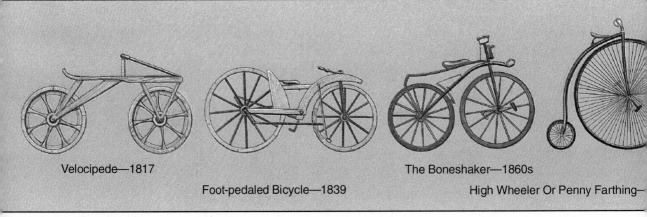

Velocipede—1817

Foot-pedaled Bicycle—1839

The Boneshaker—1860s

High Wheeler Or Penny Farthing—

Additional Examples

Use prime factorizations to find the GCF.

a. 35 and 42
$$35 = 5 \cdot \boxed{7}$$
$$42 = 2 \cdot 3 \cdot \boxed{7}$$
GCF = 7 ◄ Seven is the only
common factor.

b. 40 and 100
$$40 = \boxed{2} \cdot \boxed{2} \cdot 2 \cdot \boxed{5}$$
$$100 = \boxed{2} \cdot \boxed{2} \cdot \boxed{5} \cdot 5$$
GCF = 2 · 2 · 5 ◄ Multiply the common
= 20 factors.

☑ SKILL CHECK

List the common factors of each pair of numbers. Find the GCF; then indicate the numbers that are relatively prime.

1. 14, 35   **2.** 12, 18   **3.** 9, 20   **4.** 30, 75

Use the prime factorizations to find the GCF.

5. $12 = 2 \cdot 2 \cdot 3$
$18 = 2 \cdot 3 \cdot 3$

6. $42 = 2 \cdot 3 \cdot 7$
$105 = 3 \cdot 5 \cdot 7$

7. $60 = 2 \cdot 2 \cdot 3 \cdot 5$
$90 = 2 \cdot 3 \cdot 3 \cdot 5$

Exercises

Find the GCF by listing the factors of each pair of numbers.

1. 9, 12   **2.** 14, 21   **3.** 20, 32   **4.** 16, 24

Safety Bicycle—1880s

Tandem Bicycle (built for two)—1890s

Raleigh Safety Bicycle—1901

Number Theory—Developing Fractions

Find the GCF by using the prime factorizations of each pair of numbers.

5. $9 = 3 \cdot 3$
$15 = 3 \cdot 5$

6. $8 = 2 \cdot 2 \cdot 2$
$12 = 2 \cdot 2 \cdot 3$

7. $24 = 2 \cdot 2 \cdot 2 \cdot 3$
$30 = 2 \cdot 3 \cdot 5$

8. $42 = 2 \cdot 3 \cdot 7$
$63 = 3 \cdot 3 \cdot 7$

9. $18 = 2 \cdot 3 \cdot 3$
$54 = 2 \cdot 3 \cdot 3 \cdot 3$

10. $90 = 2 \cdot 3 \cdot 3 \cdot 5$
$60 = 2 \cdot 2 \cdot 3 \cdot 5$

11. $150 = 2 \cdot 3 \cdot 5 \cdot 5$
$175 = 5 \cdot 5 \cdot 7$

12. $108 = 2 \cdot 2 \cdot 3 \cdot 3 \cdot 3$
$126 = 2 \cdot 3 \cdot 3 \cdot 7$

Find the GCF of each pair of numbers.

13. 27, 36
14. 18, 24
15. 28, 32
16. 40, 60

17. 24, 36
18. 39, 52
19. 16, 48
20. 100, 250

Are the following numbers relatively prime? Write yes or no.

21. 4, 9
22. 42, 105
23. 25, 36

This forerunner of the modern motorcycle placed the passenger in a very precarious position in the event of a sudden stop.

Write the two numbers that are relatively prime.

24. 8, 12, 15

25. 24, 26, 33

26. 35, 42, 48

Application

Write true or false.

27. The GCF of 15 and 16 is 1.

28. The prime factorization of 42 is 2×21.

29. The GCF of 27 and 36 is 9.

30. If the GCF of 2 numbers is 1, the numbers have no common factors.

6.5 Least Common Multiple (LCM)

To find the multiples of a number, you multiply the number by 0, 1, 2, 3, 4, and so on. Study the multiples of 5 below.

Multiples of 5: 0×5 1×5 2×5 3×5 4×5

  0 ,   5 ,   10 ,   15 ,   20

If a number is a multiple of two or more numbers, it is called a ***common multiple.*** Study the following example.

Example

Identify the common multiples of 4 and 6.

Nonzero multiples of 4: 4, 8, 12, 16, 20, 24, 28, 32, 36, . . .

Nonzero multiples of 6: 6, 12, 18, 24, 30, 36, 42, . . .

Common multiples: 12, 24, 36

The ***least common multiple (LCM)*** of two or more numbers is the smallest nonzero number that is a multiple of each.

The example above illustrates that the LCM of 4 and 6 is 12.

You can also use prime factorizations to find the LCM. Study the steps below, which show how to find the LCM of 120 and 90.

STEP 1	STEP 2
Circle the highest power of each different prime factor.	Find the product of the prime factors with the highest power.

$$120 = 2 \cdot 2 \cdot 2 \cdot 3 \cdot 5$$
$$= \textcircled{2^3} \cdot 3 \cdot \textcircled{5}$$

$$90 = 2 \cdot 3 \cdot 3 \cdot 5$$
$$= 2 \cdot \textcircled{3^2} \cdot 5$$

$$\text{LCM} = \textcircled{2^3} \cdot \textcircled{3^2} \cdot \textcircled{5}$$
$$= 8 \cdot 9 \cdot 5$$
$$= 360$$

The LCM of 120 and 90 is 360.

☑**SKILL CHECK**

Find the LCM by listing multiples.

1. 4, 5
2. 6, 9
3. 7, 14
4. 6, 10, 15

Find the LCM by using the prime factorization.

5. $9 = 3^2$
   $12 = 2^2 \cdot 3$

6. $18 = 2 \cdot 3^2$
   $27 = 3^3$

7. $21 = 3 \cdot 7$
   $28 = 2^2 \cdot 7$

8. $20 = 2^2 \cdot 5$
   $30 = 2 \cdot 3 \cdot 5$
   $40 = 2^3 \cdot 5$

Exercises

List the first five nonzero multiples of each number.

1. 5
2. 6
3. 8
4. 10

Use the multiples from exercises 1-4 to find the LCM of each pair of numbers.

5. 5, 10
6. 6, 8
7. 8, 10
8. 6, 10

Find the LCM by listing multiples.

9. 2, 5
10. 12, 18
11. 15, 25
12. 10, 12

Find the LCM by the prime factorization method.

13. 10, 25   **14.** 9, 12   **15.** 8, 20   **16.** 18, 30

17. 24, 36   **18.** 25, 40   **19.** 12, 21   **20.** 20, 48

21. 12, 63   **22.** 3, 4, 6   **23.** 4, 12, 20   **24.** 9, 12, 15

Application

25. The Flower Nook sells roses in bunches of 4 and carnations in bunches of 6. If you want to buy an equal number of roses and carnations, what is the least number of each that you could buy?

26. A tomato plant needs to be watered every 6 days. A pepper plant needs to be watered every 9 days. If you water them both on the same first day, how often will they both need water?

6.6 Fractions

Ramona made a pepperoni pizza. She cut it into 6 equal pieces. Each piece is $\frac{1}{6}$ of the pizza.

The number $\frac{1}{6}$ is called a *fraction*. In a fraction, the top number is the *numerator,* and the bottom number is the *denominator.*

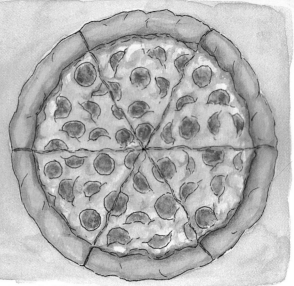

You can use a fraction to name part of a whole object.

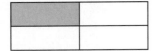

$\frac{1}{4}$ of the rectangle is shaded.

1 ◄ number of pieces shaded
¯
4 ◄ total number of equal parts

A *proper fraction* is one that represents part of a whole object or set.

$\frac{5}{9}$ and $\frac{7}{12}$ ◄ proper fractions

In a proper fraction, the numerator is less than the denominator.

You can also use a fraction to name part of a group or set.

$\frac{3}{8}$ of the squares are shaded.

3 ◄ number of squares shaded
¯
8 ◄ total number of squares

An *improper fraction* is one that represents a whole object or set or more than a whole object or set.

$\frac{6}{6}$ and $\frac{8}{3}$ ◄ improper fractions

In an improper fraction, the numerator is equal to or greater than the denominator.

You can also use fractions to show the quotient of two whole numbers. Study the following examples.

Additional Examples

Write each quotient as a fraction or whole number.

a. $2 \div 5 = \frac{2}{5}$ **b.** $6 \div 3 = \frac{6}{3} = 2$ **c.** $4 \div 4 = \frac{4}{4} = 1$

Observe that the quotient is a whole number in examples b and c.

☑ **SKILL CHECK**

Write a fraction for the shaded part in each.

1.   **2.**    **3.**

Write each quotient as a fraction or whole number.

4. $6 \div 13$ **5.** $15 \overline{)8}$ **6.** $15 \div 8$ **7.** $7 \overline{)21}$

Exercises

Write a fraction for the shaded part in each.

1.   **2.**    **3.**

4. 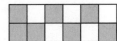   **5.**   **6.**

Write each quotient as a fraction or whole number.

7. $1 \div 7$ **8.** $2 \overline{)5}$ **9.** $3 \div 4$ **10.** $17 \overline{)7}$

11. $30 \div 13$ **12.** $50 \div 5$ **13.** $15 \div 22$ **14.** $75 \div 1$

Write a quotient for each fraction.

15. $\frac{4}{9}$ **16.** $\frac{8}{5}$ **17.** $\frac{86}{100}$ **18.** $\frac{17}{12}$

Number Theory—Developing Fractions

Tell whether each fraction is proper or improper.

19. $\dfrac{2}{3}$ **20.** $\dfrac{36}{4}$ **21.** $\dfrac{16}{20}$ **22.** $\dfrac{15}{9}$

23. Draw a circle and shade $\frac{3}{4}$ of it.

24. Draw a circle and shade $\frac{5}{8}$ of it.

25. Draw a set of squares so that $\frac{4}{6}$ of them are shaded.

26. Draw a set of squares so that $\frac{7}{9}$ of them are shaded.

Application

27. Ryan practices his trombone 5 days a week. What fraction of the days of the week does he practice?

28. The beginning band has 8 brass, 15 woodwind, and 4 percussion instruments. What fraction of the instruments are woodwinds?

6.7 Equivalent Fractions

Observe that the fractions below have the same amount of shaded area.

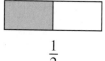

$$\frac{1}{2}$$

$$\frac{2}{4}$$

$$\frac{3}{6}$$

Fractions that represent the same part of a region, such as $\frac{1}{2}$, $\frac{2}{4}$, and $\frac{3}{6}$ are called *equivalent fractions.*

To find an equivalent fraction for a given fraction, you multiply or divide the numerator and the denominator by the same nonzero number.

$$\frac{1}{2} = \frac{1 \times 5}{2 \times 5}$$ ◄Multiply by 5.
◄Multiply by 5.

$$\frac{8}{16} = \frac{8 \div 8}{16 \div 8}$$ ◄Divide by 8.
◄Divide by 8.

$$= \frac{5}{10}$$

$$= \frac{1}{2}$$

So, $\frac{1}{2}$ and $\frac{5}{10}$ are equivalent.

So, $\frac{8}{16}$ and $\frac{1}{2}$ are equivalent.

Number Theory—Developing Fractions

You can use cross products to determine whether two fractions are equivalent.

$$\frac{4}{7} \times \frac{12}{21}$$

$$21 \times 4 = 84 \qquad 7 \times 12 = 84$$

$$\frac{4}{7} = \frac{12}{21}$$

The fractions are equivalent, since the cross products are equal.

$$\frac{5}{6} \times \frac{30}{45}$$

$$45 \times 5 = 225 \qquad 6 \times 30 = 180$$

$$\frac{5}{6} \neq \frac{30}{45}$$

The fractions are not equivalent, since the cross products are not equal.

Additional Examples

Find the missing numerator or denominator.

a. $\dfrac{3}{4} = \dfrac{n}{20}$ ◀ Think "$4 \times 5 = 20$."

$$\frac{3}{4} = \frac{3 \times 5}{4 \times 5} = \frac{15}{20}$$

$$n = 15$$

b. $\dfrac{20}{35} = \dfrac{4}{n}$ ◀ Think "$20 \div 5 = 4$."

$$\frac{20}{35} = \frac{20 \div 5}{35 \div 5} = \frac{4}{7}$$

$$n = 7$$

☑ SKILL CHECK

Determine whether each pair of fractions is equivalent. Use cross products.

1. $\dfrac{5}{7}, \dfrac{35}{49}$

2. $\dfrac{9}{24}, \dfrac{7}{16}$

3. $\dfrac{15}{40}, \dfrac{9}{24}$

Find the missing numerator or denominator.

4. $\dfrac{2}{5} = \dfrac{\square}{15}$

5. $\dfrac{12}{28} = \dfrac{3}{\square}$

6. $\dfrac{7}{9} = \dfrac{\square}{54}$

Exercises

Use cross products to determine whether each pair of fractions is equivalent. Write = or ≠.

1. $\dfrac{3}{6}, \dfrac{5}{10}$

2. $\dfrac{9}{12}, \dfrac{7}{8}$

3. $\dfrac{5}{10}, \dfrac{50}{100}$

4. $\dfrac{8}{11}, \dfrac{9}{12}$

5. $\dfrac{10}{14}, \dfrac{15}{21}$ **6.** $\dfrac{9}{30}, \dfrac{24}{80}$ **7.** $\dfrac{12}{14}, \dfrac{18}{22}$ **8.** $\dfrac{12}{44}, \dfrac{14}{55}$

Find the equivalent fraction.

9. $\dfrac{1}{4} = \dfrac{1 \times 3}{4 \times 3} = \square$ **10.** $\dfrac{3}{5} = \dfrac{3 \times 4}{5 \times 4} = \square$

11. $\dfrac{7}{21} = \dfrac{7 \div 7}{21 \div 7} = \square$ **12.** $\dfrac{25}{40} = \dfrac{25 \div 5}{40 \div 5} = \square$

Find the missing number.

13. $\dfrac{1}{3} = \dfrac{n}{12}$ **14.** $\dfrac{4}{5} = \dfrac{12}{n}$ **15.** $\dfrac{3}{8} = \dfrac{n}{40}$ **16.** $\dfrac{7}{9} = \dfrac{63}{n}$

17. $\dfrac{9}{21} = \dfrac{n}{7}$ **18.** $\dfrac{12}{18} = \dfrac{n}{3}$ **19.** $\dfrac{27}{36} = \dfrac{3}{n}$ **20.** $\dfrac{20}{60} = \dfrac{n}{30}$

21. $\dfrac{6}{13} = \dfrac{n}{39}$ **22.** $\dfrac{16}{32} = \dfrac{1}{n}$ **23.** $\dfrac{8}{12} = \dfrac{40}{n}$ **24.** $\dfrac{28}{63} = \dfrac{n}{9}$

Write the fraction that is not equivalent.

25. $\dfrac{5}{7}, \dfrac{10}{14}, \dfrac{15}{21}, \dfrac{20}{27}$ **26.** $\dfrac{2}{3}, \dfrac{3}{5}, \dfrac{6}{10}, \dfrac{9}{15}$

27. $\dfrac{3}{5}, \dfrac{6}{10}, \dfrac{10}{15}, \dfrac{12}{20}$ **28.** $\dfrac{7}{8}, \dfrac{10}{12}, \dfrac{14}{16}, \dfrac{21}{24}$

Application

29. Bill has completed $\dfrac{8}{12}$ of a 24-mile bicycle race. Randy has completed $\dfrac{15}{24}$ of the same race. Have they completed the same amount of the race?

30. Diana got 16 out of 18 correct on her first Bible quiz. She got 18 out of 24 correct on her second quiz. Did she score the same grade on each quiz?

6.8 Lowest Terms

Dick mowed his grandmother's lawn in 29 minutes, or $\frac{29}{60}$ of an hour. He mowed his neighbor's lawn in 36 minutes, or $\frac{36}{60}$ of an hour. Are these fractions in lowest terms?

A fraction is in **lowest terms** when the greatest common factor (GCF) of the numerator and the denominator is 1.

GCF of 29 and 60: 1

Yes, $\frac{29}{60}$ is in lowest terms.

GCF of 36 and 60: 12

No, $\frac{36}{60}$ is not in lowest terms.

To write $\frac{36}{60}$ in lowest terms, you can divide the numerator and denominator by their GCF, 12.

$$\frac{36}{60} = \frac{36 \div 12}{60 \div 12} = \frac{3}{5} \quad \blacktriangleleft \text{lowest terms}$$

You can also write $\frac{36}{60}$ in lowest terms by dividing the numerator and denominator by any common factor and then continuing to divide by common factors until the fraction is in lowest terms. Consider the example below.

$$\frac{36}{60} = \frac{36 \div 2}{60 \div 2} = \frac{18}{30} \longrightarrow \frac{18}{30} = \frac{18 \div 2}{30 \div 2} = \frac{9}{15} \longrightarrow \frac{9}{15} = \frac{9 \div 3}{15 \div 3} = \frac{3}{5} \quad \blacktriangleleft \text{lowest terms}$$

Additional Examples

Write each fraction in lowest terms.

a. $\frac{21}{35} = \frac{21 \div 7}{35 \div 7} = \frac{3}{5}$

b. $\frac{30}{54} = \frac{30 \div 6}{54 \div 6} = \frac{5}{9}$

c. $\frac{9}{14}$ $\blacktriangleleft$ The GCF of 9 and 14 is 1, so the fraction is in lowest terms.

☑SKILL CHECK

Is the fraction in lowest terms? Write yes or no.

1. $\frac{4}{5}$ 2. $\frac{10}{12}$ 3. $\frac{14}{19}$ 4. $\frac{30}{35}$

Write each fraction in lowest terms.

5. $\frac{4}{8}$ 6. $\frac{18}{24}$ 7. $\frac{36}{63}$ 8. $\frac{65}{100}$

Number Theory—Developing Fractions

Exercises

Is the fraction in lowest terms? Write yes or no.

1. $\dfrac{15}{18}$ 2. $\dfrac{16}{21}$ 3. $\dfrac{25}{28}$ 4. $\dfrac{32}{45}$

Write the GCF of the numerator and the denominator.

5. $\dfrac{8}{12}$ 6. $\dfrac{15}{21}$ 7. $\dfrac{18}{28}$ 8. $\dfrac{36}{60}$

Complete.

9. $\dfrac{9 \div 3}{15 \div 3} = \dfrac{3}{\square}$ 10. $\dfrac{16 \div 8}{24 \div 8} = \dfrac{\square}{3}$

11. $\dfrac{36 \div 12}{60 \div 12} = \dfrac{3}{\square}$ 12. $\dfrac{18 \div 18}{36 \div 18} = \dfrac{\square}{2}$

Write each fraction in lowest terms.

13. $\dfrac{5}{20}$ 14. $\dfrac{10}{24}$ 15. $\dfrac{12}{16}$ 16. $\dfrac{20}{35}$

17. $\dfrac{8}{24}$ 18. $\dfrac{40}{60}$ 19. $\dfrac{24}{30}$ 20. $\dfrac{35}{63}$

21. $\dfrac{40}{75}$ 22. $\dfrac{42}{48}$ 23. $\dfrac{66}{99}$ 24. $\dfrac{48}{96}$

Identify the fraction in each group that is not in lowest terms; then write it in lowest terms.

25. $\dfrac{9}{11}, \dfrac{12}{15}, \dfrac{15}{19}$ 26. $\dfrac{13}{18}, \dfrac{13}{22}, \dfrac{13}{26}$

27. $\dfrac{10}{30}, \dfrac{11}{32}, \dfrac{13}{33}$ 28. $\dfrac{32}{51}, \dfrac{27}{42}, \dfrac{22}{35}$

Application

29. Lionel saved $16 of the $36 that he earned from mowing yards. What fraction of his earnings did he save? Write the fraction in lowest terms.

30. Stephen mowed lawns for 32 weeks one year. What fractional part of the year was this? Write the fraction in lowest terms.

Problem Solving: Guess and Check

You can use the strategy "Guess and Check" to solve some word problems. In this strategy, you guess the answer and then check your guess against the conditions in the problem.

Gail is twice as old as Donna. If the sum of their ages is 39, how old are Gail and Donna?

Four-Point Check List

1 READ to understand the question and identify the needed data.

2 PLAN what to do to solve the problem.

3 SOLVE the problem by carrying out the plan.

4 CHECK to make sure the solution is reasonable.

1. READ: Understand the question.
   ■ How old are Gail and Donna?
   Identify the needed data.
   ■ Gail is twice as old as Donna.
   ■ The sum of their ages is 39.

2. PLAN: Use the strategy "Guess and Check."
   a. Guess the answer
   b. Check the guess against the conditions in the problem.

3. SOLVE: Carry out the plan.

First Guess	**Second Guess**	**Third Guess**
a. If Donna is 11, Gail must be 2 × 11 or 22.	**a.** If Donna is 14, Gail must be 2 × 14 = 28.	**a.** If Donna is 13, Gail must be 2 × 13 or 26.
b. Since 11 + 22 = 33, this guess is too small.	**b.** Since 14 + 28 = 42, this guess is too big.	**b.** Since 13 + 26 = 39, this guess is correct.

   Donna is 13 years old and Gail is 26 years old.

4. CHECK: Is the solution reasonable?
   The solution is reasonable, since Gail is twice as old as Donna, and 13 + 26 = 39.

☑SKILL CHECK

Solve.

1. Mario is half as old as David. If the sum of their ages is 24, how old are Mario and David?

2. Doug handed out 4 fewer tracts than Keith during door-to-door visitation. Together they handed out 28 tracts. How many tracts did each hand out?

Exercises

Solve using the strategy "Guess and Check."

1. Anna made three times as many muffins as Terri. Together they made 36 muffins. How many muffins did each make?

2. On the biology field trip, Carrie collected 8 more leaves than Gary. Together they collected 26 leaves. How many leaves did each collect?

Mixed review.

Solve.

3. Melba spent $1.29 for bread, $2.62 for potatoes, and $13.42 for a turkey. If she gave the cashier $20, how much change did she receive?

4. It takes Yolanda 12 minutes to get dressed and make her bed. What fractional part of an hour is this? Write the fraction in lowest terms.

5. Ron bought 6 tickets to a concert by the orchestra in his town. If he gave the cashier $75 and received $3 in change, how much did each ticket cost?

6. There are 117 boys signed up for the Junior Baseball League. They are being divided into teams with 9 boys on a team. Can they be divided equally?

7. The Drama Club sold 249 tickets at $3 each for its spring play. If the expenses for putting on the performance were $138, how much profit did the Drama Club make?

8. If Matthias's age is the sum of the first two composite numbers greater than 11, how old is he?

9. The cost of a knit shirt is $8.95. The sales tax on each shirt is $0.45. How much would 4 knit shirts cost, including tax?

10. Brenda's age minus the largest prime number less than 17 is equal to 7. How old is Brenda?

Chapter 6 Review

6.1 Indicate whether each number is divisible by 2, 3, 4, 5, 6, 9, 10, or none of these numbers.

1. 477   2. 3,920   3. 7,194   4. 15,743

6.2 List all of the factors of each number.

5. 21   6. 36   7. 47

6.3 Write the prime number in the list.   **Write the composite number in the list.**

8. 15, 23, 36, 49   9. 31, 41, 51, 61

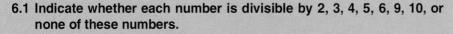

Number Theory—Developing Fractions

Write the prime factorization. Use exponents.

10. 42

11. 90

12. 168

6.4 Find the GCF of each pair of numbers.

13. 63, 70

14. 24, 42

15. 18, 54

6.5 Find the LCM of each group of numbers.

16. 8, 12

17. 6, 10

18. 3, 9, 15

6.6 Write a fraction for the shaded part of each.

19.

20.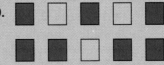

Write the quotient as a fraction or whole number.

21. Write the quotient $9\overline{)4}$ as a fraction.

22. Write a quotient for the fraction $\dfrac{19}{8}$.

6.7 Use cross products to determine whether the pair of fractions is equivalent. Write = or ≠.

23. $\dfrac{7}{9}, \dfrac{9}{13}$

24. $\dfrac{6}{14}, \dfrac{15}{35}$

Find the missing number.

25. $\dfrac{1}{4} = \dfrac{n}{20}$

26. $\dfrac{5}{9} = \dfrac{30}{n}$

27. $\dfrac{24}{56} = \dfrac{n}{7}$

6.8 Write each fraction in lowest terms.

28. $\dfrac{7}{49}$

29. $\dfrac{12}{18}$

30. $\dfrac{24}{56}$

Identify the fraction in the group that is not in lowest terms; then write it in lowest terms.

31. $\dfrac{2}{3}, \dfrac{3}{5}, \dfrac{4}{6}$

32. $\dfrac{12}{13}, \dfrac{15}{17}, \dfrac{18}{21}$

Chapter 6 Cumulative Review

1. Give the standard form for
$0.3 + 0.05 + 0.0002$.
- **a.** 0.352
- **b.** 0.3502
- **c.** 0.3052
- **d.** not given

2. Write in order from least to greatest:
0.2354, 0.2348, 0.2295.
- **a.** 0.2348, 0.2295, 0.2354
- **b.** 0.2295, 0.2354, 0.2348
- **c.** 0.2295, 0.2348, 0.2354
- **d.** not given

3. Round 0.0751 to the nearest hundredth.
- **a.** 0.1
- **b.** 0.08
- **c.** 0.75
- **d.** not given

4. Estimate; then compare using >, < or =.
$38.94 + 41.37 + 17.25 \square 110$
- **a.** >
- **b.** <
- **c.** =
- **c.** not given

5. Simplify. $42.57 + (7 - 3.674)$
- **a.** 45.896
- **b.** 46.895
- **c.** 47.244
- **d.** not given

6. Place the decimal point.
$$\begin{array}{r} 0.58 \\ \times\ 3.2 \\ \hline 1856 \end{array}$$
- **a.** 1.856
- **b.** 18.56
- **c.** 185.6
- **d.** not given

7. Multiply 0.08×0.529.
- **a.** 0.03232
- **b.** 0.04232
- **c.** 0.04222
- **d.** not given

8. Divide. Round to the nearest tenth.
$13)\overline{25}$
- **a.** 1.9
- **b.** 1.92
- **c.** 2.0
- **d.** not given

9. Place the decimal point. $23)\overline{105.11}^{\,457}$
- **a.** 4.57
- **b.** 45.7
- **c.** 457.0
- **d.** not given

10. Write 7,540,000 in scientific notation.
- **a.** 7.54×10^6
- **b.** 75.4×10^5
- **c.** 7.54×10^4
- **d.** not given

11. Identify the following basic geometric figure:
- **a.** point
- **b.** segment
- **c.** ray
- **d.** line

12. Classify the following angle:
- **a.** acute
- **b.** right
- **c.** obtuse
- **d.** straight

13. Classify the following pair of lines: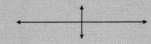
- **a.** perpendicular
- **b.** parallel
- **c.** neither

14. Name the polygon: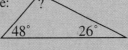
- **a.** regular pentagon
- **b.** regular heptagon
- **c.** regular hexagon
- **d.** not given

15. Find the missing measure in the following triangle: $48°$ $26°$?
- **a.** 16
- **b.** 106
- **c.** 116
- **d.** not given

Number Theory—Developing Fractions

PIERRE & MARIE CURIE
RADIOACTIVITY

Although the marriage of Pierre Curie, a respected French physicist, and Marie Sklodowska, a young physics student from Poland, may have seemed insignificant at the time, this union resulted in some of the greatest advances that were made in the study of physics in the early twentieth century.

In 1896 Henri Becquerel discovered rays which appeared to emanate spontaneously from uranium. Marie Curie would later name this phenomenon radioactivity. Inspired by Becquerel's discovery, the Curies set out to determine if there were other substances that emitted this curious type of radiation.

After two years of experimenting with the highly radioactive mineral pitchblende, their research culminated in the discovery of two new elements. In 1898, the Curies isolated a new element which they named polonium in honor of Marie's homeland. Just a few months later, they discovered a second element which they called radium. The discovery of these two new elements earned them, along with Becquerel, a Nobel Prize in 1903.

While Marie devoted herself to the task of isolating pure radium from pitchblende ore, Pierre studied the physical aspects of these new radioactive elements. He was able to prove that the radiation emitted three different types of particles. Scientists later named these particles alpha, beta, and gamma rays.

Pierre's accidental death in 1906 left Marie alone to continue their work with radium and to raise their two young daughters. Devastated by the loss of her beloved husband, Marie threw herself into their unfinished experiments in an effort to ease her pain. Her dedication to her work with radium was again rewarded with

1867-1934

another Nobel Prize in 1911. This accomplishment made Marie the first person to receive two Nobel Prizes in science.

Marie spent much of the remainder of her life developing a new technology based on her research with radioactivity. X-radiography was designed to enable doctors to see inside the human body. At the advent of World War I, Marie realized that military doctors could use radiation to aid them in locating bullets, shrapnel, and broken bones in wounded soldiers. If doctors could pinpoint these problems at the battle site, the potential for saving lives would be great.

Working with her daughter Irène, Marie constructed a radiological car equipped with x-ray equipment that could move quickly and easily along the battlefield. She soon discovered that these cars were extremely

1859-1906

beneficial to doctors, but there were not enough men available to operate the equipment. To solve this problem, she established a school dedicated to teaching young women the techniques of using x-radiography. After receiving basic instruction in math, physics, and anatomy, the girls were sent to the front lines where they operated the radiological cars.

During the last decade of her life, Marie suffered constantly from a mysterious illness. Unacquainted with the symptoms of radiation sickness, her doctors attributed her ailments to fatigue. Even as scientists began to realize that working with radium posed potential health problems, Marie continued to insist that her poor health was due merely to years of overwork. However, on July 4, 1934, the frail scientist died from leukemia, a disease caused by her lifelong work with radium.

ADDING AND SUBTRACTING FRACTIONS

SERVICE RADIOLOSIQUE

7.1 Mixed Numbers

A ***mixed number,*** such as $2\frac{1}{3}$, consists of a whole number and a fraction.

$2\frac{1}{3}$ ⟵——— fraction
⌐——— whole number

Consider the model for $2\frac{1}{3}$ below.

You can also express $2\frac{1}{3}$ as an improper fraction. Since there are 7 one-third parts shaded above, $2\frac{1}{3}$ can be renamed as $\frac{7}{3}$.

To rename a mixed number as an improper fraction, follow the steps in the short cut below.

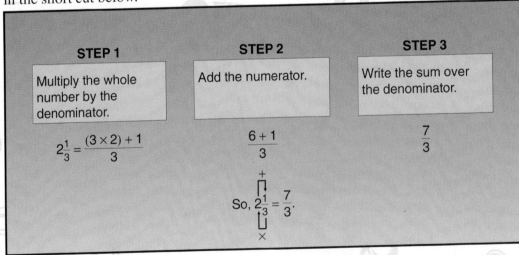

STEP 1

Multiply the whole number by the denominator.

$$2\frac{1}{3} = \frac{(3 \times 2) + 1}{3}$$

STEP 2

Add the numerator.

$$\frac{6 + 1}{3}$$

So, $2\frac{1}{3} = \frac{7}{3}$.

STEP 3

Write the sum over the denominator.

$$\frac{7}{3}$$

To write an improper fraction as a mixed number (or whole number), follow these steps.

STEP 1	STEP 2
Divide the numerator by the denominator.	Write the remainder as a fraction.

$$\frac{14}{9} \rightarrow 9\overline{)14} \quad \begin{array}{r} 1 \\ \end{array}$$
$$\begin{array}{r} -\ 9 \\ \hline 5 \end{array}$$

$$1\frac{5}{9}$$

$$\text{So, } \frac{14}{9} = 1\frac{5}{9}.$$

Additional Examples

Write each as an improper fraction, whole number, or mixed number in lowest terms.

a. $10\frac{3}{4} = \dfrac{(4 \times 10) + 3}{4}$

$= \dfrac{40 + 3}{4}$

$= \dfrac{43}{4}$

b. $\dfrac{27}{9} \rightarrow 9\overline{)27}^{\,3}$

So, $\dfrac{27}{9} = 3.$

c. $\dfrac{34}{6} \rightarrow 6\overline{)34}^{\,5} \rightarrow 5\frac{4}{6}$

$\begin{array}{r} -\ 30 \\ \hline 4 \end{array}$

$5\frac{4 \div 2}{6 \div 2} = 5\frac{2}{3}$

So, $\dfrac{34}{6} = 5\frac{2}{3}.$

☑ **SKILL CHECK**

Write each as an improper fraction.

1. $1\frac{3}{5}$ **2.** $3\frac{1}{4}$ **3.** $6\frac{5}{9}$ **4.** $5\frac{7}{16}$

Write each as a whole number or mixed number in lowest terms.

5. $\dfrac{19}{6}$ **6.** $\dfrac{24}{4}$ **7.** $\dfrac{41}{7}$ **8.** $\dfrac{30}{12}$

Adding and Subtracting Fractions

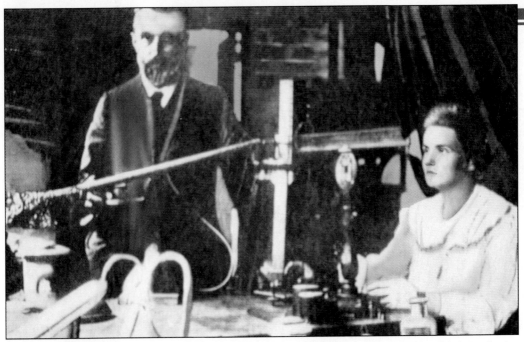

The scientific careers of Pierre Curie and his wife, Marie, were closely intertwined. In 1903 they jointly received the Nobel Prize in physics for their work with radioactivity.

Exercises

Complete.

1. $1\frac{2}{3} = \frac{\square}{3}$

2. $3\frac{1}{4} = \frac{\square}{4}$

3. $5\frac{2}{7} = \frac{\square}{7}$

Write each as an improper fraction.

4. $2\frac{1}{5}$

5. $4\frac{3}{7}$

6. $1\frac{8}{9}$

7. $3\frac{7}{12}$

8. $5\frac{3}{11}$

9. $12\frac{4}{5}$

10. $10\frac{3}{10}$

11. $18\frac{5}{8}$

Complete.

12. $\frac{5}{4} = 1\frac{\square}{4}$

13. $\frac{13}{5} = 2\frac{\square}{5}$

14. $\frac{20}{7} = 2\frac{\square}{7}$

Write each as a whole number or mixed number in lowest terms.

15. $\frac{9}{5}$

16. $\frac{14}{3}$

17. $\frac{16}{9}$

18. $\frac{25}{7}$

19. $\frac{53}{10}$

20. $\frac{47}{8}$

21. $\frac{59}{16}$

22. $\frac{87}{13}$

23. $\dfrac{15}{6}$ **24.** $\dfrac{36}{3}$ **25.** $\dfrac{68}{12}$ **26.** $\dfrac{54}{18}$

Application

27. Karen cut each of two pizzas into fourths. She ate 5 of those fourths. Write a mixed number that tells what part of the pizzas she ate.

28. Josh bought a large pizza and cut it into sixths. If each sixth would feed one boy, then how many pizzas would he need to feed 18 boys?

7.2 Comparing and Ordering Fractions

One recipe for bran muffins calls for $\frac{1}{2}$ cup of sugar. A second recipe calls for $\frac{2}{3}$ cup of sugar. Which recipe uses less sugar?

You compare $\frac{1}{2}$ and $\frac{2}{3}$ to determine which recipe uses less sugar. Fractions such as $\frac{1}{2}$ and $\frac{2}{3}$ that have different denominators are called **unlike fractions**.

To compare unlike fractions, you must first rename them as equivalent fractions with a common denominator.

Consider the comparison of $\frac{1}{2}$ and $\frac{2}{3}$ below.

$$\frac{1}{2} = \frac{1 \times 3}{2 \times 3} = \frac{3}{6}, \text{ and } \frac{2}{3} = \frac{2 \times 2}{3 \times 2} = \frac{4}{6}$$

$$\frac{3}{6} < \frac{4}{6}, \text{ so } \frac{1}{2} < \frac{2}{3}$$

The first recipe uses less sugar, since $\frac{1}{2} < \frac{2}{3}$.

You can also use cross products to compare unlike fractions. Observe below that the fractions compare as their cross products compare.

$$\frac{3}{4} \square \frac{7}{8} \qquad\qquad \frac{4}{5} \square \frac{12}{15}$$

$$\frac{3}{4} \times \frac{7}{8} \qquad\qquad \frac{4}{5} \times \frac{12}{15}$$

$$8 \cdot 3 \square 4 \cdot 7 \qquad\quad 15 \cdot 4 \square 5 \cdot 12$$
$$24 < 28 \qquad\qquad\quad 60 = 60$$

$$\text{So, } \frac{3}{4} < \frac{7}{8}. \qquad \text{So, } \frac{4}{5} = \frac{12}{15}.$$

Additional Example

Write $2\frac{2}{3}$, $2\frac{1}{4}$, and $2\frac{5}{6}$ in order from least to greatest.

Rename as equivalent fractions with a common denominator:

$$2\frac{2}{3} = 2\frac{8}{12}, \qquad 2\frac{1}{4} = 2\frac{3}{12}, \qquad 2\frac{5}{6} = 2\frac{10}{12}$$

From least to greatest: $2\frac{1}{4}$, $2\frac{2}{3}$, $2\frac{5}{6}$

☑ SKILL CHECK

Compare. Write >, <, or =.

1. $\frac{1}{2} \square \frac{3}{5}$ 2. $\frac{3}{4} \square \frac{11}{16}$ 3. $\frac{5}{8} \square \frac{15}{24}$ 4. $1\frac{1}{3} \square 1\frac{1}{4}$

Write in order from least to greatest.

5. $\frac{1}{2}, \frac{2}{3}, \frac{4}{9}$ 6. $3\frac{1}{3}, 3\frac{2}{5}, 3\frac{4}{15}$

Exercises

Find the LCD of each pair of fractions.

1. $\frac{3}{4}, \frac{5}{8}$ 2. $\frac{2}{3}, \frac{3}{5}$ 3. $\frac{5}{6}, \frac{7}{8}$ 4. $\frac{3}{10}, \frac{4}{15}$

Use the LCD to compare the fractions. Write >, <, or =.

5. $\frac{2}{3} \square \frac{5}{6}$ 6. $\frac{1}{2} \square \frac{2}{5}$ 7. $\frac{7}{8} \square \frac{3}{4}$ 8. $\frac{7}{10} \square \frac{4}{5}$

9. $\frac{3}{4} \square \frac{7}{10}$ 10. $3\frac{3}{4} \square 3\frac{11}{12}$ 11. $\frac{7}{10} \square \frac{4}{5}$ 12. $1\frac{15}{16} \square 1\frac{7}{8}$

Use cross products to compare the fractions. Write >, <, or =.

13. $\frac{1}{2} \square \frac{5}{9}$

14. $\frac{4}{5} \square \frac{7}{9}$

15. $\frac{5}{8} \square \frac{3}{4}$

16. $\frac{6}{7} \square \frac{5}{6}$

17. $\frac{5}{7} \square \frac{4}{5}$

18. $3\frac{1}{2} \square 3\frac{5}{9}$

19. $\frac{3}{4} \square \frac{17}{24}$

20. $7\frac{5}{8} \square 7\frac{5}{12}$

Write in order from least to greatest.

21. $\frac{1}{2}, \frac{2}{3}, \frac{2}{6}$

22. $\frac{2}{3}, \frac{1}{4}, \frac{3}{6}$

23. $\frac{3}{4}, \frac{5}{6}, \frac{7}{12}$

24. $\frac{1}{2}, \frac{4}{5}, \frac{7}{10}$

25. $\frac{2}{4}, \frac{3}{8}, \frac{5}{16}$

26. $\frac{2}{3}, \frac{3}{5}, \frac{7}{10}$

Application

27. Which is greater, $\frac{3}{4}$ of a pound of flour, or $\frac{5}{8}$ of a pound of flour?

28. Three jars of cinnamon contain $4\frac{3}{4}$ ounces, $4\frac{5}{8}$ ounces, and $4\frac{7}{16}$ ounces. List the mixed numbers in order from least to greatest.

M I N D ❓ B O G G L E R

A hungry deer ate 100 apples in 5 days. Each day he ate 6 more than on the previous day. How many apples did he eat on each of the 5 days?

Adding and Subtracting Fractions

7.3 Adding and Subtracting Like Fractions

At the youth group fellowship, the girls drank $\frac{5}{8}$ of a gallon of punch. If the boys drank $\frac{7}{8}$ of a gallon, how much punch did they drink in all?

You add $\frac{5}{8}$ and $\frac{7}{8}$ to determine how much punch they drank. Fractions like $\frac{5}{8}$ and $\frac{7}{8}$ that have the same denominator are called *like fractions*.

To add or subtract like fractions, follow these steps.

STEP 1	STEP 2	STEP 3
Write the sum or difference of the numerators over the denominator.	Add or subtract.	Write any improper fraction as a mixed number and rename in lowest terms.
$\frac{5}{8} + \frac{7}{8} = \frac{5+7}{8}$	$\frac{12}{8}$	$1\frac{4}{8} = 1\frac{1}{2}$

The girls and boys drank a total of $1\frac{1}{2}$ gallons of punch.

Additional Examples

Add or subtract.

a.
$$\frac{17}{18} - \frac{5}{18} \blacktriangleleft \frac{17-5}{18}$$
$$\frac{12 \div 6}{18 \div 6} = \frac{2}{3}$$

b.
$$\frac{3}{14} + \frac{9}{14} + \frac{2}{14} \blacktriangleleft \frac{3+9+2}{14}$$
$$\frac{14}{14} = 1$$

c.
$$\frac{9}{10} + \frac{7}{10} + \frac{8}{10} \blacktriangleleft \frac{9+7+8}{10}$$
$$\frac{24}{10} = 2\frac{4 \div 2}{10 \div 2} = 2\frac{2}{5}$$

☑**SKILL CHECK**

Add or subtract. Write the answer in lowest terms.

1. $\dfrac{5}{8} + \dfrac{1}{8}$

2. $\dfrac{11}{12} + \dfrac{5}{12} + \dfrac{1}{12}$

3. $\dfrac{13}{10} - \dfrac{7}{10} - \dfrac{4}{10}$

4. $\begin{array}{r} \dfrac{6}{7} \\ + \dfrac{4}{7} \\ \hline \end{array}$

5. $\begin{array}{r} \dfrac{15}{16} \\ - \dfrac{7}{16} \\ \hline \end{array}$

6. $\begin{array}{r} \dfrac{9}{10} \\ + \dfrac{1}{10} \\ \hline \end{array}$

7. $\begin{array}{r} \dfrac{17}{18} \\ - \dfrac{11}{18} \\ \hline \end{array}$

Exercises

Complete.

1. $\dfrac{3}{4} - \dfrac{1}{4} = \dfrac{\square - 1}{4}$

2. $\dfrac{2}{7} + \dfrac{3}{7} + \dfrac{1}{7} = \dfrac{2 + \square + 1}{\square}$

Add or subtract. Write the answer in lowest terms.

3. $\dfrac{1}{7} + \dfrac{3}{7}$

4. $\dfrac{5}{8} - \dfrac{1}{8}$

5. $\dfrac{7}{9} + \dfrac{3}{9}$

6. $\dfrac{11}{12} - \dfrac{3}{12}$

7. $\dfrac{13}{16} - \dfrac{3}{16}$

8. $\dfrac{7}{15} + \dfrac{11}{15}$

9. $\dfrac{9}{20} + \dfrac{11}{20}$

10. $\dfrac{13}{15} - \dfrac{4}{15}$

Adding and Subtracting Fractions

11. $\frac{3}{10}$
$+\frac{9}{10}$

12. $\frac{7}{12}$
$-\frac{4}{12}$

13. $\frac{17}{20}$
$-\frac{3}{20}$

14. $\frac{5}{18}$
$+\frac{17}{18}$

15. $\frac{7}{9}$
$+\frac{8}{9}$

16. $\frac{16}{21}$
$-\frac{1}{21}$

17. $\frac{15}{16}$
$-\frac{3}{16}$

18. $\frac{37}{50}$
$+\frac{19}{50}$

19. $\frac{2}{5} + \frac{1}{5} + \frac{3}{5}$

20. $\frac{5}{8} + \frac{7}{8} + \frac{4}{8}$

21. $\frac{14}{9} - \frac{4}{9} - \frac{2}{9}$

22. $\frac{9}{20} + \frac{3}{20} + \frac{6}{20}$

23. $\frac{11}{15} + \frac{7}{15} + \frac{14}{15}$

24. $\frac{20}{21} - \frac{6}{21} - \frac{5}{21}$

Application

25. Barbara has a sack of mints that is $\frac{5}{6}$ full. Steve has a sack that is $\frac{1}{6}$ full. How much more of a sack of mints does Barbara have?

26. On each of the following nights, the Patel family drank part of a gallon of milk: Monday, $\frac{3}{8}$; Tuesday, $\frac{1}{8}$; Wednesday, $\frac{5}{8}$. How much milk did they drink in three nights?

7.4 Adding and Subtracting Unlike Fractions

At their Fourth of July picnic, the Roberts family ate $\frac{1}{3}$ of a gallon of vanilla ice cream and $\frac{3}{4}$ of a gallon of chocolate ice cream. How much ice cream did they eat in all?

You add $\frac{1}{3} + \frac{3}{4}$ to find the total amount.

To add or subtract fractions with unlike denominators, follow these steps.

STEP 1

Rename the fractions as equivalent fractions. Use the LCM of the denominators as the least common denominator (LCD).

LCM of 3 and 4:
3, 6, 9, ⑫ 15 . . .
4, 8, ⑫ 16, 20 . . .
LCD = 12

STEP 2

Add or subtract. If necessary, rename the answer in lowest terms.

$$\frac{1}{3} = \frac{1 \times 4}{3 \times 4} = \frac{4}{12}$$
$$+\frac{3}{4} = \frac{3 \times 3}{4 \times 3} = \frac{9}{12}$$

$$\frac{13}{12}, \text{ or } 1\frac{1}{12}$$

The Roberts family ate a total of $1\frac{1}{12}$ gallons of ice cream.

Additional Examples

a. Subtract. $\frac{11}{12} - \frac{1}{4}$

LCD of 12 and 4 = 12.

$$\frac{11}{12} = \frac{11}{12}$$
$$-\frac{1}{4} = \frac{3}{12}$$

$$\frac{8}{12} = \frac{8 \div 4}{12 \div 4} = \frac{2}{3}$$

b. Add. $\frac{2}{3} + \frac{1}{6} + \frac{4}{9}$

LCD of 3, 6, and 9 = 18.

$$\frac{2}{3} = \frac{12}{18}$$
$$\frac{1}{6} = \frac{3}{18}$$
$$+\frac{4}{9} = \frac{8}{18}$$

$$\frac{23}{18}, \text{ or } 1\frac{5}{18}$$

Adding and Subtracting Fractions

A spectroscope is an instrument used to study the rainbow patterns (spectra) given off by elements heated to high temperatures. No two elements have the same spectrum. The spectroscope confirmed the Curies' discovery of radium because its spectrum was like that of no other element.

☑SKILL CHECK

Add or subtract.

1.
$$\begin{array}{r} \frac{1}{2} \\ +\frac{1}{4} \\ \hline \end{array}$$

2.
$$\begin{array}{r} \frac{5}{6} \\ -\frac{1}{3} \\ \hline \end{array}$$

3.
$$\begin{array}{r} \frac{4}{5} \\ +\frac{3}{4} \\ \hline \end{array}$$

4.
$$\begin{array}{r} \frac{7}{9} \\ -\frac{1}{6} \\ \hline \end{array}$$

5. $\frac{3}{4} + \frac{2}{3}$

6. $\frac{11}{12} - \frac{1}{4}$

7. $\frac{5}{6} - \frac{2}{5}$

8. $\frac{2}{3} + \frac{1}{4} + \frac{7}{12}$

Exercises

Find the LCD for each pair of fractions.

1. $\frac{1}{2}, \frac{2}{3}$

2. $\frac{3}{4}, \frac{5}{6}$

3. $\frac{7}{10}, \frac{4}{15}$

Complete.

4.
$$\begin{array}{r} \frac{2}{3} = \frac{\square}{6} \\ +\frac{1}{6} = \frac{\square}{6} \\ \hline \frac{\square}{6} \end{array}$$

5.
$$\begin{array}{r} \frac{3}{4} = \frac{\square}{12} \\ -\frac{1}{3} = \frac{\square}{12} \\ \hline \frac{\square}{12} \end{array}$$

6.
$$\begin{array}{r} \frac{5}{6} = \frac{\square}{12} \\ +\frac{3}{4} = \frac{\square}{12} \\ \hline \frac{\square}{12} = 1\frac{\square}{12} \end{array}$$

Add or subtract. Write the answer in lowest terms.

7. $\dfrac{5}{9}$
$+\dfrac{1}{3}$

8. $\dfrac{2}{3}$
$+\dfrac{1}{6}$

9. $\dfrac{4}{5}$
$-\dfrac{3}{4}$

10. $\dfrac{8}{10}$
$-\dfrac{2}{5}$

11. $\dfrac{3}{4}$
$+\dfrac{2}{3}$

12. $\dfrac{5}{6}$
$-\dfrac{3}{10}$

13. $\dfrac{7}{10}$
$-\dfrac{4}{15}$

14. $\dfrac{5}{8}$
$+\dfrac{3}{12}$

15. $\dfrac{3}{15}$
$+\dfrac{4}{9}$

16. $\dfrac{57}{100}$
$-\dfrac{3}{10}$

17. $\dfrac{17}{20}$
$+\dfrac{5}{8}$

18. $\dfrac{21}{25}$
$-\dfrac{7}{10}$

19. $\dfrac{1}{8} + \dfrac{1}{3} + \dfrac{1}{2}$

20. $\dfrac{3}{8} + \dfrac{1}{4} + \dfrac{5}{12}$

21. $\dfrac{13}{15} + \dfrac{7}{10} + \dfrac{2}{5}$

22. $\left(\dfrac{11}{15} - \dfrac{3}{10}\right) + \dfrac{1}{3}$

23. $\left(\dfrac{3}{8} + \dfrac{1}{2}\right) - \dfrac{5}{16}$

24. $\left(\dfrac{9}{10} - \dfrac{1}{4}\right) - \dfrac{1}{2}$

Application

25. It takes Ming $\dfrac{7}{8}$ of an hour to practice his piano and walk the dog. If it takes him $\dfrac{1}{6}$ of an hour to walk the dog, then how long does it take him to practice the piano?

26. One Saturday, Jesse practiced the piano $\dfrac{1}{2}$ of an hour in the morning and $\dfrac{3}{5}$ of an hour in the afternoon. How long did he practice the piano that day?

Adding and Subtracting Fractions

7.5 Adding Mixed Numbers

Mrs. Leedy canned $3\frac{9}{10}$ bushels of green beans and $4\frac{4}{5}$ bushels of tomatoes. How many bushels of produce did she can in all?

You add $3\frac{9}{10} + 4\frac{4}{5}$ to find the total number of bushels.

To add mixed numbers with unlike denominators, follow these steps.

STEP 1	STEP 2	STEP 3
Rename the fractions as equivalent fractions. Use the LCM of the denominators as the LCD.	Add the fractions.	Add the whole numbers. If necessary, rename the answer in lowest terms.

LCM of 5 and 10:
5, ⑩, 15, . . .
⑩, 20, 30, . . .
LCD = 10

$$3\frac{9}{10} = 3\frac{\mathbf{9}}{\mathbf{10}}$$
$$+4\frac{4}{5} = 4\frac{\mathbf{8}}{\mathbf{10}}$$
$$\overline{\qquad}$$
$$\frac{\mathbf{17}}{\mathbf{10}} = 1\frac{7}{10}$$

$$3\frac{9}{10} = \mathbf{3}\frac{9}{10}$$
$$+4\frac{4}{5} = \mathbf{4}\frac{8}{10}$$
$$\overline{\qquad}$$
$$\mathbf{7} + 1\frac{7}{10} = 8\frac{7}{10}$$

Mrs. Leedy canned a total of $8\frac{7}{10}$ bushels of produce.

Additional Examples

Add.

a.
$$2\frac{4}{7}$$
$$+3\frac{3}{7}$$
$$5\frac{7}{7} = 6$$

b.
$$9\frac{2}{3} = 9\frac{8}{12}$$
$$+4\frac{3}{4} = 4\frac{9}{12}$$
$$13\frac{17}{12} = 14\frac{5}{12}$$

c.
$$14\frac{1}{3} = 14\frac{4}{12}$$
$$5\frac{3}{4} = 5\frac{9}{12}$$
$$+3\frac{5}{6} = 3\frac{10}{12}$$
$$22\frac{23}{12} = 23\frac{11}{12}$$

☑SKILL CHECK

Add. Write the answer in lowest terms.

1.
$$4\frac{1}{8}$$
$$+2\frac{3}{8}$$

2.
$$5\frac{5}{7}$$
$$+1\frac{3}{7}$$

3.
$$9\frac{5}{12}$$
$$+6\frac{11}{12}$$

4.
$$12\frac{7}{9}$$
$$6\frac{5}{9}$$
$$+8\frac{4}{9}$$

5.
$$10\frac{2}{3}$$
$$+3\frac{1}{6}$$

6.
$$7\frac{3}{5}$$
$$+2\frac{3}{4}$$

7.
$$19\frac{3}{8}$$
$$+13\frac{7}{12}$$

8.
$$6\frac{1}{3}$$
$$5\frac{3}{4}$$
$$+8\frac{5}{6}$$

Exercises

Complete.

1. $3\frac{9}{7} = 3 + 1\frac{\square}{7}$

2. $5\frac{7}{3} = 5 + \square\frac{1}{3}$

3. $6\frac{8}{5} = \square\frac{3}{5}$

4. $8\frac{10}{6} = 9\frac{\square}{6} = 9\frac{2}{\square}$

Adding and Subtracting Fractions

Add. Write the answer in lowest terms.

5. $2\frac{3}{10}$
    $+5\frac{1}{10}$

6. 13
    $+5\frac{7}{12}$

7. $3\frac{1}{6}$
    $+4\frac{5}{6}$

8. $7\frac{8}{9}$
    $+3\frac{5}{9}$

9. $12\frac{6}{7}$
    $+\ 3\frac{5}{7}$

10. $4\frac{1}{2}$
    $+6\frac{1}{4}$

11. $5\frac{3}{14}$
    $+9\frac{2}{7}$

12. $7\frac{2}{5}$
    $+2\frac{3}{4}$

13. $14\frac{9}{20}$
    $+9\frac{3}{4}$

14. $13\frac{3}{4}$
    $+6\frac{5}{6}$

15. $8\frac{5}{6}$
    $+2\frac{2}{3}$

16. $17\frac{2}{8}$
    $+7\frac{5}{12}$

17. $3\frac{5}{8}+8\frac{1}{2}+4\frac{1}{4}$

18. $4\frac{4}{9}+2\frac{2}{3}+1\frac{1}{2}$

19. $7\frac{2}{5}+3\frac{3}{8}+6\frac{1}{4}$

20. $5\frac{3}{4}+12\frac{2}{3}+3\frac{1}{2}$

21. $13\frac{2}{3}+2\frac{1}{4}+7\frac{5}{12}$

22. $8\frac{2}{3}+4\frac{1}{4}+2\frac{5}{6}$

Application

23. At a roadside stand, a farmer sold all of his produce except for $3\frac{2}{3}$ bushels of corn and $1\frac{1}{2}$ bushels of green beans. How many bushels of produce did he have left over?

24. Daria used 3 lengths of treated timbers to landscape her back yard. The lengths of the timbers were $7\frac{2}{3}$ ft., $6\frac{3}{4}$ ft., and $7\frac{1}{12}$ ft. What was the combined length of the timbers?

7.6 Subtracting Mixed Numbers

Carl had a piece of plywood that was $42\frac{7}{8}$ inches long. He cut $17\frac{1}{4}$ inches off one end of that piece. How long was the remaining piece of plywood?

You subtract $42\frac{7}{8} - 17\frac{1}{4}$ to find the length of the remaining piece.

To subtract mixed numbers with unlike denominators, follow these steps.

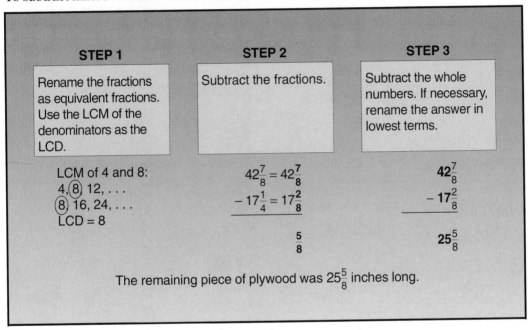

STEP 1

Rename the fractions as equivalent fractions. Use the LCM of the denominators as the LCD.

LCM of 4 and 8:
4, ⑧ 12, . . .
⑧ 16, 24, . . .
LCD = 8

STEP 2

Subtract the fractions.

$$42\frac{7}{8} = 42\frac{7}{8}$$
$$-17\frac{1}{4} = 17\frac{2}{8}$$
$$\phantom{-17\frac{1}{4} = 17}\frac{5}{8}$$

STEP 3

Subtract the whole numbers. If necessary, rename the answer in lowest terms.

$$42\frac{7}{8}$$
$$-17\frac{2}{8}$$
$$25\frac{5}{8}$$

The remaining piece of plywood was $25\frac{5}{8}$ inches long.

Additional Examples

Subtract.

a.
$$5\frac{7}{8}$$
$$-2$$
$$\overline{3\frac{7}{8}}$$

b.
$$14\frac{4}{5} = 14\frac{8}{10}$$
$$-4\frac{1}{2} = 4\frac{5}{10}$$
$$\overline{\phantom{-4\frac{1}{2} = }10\frac{3}{10}}$$

c.
$$11\frac{5}{6} = 11\frac{25}{30}$$
$$-5\frac{3}{10} = 5\frac{9}{30}$$
$$\overline{\phantom{-5\frac{3}{10} = }6\frac{16}{30} = 6\frac{8}{15}}$$

Adding and Subtracting Fractions

☑SKILL CHECK

Subtract. Write the answer in lowest terms.

1. $7\frac{6}{7}$
    $-\ 3\frac{1}{7}$

2. $12\frac{8}{9}$
    $-\ 5$

3. $14\frac{9}{10}$
    $-\ 7\frac{3}{10}$

4. $9\frac{2}{3}$
    $-\ 4\frac{1}{5}$

5. $20\frac{3}{8}$
    $-\ 17\frac{1}{4}$

6. $15\frac{5}{6}$
    $-\ 6\frac{3}{4}$

7. $18\frac{2}{3}$
    $-\ 13\frac{1}{6}$

8. $16\frac{5}{6}$
    $-\ 7\frac{1}{2}$

Marie Curie had two daughters. Her elder daughter, Irène, trained as a physicist and joined Marie in her Paris laboratory. Her younger daughter, Eve, became an accomplished concert pianist and later wrote a biography of her mother.

Exercises

Subtract. Write the answer in lowest terms.

1. $8\frac{7}{9}$
    $-\ 5\frac{3}{9}$

2. $7\frac{5}{8}$
    $-\ 2\frac{3}{8}$

3. $6\frac{3}{7}$
    $-\ 4$

4. $15\frac{14}{15}$
    $-\ 9\frac{4}{15}$

Find the LCD of the given mixed numbers.

5. $5\frac{1}{2},\ 2\frac{5}{6}$

6. $8\frac{3}{4},\ 3\frac{1}{3}$

7. $13\frac{1}{6},\ 4\frac{7}{9}$

8. $6\frac{2}{5},\ 4\frac{6}{7}$

Subtract. Write the answer in lowest terms.

9. $9\frac{1}{2}$
    $-\ 6\frac{1}{3}$

10. $12\frac{1}{2}$
    $-\ 1\frac{3}{10}$

11. $15\frac{7}{8}$
    $-\ 7\frac{3}{4}$

12. $17\frac{5}{6}$
    $-\ 9\frac{3}{8}$

13. $10\frac{4}{5}$
$\ \ -\ 3\frac{1}{2}$

14. $13\frac{3}{4}$
$\ \ -\ 5\frac{1}{8}$

15. $17\frac{8}{15}$
$\ \ -\ 4\frac{1}{3}$

16. $21\frac{4}{5}$
$\ \ -\ 3\frac{1}{6}$

17. $24\frac{5}{6} - 6\frac{7}{10}$

18. $23\frac{8}{9} - 16\frac{4}{5}$

19. $25\frac{13}{15} - 19\frac{7}{12}$

20. $18\frac{3}{10} - 11\frac{7}{100}$

21. $16\frac{5}{6} - 8\frac{8}{15}$

22. $13\frac{2}{3} - 4\frac{5}{11}$

Marie Curie spearheaded a plan to equip and staff mobile x-ray cars, which were later nicknamed "Little Curies,"
for the battlefields of France during World War I. These cars saved many lives by allowing wounded soldiers to
be treated quickly on the battlefield, instead of having to be transported to hospitals before they could get help.

Application

23. Harold's lawn takes $5\frac{2}{3}$ hours to mow. He mowed for $3\frac{1}{2}$ hours one morning. How long must Harold mow to finish the job?

24. Gary lives $4\frac{4}{5}$ miles from Jeff's house. One morning Gary ran $2\frac{3}{10}$ miles toward Jeff's house and then stopped to rest. How much farther must Gary go to get to Jeff's house?

Adding and Subtracting Fractions

7.7 Subtracting Mixed Numbers with Renaming

In two days, Ron hiked a total of $12\frac{1}{8}$ miles along the Chattooga river. If he spent the first night at a campsite $4\frac{7}{8}$ miles from the trail head, how far did Ron hike the next day?

You subtract $12\frac{1}{8} - 4\frac{7}{8}$ to find the distance.

Since it is not possible to subtract $\frac{7}{8}$ from $\frac{1}{8}$, you must first rename $12\frac{1}{8}$; then subtract as with mixed numbers.

Consider the example below.

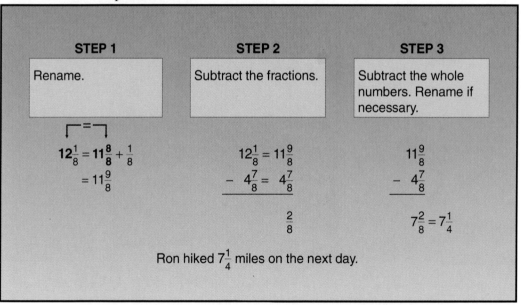

STEP 1	STEP 2	STEP 3
Rename.	Subtract the fractions.	Subtract the whole numbers. Rename if necessary.

$$12\frac{1}{8} = 11\frac{8}{8} + \frac{1}{8}$$
$$= 11\frac{9}{8}$$

$$12\frac{1}{8} = 11\frac{9}{8}$$
$$- \ 4\frac{7}{8} = \ 4\frac{7}{8}$$
$$\frac{2}{8}$$

$$11\frac{9}{8}$$
$$- \ 4\frac{7}{8}$$
$$7\frac{2}{8} = 7\frac{1}{4}$$

Ron hiked $7\frac{1}{4}$ miles on the next day.

Additional Examples

Subtract.

a.
$$8 = 7\frac{5}{5}$$
$$-\ 3\frac{2}{5} = 3\frac{2}{5}$$
$$\overline{\phantom{-3\frac{2}{5}}}$$
$$4\frac{3}{5}$$

b.
$$12\frac{3}{4} = 12\frac{15}{20} = 11\frac{35}{20}$$
$$-\ 7\frac{9}{10} =\ 7\frac{18}{20} =\ 7\frac{18}{20}$$
$$\overline{\phantom{-7\frac{9}{10}}}$$
$$4\frac{17}{20}$$

☑SKILL CHECK

Subtract. Write each answer in lowest terms.

1.
$$17$$
$$-\ \ 3\frac{7}{12}$$
$$\overline{\phantom{-3\frac{7}{12}}}$$

2.
$$5\frac{1}{8}$$
$$-2\frac{5}{8}$$
$$\overline{\phantom{-2\frac{5}{8}}}$$

3.
$$9\frac{1}{3}$$
$$-4\frac{5}{9}$$
$$\overline{\phantom{-4\frac{5}{9}}}$$

4. $16\frac{2}{5} - 10\frac{3}{4}$

5. $11\frac{1}{4} - 7\frac{5}{6}$

6. $18\frac{4}{25} - 12\frac{7}{10}$

Exercises

Complete.

1. $5 = 4\frac{\square}{7}$

2. $14 = \square\frac{5}{5}$

3. $\square = 7\frac{10}{10}$

Subtract.

4.
$$12$$
$$-\ \ 7\frac{3}{4}$$
$$\overline{\phantom{-7\frac{3}{4}}}$$

5.
$$9$$
$$-2\frac{1}{6}$$
$$\overline{\phantom{-2\frac{1}{6}}}$$

6.
$$14$$
$$-\ \ 8\frac{5}{9}$$
$$\overline{\phantom{-8\frac{5}{9}}}$$

7.
$$24$$
$$-\ 15\frac{11}{16}$$
$$\overline{\phantom{-15\frac{11}{16}}}$$

Adding and Subtracting Fractions

Complete.

8. $8\frac{1}{5} = 7\frac{\square}{5}$

    $- 3\frac{3}{5} = 3\frac{\square}{5}$

          $4\frac{\square}{5}$

9. $6\frac{3}{8} = 5\frac{\square}{8}$

    $- 1\frac{5}{8} = 1\frac{5}{8}$

          $4\frac{\square}{8} = 4\frac{\square}{4}$

10. $9\frac{5}{13} = 8\frac{\square}{13}$

    $- 3\frac{11}{13} = 3\frac{11}{13}$

          $5\frac{\square}{13}$

Subtract. Write the answer in lowest terms.

11. $9\frac{1}{7}$

    $- 5\frac{3}{7}$

12. $4\frac{2}{9}$

    $- 1\frac{5}{9}$

13. $16\frac{2}{5}$

    $- 7\frac{4}{5}$

14. $12\frac{1}{8}$

    $- 4\frac{7}{8}$

15. $8\frac{1}{5}$

    $- 6\frac{9}{10}$

16. $13\frac{3}{8}$

    $- 7\frac{1}{2}$

17. $9\frac{1}{4}$

    $- 2\frac{1}{3}$

18. $10\frac{3}{4}$

    $- 5\frac{9}{10}$

19. $9\frac{1}{10} - 6\frac{3}{5}$

20. $15\frac{1}{4} - 7\frac{5}{8}$

21. $16\frac{5}{6} - 13\frac{9}{10}$

22. $17\frac{2}{3} - 11\frac{7}{8}$

Application

23. Roger bought IBC stock at a price of 36. He sold the stock when its price fell by $2\frac{3}{8}$. At what price did he sell the stock?

24. Bonita bought BTT stock at a price of $29\frac{3}{4}$. One week later she bought more of the same stock at $31\frac{1}{8}$. How much did the price of the stock rise in one week?

7.8 Estimating with Fractions

You can determine whether a fraction is closer to 0, $\frac{1}{2}$, or 1 by examining its numerator and denominator.

Consider the following examples.

Fractions close to 1:

$$\frac{7}{8}, \frac{11}{13}, \frac{71}{75}, \frac{10}{9} \qquad \blacktriangleleft \text{The numerator and the denominator are about the same size.}$$

Fractions close to $\frac{1}{2}$:

$$\frac{4}{9}, \frac{7}{13}, \frac{23}{50}, \frac{57}{100} \qquad \blacktriangleleft \text{The numerator is about } \frac{1}{2} \text{ the size of the denominator.}$$

Fractions close to 0:

$$\frac{1}{6}, \frac{2}{9}, \frac{3}{40}, \frac{9}{100} \qquad \blacktriangleleft \text{The numerator is very small in comparison to the denominator.}$$

You can estimate sums and differences of fractions by rounding each fraction to 0, $\frac{1}{2}$, or 1.

Estimate $\frac{7}{8} - \frac{5}{12}$.

$$\frac{7}{8} \xrightarrow{\text{rounds to}} 1$$
$$-\frac{5}{12} \xrightarrow{\text{rounds to}} -\frac{1}{2}$$
$$\overline{\phantom{-\frac{5}{12}}} \qquad \overline{\frac{1}{2}}$$

The difference is about $\frac{1}{2}$.

Estimate $\frac{19}{20} + \frac{1}{6} + \frac{5}{8}$.

$$\frac{19}{20} + \frac{1}{6} + \frac{5}{8}$$
$$\downarrow \quad \downarrow \quad \downarrow$$
$$1 + 0 + \frac{1}{2} = 1\frac{1}{2}$$

The sum is about $1\frac{1}{2}$.

You can also estimate sums and differences of mixed numbers.

Additional Examples

Estimate.

a.
$$2\frac{3}{4} + 1\frac{9}{16}$$
$$\downarrow \quad \downarrow$$
$$3 + 1\frac{1}{2} = 4\frac{1}{2}$$

b.
$$9\frac{11}{12} - 3\frac{1}{10}$$
$$\downarrow \quad \downarrow$$
$$10 - 3 = 7$$

Adding and Subtracting Fractions

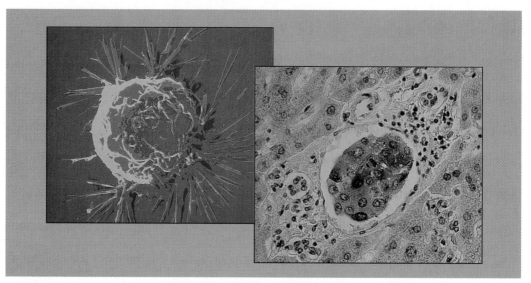

Following the discovery of radium in 1898, radiation was used to destroy cancerous cells such as the ones pictured here. Much of the early work was crude, destroying healthy cells along with diseased ones.

✓SKILL CHECK

Round each fraction to 0, $\frac{1}{2}$, or 1.

1. $\frac{8}{9}$ **2.** $\frac{8}{15}$ **3.** $\frac{1}{5}$ **4.** $\frac{9}{20}$

Estimate each sum or difference.

5. $\frac{5}{8} + \frac{11}{13}$ **6.** $\frac{17}{19} - \frac{1}{7}$ **7.** $4\frac{9}{10} + 5\frac{4}{9}$ **8.** $8\frac{6}{7} - \frac{5}{8}$

Exercises

Tell whether each fraction rounds to 0, $\frac{1}{2}$, or 1.

1. $\frac{3}{5}$ **2.** $1\frac{1}{6}$ **3.** $\frac{2}{11}$ **4.** $\frac{19}{20}$

Tell whether each fraction rounds to $1\frac{1}{2}$, 2, or $2\frac{1}{2}$.

5. $2\frac{1}{8}$ **6.** $1\frac{4}{9}$ **7.** $1\frac{11}{12}$ **8.** $2\frac{9}{16}$

Estimate the sum or difference.

9. $\begin{array}{r} \frac{4}{7} \\ + \frac{9}{10} \\ \hline \end{array}$ **10.** $\begin{array}{r} 6\frac{4}{5} \\ + 2\frac{1}{4} \\ \hline \end{array}$ **11.** $\begin{array}{r} \frac{6}{7} \\ - \frac{1}{2} \\ \hline \end{array}$ **12.** $\begin{array}{r} 13\frac{9}{17} \\ - 2\frac{8}{9} \\ \hline \end{array}$

13. $6\frac{7}{8}$
$-\ \ \frac{11}{12}$

14. $3\frac{14}{15}$
$+\ \ \frac{7}{12}$

15. $\frac{2}{9}$
$+\ \frac{9}{10}$

16. $9\frac{1}{8}$
$+5\frac{1}{7}$

17. $4\frac{1}{9} + 8\frac{1}{5}$

18. $7\frac{2}{4} - 2\frac{8}{9}$

19. $3\frac{4}{7} - 1\frac{5}{9}$

Estimate; then choose the correct answer.

20. $5\frac{1}{8} + 7\frac{7}{8}$
a. 7
b. $7\frac{3}{8}$
c. 13

21. $9\frac{1}{2} - 3\frac{1}{6}$
a. 6
b. $6\frac{1}{3}$
c. 7

22. $4\frac{3}{8} + 2\frac{1}{4}$
a. $6\frac{5}{8}$
b. 7
c. $7\frac{5}{8}$

Application

23. Terry studied for $2\frac{3}{8}$ hours on Monday night and $3\frac{1}{4}$ hours on Tuesday night. Estimate how much longer he studied on Tuesday night.

24. Jasmine typed for $1\frac{5}{6}$ hours in the afternoon and $2\frac{3}{4}$ hours in the evening. Estimate how many hours she typed in all.

In World War I x-ray machines were used for locating the position of bullets in wounded soldiers. While x-ray machines were relatively rare in the early 1900s, their use for everything from photographing teeth to pinpointing bone injuries has become commonplace today.

Adding and Subtracting Fractions

Problem Solving: Draw a Picture

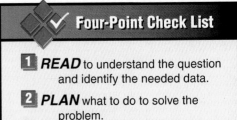

Four-Point Check List

1 READ to understand the question and identify the needed data.

2 PLAN what to do to solve the problem.

3 SOLVE the problem by carrying out the plan.

4 CHECK to make sure the solution is reasonable.

You can use the strategy "Draw a Picture" to solve some word problems. In this strategy, you draw a picture to help you understand how the data in the problem are related.

Andrew built a rectangular kennel for his golden retriever. The kennel was 15 feet long and 9 feet wide. He placed one post at each of the corners and then spaced the remaining posts 3 feet apart. How many posts did Andrew use?

1. READ: Understand the question.
   - How many posts did Andrew use?

   Identify the needed data.
   - The rectangular kennel was 15 feet by 9 feet.
   - There was a post at each corner.
   - The remaining posts were spaced 3 feet apart.

2. PLAN: Use the strategy "Draw a Picture."

3. SOLVE: Draw an accurate picture to represent the data in the problem.

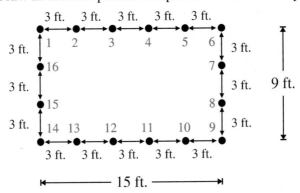

Andrew used a total of 16 posts.

4. CHECK: Is the solution reasonable?

   The picture accurately represents the placement of the posts spaced 3 feet apart in a 9 ft. × 15 ft. rectangle; so the solution is reasonable.

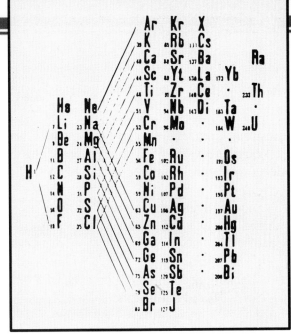

This periodic chart was prepared in 1898 by a chemist named Julius Thomsen. A total of 72 elements are listed on the chart. There are more than 100 elements recorded in the modern periodic table. Note that the atomic weight for radium is not given on this chart. Radium's atomic weight was not worked out until several years later.

☑SKILL CHECK

Draw a Picture. Solve.

1. Laura cut a candy bar into 8 equal pieces. How many cuts did she make?

2. Kane was stacking 21 bales of hay. Each row had 1 bale fewer than the row below it. If there was only 1 bale in the top row, how many rows were there in all?

Exercises

Draw a picture. Solve.

1. Lenny was stacking 25 boxes of apples in the pattern depicted on the right. How many boxes should he place in the bottom row?

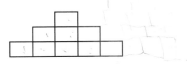

2. Anne was planting 15 tomato plants in 3 rows. The first row had 1 fewer than the second row, which had 1 fewer than the third row. How many tomato plants were in the first row?

Adding and Subtracting Fractions

Mixed Review

Solve.

3. There are 392 students enrolled at Calvary Christian Academy. Last year there were 68 fewer students enrolled. How many students were enrolled in the school last year?

4. Sarah practiced the piano twice as long as Ashley. If their combined practice time was 60 minutes, how long did Sarah practice?

5. Dan's checking account had a balance of $193.46. He made a deposit of $250 and wrote a check for $21.73. What was his new balance?

6. Mr. Davis rented a car for $29 per day plus $0.15 per mile. If he kept the car for 3 days and drove 180 miles, what was his total rental cost?

7. A commuter airplane has a seating capacity of 68 passengers. How many passengers could the plane transport in 12 flights?

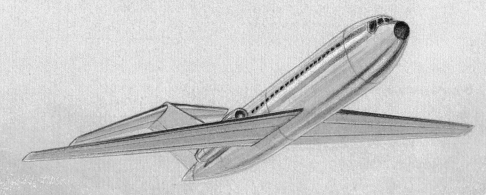

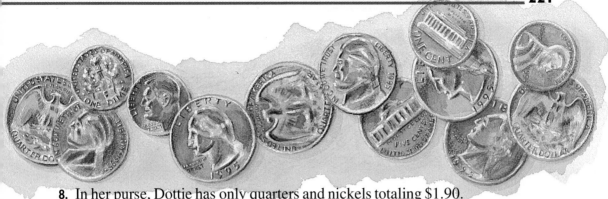

8. In her purse, Dottie has only quarters and nickels totaling $1.90. If she has 3 nickels, how many quarters does she have?

9. The members of the 1,600 m relay team had these times for 400 m: Chad, 65.1 s; Jason 64.5 s ; Aaron, 63.9 s; and John 65.4 s. List the times in order from least to greatest.

10. There were 22 female singers and 17 male singers in the school choir. If they were divided into 3 equal groups, how many students were in each group?

Chapter 7 Review

7.1 Write each as an improper fraction.

1. $2\frac{1}{5}$

2. $4\frac{5}{13}$

3. $12\frac{6}{7}$

Write each as a whole number or mixed number in lowest terms.

4. $\dfrac{23}{8}$

5. $\dfrac{40}{12}$

6. $\dfrac{56}{14}$

7.2 Compare the fractions. Write >, <, or =

7. $\dfrac{7}{12} \square \dfrac{4}{7}$

8. $8\frac{4}{5} \square 8\frac{11}{13}$

9. $\dfrac{10}{16} \square \dfrac{15}{24}$

Write in order from least to greatest.

10. $\dfrac{7}{8}, \dfrac{11}{12}, \dfrac{5}{6}$

11. $\dfrac{2}{3}, \dfrac{4}{5}, \dfrac{8}{15}$

Adding and Subtracting Fractions

7.3 - 7.7 Add or subtract. Write the answer in lowest terms.

12. $\dfrac{8}{9} - \dfrac{2}{9}$

13. $\dfrac{7}{11} + \dfrac{9}{11}$

14. $\dfrac{19}{21} + \dfrac{5}{21}$

15. $\begin{array}{r} \frac{1}{4} \\ + \frac{5}{8} \\ \hline \end{array}$

16. $\begin{array}{r} \frac{4}{5} \\ - \frac{2}{3} \\ \hline \end{array}$

17. $\begin{array}{r} \frac{7}{10} \\ + \frac{11}{15} \\ \hline \end{array}$

18. $\dfrac{13}{18} + \dfrac{6}{18} + \dfrac{17}{18}$

19. $\dfrac{3}{4} + \dfrac{1}{6} + \dfrac{7}{12}$

20. $\begin{array}{r} 9\frac{7}{9} \\ + 4\frac{5}{9} \\ \hline \end{array}$

21. $\begin{array}{r} 5\frac{3}{16} \\ + 2\frac{5}{8} \\ \hline \end{array}$

22. $\begin{array}{r} 3\frac{2}{8} \\ + 8\frac{7}{12} \\ \hline \end{array}$

23. $\begin{array}{r} 8\frac{3}{4} \\ - 5\frac{1}{3} \\ \hline \end{array}$

24. $\begin{array}{r} 14\frac{5}{8} \\ - 6\frac{1}{6} \\ \hline \end{array}$

25. $\begin{array}{r} 17\frac{11}{15} \\ - 13\frac{2}{5} \\ \hline \end{array}$

26. $22\frac{9}{10} - 8\frac{5}{6}$

27. $4\frac{1}{2} + 3\frac{3}{5} + 2\frac{5}{6}$

28. $\begin{array}{r} 8\frac{1}{8} \\ - 2\frac{3}{8} \\ \hline \end{array}$

29. $\begin{array}{r} 14\frac{1}{3} \\ - 6\frac{7}{9} \\ \hline \end{array}$

30. $\begin{array}{r} 8\frac{3}{10} \\ - 3\frac{3}{4} \\ \hline \end{array}$

31. $16\frac{14}{15} - 9\frac{5}{6}$

32. $8\frac{3}{10} - 1\frac{4}{5}$

7.8 Estimate each sum or difference.

33. $\dfrac{5}{9} + \dfrac{2}{11}$

34. $2\frac{13}{15} - 1\frac{4}{7}$

35. $6\frac{11}{20} - \dfrac{9}{10}$

Chapter 7 Cumulative Review

1. Multiply. $1.7 \times 0.4 \times 3.48$
   a. 2.3654
   b. 2.3664
   c. 2.4664
   d. not given

2. Multiply. Round to the nearest cent.
   3.79×0.48
   a. $1.81
   b. $1.82
   c. $1.80
   d. not given

3. Write 1,000 as a power of 10 using exponents.
   a. 10^2
   b. 10^3
   c. 10^4
   d. not given

4. Divide. $27 \overline{)8.316}$
   a. 0.038
   b. 0.308
   c. 0.38
   d. not given

5. Write 6.32×10^5 in standard form.
   a. 6,320
   b. 63,200
   c. 632,000
   d. not given

6. Choose the name that best describes the following quadrilateral.

   a. square
   b. trapezoid
   c. parallelogram
   d. rhombus

7. Choose the segment that is not a radius of the circle.

   a. $\overline{AB}$
   b. $\overline{CA}$
   c. $\overline{DC}$
   d. not given

8. $\triangle ABC$ and $\triangle XYZ$ are congruent. Compare. $\overline{BC} \cong$ ____.
   a. $\overline{XY}$
   b. $\overline{YZ}$
   c. $\overline{XZ}$
   d. not given

9. Which is *not* a name for the angle?

   a. $\angle GHI$
   b. $\angle GIH$
   c. $\angle IHG$
   d. $\angle H$

10. Choose the measure of the complement of a 67° angle.
   a. 13°
   b. 23°
   c. 113°
   d. not given

11. Tell whether 300 is divisible by 2, 4, 5, 10, or none of these numbers.
   a. 2, 4
   b. 2, 5, 10
   c. 2, 4, 5, 10
   d. none

12. Choose the number that is not a factor of 18.
   a. 2
   b. 6
   c. 8
   d. not given

13. Choose the composite number in the list. 23, 33, 43, 53
   a. 23
   b. 33
   c. 43
   d. 53

14. Find the GCF of 24 and 30.
   a. 4
   b. 6
   c. 12
   d. not given

15. Find the LCM of 9 and 12.
   a. 3
   b. 24
   c. 36
   d. not given

Adding and Subtracting Fractions

CHARLES BABBAGE
COMPUTER

Charles Babbage, English mathematician and inventor, is best known for the invention of a device which he never completed—the computer. Often referred to as the "Father of Computers," he developed a detailed set of plans for an advanced calculating machine. The design of this machine foreshadowed many of the features of modern-day computers, including the ability to program it to perform mathematical operations.

Charles developed his interest in mathematics at an early age. As a young schoolboy, he awoke every morning at three o'clock for several consecutive months to teach himself algebra. By the time he was old enough to attend England's renowned Cambridge University, he had already mastered the principles of calculus through self study. At Cambridge, he soon discovered that his mathematical abilities surpassed those of many of his classmates and even some of his professors.

Somewhat disappointed, he founded Cambridge's Analytical Society for students who desired to learn more than their professors could teach them. The purpose of the society was to analyze and study the mathematical developments promoted by the top European mathematicians of the day. It was during one of these meetings that Charles first considered the possibility of using a machine to calculate mathematical formulas. After examining a set of tables which were riddled with errors, Charles turned to a classmate and exclaimed, "I am thinking that all these mathematical tables might be calculated by machinery!"

This idea became an obsession with Charles for the rest of his life. In 1822 he developed a small machine powered by a hand crank which could perform mathematical calculations rapidly and accurately. Using this invention as a springboard, he secured financial backing from the British government to produce a large machine which he called a "difference engine."

Ten years later he abandoned work on this project to begin work on an even more complicated device. This forerunner of the computer, called an "analytical engine," would be capable of storing numbers. It would also be programmable, using a series of punched cards. In this respect, it was similar to the jacquard loom, which used a series of punched cards to program the loom to weave a pattern in cloth. It was Countess Ada Lovelace, a fellow mathematician and daughter of

1792 - 1871

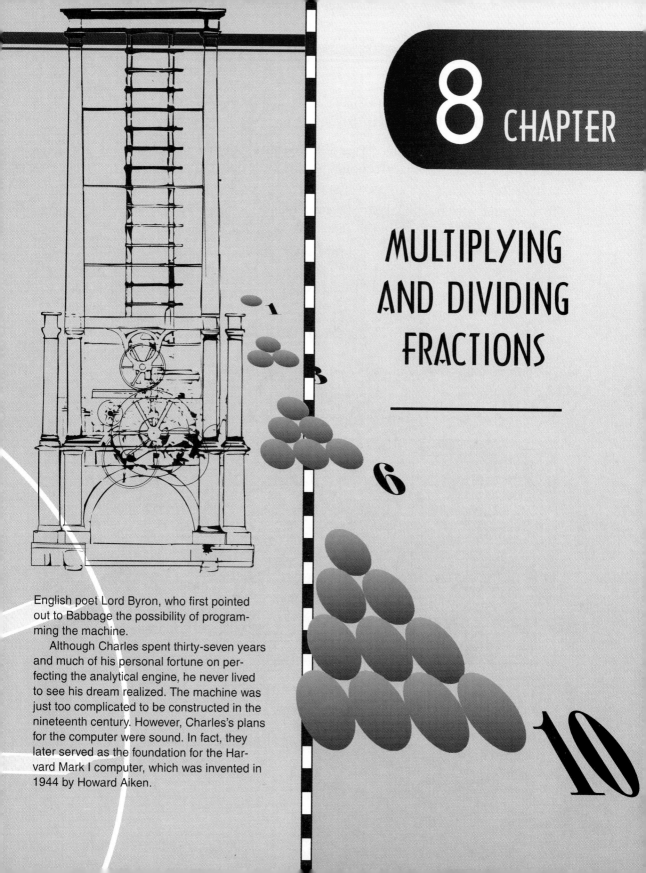

8 CHAPTER

MULTIPLYING AND DIVIDING FRACTIONS

English poet Lord Byron, who first pointed out to Babbage the possibility of programming the machine.

Although Charles spent thirty-seven years and much of his personal fortune on perfecting the analytical engine, he never lived to see his dream realized. The machine was just too complicated to be constructed in the nineteenth century. However, Charles's plans for the computer were sound. In fact, they later served as the foundation for the Harvard Mark I computer, which was invented in 1944 by Howard Aiken.

8.1 Multiplying Fractions

Mrs. Sanchez has $\frac{3}{4}$ of a pan of cake left. She gave $\frac{1}{3}$ of the remaining cake to her children. What fractional part of the whole cake did she give them?

To determine what fractional part she gave them, you find $\frac{1}{3}$ of $\frac{3}{4}$. Study the following diagrams.

 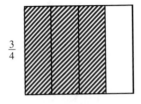 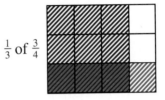

According to the above diagrams, $\frac{1}{3}$ of $\frac{3}{4}$ is equal to $\frac{3}{12}$ or $\frac{1}{4}$.

You can also multiply $\frac{1}{3} \times \frac{3}{4}$ to find $\frac{1}{3}$ of $\frac{3}{4}$.

To multiply fractions, follow these steps.

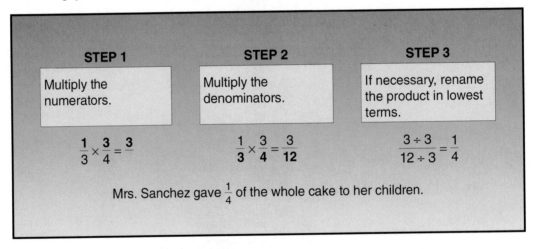

STEP 1	STEP 2	STEP 3
Multiply the numerators.	Multiply the denominators.	If necessary, rename the product in lowest terms.
$\frac{1}{3} \times \frac{3}{4} = \frac{3}{}$	$\frac{1}{3} \times \frac{3}{4} = \frac{3}{12}$	$\frac{3 \div 3}{12 \div 3} = \frac{1}{4}$

Mrs. Sanchez gave $\frac{1}{4}$ of the whole cake to her children.

To find the product of a whole number and a fraction, you rename the whole number as a fraction and then multiply.

Additional Examples

Multiply.

a. $\dfrac{3}{4} \times 5 = \dfrac{3}{4} \times \dfrac{5}{1}$

$\qquad = \dfrac{15}{4}$

$\qquad = 3\frac{3}{4}$

b. $\dfrac{1}{2} \times \dfrac{2}{3} \times 9 = \dfrac{1}{2} \times \dfrac{2}{3} \times \dfrac{9}{1}$

$\qquad = \dfrac{18 \div 6}{6 \div 6}$

$\qquad = \dfrac{3}{1}, \text{ or } 3$

☑ **SKILL CHECK**

Multiply. Write the product in lowest terms.

1. $\dfrac{3}{4} \times \dfrac{1}{8}$ **2.** $\dfrac{1}{4} \times \dfrac{4}{5}$ **3.** $\dfrac{5}{6} \times \dfrac{3}{4}$ **4.** $\dfrac{6}{7} \times \dfrac{5}{12}$

5. $\dfrac{4}{7} \times 5$ **6.** $6 \times \dfrac{1}{4}$ **7.** $\dfrac{5}{6} \times \dfrac{1}{2} \times \dfrac{3}{4}$ **8.** $\dfrac{5}{8} \times 8 \times \dfrac{3}{10}$

Multiplying and Dividing Fractions

Exercises

Complete.

1. $\dfrac{4}{5} \times \dfrac{1}{3} = \dfrac{4 \times \square}{5 \times \square} = \dfrac{4}{15}$

2. $\dfrac{1}{5} \times \dfrac{2}{7} = \dfrac{\square \times 2}{\square \times 7} = \dfrac{2}{35}$

3. $\dfrac{7}{8} \times \dfrac{1}{4} = \dfrac{\square \times \square}{8 \times 4} = \dfrac{7}{32}$

4. $\dfrac{5}{11} \times \dfrac{3}{8} = \dfrac{5 \times 3}{\square \times \square} = \dfrac{15}{88}$

Multiply. Write the product in lowest terms.

5. $\dfrac{9}{10} \times \dfrac{3}{5}$

6. $\dfrac{4}{5} \times \dfrac{5}{8}$

7. $4 \times \dfrac{3}{5}$

8. $\dfrac{2}{7} \times \dfrac{5}{8}$

9. $\dfrac{3}{4} \times \dfrac{1}{8}$

10. $\dfrac{5}{6} \times \dfrac{3}{10}$

11. $\dfrac{3}{20} \times 5$

12. $\dfrac{6}{7} \times \dfrac{2}{3}$

13. $\dfrac{4}{11} \times \dfrac{2}{5}$

14. $\dfrac{2}{9} \times 13$

15. $\dfrac{3}{10} \times \dfrac{5}{1}$

16. $\dfrac{5}{6} \times 12$

17. $\dfrac{4}{7} \times \dfrac{1}{3} \times \dfrac{2}{5}$

18. $\dfrac{5}{9} \times \dfrac{1}{2} \times \dfrac{3}{10}$

19. $\dfrac{3}{5} \times \dfrac{1}{4} \times \dfrac{5}{8}$

20. $\dfrac{4}{9} \times \dfrac{1}{2} \times 6$

21. $\dfrac{3}{10} \times \dfrac{2}{3} \times \dfrac{5}{1}$

22. $\dfrac{5}{6} \times 6 \times \dfrac{2}{3}$

Application

23. Mrs. Casillas had $\frac{2}{3}$ of a gallon of milk. She used $\frac{3}{4}$ of it. What fractional part of a gallon of milk did she use?

24. Mrs. Cates had a container full of 36 cookies. She gave $\frac{4}{9}$ of them to her neighbor. How many cookies did she give away?

8.2 Simplifying Before Multiplying

In the previous lesson, you learned to find the product of fractions by multiplying first and then simplifying. Consider the following example.

$$\frac{5}{6} \times \frac{3}{4} = \frac{15}{24}$$
$$= \frac{15 \div 3}{24 \div 3}$$
$$= \frac{5}{8}$$

In some products you can simplify first by dividing the numerator and denominator by common factors. To use this short cut for multiplying fractions, follow these steps.

STEP 1	STEP 2	STEP 3
Identify a common factor of any numerator and any denominator.	Divide the numerator and the denominator by the common factor.	Multiply the resulting numerators and denominators.

$\dfrac{5}{6} \times \dfrac{3}{4}$ ◀ 3 is the GCF of 3 and 6.

$\dfrac{5}{\underset{2}{\cancel{6} \div 3}} \times \dfrac{\overset{1}{\cancel{3} \div 3}}{4}$ ◀ Divide by 3.

$\dfrac{5}{\underset{2}{\cancel{6}}} \times \dfrac{\overset{1}{\cancel{3}}}{4} = \dfrac{5}{8}$

The above product was simplified in one step by dividing by the GCF. However, you can also simplify by dividing several times by any common factor. Consider the following product.

$$\frac{18}{19} \times \frac{7}{12} \longrightarrow \frac{\overset{9}{\cancel{18} \div 2}}{19} \times \frac{7}{\underset{6}{\cancel{12} \div 2}} \longrightarrow \frac{\overset{\overset{3}{\cancel{9} \div 3}}{\cancel{18}}}{19} \times \frac{7}{\underset{\underset{2}{\cancel{6} \div 3}}{\cancel{12}}} = \frac{21}{38}$$

Additional Example

Multiply. Use the short cut.

$$\frac{3}{8} \times 32 \times \frac{5}{6} \longrightarrow \frac{\overset{1}{\cancel{3}} \div 3}{\overset{}{\cancel{8}} \div 8} \times \frac{\overset{4}{\cancel{32}} \div 8}{1} \times \frac{5}{\overset{}{\cancel{6}} \div 3} \longrightarrow \frac{\overset{1}{\cancel{3}}}{\cancel{8}} \times \frac{\overset{4 \div 2}{\cancel{32}}}{1} \times \frac{5}{\overset{\cancel{6}}{2 \div 2}} = \frac{10}{1}, \text{ or } 10$$

☑**SKILL CHECK**

Complete.

1. $\dfrac{1}{\underset{\div 5}{\cancel{10}}} \times \dfrac{\overset{\square}{\cancel{15}} \div 5}{16} = \dfrac{\square}{\square}$

2. $\dfrac{\overset{\square}{\cancel{3}} \div 3}{\underset{\div 2}{\cancel{8}}} \times \dfrac{\overset{\square}{\cancel{2}} \div 2}{\underset{\div 3}{\cancel{9}}} = \dfrac{\square}{\square}$

Multiply. Use the short cut where possible.

3. $\dfrac{3}{10} \times 12$ 4. $\dfrac{3}{4} \times \dfrac{14}{9}$ 5. $15 \times \dfrac{13}{20}$ 6. $\dfrac{6}{7} \times \dfrac{18}{24} \times \dfrac{8}{9}$

Exercises

Multiply. Use the short cut where possible.

1. $\dfrac{7}{8} \times \dfrac{8}{9}$ 2. $\dfrac{2}{7} \times \dfrac{5}{6}$ 3. $\dfrac{3}{8} \times \dfrac{4}{21}$ 4. $9 \times \dfrac{7}{18}$

5. $\dfrac{7}{8} \times \dfrac{3}{14}$ 6. $\dfrac{5}{6} \times \dfrac{3}{10}$ 7. $\dfrac{11}{16} \times \dfrac{6}{7}$ 8. $\dfrac{8}{15} \times \dfrac{5}{28}$

9. $\dfrac{9}{20} \times \dfrac{10}{13}$ 10. $\dfrac{9}{10} \times \dfrac{6}{7}$ 11. $18 \times \dfrac{7}{12}$ 12. $\dfrac{9}{16} \times \dfrac{8}{15}$

13. $32 \times \dfrac{5}{8}$ 14. $\dfrac{4}{15} \times \dfrac{5}{8}$ 15. $\dfrac{11}{21} \times \dfrac{14}{22}$ 16. $\dfrac{9}{10} \times \dfrac{20}{21}$

17. $\dfrac{6}{7} \times \dfrac{5}{11} \times \dfrac{7}{8}$ 18. $\dfrac{9}{10} \times 3 \times \dfrac{5}{12}$ 19. $\dfrac{5}{8} \times \dfrac{2}{9} \times \dfrac{4}{5}$

20. $\dfrac{14}{3} \times \dfrac{3}{4} \times \dfrac{6}{7}$ 21. $\dfrac{3}{12} \times \dfrac{5}{9} \times 6$ 22. $\dfrac{7}{10} \times \dfrac{4}{7} \times \dfrac{5}{8}$

Application

23. In math class, $\frac{3}{4}$ of the students got A's on a test. Of the students who got A's, $\frac{4}{9}$ were girls. What fraction of students were girls who got A's?

24. Terry is $\frac{5}{6}$ the age of Ron. Ron is 30 years old. How old is Terry?

8.3 Estimating Products of Mixed Numbers

Hal is riding his bike along the Blue Ridge Parkway. If he can average $12\frac{9}{10}$ miles per hour, about how far can he travel in $5\frac{1}{2}$ hours?

Since the question does not ask for an exact answer, you can estimate the product $12\frac{9}{10} \times 5\frac{1}{2}$ to get an approximate answer.

To estimate products with mixed numbers, follow these steps.

STEP 1	STEP 2
Round each factor to the nearest whole number. If the fraction is $\frac{1}{2}$ or greater, round up.	Multiply the rounded factors.

$12\frac{9}{10} \xrightarrow{\text{rounds to}} 13$

$5\frac{1}{2} \xrightarrow{\text{rounds to}} 6$

$13 \times 6 = 78$

Hal can travel about 78 miles in $5\frac{1}{2}$ hours.

Multiplying and Dividing Fractions

When estimating products with fractions less than 1, you generally round these fractions to $\frac{1}{2}$ or 1. Study the examples below.

Additional Examples

Estimate.

a. $\dfrac{3}{8} \times 9\frac{9}{16}$

$\downarrow \quad \downarrow$

$\dfrac{1}{2} \times 10 = 5$

b. $\dfrac{13}{16} \times 12\frac{1}{8}$

$\downarrow \quad \downarrow$

$1 \times 12 = 12$

c. $\dfrac{1}{6} \times 11\frac{7}{9}$

$\downarrow \quad \downarrow$

$\dfrac{1}{6} \times 12 = 2$

◀ Do not round $\frac{1}{6}$, since $\frac{1}{6}$ is compatible with 12.

d. $4\frac{2}{3} \times 18\frac{7}{10}$

$\downarrow \quad \downarrow$

$5 \times 20 = 100$

◀ Round $18\frac{7}{10}$ to 20, since it is an easy number to compute with mentally.

☑ SKILL CHECK

Estimate.

1. $6\frac{9}{10} \times 3\frac{1}{7}$ 2. $8\frac{4}{5} \times 4\frac{7}{8}$ 3. $4\frac{1}{9} \times 15\frac{2}{5}$ 4. $\dfrac{5}{9} \times 17\frac{7}{8}$

Choose the best estimate.

5. $9\frac{1}{3} \times 6\frac{1}{2}$ a. about 54   b. about 63   c. about 70

Exercises

Estimate.

1. $2\frac{1}{3} \times 7\frac{1}{3}$ 2. $9\frac{3}{4} \times 5\frac{5}{6}$ 3. $8\frac{9}{10} \times 2\frac{1}{4}$

4. $11\frac{1}{8} \times 5$ 5. $\dfrac{9}{11} \times 3\frac{15}{16}$ 6. $3\frac{1}{4} \times 3\frac{7}{8}$

7. $8\frac{3}{16} \times 7\frac{2}{5}$ 8. $\dfrac{1}{4} \times 16\frac{1}{8}$.   9. $8\frac{5}{6} \times \dfrac{15}{16}$

10. $2\frac{5}{6} \times 7\frac{2}{5}$ **11.** $\frac{1}{7} \times 13\frac{7}{8}$ **12.** $8 \times 7\frac{8}{11}$

13. $13\frac{1}{5} \times 10\frac{1}{8}$ **14.** $4\frac{8}{9} \times 20\frac{1}{7}$ **15.** $6\frac{11}{12} \times 29\frac{6}{7}$

Choose the best estimate.

16. $7\frac{1}{3} \times 3\frac{1}{2}$ **a.** about 21   **b.** about 28   **c.** about 35

17. $9\frac{1}{8} \times \frac{9}{10}$ **a.** about 7   **b.** about 9   **c.** about 11

18. $\frac{1}{5} \times 14\frac{2}{3}$ **a.** about 2   **b.** about 3   **c.** about 5

Estimate. Write > or < for each ☐.

19. $6 \times 9\frac{4}{11}$ ☐ 54   **20.** $4\frac{3}{4} \times 5\frac{5}{6}$ ☐ 30

21. $7\frac{1}{10} \times 8\frac{5}{6}$ ☐ 65   **22.** $9\frac{2}{7} \times 7\frac{3}{4}$ ☐ 70

23. $19\frac{5}{6} \times 4\frac{4}{5}$ ☐ 100   **24.** $8 \times 20\frac{3}{7}$ ☐ 160

25. $6\frac{2}{3} \times 7\frac{1}{16}$ ☐ 50   **26.** $12\frac{1}{4} \times 10\frac{3}{8}$ ☐ 120

Application

Estimate.

27. Ted drank $\frac{1}{16}$ of a gallon of water during the first hour of his ride. At this rate, about how many gallons of water will Ted drink during a ride of $5\frac{5}{6}$ hours?

28. Malik planned to ride a total of 195 miles along the Parkway. If he can ride $39\frac{8}{10}$ miles per day, how many days will it take him to ride this distance?

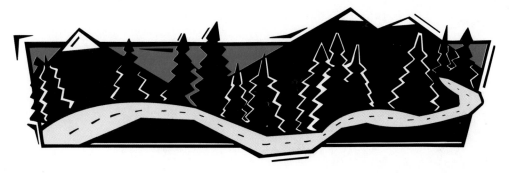

Multiplying and Dividing Fractions

8.4 Multiply Mixed Numbers

Mrs. Valquez is making bran muffins for a women's prayer breakfast. The recipe calls for $1\frac{2}{3}$ cups of flour to make 1 dozen muffins. If Mrs. Valquez wants to make $2\frac{1}{2}$ dozen muffins, how much flour does she need?

You multiply $2\frac{1}{2} \times 1\frac{2}{3}$ to determine how much flour she needs.

To multiply mixed numbers, follow these steps.

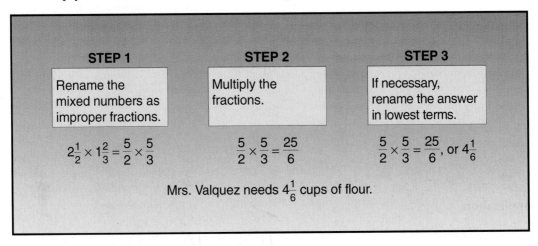

STEP 1	STEP 2	STEP 3
Rename the mixed numbers as improper fractions.	Multiply the fractions.	If necessary, rename the answer in lowest terms.
$2\frac{1}{2} \times 1\frac{2}{3} = \frac{5}{2} \times \frac{5}{3}$	$\frac{5}{2} \times \frac{5}{3} = \frac{25}{6}$	$\frac{5}{2} \times \frac{5}{3} = \frac{25}{6}$, or $4\frac{1}{6}$

Mrs. Valquez needs $4\frac{1}{6}$ cups of flour.

Additional Examples

Multiply. Write the answer in lowest terms.

a. $5\frac{1}{5} \times 1\frac{2}{13} = \frac{26}{5} \times \frac{15}{13}$

$= \frac{\overset{2}{\cancel{26}}}{\underset{1}{\cancel{5}}} \times \frac{\overset{3}{\cancel{15}}}{\underset{1}{\cancel{13}}}$

$= \frac{6}{1}$

$= 6$

b. $2\frac{2}{3} \times \frac{7}{12} = \frac{8}{3} \times \frac{7}{12}$

$= \frac{\overset{2}{\cancel{8}}}{3} \times \frac{7}{\underset{3}{\cancel{12}}}$

$= \frac{14}{9}$, or $1\frac{5}{9}$

c. $1\frac{3}{4} \times 10 = \frac{7}{4} \times \frac{10}{1}$

$$= \frac{7}{\overset{}{\underset{2}{4}}} \times \frac{\overset{5}{10}}{1}$$

$$= \frac{35}{2}, \text{ or } 17\frac{1}{2}$$

d. $6\frac{2}{3} \times 6 \times \frac{3}{16} = \frac{20}{3} \times \frac{6}{1} \times \frac{3}{16}$

$$= \frac{\overset{5}{20}}{\underset{1}{3}} \times \frac{\overset{\overset{1}{2}}{6}}{1} \times \frac{3}{\underset{\underset{2}{4}}{16}}$$

$$= \frac{15}{2}, \text{ or } 7\frac{1}{2}$$

The Mark I computer was the first large-scale automatic digital computer. It consisted of more than 750,000 parts, most of which were mechanical.

Multiplying and Dividing Fractions

☑**SKILL CHECK**

Complete.

1. $5\frac{3}{4} = \dfrac{\square}{4}$

2. $2\frac{5}{6} \times 1\frac{2}{3} = \dfrac{\square}{6} \times \dfrac{\square}{3}$

3. $4\frac{1}{2} \times 1\frac{2}{3}$

Multiply. Write the answer in lowest terms.

4. $\dfrac{5}{6} \times 7\frac{1}{2}$

5. $3\frac{4}{7} \times 14$

6. $1\frac{1}{9} \times 1\frac{1}{5}$

Exercises

Multiply. Write the product in lowest terms.

1. $\dfrac{1}{3} \times 2\frac{3}{8}$

2. $1\frac{5}{6} \times 9$

3. $2\frac{1}{3} \times 1\frac{1}{5}$

4. $\dfrac{3}{7} \times 4\frac{2}{3}$

5. $3\frac{1}{2} \times 1\frac{1}{4}$

6. $\dfrac{5}{12} \times 3\frac{1}{5}$

7. $6 \times 4\frac{2}{3}$

8. $\dfrac{6}{7} \times 3\frac{8}{9}$

9. $3\frac{5}{8} \times 2\frac{2}{3}$

10. $4\frac{2}{5} \times 1\frac{7}{8}$

11. $1\frac{4}{5} \times 2\frac{2}{9}$

12. $3\frac{3}{4} \times 1\frac{1}{9}$

13. $8\frac{1}{3} \times 2\frac{1}{10}$

14. $5\frac{4}{9} \times \dfrac{9}{14}$

15. $5\frac{1}{3} \times 3\frac{3}{4}$

16. $3\frac{1}{8} \times 1\frac{1}{15}$

17. $2 \times \dfrac{2}{3} \times 3\frac{1}{2}$

18. $4\frac{1}{6} \times 2 \times \dfrac{3}{8}$

19. $1\frac{3}{4} \times \dfrac{2}{5} \times 1\frac{3}{14}$

20. $2\frac{1}{4} \times 4 \times 2\frac{5}{6}$

21. $3\frac{1}{12} \times 2\frac{1}{2} \times 3\frac{3}{5}$

22. $7\frac{1}{2} \times \dfrac{4}{15} \times 1\frac{7}{12}$

Today's laptop computers are many times more powerful than the early computers of the 1950s, which took up whole rooms.

The computers of today are so user-friendly that even a child can operate one. Today, students become computer literate at an early age.

Application

23. A church bus traveled $4\frac{2}{3}$ hours at 48 miles per hour. How far did the bus travel?

24. The bus's engine had an oil capacity of $5\frac{3}{4}$ quarts. The oil level dropped to $\frac{4}{5}$ of that capacity. How many quarts of oil were still in the engine?

8.5 Dividing Fractions

Two numbers are **reciprocals** if their product is 1. Consider the following examples.

$$\frac{3}{4} \times \frac{4}{3} = \frac{12}{12}, \text{ or } 1 \qquad\qquad 6 \times \frac{1}{6} = \frac{6}{6}, \text{ or } 1$$

$\frac{3}{4}$ and $\frac{4}{3}$ are reciprocals. $\qquad\qquad$ 6 and $\frac{1}{6}$ are reciprocals.

The number zero has no reciprocal: $0 \times ? = 1$. Can you explain why?

You can find the reciprocal of a fraction by exchanging the numerator and the denominator.

Fraction: $\dfrac{5}{9} \times \dfrac{9}{5}$ ◀ The reciprocal of $\frac{5}{9}$ is $\frac{9}{5}$.

To find the reciprocal of a whole number, first write the whole number in fraction form; then exchange the numerator and the denominator.

Whole number: $4 = \dfrac{4}{1} \times \dfrac{1}{4}$ ◀ The reciprocal of 4 is $\frac{1}{4}$.

Notice in the example below that dividing by a number gives the same result as multiplying by the reciprocal of the number.

$$12 \div 4 = 3 \qquad\qquad 12 \times \frac{1}{4} = 3$$

reciprocals

To divide with fractions, you multiply by the reciprocal of the divisor. Study the examples below.

reciprocals

$$\frac{5}{8} \div \frac{3}{5} = \frac{5}{8} \times \frac{5}{3}$$
$$= \frac{25}{24}, \text{ or } 1\frac{1}{24}$$

reciprocals

$$\frac{4}{9} \div 3 = \frac{4}{9} \times \frac{1}{3}$$
$$= \frac{4}{27}$$

Additional Examples

Divide. Write the answer in lowest terms.

a. $\dfrac{3}{10} \div \dfrac{9}{16} = \dfrac{\overset{1}{\cancel{3}}}{\underset{5}{\cancel{10}}} \times \dfrac{\overset{8}{\cancel{16}}}{\underset{3}{\cancel{9}}}$

$$= \frac{8}{15}$$

b. $8 \div \dfrac{4}{13} = \dfrac{8}{1} \times \dfrac{13}{\underset{1}{\cancel{4}}}\overset{2}{}$

$$= \frac{26}{1}, \text{ or } 26$$

☑**SKILL CHECK**

Divide. Write the quotient in lowest terms.

1. $\dfrac{2}{5} \div \dfrac{3}{4}$

2. $\dfrac{3}{8} \div \dfrac{1}{6}$

3. $\dfrac{11}{12} \div \dfrac{1}{4}$

4. $\dfrac{7}{10} \div \dfrac{8}{15}$

5. $2 \div \dfrac{1}{3}$

6. $\dfrac{5}{6} \div \dfrac{5}{9}$

7. $8 \div \dfrac{6}{7}$

8. $\dfrac{4}{13} \div 6$

Exercises

Write the reciprocal.

1. $\dfrac{3}{7}$

2. $\dfrac{1}{8}$

3. 5

4. $\dfrac{9}{4}$

Divide. Write the quotient in lowest terms.

5. $\dfrac{3}{4} \div \dfrac{1}{5}$

6. $\dfrac{8}{9} \div 3$

7. $\dfrac{13}{14} \div \dfrac{1}{7}$

8. $\dfrac{7}{9} \div 2$

9. $\dfrac{4}{7} \div 3$

10. $\dfrac{3}{8} \div \dfrac{3}{8}$

11. $16 \div \dfrac{4}{15}$

12. $\dfrac{5}{6} \div \dfrac{2}{7}$

13. $\dfrac{4}{5} \div \dfrac{1}{2}$

14. $\dfrac{5}{12} \div \dfrac{5}{9}$

15. $6 \div \dfrac{2}{3}$

16. $\dfrac{4}{7} \div \dfrac{3}{5}$

17. $\dfrac{5}{9} \div \dfrac{5}{6}$

18. $\dfrac{8}{15} \div \dfrac{4}{9}$

19. $12 \div \dfrac{8}{9}$

20. $\dfrac{3}{4} \div \dfrac{3}{8}$

21. $\left(\dfrac{3}{4} \div \dfrac{2}{5} \right) \div \dfrac{5}{7}$

22. $\left(1 \div \dfrac{5}{8} \right) \div 10$

23. $\left(\dfrac{6}{7} \div 3 \right) \div \dfrac{3}{14}$

24. $\left(\dfrac{3}{8} \div 3 \right) \div \dfrac{3}{8}$

25. $12 \div \left(\dfrac{4}{5} \times \dfrac{2}{3} \right)$

26. $\dfrac{15}{16} \div \left(\dfrac{1}{8} + \dfrac{1}{4} \right)$

Application

27. Mrs. Matthews is cooking a ham for Sunday dinner. If a serving of ham is $\frac{3}{8}$ of a pound, how many servings are there in a 9-pound ham?

28. Mr. Seeley has $\frac{3}{4}$ of a gallon of milk in a pitcher. If each glass holds $\frac{1}{12}$ of a gallon, how many glasses can he fill?

8.6 Dividing with Mixed Numbers

Joan has 14 yards of ribbon. She plans to cut the ribbon into pieces $1\frac{3}{4}$ yard long. How many pieces of ribbon can she make?

You divide $14 \div 1\frac{3}{4}$ to determine how many pieces of ribbon Joan can make.

To divide with mixed numbers, follow these steps.

STEP 1	STEP 2	STEP 3
Rename the whole numbers or mixed numbers as improper fractions.	Multiply by the reciprocal of the divisor.	Use the multiplication short cut where applicable. If necessary, rename the answer in lowest terms.

$$14 \div 1\frac{3}{4} = \frac{14}{1} \div \frac{7}{4}$$

$$\frac{14}{1} \div \frac{7}{4} = \frac{14}{1} \times \frac{4}{7}$$

$$\frac{\overset{2}{\cancel{14}}}{1} \times \frac{4}{\underset{1}{\cancel{7}}} = \frac{8}{1}, \text{ or } 8$$

Joan can make 8 pieces of ribbon $1\frac{3}{4}$ yd. long.

Additional Examples

Divide.

a. $6\frac{2}{3} \div 4 = \dfrac{20}{3} \div \dfrac{4}{1}$

$\qquad = \dfrac{20}{3} \times \dfrac{1}{4}$

$\qquad = \dfrac{5}{3}, \text{ or } 1\frac{2}{3}$

b. $4\frac{4}{5} \div 3\frac{1}{5} = \dfrac{24}{5} \div \dfrac{16}{5}$

$\qquad = \dfrac{24}{5} \times \dfrac{5}{16}$

$\qquad = \dfrac{3}{2}, \text{ or } 1\frac{1}{2}$

c. $\dfrac{7}{15} \div 1\frac{3}{5} = \dfrac{7}{15} \div \dfrac{8}{5}$

$\qquad = \dfrac{7}{15} \times \dfrac{5}{8}$

$\qquad = \dfrac{7}{24}$

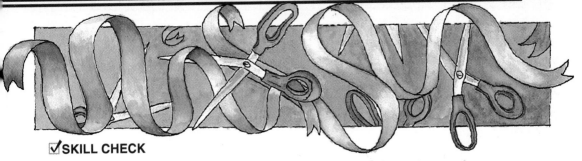

☑**SKILL CHECK**

Divide. Express the answer in lowest terms.

1. $\dfrac{3}{5} \div 2\dfrac{2}{5}$

2. $4 \div 2\dfrac{1}{3}$

3. $5\dfrac{1}{2} \div 1\dfrac{3}{4}$

4. $5 \div 6\dfrac{2}{3}$

5. $3\dfrac{1}{3} \div \dfrac{3}{4}$

6. $6 \div 1\dfrac{1}{9}$

7. $1\dfrac{3}{4} \div 6$

8. $5\dfrac{1}{3} \div 2\dfrac{1}{2}$

Exercises

Write the reciprocal.

1. $1\dfrac{2}{5}$

2. $2\dfrac{3}{7}$

3. $4\dfrac{1}{3}$

4. $5\dfrac{7}{12}$

Divide. Express the answer in lowest terms.

5. $\dfrac{2}{3} \div 2\dfrac{2}{5}$

6. $7 \div 4\dfrac{1}{2}$

7. $2\dfrac{1}{2} \div \dfrac{1}{8}$

8. $2\dfrac{1}{8} \div 4\dfrac{1}{8}$

9. $1\dfrac{3}{10} \div \dfrac{1}{5}$

10. $1\dfrac{3}{4} \div 1\dfrac{7}{8}$

11. $2\dfrac{1}{2} \div \dfrac{2}{3}$

12. $2\dfrac{1}{2} \div 1\dfrac{1}{4}$

13. $4\dfrac{1}{4} \div 3$

14. $1\dfrac{1}{2} \div 1\dfrac{1}{8}$

15. $11\dfrac{1}{4} \div 4\dfrac{1}{2}$

16. $7\dfrac{1}{3} \div 11$

17. $3\dfrac{2}{3} \div 1\dfrac{2}{9}$

18. $9\dfrac{2}{7} \div 1\dfrac{1}{4}$

19. $8\dfrac{1}{8} \div \dfrac{5}{16}$

20. $4\dfrac{1}{6} \div 1\dfrac{4}{9}$

Perform the operations.

21. $(4\dfrac{2}{3} \div 8) \div 14$

22. $1\dfrac{5}{7} \div (4 \div 3\dfrac{1}{2})$

23. $(2\dfrac{2}{3} \div 1\dfrac{1}{2}) \div 2\dfrac{2}{15}$

Application

24. Tanya jogged $4\dfrac{1}{8}$ miles in $\dfrac{3}{4}$ of an hour. What was her average speed in miles per hour?

25. Ramón sprinted the last 60 feet of his run. If each of his strides was $3\dfrac{1}{3}$ feet long, how many strides did he sprint?

Multiplying and Dividing Fractions

8.7 Fractions and Decimals

There were 10 questions on a math quiz. If Rafael answered 8 of the 10 questions correctly, what fractional part of his answers were correct?

Eight tenths of his answers were correct.

You can express 8 tenths as a fraction or a decimal.

$$\overbrace{\qquad\qquad}^{\text{8 tenths}}$$

Fraction: $\dfrac{8}{10} = \dfrac{8 \div 2}{10 \div 2}$ $\qquad\qquad$ Decimal: 0.8

$$= \dfrac{4}{5} \; \blacktriangleleft \text{lowest terms}$$

When the denominator of the fraction is a power of 10, you can easily write a fraction or mixed number as a decimal.

$$\dfrac{3}{10} = 0.3 \qquad\qquad 4\dfrac{55}{100} = 4.55 \qquad\qquad \dfrac{375}{1,000} = 0.375$$

When the denominator of the fraction is not a power of 10, you can often rename it as an equivalent fraction with a denominator that is a power of 10. Study the following examples.

$$\overbrace{\qquad\qquad}^{\substack{\text{equivalent}\\\text{fractions}}}$$

$$\dfrac{2}{5} = \dfrac{2 \times 2}{5 \times 2} = \dfrac{4}{10}$$

$$\overbrace{\qquad\qquad}^{\substack{\text{equivalent}\\\text{fractions}}}$$

$$6\dfrac{8}{25} = 6\dfrac{8 \cdot 4}{25 \cdot 4} = 6\dfrac{32}{100}$$

$$= 0.4 \; \blacktriangleleft \text{decimal} \qquad\qquad\qquad = 6.32 \; \blacktriangleleft \text{decimal}$$

You can also write decimals as fractions or mixed numbers. Study the following examples.

Additional Examples

Express each as a lowest-term fraction or mixed numeral.

a. $0.24 \xrightarrow{\text{means}} 24$ hundredths

$0.24 = \dfrac{24}{100} = \dfrac{6}{25}$ ◄ lowest terms

b. $2.375 \xrightarrow{\text{means}} 2$ and 375 thousandths

$2.375 = 2\frac{375}{1,000} = 2\frac{3}{8}$ ◄ lowest terms

☑ **SKILL CHECK**

Express each as a decimal.

1. $\dfrac{7}{10}$

2. $6\frac{17}{20}$

3. $\dfrac{11}{25}$

4. $9\frac{3}{5}$

Express each as a lowest-term fraction or mixed numeral.

5. 0.6

6. 0.47

7. 23.75

8. 7.125

Exercises

Write each word name as a decimal and a lowest-term fraction or mixed number.

1. 7 tenths

2. 36 hundredths

3. 4 and 75 hundredths

4. 19 and 500 thousandths

Multiplying and Dividing Fractions

Write each as a decimal.

5. $\dfrac{47}{100}$ 6. $\dfrac{2}{10}$ 7. $\dfrac{4}{5}$ 8. $\dfrac{1}{20}$

9. $\dfrac{3}{4}$ 10. $2\frac{1}{2}$ 11. $\dfrac{9}{100}$ 12. $8\frac{12}{25}$

13. $27\frac{39}{50}$ 14. $\dfrac{438}{1,000}$ 15. $13\frac{118}{250}$ 16. $\dfrac{3}{50}$

Write each as a fraction or mixed number in lowest terms.

17. 0.3 18. 0.08 19. 0.250 20. 0.45

21. 0.60 22. 3.75 23. 0.002 24. 24.6

25. 5.250 26. 0.0001 27. 17.12 28. 0.375

Application

29. A final exam had 100 questions. Robert answered 0.95 of all the questions correctly. What lowest-term fraction expresses the fractional portion of questions that Robert answered correctly?

30. Of the 75 students who took the final exam, $\frac{17}{50}$ of them made A's. What decimal expresses the fractional portion of students who made A's?

8.8 Terminating and Repeating Decimals

You can also use division to write a fraction as a decimal. Recall that $\frac{a}{b}$ means $a \div b$ or $b\overline{)a}$.

To write a fraction as a decimal, divide the numerator by the denominator. Consider the following examples.

$$\frac{3}{8} = 3 \div 8 \quad \begin{array}{r} 0.375 \\ 8\overline{)3.000} \\ -24 \\ \hline 60 \\ -56 \\ \hline 40 \\ -40 \\ \hline 0 \end{array}$$

$$\frac{1}{3} = 1 \div 3 \quad \begin{array}{r} 0.333\ldots \\ 3\overline{)1.000} \\ -9 \\ \hline 10 \\ -9 \\ \hline 10 \\ -9 \\ \hline 1 \end{array}$$

The decimal 0.375 is a *terminating decimal* because the remainder is 0.

So, $\frac{3}{8} = 0.375$

The decimal 0.333 . . . is a *repeating decimal* because the remainder is never zero.

So, $\frac{1}{3} = 0.333\ldots = 0.\overline{3}$

Observe that, in a repeating decimal, you draw a bar over the repeating digit or digits.

Additional Examples

a. Write $\frac{3}{11}$ as a decimal.

$$\frac{3}{11} \rightarrow \begin{array}{r} 0.2727\ldots \\ 11\overline{)3.0000} \end{array}$$

$$\frac{3}{11} = 0.2727\ldots = 0.\overline{27}$$

b. Write $\frac{1}{6}$ as a decimal.

$$\frac{1}{6} \rightarrow \begin{array}{r} 0.1666\ldots \\ 6\overline{)1.0000} \end{array}$$

$$\frac{1}{6} = 0.1666\ldots = 0.1\overline{6}$$

c. Compare $\frac{5}{9}$ and $\frac{7}{15}$ by comparing their decimals.

$$\frac{5}{9} = 0.5555\ldots$$
$$= 0.\overline{5}$$

$$\frac{7}{15} = 0.4666\ldots$$
$$= 0.4\overline{6}$$

$$0.\overline{5} > 0.4\overline{6}$$

So, $\frac{5}{9} > \frac{7}{15}$

Multiplying and Dividing Fractions

☑SKILL CHECK

Use a bar to show each repeating decimal.

1. 0.454545 2. 0.583333 3. 0.296296 4. 0.541666

Write each as a decimal. Draw a bar over the repeating digit or digits.

5. $\dfrac{1}{4}$ 6. $\dfrac{7}{11}$ 7. $\dfrac{5}{8}$ 8. $\dfrac{4}{15}$

Exercises

Write the terminating decimal for each fraction.

1. $\dfrac{4}{5}$ 2. $\dfrac{3}{4}$ 3. $\dfrac{1}{8}$ 4. $\dfrac{2}{25}$

5. $\dfrac{21}{40}$ 6. $\dfrac{27}{50}$ 7. $\dfrac{19}{25}$ 8. $\dfrac{13}{52}$

Write the repeating decimal for each fraction.

9. $\dfrac{1}{3}$ 10. $\dfrac{7}{9}$ 11. $\dfrac{5}{6}$ 12. $\dfrac{4}{11}$

13. $\dfrac{3}{22}$ 14. $\dfrac{13}{18}$ 15. $\dfrac{5}{27}$ 16. $\dfrac{1}{7}$

Write each fraction as a decimal.

17. $\dfrac{9}{50}$ 18. $\dfrac{2}{15}$ 19. $\dfrac{18}{25}$ 20. $\dfrac{1}{6}$

21. $\dfrac{10}{11}$ 22. $\dfrac{7}{8}$ 23. $\dfrac{1}{27}$ 24. $\dfrac{21}{28}$

Compare. Use > or <.

25. $\dfrac{3}{5}\ \square\ 0.59$ 26. $\dfrac{7}{8}\ \square\ 0.88$ 27. $\dfrac{6}{9}\ \square\ 0.625$

28. $\dfrac{1}{3}\ \square\ 0.36$ 29. $\dfrac{2}{11}\ \square\ 0.2$ 30. $\dfrac{19}{20}\ \square\ 0.9\overline{3}$

Problem Solving: Make an Organized List

To solve word problems in which you must find all the different ways something can be done, you can use the strategy "Make an Organized List."

Study the following example.

Maurice placed 10 coins with a value of $1.45 in the offering plate. The coins included only quarters and dimes. How many quarters did Maurice give? How many dimes?

1. **READ:** Understand the question.
    - How many quarters did Maurice give?
    - How many dimes did he give?

    Identify the needed data.
    - Maurice placed 10 coins in the offering plate.
    - The value of the coins was $1.45.
    - The coins were quarters and dimes.

> **✓ Four-Point Check List**
>
> **1 READ** to understand the question and identify the needed data.
>
> **2 PLAN** what to do to solve the problem.
>
> **3 SOLVE** the problem by carrying out the plan.
>
> **4 CHECK** to make sure the solution is reasonable.

2. **PLAN:** Use the strategy "Make an Organized List."

3. **SOLVE:** Make an organized list beginning with 0 quarters and 10 dimes

Quarters	Dimes	Total
0	10	$1.00
1	9	$0.25 + $0.90 = $1.15
2	8	$0.50 + $0.80 = $1.30
3	7	$0.75 + $0.70 = $1.45

Maurice placed 3 quarters and 7 dimes in the offering plate.

Multiplying and Dividing Fractions

4. CHECK: Is the solution reasonable?

The sum of 3 quarters + 7 dimes is equal to 10 coins. The value of the coins is $1.45, so the solution is reasonable.

Make an organized list. Solve.

1. Josie has 2 more dimes than quarters. If the total value of her coins is $0.90, how many quarters does Josie have? How many dimes?

2. Alyssa plans to take 2 jackets (navy, tan) and 3 skirts (red, green, and blue) on a trip. How many different combinations of jacket and skirt can she make from these choices?

Exercises

Make an organized list. Solve.

1. Lori removed 12 coins with a value of $1.00 from her piggy bank. The coins included only nickels and dimes. How many nickels did Lori remove? How many dimes?

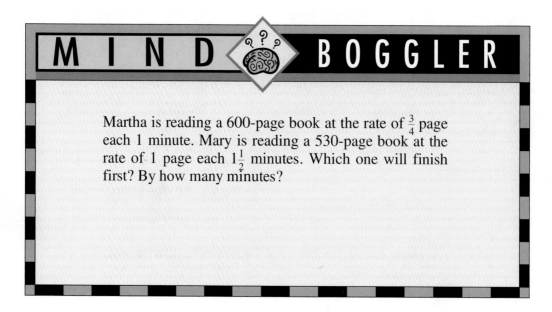

Martha is reading a 600-page book at the rate of $\frac{3}{4}$ page each 1 minute. Mary is reading a 530-page book at the rate of 1 page each $1\frac{1}{2}$ minutes. Which one will finish first? By how many minutes?

2. Chen has 4 dress shirts (white, tan, gray, and blue) and 2 pairs of dress pants (navy, black). How many different combinations can he make from these choices?

Mixed Review

Solve.

3. Gail would like to double her recipe for banana muffins. The original recipe calls for $1\frac{2}{3}$ cups of flour. How much flour should Gail use?

4. Leon walked $1\frac{3}{8}$ miles from home to school, $\frac{5}{6}$ of a mile from school to church, and $1\frac{2}{3}$ miles from church to home. How many miles did he walk in all?

5. The cost of renting a room at the Grove Park Lodge is $63 for two people per night. To have children in the room, there is an extra charge of $6.50 per child. How much does it cost a family of two adults and three children to stay for two nights?

6. Kristi cut a pie into 8 equal pieces by making edge-to-edge cuts through the center. How many cuts did she make?

7. A cookie recipe calls for $2\frac{1}{3}$ cups of sugar. If Amy has only $1\frac{1}{2}$ cups of sugar left, how much sugar does she need to borrow?

8. John handed out 8 more tracts at the mall than David did. Altogether they handed out 30 tracts. How many tracts did John hand out?

9. Nichelle's age plus the largest prime number less than 17 is equal to 30. How old is Nichelle?

10. Joel bought two sleeping bags on sale for $54.95 each, a tent for $129.95, and a stove for $17.95. How much did he spend for all four items?

Multiplying and Dividing Fractions

Chapter 8 Review

8.1 Multiply. Write the product in lowest terms.

1. $\dfrac{7}{8} \times \dfrac{3}{5}$
2. $3 \times \dfrac{5}{7}$
3. $\dfrac{8}{11} \times \dfrac{3}{4}$
4. $\dfrac{5}{8} \times 6 \times \dfrac{2}{5}$

8.2 Multiply. Use the short cut where possible.

5. $\dfrac{5}{6} \times \dfrac{6}{11}$
6. $\dfrac{4}{7} \times \dfrac{1}{6}$
7. $8 \times \dfrac{7}{16}$
8. $\dfrac{6}{7} \times \dfrac{5}{9} \times \dfrac{7}{8}$

8.3 Estimate.

9. $9\frac{5}{8} \times 3\frac{2}{7}$
10. $\dfrac{15}{16} \times 14\frac{2}{9}$
11. $11\frac{8}{9} \times \dfrac{1}{6}$
12. $3\frac{7}{8} \times 25\frac{2}{5}$

8.4 Multiply. Write the product in lowest terms.

13. $1\frac{5}{8} \times 12$
14. $1\frac{2}{5} \times 2\frac{1}{7}$
15. $4\frac{1}{5} \times 1\frac{1}{4}$
16. $2\frac{2}{5} \times \dfrac{5}{1} \times 1\frac{2}{9}$

8.5 Divide.

17. $\dfrac{11}{12} \div \dfrac{1}{6}$
18. $15 \div \dfrac{5}{13}$
19. $\dfrac{5}{8} \div \dfrac{5}{6}$
20. $\left(\dfrac{6}{7} \div 2\right) \div \dfrac{2}{7}$

8.6 Divide.

21. $4\frac{2}{3} \div 8$
22. $2\frac{1}{3} \div 1\frac{1}{6}$
23. $6\frac{3}{7} \div 1\frac{2}{3}$
24. $1\frac{5}{7} \div (5\frac{1}{3} \div 6)$

8.7 Write each fraction as a decimal.   **Write each decimal as a fraction in lowest terms.**

25. $\dfrac{3}{20}$
26. $2\frac{3}{4}$
27. 0.15
28. 23.8

8.8 Write each as a decimal. Use a bar for the repeating decimals.

29. $\dfrac{4}{5}$
30. $\dfrac{2}{3}$
31. $\dfrac{17}{20}$
32. $\dfrac{11}{18}$

Chapter 8 Cumulative Review

1. Identify the vertex in the given angle.

  a. R **b.** S

  c. T **d.** not given

2. Give the measure of the supplement to a 124° angle.

  a. 34°   **b.** 56°

  c. 66°   **d.** not given

3. How many diagonals can you draw from vertex A in the figure on the right?

  a. 0   **b.** 1

  c. 2   **d.** not given

4. Classify the triangle according to the length of its sides: 24 cm, 15 cm, 19 cm.

  a. scalene   **b.** equilateral

  c. isosceles   **d.** not given

5. If the length of $\overline{EF}$ is 7 cm, how long is $\overline{EG}$?

  a. 7 cm   **b.** 10 cm

  c. 14 cm   **d.** not given

6. Give the lowest-term fraction for $\frac{16}{40}$.

  a. $\frac{2}{3}$ **b.** $\frac{2}{5}$

  c. $\frac{3}{5}$ **d.** not given

7. Find the missing number. $\frac{3}{8} = \frac{n}{32}$

  a. 4   **b.** 8

  c. 12   **d.** not given

8. Write $\frac{18}{42}$ in lowest terms.

  a. $\frac{9}{21}$ **b.** $\frac{6}{14}$

  c. $\frac{3}{7}$ **d.** not given

9. Is 615 divisible by 3, 9, or neither of these numbers?

  a. 3   **b.** 9

  c. 3, 9   **d.** neither

10. Which number has 9 for a factor?

  a. 174   **b.** 276

  c. 387   **d.** not given

11. Write $2\frac{4}{7}$ as an improper fraction.

  a. $\frac{14}{7}$ **b.** $\frac{18}{7}$

  c. $\frac{24}{7}$ **d.** not given

12. Compare. Write >, <, or =. $\frac{4}{5} \,\square\, \frac{17}{20}$

  a. >   **b.** <

  c. =   **d.** not given

13. Subtract. $\frac{19}{20} - \frac{3}{20}$

  a. $\frac{16}{20}$ **b.** $\frac{8}{10}$

  c. $\frac{4}{5}$ **d.** not given

14. Add. $\frac{5}{6} + \frac{3}{8}$

  a. $1\frac{5}{24}$ **b.** $\frac{29}{24}$

  c. $\frac{11}{14}$ **d.** not given

15. Add. $13\frac{3}{8} + 6\frac{5}{12}$

  a. $19\frac{4}{5}$ **b.** $19\frac{19}{24}$

  c. $19\frac{38}{48}$ **d.** not given

Multiplying and Dividing Fractions

INNOVATORS

WERNHER VON BRAUN
ROCKET SCIENCE

A childhood fascination with astronomy evolved into a lifelong interest in outer space for Wernher von Braun (VEHR nur fohn broun). As a young boy in Berlin, Wernher exhibited more than a passing interest in science. Believing that scientific inquiry was important for future generations, his mother encouraged her son's experiments. Wernher's boarding school fostered his interest even further by allowing the young boy to plan and construct an observatory on the school campus.

Despite this encouragement in the area of science, young Wernher performed poorly in mathematics. In 1925 he read *The Rocket into Interplanetary Space,* written by Hermann Oberth, a pioneer in rocket science. After reading this book, Wernher realized that an understanding of math was essential for him to realize his dream of exploring the heavens. He then began to concentrate on learning the mathematical principles which had previously eluded him. Within a few months, he was at the top of his math class.

After he obtained a doctorate in physics from the University of Berlin, the Nazi government asked Wernher to direct the development of the V-2 ballistic missile. The V-2 was the most advanced missile of its day. Traveling at speeds of up to 3,500 miles per hour, it was used to destroy much of southern England during the last year of World War II. The effectiveness of these missiles convinced the United States that it needed the ability to produce missiles capable of carrying atomic warheads.

After it became apparent that the Nazis would lose the war, Wernher and many of his fellow scientists surrendered to the United States. They brought with them much valuable experience in the field of rocket science. This included nearly fourteen tons of documents detailing their research and experiments conducted between 1932 and 1945.

This group of talented men became the backbone of the United States' rocket and space programs. The German scientists were far more accomplished in the field of rocketry than their American counterparts. However, Wernher was quick to admit that his team's success was due to their years of experience. "After all," he once said, "if we are good, it's because we've had fifteen more years of experience in making mistakes and learning from them!"

Wernher's work with the United States' missile programs between 1950 and 1955 led to the development of the Redstone

1912-1977

ballistic missile. Just three years later, a modified version of this missile was used to launch the United States' first artificial satellite, the *Explorer I*.

In 1960 Wernher was asked to serve as director of NASA's George C. Marshall Space Flight Center in Huntsville, Alabama. Under von Braun's watchful eye, the center focused its efforts on creating a rocket capable of carrying men to the moon. As the world watched in July of 1969, a Saturn V rocket powered the craft which allowed Neil Armstrong and Buzz Aldrin to take "one giant leap for mankind" as they landed safely on the moon.

In the end, it was the expertise of one man, Wernher von Braun, that enabled the United States to win the race to the moon, and in doing so helped the United States establish itself as a world leader in the exploration of space.

9 CHAPTER

EQUATIONS

9.1 Order of Operations

A mathematical phrase made up of numbers and operations is called a *numerical expression.*

To simplify a numerical expression, you perform the operations. Consider the numerical expressions below.

$16 + 4$	$16 - 4$	16×4	$16 \div 4$
$\downarrow$	$\downarrow$	$\downarrow$	$\downarrow$
20	12	64	4

When a numerical expression has more than one operation, you need to know which operation to perform first.

Study the following rules for "Order of Operations."

Rules: Order of Operations
1. Do all operations inside parentheses first.
2. Next do all the multiplication and division in order from left to right.
3. Then do all the addition and subtraction in order from left to right.

If one of the rules does not apply to a particular expression, simply proceed to the next rule.

Evaluate $18 - 12 \div 4$ according to the rules for Order of Operations.

$$18 - \underline{12 \div 4} \quad \blacktriangleleft \text{Divide first.}$$
$$\downarrow$$
$$\underline{18 - 3} \quad \blacktriangleleft \text{Subtract next.}$$
$$\downarrow$$
$$15$$

Other Examples

Perform the operations.

a. $6 + (9 - 4) \times 3$
$6 + 5 \times 3$
$6 + 15$
21

b. $8 \times 3 - 10 \div 5$
$24 - 2$
22

c. $5 + 12 \div 6 - 3 \times 2$
$5 + 2 - 6$
$7 - 6$
1

 SKILL CHECK

Perform the operations.

1. $7 + 3 \times 5$

2. $(6 + 2) \div 4$

3. $36 \div 6 \times 2$

4. $27 \div 3 + 6 \times 2$

5. $36 \div (3 + 9) \times 2$

6. $27 + 3 \times 6 \div 2$

Exercises

Perform the operations.

1. $17 - 8 + 4$

2. $17 - (8 + 4)$

3. $5 \times 6 \div 2$

4. $6 + 24 \div 3$

5. $28 \div 7 - 3$

6. $30 - 16 \div 4$

7. $12 + 3 + 2 \times 6$

8. $30 - (3 + 15) \div 6$

9. $27 + 5 + 14 \div 7$

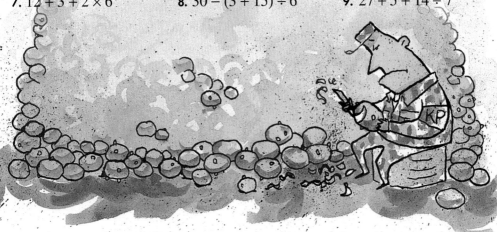

10. $(16 - 4) \times (9 - 5)$ **11.** $36 \div 4 + 7 - 2$ **12.** $35 - 15 \div 3 - 5$

13. $18 \div 6 + 2 \times 7$ **14.** $19 - 5 \times 2 + (8 \div 4)$

15. $2 \times 5 \times 7 - 6 \div 3$ **16.** $9 \times 2 + 5 + 4 - 6$

17. $(15 \div 5) + (2 \times 8) - 7$ **18.** $21 - 3 \times 2 + (9 \div 3)$

Write true or false.

19. $9 + 7 - 4 = 9 + (7 - 4)$

20. $(4 + 5) \times 7 = 4 + 5 \times 7$

21. $6 + 8 \div 4 - 3 = 6 + 8 \div (4 - 3)$

22. $8 \times (10 \times 3) = 8 \times 10 \times 3$

23. $16 - 4 \div 2 \times 8 = 16 - (4 \div 2) \times 8$

24. $(7 + 4) \times (25 \div 5) = 7 + 4 \times 25 \div 5$

Application

Write each as a numerical statement; then perform the operations.

25. Subtract the product of 3 and 6 from 35.

26. Add 9 to 15; then divide the sum by 8.

27. Multiply 7 and the difference of 15 and 6.

28. Subtract the sum of 6 and 9 from the product of 4 and 7.

The space shuttle Columbia *lifts off at 8:37 A.M. from Kennedy Space Center in Florida. While daytime launches are awe-inspiring, nighttime launches can be even more spectacular.*

Wernher von Braun with the television camera used on Apollo 15, the fourth manned lunar landing mission. This camera was left behind on the moon and was eventually the first to show the lunar module's liftoff from the moon.

9.2 Variables and Expressions

Reggie is 5 inches taller than his sister Jill. How do you write a mathematical expression to represent Reggie's height?

To express Reggie's height in terms of Jill's height, you must use a variable. A *variable* is a letter used to represent a number in an expression.

Let j = Jill's height. Then, $j + 5$ = Reggie's height. The expression $j + 5$ contains the variable j. If a mathematical expression contains at least one variable, it is called an *algebraic expression.*

To evaluate an algebraic expression like $j + 5$, you replace the variable with a given number and then perform the operation. Consider the following examples.

Let $j = 40$.	Let $j = 57$.	Let $j = 63$.
$j + 5 = 40 + 5$	$j + 5 = 57 + 5$	$j + 5 = 63 + 5$
$\quad = 45$	$\quad = 62$	$\quad = 68$

In algebraic expressions, the multiplication symbol is often left out. For example, the expression $3 \times n$ is often written as $3n$.

Equations

Additional Examples

Evaluate each expression. Let $r = 12$, $s = 28$, and $w = 7$.

a. $30 - r$
$30 - r = 30 - 12$
$\quad = 18$

b. $\dfrac{s}{4}$
$\dfrac{s}{4} = \dfrac{28}{4}$
$\quad = 7$

c. $3w + 5$
$3w + 5 = 3(7) + 5$
$\quad = 21 + 5$
$\quad = 26$

☑ SKILL CHECK

Evaluate each expression. Let $n = 6$.

1. $7n$
2. $\dfrac{30}{n}$
3. $13 - n$
4. $3n + 2$

Evaluate each expression. Let $x = 4$, $y = 7$, and $z = 11$.

5. $36 \div x$
6. $z - x$
7. $x + 3y$
8. $2(z - 3)$

Exercises

Evaluate each expression. Let $n = 6$.

1. $4n$
2. $n + 8$
3. $\dfrac{18}{n}$
4. $n - 1$

5. $3n + 2$
6. $15 - n$
7. $5n - 13$
8. $19 + n$

Evaluate each expression. Let $x = 5$, $y = 8$, and $z = 12$.

9. $y + 12$
10. $6x$
11. $36 \div z$
12. $30 - y$

13. $13 + z$
14. $z - x$
15. $4x + 3$
16. $x + 3y$

17. $3(x + 2)$
18. $50 - 4y$
19. $2z + 2x$
20. $\dfrac{z}{4} + 5$

Write true or false.

21. $35 + x = 64$, if $x = 29$
22. $y - 43 = 38$, if $y = 71$

23. $59 - z = 36$, if $z = 33$
24. $w + 64 = 102$, if $w = 38$

Complete each table.

	a	$a + 14$
25.	9	
26.	17	

	b	$6b$
27.	8	
28.	13	

	c	$19 - c$
29.	7	
30.	13	

Prior to space shuttles, Saturn V rockets such as this one transported into space the space vehicles for the Apollo and Skylab missions.

9.3 Writing Addition and Subtraction Expressions

Study the word phrases which indicate the operations of addition and subtraction in the tables below.

Addition	
Word Phrase	Numerical Expression
the sum of 2 and 3 2 increased by 3 3 more than 2	2 + 3

Subtraction	
Word Phrase	Numerical Expression
the difference of 7 and 4 4 subtracted from 7 4 less than 7	7 − 4

If a word phrase indicates a variable, you can express the phrase as an algebraic expression. Consider the following examples.

	Word Phrase	Variable	Algebraic Expression
a.	a number a decreased by 5	a	$a - 5$
b.	the sum of a number n and 8	n	$n + 8$
c.	75 minus a number k	k	$75 - k$
d.	\$3 less than a number of dollars x	x	$x - \$3$
e.	a number p plus 19	p	$p + 19$

Equations

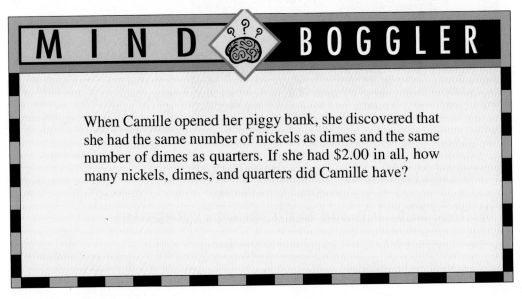

MIND ??? BOGGLER

When Camille opened her piggy bank, she discovered that she had the same number of nickels as dimes and the same number of dimes as quarters. If she had $2.00 in all, how many nickels, dimes, and quarters did Camille have?

☑ SKILL CHECK

Choose the correct expression for each word phrase.

1. 14 decreased by 8   **a.** $14 - 8$ **b.** $8 - 14$

2. 8 more than a   **a.** $n + 8$ **b.** $8 + n$
    number n

3. A number j sub-   **a.** $j - 17$ **b.** $17 - j$
    tracted from 17

Write the numerical or algebraic expression for each word phrase.

4. eight increased by thirty   **5.** fourteen less than twenty-five

6. 38 minus a number k **7.** the sum of 19 and a number b

Exercises

Write a numerical expression for each word phrase.

1. the sum of five and nine

2. thirteen minus four

3. twenty decreased by twelve

4. five added to sixteen

5. the difference between nineteen and three

6. nine more than six

Write an algebraic expression for each word phrase.

7. a number k increased by 25

8. the sum of 17 and a number n

9. the result of subtracting 8 from a number p

10. a number k plus 27

11. 19 decreased by a number w

12. the difference when a number s is subtracted from 21

13. a number n subtracted from 16

14. 23 plus a number n

15. 24 more than a number r

16. a number z decreased by 18

17. $27 minus a number of dollars b

18. The result of subtracting a number j from 13

Write as a word phrase.

19. $17 + 24$

20. $30 - 17$

21. $n + 5$

22. $16 - c$

Application

23. Hank hit a total of h home runs during the season. He hit 4 more triples than home runs. What algebraic expression represents the number of triples that Hank hit?

24. Felipe's team played a total of 18 games. They won w of those games. What algebraic expression represents the number of games that they lost?

9.4 Writing Multiplication and Division Expressions

Study the word phrases which indicate the operations of multiplication and division in the tables below.

Multiplication	
Word Phrase	Numerical Expressions
2 multiplied by 6	2×6 or
2 times 6	$2 \cdot 6$ or
the product of 2 and 6	$2(6)$

Division	
Word Phrase	Numerical Expressions
10 divided by 5	$10 \div 5$ or
the quotient of 10 and 5	$\dfrac{10}{5}$ or $5\overline{)10}$

Some word phrases for algebraic expressions suggest more than one operation. Consider the following examples.

	Word Phrase	Variable	Algebraic Expression
a.	4 times a number j, increased by 3	j	$4j + 3$
b.	$\dfrac{1}{3}$ of a number y, minus 2	y	$\dfrac{1}{3}y - 2$
c.	4, added to 5 multiplied by a number p	p	$5p + 4$
d.	a number n divided by 8, decreased by 4	n	$\dfrac{n}{8} - 4$
e.	the sum of a number y and 5, divided by 4	y	$\dfrac{y + 5}{4}$

☑SKILL CHECK

Choose the expression which best translates the word phrase.

1. the product of 7 and a number m **a.** $7 \times m$ or $7m$ **b.** $m \times 7$ or $m7$

2. the quotient of a number y and 15   **a.** $\dfrac{y}{15}$ **b.** $\dfrac{15}{y}$

3. a number y multiplied by 7, decreased by 9   **a.** $9 - 7y$ **b.** $7y - 9$

Write a numerical or algebraic expression for each word phrase.

4. fourteen less than twenty-five

5. the sum of 19 and a number b.

6. 2 more than a number r times 5

Exercises

Write a numerical expression for each word phrase.

1. fifteen divided by three

2. twice nine

3. the product of five and thirteen

4. the quotient of fourteen and seven

This is a full-scale mockup (model) of a space shuttle. Models are necessary to detect design problems before investing resources in the real product.

Equations

Write an algebraic expression for each word phrase.

5. a number r multiplied by 37

6. a number b divided by 3, decreased by 7

7. the quotient of a number c and 25

8. 12, added to 6 times a number z

9. $\frac{1}{2}$ of a number k, plus 3

10. a number c tripled

11. 9 less than 3 times a number n

12. 6, subtracted from a number p divided by 15

13. 45 divided by a number n

14. a number y times 13

15. a number y multiplied by 4, decreased by 1

16. 17, added to 8 times a number a

17. $\frac{1}{3}$ of a number c, plus 32

18. five times the difference of a number f and 2

Write as a word phrase.

19. 13×9

20. $72 \div 6$

21. $\dfrac{a}{16}$

22. $3e + 11$

Application

23. The land area of Colorado is about 2 times the land area of Florida. Let f = the land area of Florida. What algebraic expression represents the land area of Colorado?

24. The population of Florida is about 4 times the population of Colorado. Let f = the population of Florida. What algebraic expression represents the population of Colorado?

9.5 Writing Equations

The Junior High Choir has a total of 37 members. Of this total, 23 members are eighth graders and the remaining members are seventh graders. How many members are seventh graders?

You can represent the information in the above problem by writing an equation. An *equation* is a mathematical sentence that contains an equal sign.

Study the following example.

seventh graders + eighth graders = total members

Let n = the number of seventh grade choir members.

$$n + 23 = 37$$

In an equation, a number that replaces the variable to make the equation true is called a *solution.* Is 14 a solution of the above equation?

To determine whether 14 is the solution of $n + 23 = 37$, you substitute 14 for n in the equation.

$$n + 23 = 37$$
$$(14) + 23 \stackrel{?}{=} 37 \quad \blacktriangleleft \text{Substitute 14 for } n.$$
$$37 = 37 \quad \blacktriangleleft \text{true}$$

Yes, 14 is the solution of $n + 23 = 37$

Additional Examples

Write an equation for the following word sentences.

a. A number n increased by 8 is 12. $\longrightarrow$ $n + 8 = 12$

b. Nine less than a number y is 5. $\longrightarrow$ $y - 9 = 5$

c. A number f divided by 4 is 9. $\longrightarrow$ $f \div 4 = 9$, or $\frac{f}{4} = 9$

d. Ten more than 3 times a number p is 28. $\longrightarrow$ $3p + 10 = 28$

Equations

☑ **SKILL CHECK**

Write an equation for the following word sentences.

1. The product of 7 and a number b is 63.
2. 15 divided by a number r is 3.
3. The difference of 3 times a number y and 2 equals 19.
4. Two increased by the quotient of a number p and 3 is 5.

Exercises

Fill in the blanks to write a word sentence for the following equations.

1. $\frac{40}{x} = 8$; _____ divided by _____ is equal to _____
2. $6s + 4 = 22$; _____ more than _____ times _____ is equal to _____

Write an equation for the following word sentences.

3. A number e minus 6 is 23.
4. 6 more than a number r is 108.
5. 15 times a number z is equal to 75.
6. The difference of 17 and a number s equals 8.
7. A number g divided by 6 is 12.
8. Twice a number j is equal to 38.
9. 8 less than 4 times a number k equals 36.
10. The sum of 2 times a number y and 1 is equal to 19.
11. 3 more than the quotient of a number f and 2 is 12.
12. 17 decreased by the product of 3 and a number c equals 5.

Determine whether the given value of the variable is a solution of the equation. Write yes or no.

13. $n + 17 = 32, n = 16$

14. $6a = 78, a = 13$

15. $r - 15 = 12, r = 27$

16. $33 - w = 24, w = 8$

17. $\dfrac{f}{4} = 13, f = 52$

18. $3x + 7 = 31, x = 8$

19. $\dfrac{g}{3} - 10 = 2, g = 39$

20. $8m - 14 = 42, m = 7$

Application

Write an equation for each.

21. Of the 37 members in the choir, 21 were girls. Let b represent the number of boys in the choir.

22. There are 14 sopranos in the choir. This is 4 less than twice the number of altos. Let a represent the number of altos.

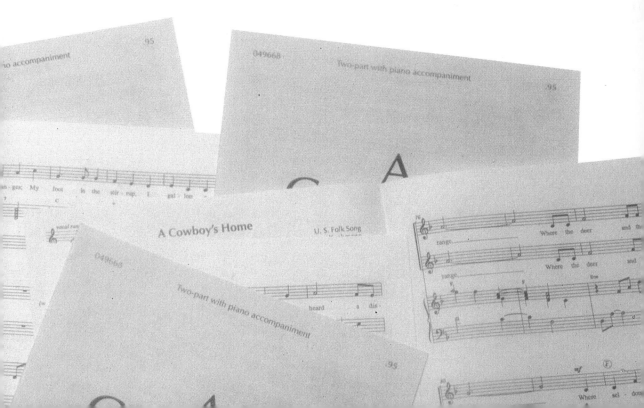

9.6 Solving Addition and Subtraction Equations

Addition and subtraction are inverse operations. Each operation can undo the other. Study the following examples.

Subtraction can undo addition.

$$5 + 8 = 13 \rightarrow 13 - 8 = 5$$
$$\underbrace{\qquad}_{\text{same}}$$

Addition can undo subtraction.

$$16 - 7 = 9 \rightarrow 9 + 7 = 16$$
$$\underbrace{\qquad}_{\text{same}}$$

You can use inverse operations to solve equations involving addition and subtraction.

To solve an addition equation, subtract the same number from both sides of the equation. Consider the example below.

$$y + 13 = 29$$
$$y + 13 - \mathbf{13} = 29 - \mathbf{13}$$
$$y = 16$$

Solution: 16

Check: Is 16 the solution?
$$y + 13 = 29$$
$$(16) + 13 \overset{?}{=} 29 \quad \blacktriangleleft \text{Substitute 16 for } y.$$
$$29 = 29 \quad \blacktriangleleft \text{true}$$

Yes. The solution is 16.

To solve a subtraction equation, add the same number to both sides of the equation. Consider the following example.

$$b - 27 = 65$$
$$b - 27 + \mathbf{27} = 65 + \mathbf{27}$$
$$b = 92$$

Solution: 92

Check: Is 92 the solution?
$$b - 27 = 65$$
$$(92) - 27 \overset{?}{=} 65 \quad \blacktriangleleft \text{Substitute 92 for } y.$$
$$65 = 65 \quad \blacktriangleleft \text{true}$$

Yes. The solution is 92.

Additional Examples

Solve each equation.

a.
$$9 + n = 32$$
$$9 - \mathbf{9} + n = 32 - \mathbf{9}$$
$$n = 23$$

Check: $9 + 23 \overset{?}{=} 32$
$$32 = 32$$

b.
$$47 = a - 18$$
$$47 + \mathbf{18} = a - 18 + \mathbf{18}$$
$$65 = a$$

Check: $47 \overset{?}{=} 65 - 18$
$$47 = 47$$

☑SKILL CHECK

Solve each equation.

1. $b + 7 = 22$ 2. $n + 13 = 40$ 3. $9 + w = 35$ 4. $f + 17 = 61$
5. $c - 8 = 25$ 6. $r - 14 = 32$ 7. $48 = h - 12$ 8. $z - 24 = 57$

Exercises

Solve each equation.

1. $w + 8 = 19$ 2. $b + 13 = 27$
3. $g + 7 = 32$ 4. $k + 24 = 40$
5. $18 + r = 45$ 6. $v + 29 = 64$
7. $c - 5 = 17$ 8. $j - 16 = 8$
9. $n - 23 = 27$ 10. $g - 19 = 19$
11. $32 = y - 24$ 12. $z - 28 = 33$
13. $a + 27 = 48$ 14. $f - 41 = 15$
15. $58 + r = 73$ 16. $r - 42 = 59$
17. $x + 27 = 62$ 18. $e - 49 = 18$
19. $j + 38 = 117$ 20. $x - 67 = 88$
21. $p - 137 = 115$ 22. $m + 23 = 132$
23. $h - 120 = 97$ 24. $s + 128 = 172$

The command module ("space capsule") and service module (the cylindrical part below the capsule) orbited the moon while the lunar module landed on the moon's surface.

Application

Write an equation. Solve.

25. A number increased by 14 is equal to 33. What is the number?

26. 18 less than a number is equal to 32. What is the number?

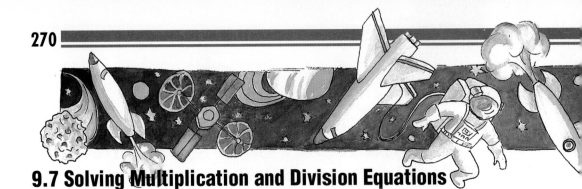

9.7 Solving Multiplication and Division Equations

Multiplication and division are inverse operations. Each operation can undo the other. Study the following examples.

Multiplication can undo division.	Division can undo multiplication.

$$27 \div \mathbf{9} = 3 \rightarrow 3 \times \mathbf{9} = 27$$
$$\underset{\text{same}}{\underline{\qquad\qquad\qquad}}$$

$$12 \times \mathbf{4} = 48 \rightarrow 48 \div \mathbf{4} = 12$$
$$\underset{\text{same}}{\underline{\qquad\qquad\qquad}}$$

You can use inverse operations to solve equations involving multiplication and division.

To solve a multiplication equation, divide both sides by the same number. Consider the following example.

$$6a = 78$$

$$\frac{6a}{6} = \frac{78}{6}$$

$$a = 13$$

Solution: 13

Check: Is 13 the solution?

$$6a = 78$$

$$6(13) \stackrel{?}{=} 78 \qquad \blacktriangleleft \text{Substitute 13 for } a.$$

$$78 = 78 \qquad \blacktriangleleft \text{true}$$

Yes. The solution is 13.

To solve a division equation, multiply both sides of the equation by the same number. Consider the following example.

$$\frac{w}{7} = 9$$

$$\frac{w}{7} \cdot \mathbf{7} = 9 \cdot \mathbf{7}$$

$$w = 63$$

Solution: 63

Check: Is 63 the solution?

$$\frac{w}{7} = 9$$

$$\frac{(63)}{7} \stackrel{?}{=} 9 \qquad \blacktriangleleft \text{Substitute 63 for } w.$$

$$9 = 9 \qquad \blacktriangleleft \text{true}$$

Yes. The solution is 63.

Additional Examples

Solve each equation.

a.
$$112 = r \times 14$$
$$112 \div \mathbf{14} = r \times 14 \div \mathbf{14}$$
$$8 = r$$

Check: $112 \overset{?}{=} 8 \times 14$

$112 = 112$ ◀ true

b.
$$13 = d \div 12$$
$$13 \times \mathbf{12} = d \div 12 \times \mathbf{12}$$
$$156 = d$$

Check: $13 \overset{?}{=} 156 \div 12$

$13 = 13$ ◀ true

☑ SKILL CHECK

Solve each equation.

1. $7f = 21$
2. $4b = 32$
3. $135 = 9m$
4. $12 \times s = 96$

5. $\dfrac{h}{2} = 19$
6. $\dfrac{n}{5} = 14$
7. $16 = \dfrac{p}{8}$
8. $y \div 13 = 7$

Exercises

Solve each equation.

1. $2v = 18$
2. $5w = 75$
3. $8 \times f = 96$

4. $112 = 7v$
5. $12j = 120$
6. $35n = 245$

7. $\dfrac{d}{3} = 7$
8. $\dfrac{y}{6} = 6$
9. $h \div 9 = 8$

10. $\dfrac{s}{11} = 5$
11. $18 = \dfrac{r}{4}$
12. $\dfrac{p}{19} = 7$

13. $8z = 64$
14. $\dfrac{g}{9} = 3$
15. $72 = 6e$

16. $\dfrac{v}{17} = 5$
17. $23 \times m = 115$
18. $k \div 16 = 10$

19. $37b = 111$
20. $45g = 270$
21. $6 = \dfrac{j}{27}$

22. $\dfrac{d}{27} = 5$
23. $780 = 52w$
24. $\dfrac{n}{32} = 14$

Equations

Application

Write an equation. Solve.

25. A number divided by 7 is 19. What is the number?

26. The product of 12 and a number is 204. What is the number?

9.8 Solving Two-Step Equations

Tyrone bought 2 shirts and a tie. Each shirt cost the same amount, and the tie cost $11. If the total bill was $43, how much did each shirt cost?

You can write and solve an equation to determine how much each shirt cost.

If $s =$ the cost of one shirt, then $2s =$ the cost of 2 shirts.

Equation: $2s + 11 = 43$.   ◄ Two shirts and an $11 tie cost $43.

The equation $2s + 11 = 43$ is a two-step equation because it contains two operations. To solve a two-step equation, follow these steps.

STEP 1	STEP 2
Undo the addition or subtraction.	Undo the multiplication or division.

STEP 1

$2s + 11 = 43$

$2s + 11 - \mathbf{11} = 43 - \mathbf{11}$ ◀ Subtract 11 from both sides.

$2s = 32$

STEP 2

$\dfrac{2s}{\mathbf{2}} = \dfrac{32}{\mathbf{2}}$ ◀ Divide both sides by 2.

$s = 16$

Each shirt cost $16.

Check: Is 16 the solution?

$2s + 11 = 43$

$2 \cdot \mathbf{16} + 11 \overset{?}{=} 43$ ◀ Substitute 16 for *s*.

$32 + 11 \overset{?}{=} 43$

$43 = 43$ ◀ true

Yes. The solution is 16.

Additional Examples

Solve each equation.

a. $\dfrac{a}{3} - 5 = 2$

$\dfrac{a}{3} - 5 + \mathbf{5} = 2 + \mathbf{5}$

$\dfrac{a}{3} = 7$

$\mathbf{3} \cdot \dfrac{a}{3} = 7 \cdot \mathbf{3}$

$a = 21$

Check: $\dfrac{21}{3} - 5 \overset{?}{=} 2$

$7 - 5 \overset{?}{=} 2$

$2 = 2$

b. $5x - 3 = 27$

$5x - 3 + \mathbf{3} = 27 + \mathbf{3}$

$5x = 30$

$\dfrac{5x}{5} = \dfrac{30}{5}$

$x = 6$

Check: $5 \cdot 6 - 3 \overset{?}{=} 27$

$30 - 3 \overset{?}{=} 27$

$27 = 27$

Equations

☑SKILL CHECK

Solve each equation.

1. $3f + 7 = 25$ 2. $4n - 12 = 20$ 3. $\dfrac{r}{5} + 10 = 20$ 4. $\dfrac{y}{13} - 1 = 2$

Exercises

Solve each equation.

1. $6a + 3 = 15$ 2. $8m - 5 = 43$ 3. $2f + 7 = 25$

4. $3k + 8 = 44$ 5. $15y - 30 = 15$ 6. $20s + 5 = 145$

Solve each equation.

7. $\dfrac{b}{5} + 7 = 10$ 8. $\dfrac{y}{8} - 4 = 2$ 9. $\dfrac{v}{10} + 14 = 22$

10. $\dfrac{p}{12} - 4 = 1$ 11. $\dfrac{c}{3} + 17 = 25$ 12. $\dfrac{e}{15} - 3 = 3$

Solve each equation.

13. $6x + 25 = 73$ 14. $\dfrac{g}{14} - 2 = 5$ 15. $12x - 8 = 100$

16. $\dfrac{w}{11} - 3 = 1$ 17. $97 = 18r + 7$ 18. $\dfrac{s}{9} + 4 = 4$

19. $16z - 20 = 28$ 20. $20f + 10 = 170$ 21. $\dfrac{a}{16} + 24 = 29$

22. $12 = \dfrac{j}{12} - 18$ 23. $25g - 65 = 110$ 24. $\dfrac{n}{16} + 30 = 45$

Application

Solve by writing an equation.

25. Mr. Wilson bought a suit on sale for $\frac{1}{2}$ price. He also bought a belt for $13. The total bill was $97. What was the original price of the suit?

26. Gail bought 3 new dresses at a department store. The price of each dress was the same. After the cashier deducted $15 for a discount coupon, her total bill was $87. What was the price of each dress?

Problem Solving: Work Backwards

In some word problems, you are given the end result and asked to find a missing fact. To solve problems like these, you can use the strategy "Work Backwards." Study the following example.

Anna baked 3 batches of Christmas cookies. She gave a plate of 9 cookies to her neighbor. On Sunday, she sent 2 dozen cookies to the teen fellowship. If there were 51 cookies left, how many cookies were in each batch?

Four-Point Check List

1 READ to understand the question and identify the needed data.

2 PLAN what to do to solve the problem.

3 SOLVE the problem by carrying out the plan.

4 CHECK to make sure the solution is reasonable.

1. READ: Understand the question.
   ■ How many cookies were in each batch?
   Identify the needed data.
   ■ Anna baked 3 batches of cookies.
   ■ She gave away 9 cookies and sent 2 dozen, or 24, cookies to the teen fellowship.
   ■ There were 51 cookies left.

2. PLAN: Use the strategy "Work Backwards."

3. SOLVE: Write the steps in the order stated in the problem.

$$\boxed{\text{number of cookies in a batch}} \rightarrow \boxed{\times 3} \rightarrow \boxed{-9} \rightarrow \boxed{-24} \rightarrow \boxed{51}$$

Then, work backwards. Follow the steps in reverse order and use the opposite operation.

$$\boxed{51} \rightarrow \boxed{+24} \rightarrow \boxed{+9} \rightarrow \boxed{\div 3} \rightarrow \boxed{28}$$

$$\begin{array}{r} 51 \\ +24 \\ \hline 75 \end{array} \qquad \begin{array}{r} 75 \\ +\ 9 \\ \hline 84 \end{array} \qquad \begin{array}{r} 28 \\ 3\overline{)84} \end{array}$$

There were 28 cookies in each batch.

Equations

4. CHECK: Is the solution reasonable?

The expression $28 \times 3 - 9 - 24$ is equal to 51, so the solution is reasonable.

☑ SKILL CHECK

Solve. Use the strategy "Work Backwards."

1. On Saturday, Sandy bought a sweater for $19.95 and spent $13.75 for supper. After she put $5.00 in the offering on Sunday, she had $3.30 left. How much money did she have on Friday?

2. Gary said, "If you divide my age by 2, add 4 to the quotient, and then multiply by 3, the result is 90." What is Gary's age?

Exercises

Solve. Use the strategy "Work Backwards."

1. After Aaron wrote checks for $43, $28, and $56, his account had a balance of $169. What was the balance in his account before he wrote the checks?

2. Larissa said, "If you multiply my age by 3, subtract 6 from the product, then divide the difference by 5, the result is 9." What is Larissa's age?

Mixed Review

Solve.

3. A number increased by 13 is equal to 58. What is the number?

4. The church, the school, and the bank are located along the same straight road. The church is 3.2 miles from the bank, and the school is 1.9 miles from the church. If the school is located between the church and the bank, how far is it from the school to the bank?

5. George and John ordered carryout food from the Barbecue Shack. George paid the total bill of $10.65. If George's share of the bill was $5.17, how much does John owe George?

6. Dr. Horton bought 4 pounds of apples at $0.89 per pound, 2 pounds of bananas at $0.59 per pound, and 3 pounds of grapes at $1.29 per pound. How much change did he receive from a $10 bill?

7. This week Table Rock park issued 64 camping permits. Last week they issued $2\frac{1}{2}$ times that number. How many permits did they issue last week?

8. Allen, Bonnie, and Carson are to be appointed to the offices of president, vice president, and secretary of their youth group. How many different possibilities are there for appointing them to these offices?

9. Stan painted $8\frac{7}{12}$ yards of fence on Friday and $9\frac{5}{6}$ yards on Saturday. If the fence is 30 yards long, how much fence is left to be painted?

10. Tia purchased a magazine subscription for 26 issues at $49.95. The newsstand price of the magazine is $2.95 per issue. How much will Tia save by purchasing the subscription instead of buying 26 issues at the newsstand?

Equations

Chapter 9 Review

9.1 Perform the Operations.

1. $6 + 21 \div 3$
2. $30 - (4 + 7) \times 2$
3. $25 - 15 \div 3 + 2$

9.2 Evaluate each expression for $a = 5$, $b = 12$, and $c = 9$.

4. $b + 9$
5. $30 - 4a$
6. $\dfrac{c}{3} + 2b$

9.3 - 9.4 Write a numerical or algebraic expression for each word phrase.

7. thirty increased by seven
8. the quotient of nine and three
9. a number n subtracted from 15
10. 8 more than 3 times a number n
11. a number y tripled
12. the result of subtracting 17 from $\frac{1}{2}$ of a number x

9.5 Write an equation for the following word sentences.

13. Twice a number k is equal to 28.
14. 15 increased by the product of 2 and a number y is 23.
15. 6 less than the quotient of a number f and 2 is 12.

Determine whether the given value of the variable is a solution of the equation. Write yes or no.

16. $x + 14 = 33$; $x = 18$
17. $4y = 68$; $y = 17$

18. $36 - z = 17$; $z = 19$
19. $\dfrac{w}{4} - 3 = 5$; $w = 28$

9.6 - 9.8 Solve each equation.

20. $a + 19 = 34$
21. $k - 42 = 76$
22. $r + 84 = 121$

23. $\dfrac{b}{4} = 9$
24. $6y = 84$
25. $18 = \dfrac{w}{12}$

26. $5x + 28 = 73$
27. $\dfrac{f}{7} - 13 = 2$
28. $79 = 14p + 23$

Solve by writing an equation.

29. A number decreased by 14 is equal to 27. What is the number?

30. 23 more than the product of 5 and a number is 48. What is the number?

Chapter 9 Cumulative Review

1. Choose the prime factorization for 72.
   - **a.** $2^2 \cdot 3^2$
   - **b.** $2^2 \cdot 3^3$
   - **c.** $2^3 \cdot 3^2$
   - **d.** not given

2. Choose the two numbers that are relatively prime. 9, 14, 21
   - **a.** 9, 14
   - **b.** 9, 21
   - **c.** 14, 21
   - **d.** not given

3. Find the LCM of 6, 8, and 16.
   - **a.** 24
   - **b.** 32
   - **c.** 48
   - **d.** not given

4. Identify the fraction that is not equivalent: $\frac{5}{8}, \frac{10}{16}, \frac{15}{24}, \frac{20}{36}$.
   - **a.** $\frac{5}{8}$
   - **b.** $\frac{10}{16}$
   - **c.** $\frac{15}{24}$
   - **d.** $\frac{20}{36}$

5. Identify the fraction that is not in lowest terms: $\frac{4}{11}, \frac{5}{14}, \frac{10}{15}, \frac{18}{25}$.
   - **a.** $\frac{4}{11}$
   - **b.** $\frac{5}{14}$
   - **c.** $\frac{10}{15}$
   - **d.** $\frac{18}{25}$

6. Complete. $\frac{19}{7} = 2\frac{\square}{7}$
   - **a.** 4
   - **b.** 5
   - **c.** 6
   - **d.** not given

7. Order the fractions from least to greatest: $\frac{1}{2}, \frac{3}{8}, \frac{5}{16}$.
   - **a.** $\frac{3}{8}, \frac{5}{16}, \frac{1}{2}$
   - **b.** $\frac{3}{8}, \frac{1}{2}, \frac{5}{16}$
   - **c.** $\frac{5}{16}, \frac{3}{8}, \frac{1}{2}$
   - **d.** not given

8. Subtract. $9\frac{3}{4} - 5\frac{1}{5}$
   - **a.** $3\frac{11}{20}$
   - **b.** $4\frac{19}{20}$
   - **c.** $4\frac{11}{20}$
   - **d.** not given

9. Subtract. $13 - 4\frac{7}{9}$
   - **a.** $8\frac{2}{9}$
   - **b.** $9\frac{2}{9}$
   - **c.** $9\frac{7}{9}$
   - **d.** not given

10. Estimate. $7\frac{5}{6} + 2\frac{1}{5}$
    - **a.** 9
    - **b.** 10
    - **c.** 11
    - **d.** not given

11. Multiply. $\frac{7}{8} \times \frac{3}{5}$
    - **a.** $\frac{10}{13}$
    - **b.** $1\frac{19}{21}$
    - **c.** $\frac{21}{40}$
    - **d.** not given

12. Multiply. $\frac{6}{7} \times \frac{7}{9}$
    - **a.** $\frac{2}{3}$
    - **b.** $\frac{6}{9}$
    - **c.** $\frac{14}{21}$
    - **d.** not given

13. Multiply. $8\frac{3}{4} \times 3\frac{2}{5}$
    - **a.** 24
    - **b.** 27
    - **c.** 36
    - **d.** not given

14. Multiply. $2\frac{5}{8} \times 1\frac{7}{9}$
    - **a.** $\frac{3}{18}$
    - **b.** $4\frac{2}{3}$
    - **c.** $3\frac{35}{72}$
    - **d.** not given

15. Divide. $\frac{5}{8} \div \frac{3}{7}$
    - **a.** $\frac{24}{35}$
    - **b.** $1\frac{11}{24}$
    - **c.** $\frac{15}{56}$
    - **d.** not given

Equations

JOHN PHILIP SOUSA
MUSIC

As a boy growing up in Washington, D.C., John Philip Sousa was somewhat of a musical genius. By the age of thirteen, John Philip was an accomplished musician who could sing and play the piano, violin, and flute.

In 1867 a traveling circus band offered the teenager a job as a musician. Although John Philip was delighted to accept the offer, his father thought otherwise. Antonio Sousa made arrangements for his headstrong son to serve as an apprentice in the United States Marine Band instead.

John Philip stayed with the Marine band for seven years. He left in 1874 to travel the country and play in theater orchestras. Just six years later, the 26-year old musician eagerly accepted an offer to return to Washington as conductor of the Marine Band. In 1892 John Philip left again to form his own musical group, the Sousa Band. For the next forty years, the Sousa Band played in big cities and small towns throughout the world.

As a composer, John Philip developed his own unique musical style. This style, noted for its mathematical rhythm and precision, became John Philip's hallmark throughout his life. A prolific composer, he wrote over a hundred marches, seventy songs, several operettas, and numerous concert pieces.

Of all Sousa's compositions, the most well known and best loved were his marches. The stirring refrains of *El Capitan* and *The Washington Post March* echoed in concert halls throughout the country. The United States Marine Corps adopted *Semper Fidelis* as its official march. And Americans swelled with pride for their country whenever they heard the band begin to play *The Stars and Stripes Forever.*

The Stars and Stripes Forever proved to be John Philip's most popular composition. This flag-waving patriotic march was composed on board a ship as John Philip returned from a tour of Europe. He once said, "Day after day as I walked, it persisted in crashing into my very soul." He considered this march, written on Christmas day, 1896, as his gift to his country, and his country received it with open arms. Audiences demanded that it be played at every performance of the Sousa Band.

John Philip's musical abilities extended beyond composition and conducting. To

1854-1932

improve the musical quality of his band, John Philip designed a brass instrument similar to a tuba. This instrument, called the sousaphone, comprised a tube which snaked around the musician's body and ended in a large bell. Sousa claimed that it would allow the music to "diffuse over the entire band like the frosting on a cake."

John Philip's reputation as America's March King flourished well into the twentieth century. He scorned retirement, saying that "the first you'll hear of Sousa's retirement is when you'll hear 'Sousa dead.'" When death called for the March King, it came as he would have wanted—immediately after a rehearsal of *The Stars and Stripes Forever*.

10 CHAPTER

RATIO

•

PROPORTION

•

PERCENT

10.1 Ratio

A soccer team won 10 games and lost 6 games. What is the ratio of wins to losses?

A *ratio* is a pair of numbers used to compare one quantity to another.

In the above example, the ratio of wins to losses is 10 to 6.

You can also write this ratio as 10:6 or $\frac{10}{6}$. The numbers 10 and 6 are called the *terms* of the ratio.

Observe below that if a ratio is in fraction form, it can be renamed in lowest terms.

$$\frac{10}{6} = \frac{10 \div 2}{6 \div 2} = \frac{5}{3} \quad \blacktriangleleft \text{lowest terms}$$

To find equal ratios, you can multiply or divide both terms of the ratio by the same nonzero number. Consider the following examples.

$$\frac{3}{8} = \frac{3 \times 4}{8 \times 4} = \frac{12}{32}$$ ◄ 3:8 and 12:32 are equal ratios.

$$\frac{45}{63} = \frac{45 \div 9}{63 \div 9} = \frac{5}{7}$$ ◄ 45:63 and 5:7 are equal ratios.

A ratio that compares different kinds of units, like miles and hours, is called a *rate.*

If the second term of a rate is 1, it is called a ***unit rate.*** Consider the following example which illustrates the concept of a unit rate.

$$\frac{54 \text{ miles}}{3 \text{ hours}} = \frac{54 \div 3}{3 \div 3} = \frac{18 \text{ miles}}{1 \text{ hour}}$$

The unit rate is 18 miles per 1 hour, or 18 miles/hour.

☑SKILL CHECK

Write each ratio as a fraction in lowest terms.

1. 8 to 12   **2.** 18:9   **3.** 50 to 60

Write a ratio equal to the given one.

4. $\frac{1}{4}$ **5.** 7 to 12   **6.** 14:6

Write the unit rate. Use fraction form.

7. 315 miles in 5 hours   **8.** $27 for 3 compact discs

Exercises

Write each ratio in fraction form.

1. 4 to 9   **2.** 3:1   **3.** 15 to 7   **4.** 91:100

5. 5 hits in 13 at bats   **6.** 455 copies in 7 minutes

Write each ratio as a fraction in lowest terms.

7. 9 out of 15   **8.** 14 to 7   **9.** 25:100   **10.** 60 to 70

11. 24:60   **12.** 80 out of 100   **13.** 65 to 50   **14.** 36:120

Write a ratio equal to the given one.

15. $\frac{1}{3}$ **16.** 5:2   **17.** 3 to 7   **18.** $\frac{18}{12}$

Write the unit rate. Use fraction form.

19. 150 pages in 3 hours   **20.** 72 hours of work in 6 days

21. 1,310 miles in 5 days   **22.** 344 words in 8 minutes

23. $75 for 15 piano lessons   **24.** $268 for 4 tires

Application

The table lists the number of members in each section of the choir. Write each ratio as a fraction in lowest terms.

25. tenors to altos

26. altos to basses

27. sopranos to tenors

28. altos to total members

Junior High Choir	
Sopranos	12
Altos	9
Tenors	8
Basses	7
Total	36

Sousa always had a soprano with his band on his tours. His requirements were talent, beauty, and stage presence. From left to right, they are Marcella Lindh, Marjorie Moody, Nora Fauchald, and Estelle Liebling. Marjorie Moody, second from the left, appeared on stage more than 2,500 times.

10.2 Proportion

Ashley and Andrew are memorizing Bible verses for Sunday school. Ashley memorized 24 verses in 3 months. Andrew memorized 16 verses in 2 months. Are the ratios $\frac{24}{3}$ and $\frac{16}{2}$ equal?

Ashley memorized 24 verses in 3 months.

Andrew memorized 16 verses in 2 months.

$$\frac{24}{3} = \frac{24 \div 3}{3 \div 3}$$

$$\frac{16}{2} = \frac{16 \div 2}{2 \div 2}$$

$$= \frac{8}{1} \text{ or } 8 \quad \blacktriangleleft \text{lowest terms}$$

$$= \frac{8}{1} \text{ or } 8 \quad \blacktriangleleft \text{lowest terms}$$

Andrew and Ashley both memorized 8 verses per month; so the ratios $\frac{24}{3}$ and $\frac{16}{2}$ are equal.

A ***proportion*** is an equation which states that two ratios are equal. Observe below that there are two ways to write a proportion.

$$\frac{24}{3} = \frac{16}{2} \qquad \blacktriangleleft \text{"24 is to 3 as 16 is to 2."} \blacktriangleright \qquad 24:3 = 16:2$$

In every proportion the following statements are true.

1. The cross products are equal.

2. The product of the means is equal to the product of the extremes.

Ratio • Proportion • Percent

These statements are illustrated below using the proportion $\frac{3}{5} = \frac{6}{10}$.

$$\frac{3}{5} \bowtie \frac{6}{10}$$ ◄ cross multiplication

$$10 \cdot 3 = 5 \cdot 6$$
$$30 = 30$$

extremes
means
$$3{:}5 \;=\; 6{:}10$$

$$10 \cdot 3 = 5 \cdot 6$$
$$30 = 30$$

Additional Examples

Write = or ≠ for each ☐.

a. $\quad \dfrac{3}{8} \boxtimes \dfrac{6}{16}$

$$16 \times 3 \overset{?}{=} 8 \times 6$$
$$48 = 48$$

$$\frac{3}{8} = \frac{6}{16}$$ ◄ The cross products are equal.

b. $\quad \dfrac{2}{3} \boxtimes \dfrac{7}{10}$

$$10 \times 2 \overset{?}{=} 3 \times 7$$
$$20 \neq 21$$

$$\frac{2}{3} \neq \frac{7}{10}$$ ◄ The cross products are not equal.

☑ SKILL CHECK

State whether each is a proportion. Write yes or no.

1. $\dfrac{3}{4} = \dfrac{10}{12}$ 2. $\dfrac{15}{18} = \dfrac{5}{6}$ 3. $\dfrac{14}{6} = \dfrac{21}{9}$ 4. $\dfrac{11}{16} = \dfrac{20}{30}$

Write = or ≠ in each ☐.

5. $\dfrac{3}{4} \,\square\, \dfrac{6}{8}$ 6. $\dfrac{5}{6} \,\square\, \dfrac{16}{18}$ 7. $\dfrac{9}{6} \,\square\, \dfrac{15}{10}$ 8. $\dfrac{7}{9} \,\square\, \dfrac{9}{11}$

Exercises

State whether each is a proportion. Write yes or no.

1. $\dfrac{4}{7} = \dfrac{5}{9}$

2. $\dfrac{7}{10} = \dfrac{28}{40}$

3. $\dfrac{14}{16} = \dfrac{21}{24}$

4. $\dfrac{10}{14} = \dfrac{16}{21}$

5. $\dfrac{13}{15} = \dfrac{26}{29}$

6. $\dfrac{3}{8} = \dfrac{42}{112}$

7. $\dfrac{20}{4} = \dfrac{14}{3}$

8. $\dfrac{6}{13} = \dfrac{18}{39}$

9. $\dfrac{31}{75} = \dfrac{2}{5}$

10. $\dfrac{8}{12} = \dfrac{12}{18}$

11. $\dfrac{45}{25} = \dfrac{18}{10}$

12. $\dfrac{90}{14} = \dfrac{60}{10}$

Write = or ≠ for each ☐.

13. $\dfrac{3}{5} \ \square \ \dfrac{6}{10}$

14. $\dfrac{4}{7} \ \square \ \dfrac{9}{14}$

15. $\dfrac{6}{9} \ \square \ \dfrac{8}{12}$

16. $\dfrac{16}{8} \ \square \ \dfrac{6}{3}$

17. $\dfrac{5}{8} \ \square \ \dfrac{8}{9}$

18. $\dfrac{8}{9} \ \square \ \dfrac{7}{8}$

19. $\dfrac{20}{16} \ \square \ \dfrac{5}{4}$

20. $\dfrac{22}{7} \ \square \ \dfrac{66}{21}$

21. $\dfrac{8}{2} \ \square \ \dfrac{20}{5}$

22. $\dfrac{5}{3} \ \square \ \dfrac{35}{18}$

23. $\dfrac{13}{16} \ \square \ \dfrac{78}{96}$

24. $\dfrac{11}{5} \ \square \ \dfrac{37}{15}$

Application

25. Lewis attended 8 of 15 chess club meetings. Mario attended 11 of 15 camera club meetings. What is the combined ratio of meetings attended to total meetings for Mario and Lewis?

26. Rita played chess 20 times and won 12 games. Dolores played 15 times and won 9 games. Are their ratios of wins to losses equal?

Ratio • Proportion • Percent

10.3 Solving Proportions

A recipe calls for 2 cups of flour to make a batch of 35 cookies. If Laurie plans to make 175 cookies for vacation Bible school, how many cups of flour does she need?

You can solve this problem by writing a proportion. Study the following steps.

STEP 1

Define the variable and write a proportion.

f = number of cups of flour

$$\frac{\text{flour} \rightarrow}{\text{cookies} \rightarrow} \frac{2}{35} = \frac{f}{175}$$

STEP 2

Cross multiply and solve for the variable.

$$\frac{2}{35} = \frac{f}{175}$$

$$175 \cdot 2 = 35 \cdot f$$

$$\frac{350}{35} = \frac{35f}{35} \quad \blacktriangleleft \text{Divide both sides by 35.}$$

$$10 = f$$

Laurie needs 10 cups of flour.

Additional Examples

Solve. Use cross multiplication.

a. $\dfrac{3}{n} = \dfrac{16}{32}$

$n \cdot 16 = 32 \cdot 3$

$\dfrac{16n}{16} = \dfrac{96}{16}$

$n = 6$

Solve. Write an equal proportion.

b. $\dfrac{4}{9} = \dfrac{12}{n}$

$\dfrac{4 \cdot 3}{9 \cdot 3} = \dfrac{12}{n}$

$\dfrac{4}{9} = \dfrac{12}{27}$

$27 = n$

☑SKILL CHECK

Solve each proportion.

1. $\dfrac{3}{5} = \dfrac{12}{n}$

2. $\dfrac{n}{9} = \dfrac{20}{45}$

3. $\dfrac{8}{n} = \dfrac{10}{15}$

4. $\dfrac{24}{14} = \dfrac{n}{21}$

Exercises

Solve each proportion.

1. $\dfrac{2}{11} = \dfrac{6}{n}$

2. $\dfrac{4}{16} = \dfrac{n}{12}$

3. $\dfrac{n}{12} = \dfrac{2}{3}$

4. $\dfrac{3}{n} = \dfrac{21}{91}$

5. $\dfrac{n}{6} = \dfrac{8}{12}$

6. $\dfrac{12}{n} = \dfrac{4}{6}$

7. $\dfrac{6}{24} = \dfrac{8}{n}$

8. $\dfrac{6}{2} = \dfrac{n}{5}$

9. $\dfrac{15}{3} = \dfrac{n}{8}$

10. $\dfrac{n}{3} = \dfrac{100}{10}$

11. $\dfrac{12}{15} = \dfrac{8}{n}$

12. $\dfrac{16}{n} = \dfrac{24}{9}$

13. $\dfrac{6}{3} = \dfrac{16}{n}$

14. $\dfrac{8}{32} = \dfrac{n}{20}$

15. $\dfrac{n}{12} = \dfrac{30}{40}$

16. $\dfrac{7}{n} = \dfrac{8}{40}$

17. $\dfrac{45}{9} = \dfrac{20}{n}$

18. $\dfrac{10}{15} = \dfrac{n}{27}$

19. $\dfrac{n}{40} = \dfrac{90}{100}$

20. $\dfrac{10}{n} = \dfrac{25}{60}$

Write a proportion. Solve.

21. 1 is to 3 as n is to 18

22. 2 is to 3 as 8 is to n

23. 10 is to 12 as 15 is to n

24. 2 is to 14 as n is to 21

25. 3 is to n as 4 is to 12

26. n is to 9 as 8 is to 12

Application

Write a proportion. Solve.

27. A Sunday school class went on an outing in a bus that used 2 gallons of gas to travel 25 miles. If they traveled 175 miles, how much gas did the bus use?

28. The Sunday school program at a particular church has a ratio of 2 adults for every 3 children. If there were 88 adults in attendance one Sunday, how many children were present?

Ratio • Proportion • Percent

10.4 Ratios and Percents

In the election for student body president, 3 out of every 5 students voted for Michael. What percent of the students voted for Michael?

A **percent** is a ratio that compares a number to 100. The symbol % means "per hundred."

You can write the ratio $\frac{3}{5}$ as a percent by using an equal ratio or a proportion.

Equal ratio:

$$\frac{3}{5} = \frac{?}{100}$$

$$\frac{3}{5} = \frac{3 \times 20}{5 \times 20} = \frac{60}{100}$$

So, $\frac{3}{5} = \frac{60}{100}$, or 60%

Proportion:

$$\frac{3}{5} = \frac{n}{100}$$

$$\frac{5n}{5} = \frac{300}{5}$$

$$n = 60$$

So, $\frac{3}{5} = \frac{60}{100}$, or 60%

A total of 60% of the students voted for Michael.

To express a percent as a lowest-term ratio, follow these steps.

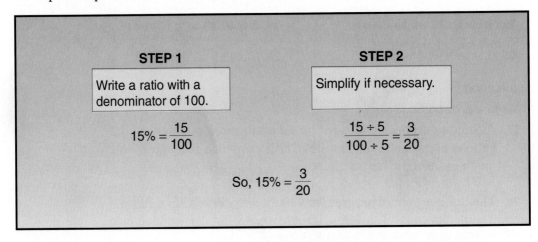

STEP 1

Write a ratio with a denominator of 100.

$$15\% = \frac{15}{100}$$

STEP 2

Simplify if necessary.

$$\frac{15 \div 5}{100 \div 5} = \frac{3}{20}$$

So, $15\% = \frac{3}{20}$

John Philip Sousa was the seventeenth director of "The President's Own," the United States Marine Band, from 1880 to 1892.

Additional Examples

a. Write $\frac{3}{10}$ as a percent.

$$\frac{3}{10} = \frac{n}{100}$$

$$10n = 300$$

$$n = 30$$

So, $\frac{3}{10} = \frac{30}{100}$, or 30%

b. Write $\frac{150}{200}$ as a percent.

$$\frac{150}{200} = \frac{150 \div 2}{200 \div 2}$$

$$= \frac{75}{100}$$

So, $\frac{150}{200} = \frac{75}{100}$, or 75%

☑SKILL CHECK

Write each fraction as a percent.

1. $\frac{39}{100}$　　　**2.** $\frac{9}{10}$　　　**3.** $\frac{1}{4}$　　　**4.** $\frac{19}{25}$

Write each percent as a lowest-term ratio.

5. 3%　　　**6.** 20%　　　**7.** 36%　　　**8.** 75%

Ratio • Proportion • Percent

Exercises

Write each ratio as a percent.

1. $\dfrac{7}{100}$ 2. $\dfrac{1}{4}$ 3. $\dfrac{4}{5}$ 4. $\dfrac{3}{10}$

5. $\dfrac{13}{20}$ 6. $\dfrac{2}{25}$ 7. $\dfrac{1}{2}$ 8. $\dfrac{19}{20}$

9. $\dfrac{18}{25}$ 10. $\dfrac{180}{200}$ 11. $\dfrac{300}{500}$ 12. $\dfrac{750}{1,000}$

13. 85 out of 100

14. 47 out of 50

15. 8¢ per 25¢

16. $50 per $200

17. 17 out of 20 students

18. 9 rows planted out of 10

Write each percent as a lowest-term ratio.

19. 1%   20. 4%   21. 19%   22. 50%

23. 32%   24. 45%   25. 73%   26. 96%

Application

27. In the school orchestra, 17 out of 50 members play brass instruments. What percent of the members play brass instruments?

28. Only 1 out of every 25 members was absent for the winter concert. What percent of the members were absent?

29. Of the 20 woodwind players in the orchestra, 3 members purchased new instruments last year. What percent did *not* purchase new instruments?

30. In the 50-member orchestra, 17 members play brass instruments and 20 members play woodwind instruments. What percent of the members play other instruments?

10.5 Percents and Decimals

In its first year of operation, the enrollment at Harvest Christian Academy was 90% full. During the second year of the school, the enrollment was 115% of the original enrollment.

You can write these two percents as decimals. Consider the table below.

Percent	Meaning	Ratio	Decimal
90%	"90 per 100"	$\frac{90}{100}$	0.90
115%	"115 per 100"	$\frac{115}{100}$	1.15

To convert a percent to a decimal, divide the percent number by 100 and omit the percent symbol (%). Study the following examples.

$$7\% = \frac{7}{100}$$
$$= 7 \div 100$$
$$= 0.07$$

$$182\% = \frac{182}{100}$$
$$= 182 \div 100$$
$$= 1.82$$

$$0.4\% = \frac{0.4}{100}$$
$$= 0.4 \div 100$$
$$= 0.004$$

Observe that moving the decimal point two places to the left is a short cut for dividing by 100.

To convert a decimal to a percent, multiply the decimal fraction by 100 and annex the percent symbol (%). Study the examples below.

$$0.36 = \frac{36}{100} \times 100$$
$$= 36\%$$

$$0.09 = \frac{9}{100} \times 100$$
$$= 9\%$$

$$0.002 = \frac{0.2}{100} \times 100$$
$$= 0.2\%$$

Observe that moving the decimal point two places to the right is a short cut for multiplying by 100.

☑ SKILL CHECK

Write each percent as a decimal.

1. 23%   **2.** 4%   **3.** 160%   **4.** 37.5%

Write each decimal as a percent.

5. 0.09   **6.** 0.5   **7.** 0.078   **8.** 1.48

Exercises

Write each percent as a decimal.

1. 44%   **2.** 3%   **3.** 15.8%   **4.** 120%

5. 5.2%   **6.** 200%   **7.** 35%   **8.** 2.75%

9. 78%   **10.** 0.04%   **11.** 395%   **12.** 99.9%

Write each decimal as a percent.

13. 0.63   **14.** 0.80   **15.** 0.02   **16.** 3.00

17. 0.002   **18.** 1.75   **19.** 0.097   **20.** 2.5

21. 1   **22.** 0.5   **23.** 0.325   **24.** 0.0008

Compare. Use >, <, or = for each box.

25. 67% ☐ 0.675   **26.** 0.3 ☐ 3%

27. 0.8% ☐ 0.08   **28.** 0.015 ☐ 1.5%

Application

29. At Harvest Christian Academy, 92.5% of the enrolled students plan to attend college. Write this percent as a decimal.

30. Music lessons at Harvest Christian Academy cost 1.3 times as much as they did 10 years ago. Write this decimal as a percent.

10.6 Percents and Fractions

In Mr. Swale's homeroom, 15% of the students play the piano. What lowest-term fraction represents the portion of students who play the piano?

To find the lowest-term fraction, you can rename the percent as a fraction with a denominator of 100 and simplify.

STEP 1	STEP 2
Rename the percent as a fraction.	Simplify the fraction.

$$15\% = 15 \text{ per hundred}$$
$$= \frac{15}{100}$$

$$\frac{15}{100} = \frac{15 \div 5}{100 \div 5}$$
$$= \frac{3}{20}$$

So, the fraction for 15% is $\frac{3}{20}$.

In Mr. Swale's homeroom, $\frac{3}{20}$ of the students play the piano.

To rename a fractional percent as a lowest-term fraction, you must use a different technique. Study the following example.

What is the lowest-term fraction for $16\frac{2}{3}\%$?

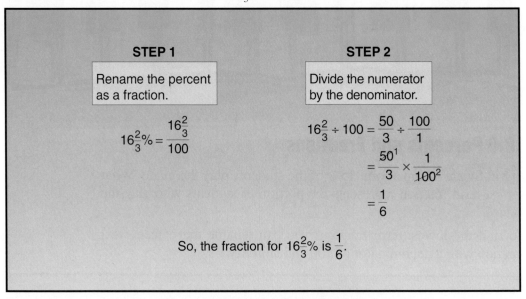

STEP 1

Rename the percent as a fraction.

$$16\frac{2}{3}\% = \frac{16\frac{2}{3}}{100}$$

STEP 2

Divide the numerator by the denominator.

$$16\frac{2}{3} \div 100 = \frac{50}{3} \div \frac{100}{1}$$
$$= \frac{50^1}{3} \times \frac{1}{100^2}$$
$$= \frac{1}{6}$$

So, the fraction for $16\frac{2}{3}\%$ is $\frac{1}{6}$.

John Philip Sousa organized the first national tour of the Marine Band in 1891. Note that there are no Sousaphones in this picture. The Sousaphone was not manufactured until 1892.

If the denominator of a fraction is not a factor of 100, you divide to rename the fraction as a decimal, and then write the decimal as a percent. Study the following example.

STEP 1	**STEP 2**	**STEP 3**
Rewrite the fraction as a quotient.	Divide. Write the remainder as a fraction and simplify.	Move the decimal point two spaces to the right.

$$\frac{3}{8} = 3 \div 8$$

$$8)\overline{3.0} \quad .37\frac{4^1}{8^2}$$
$$\underline{2\,4}$$
$$60$$
$$\underline{56}$$
$$4$$

So, $\frac{3}{8}$ is $37\frac{1}{2}\%$.

$$0.37\frac{1}{2} = 37\frac{1}{2}\%$$

If the denominator of a fraction is a factor of 100, you can easily write the fraction as a percent. Consider the example below.

What is the percent for $\frac{5}{4}$?

$$\frac{5}{4} = \frac{?}{100} \longrightarrow \frac{5 \cdot 25}{4 \cdot 25} = \frac{125}{100} \longrightarrow 125\%$$

☑ **SKILL CHECK**

Write each percent as a fraction or mixed number in lowest terms.

1. 60% 2. 48% 3. 175% 4. $12\frac{1}{2}\%$

Write each fraction as a percent.

5. $\frac{7}{20}$ 6. $1\frac{1}{2}$ 7. $\frac{4}{9}$ 8. $\frac{5}{8}$

Ratio • Proportion • Percent

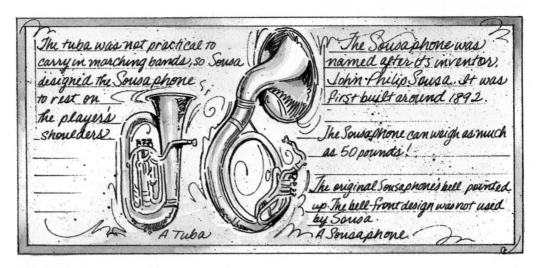

The tuba was not practical to carry in marching bands, so Sousa designed the Sousaphone to rest on the player's shoulders.

A Tuba

The Sousaphone was named after its inventor, John Philip Sousa. It was first built around 1892.

The Sousaphone can weigh as much as 50 pounds!

The original Sousaphone's bell pointed up. The bell-front design was not used by Sousa.

A Sousaphone.

Exercises

Write each percent as a fraction or mixed number in lowest terms.

1. 35% **2.** 40% **3.** 72% **4.** 130%

5. 195% **6.** $2\frac{1}{2}\%$ **7.** $18\frac{3}{4}\%$ **8.** $87\frac{1}{2}\%$

Write each fraction as a percent.

9. $\dfrac{9}{100}$ **10.** $\dfrac{4}{5}$ **11.** $\dfrac{5}{8}$ **12.** $\dfrac{3}{2}$

13. $\dfrac{8}{9}$ **14.** $\dfrac{7}{12}$ **15.** $\dfrac{3}{40}$ **16.** $2\frac{3}{4}$

Write the missing fraction or percent.

17. $\square\% = \dfrac{1}{20}$ **18.** $125\% = \square$ **19.** $\square\% = \dfrac{9}{5}$

20. $11\frac{1}{9}\% = \square$ **21.** $\square\% = \dfrac{13}{40}$ **22.** $17\frac{1}{2}\% = \square$

Application

23. In Mr. Fernando's homeroom, $\frac{1}{8}$ of the students had speaking parts in the chapel program. What percent of the students had speaking parts?

24. At the chapel program, 96% of the students' parents were in attendance. What lowest-term fraction represents the portion of students' parents who were in attendance?

Problem Solving Review

Solve, using the problem solving strategies presented in chapters 1-9.

Problem Solving Strategies		
Select the Operation	Guess and Check	Draw a Picture
Make an Organized List		Work Backwards

1. Valerie purchased 18 new stamps for her collection. That brought the total number of stamps in her collection to 93. How many stamps were in her collection before she made the purchase?

2. Miranda sold 17 pails of popcorn for the school fundraiser. This was 3 more than twice the number of pails that Sarah sold. How many pails of popcorn did Sarah sell?

3. Ramón paid $118 for a season ticket to a concert series with 9 performances. The single-ticket price was $16 per concert. How much did Ramón save by purchasing a season ticket?

4. Coach Abrams decided to cancel baseball practice because of the wet condition of the field. He called the shortstop and the catcher and told each of them to call 2 more players, and so on. Including the coach, how many players were notified by the third set of calls?

5. Mr. Jefferson is an auto mechanic. He charges $17 per hour for his labor plus the cost of the parts. The total cost of a repair was $151.75. If the parts cost $83.75, how many hours did Mr. Jefferson work on the repair?

6. Gail paid $1.45 for 5 stamps. Some of the stamps cost $0.25, and the others cost $0.35. How many $0.25 stamps did Gail buy?

The United States Marine Band has played before every president except George Washington. It has been known as "The President's Own" since July 11, 1798, when it was officially established by an act of Congress.

MIND ??? BOGGLER

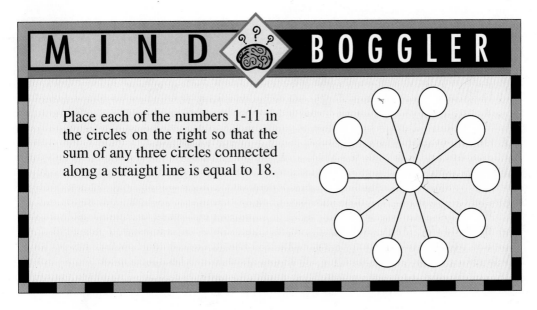

Place each of the numbers 1-11 in the circles on the right so that the sum of any three circles connected along a straight line is equal to 18.

7. Matthias ran a mile in $7\frac{3}{4}$ minutes. The following week he ran another mile in $6\frac{1}{2}$ minutes. What was his total time for the two miles?

8. Shanda paid for her breakfast with a $10 bill. Of the change she received, Shanda left a tip of $0.90 for the waitress and put the remaining $3.35 in her pocket. What was the cost of Shanda's breakfast?

9. Mr. Cox gives music lessons for $7\frac{1}{2}$ hours each day. Each of the lessons is for $\frac{3}{4}$ of an hour. How many lessons can he give in one day?

10. The enrollment in Calvary Christian School is 147 students. Of these students, 27 are in choir, 15 are in orchestra, and $\frac{1}{3}$ are in band. How many of the students are in band?

Ratio • Proportion • Percent

Chapter 10 Review

10.1 Write each ratio as a fraction in lowest terms.

1. 12 out of 18

2. $\dfrac{45}{25}$

3. 56:80

Write the unit rate.

4. 108 pages in 4 hours

5. $91 for 13 lessons

10.2 Write = or ≠ for each □.

6. $\dfrac{6}{10}$ □ $\dfrac{15}{25}$

7. $\dfrac{5}{8}$ □ $\dfrac{9}{14}$

8. $\dfrac{7}{2}$ □ $\dfrac{42}{13}$

9. $\dfrac{8}{22}$ □ $\dfrac{12}{33}$

10.3 Solve each proportion.

10. $\dfrac{3}{8} = \dfrac{15}{n}$

11. $\dfrac{10}{n} = \dfrac{35}{21}$

12. $\dfrac{8}{12} = \dfrac{n}{27}$

Write and solve a proportion.

13. 6 is to 10 as n is to 15

14. 7 is to n as 5 is to 15

10.4 Write each ratio as a percent.

15. $\dfrac{8}{20}$

16. $\dfrac{225}{300}$

17. 42 out of 50

18. $72 per $200

Write each percent as a lowest-term ratio.

19. 8%

20. 55%

10.5 Write each percent as a decimal.

21. 7%

22. 16.3%

23. 195%

Write each decimal as a percent.

24. 0.43

25. 0.086

26. 1.2

10.6 Write each percent as a fraction or mixed number in lowest terms.

27. 45%

28. 120%

29. $7\frac{1}{2}$%

Write each fraction as a percent.

30. $\dfrac{3}{20}$

31. $\dfrac{7}{4}$

32. $\dfrac{11}{12}$

Chapter 10 Cumulative Review

1. Add. $\dfrac{5}{8} + \dfrac{3}{8} + \dfrac{7}{8}$

   a. $1\dfrac{7}{8}$ **b.** 2

   c. $2\dfrac{1}{8}$ **d.** not given

2. Add. $\dfrac{7}{12} + \dfrac{2}{3} + \dfrac{1}{2}$

   a. $\dfrac{21}{12}$ **b.** $1\dfrac{9}{12}$

   c. $\dfrac{10}{17}$ **d.** not given

3. Add. $4\dfrac{5}{9} + 2\dfrac{1}{3} + 1\dfrac{1}{2}$

   a. $7\dfrac{7}{8}$ **b.** $7\dfrac{25}{18}$

   c. $8\dfrac{7}{18}$ **d.** not given

4. Subtract. $17\dfrac{5}{6} - 9\dfrac{3}{10}$

   a. $7\dfrac{16}{30}$ **b.** $8\dfrac{8}{15}$

   c. $8\dfrac{16}{30}$ **d.** not given

5. Subtract. $10\dfrac{3}{4} - 4\dfrac{4}{5}$

   a. $6\dfrac{1}{20}$ **b.** $6\dfrac{19}{20}$

   c. $5\dfrac{19}{20}$ **d.** not given

6. Divide. $11\dfrac{1}{4} \div 4\dfrac{1}{2}$

   a. $\dfrac{10}{4}$ **b.** $\dfrac{5}{2}$

   c. $2\dfrac{1}{2}$ **d.** not given

7. Write $\dfrac{3}{25}$ as a decimal.

   a. 0.3   **b.** 0.12

   c. 0.325   **d.** not given

8. Write $\dfrac{24}{25}$ as a decimal.

   a. 0.24   **b.** 0.48

   c. 0.96   **d.** not given

9. Multiply. $\dfrac{4}{9} \times 7 \times \dfrac{2}{5}$

   a. $\dfrac{56}{45}$ **b.** $1\dfrac{11}{45}$

   c. $\dfrac{8}{315}$ **d.** not given

10. Multiply. $\dfrac{5}{8} \times \dfrac{6}{7} \times \dfrac{14}{15}$

   a. $\dfrac{1}{2}$ **b.** $\dfrac{6}{12}$

   c. $\dfrac{12}{24}$ **d.** not given

11. Perform the operations. $8 + 32 \div 4 - 2$

   a. 8   **b.** 14

   c. 20   **d.** not given

12. Evaluate for $n = 7$. $4n - 3$

   a. 16   **b.** 25

   c. 44   **d.** not given

13. Write an expression for six less than nine.

   a. $6 - 9$ **b.** $6 + 9$

   c. $9 - 6$ **d.** not given

14. Solve. $f - 39 = 17$

   a. 15   **b.** 46

   c. 56   **d.** not given

15. Solve. $78 = 6f$

   a. 12   **b.** 13

   c. 14   **d.** not given

Ratio • Proportion • Percent

INNOVATORS

NATHANIEL BOWDITCH
MARINE NAVIGATION

At the age of fourteen, Nathaniel Bowditch received a gift that would change the course of his life. The gift was an algebra book which helped him to discover his aptitude for mathematics. In the late eighteenth century, books were considered a treasure—especially for an avid reader like Nathaniel. Delighted with his present, he stayed up late at night teaching himself the basic principles of algebra. He quickly fell in love with the study of mathematics.

A small, frail lad, Nathaniel was completely unsuited for the rough, physically demanding life of a sailor. Yet, in the bustling port of Salem, Massachusetts, the sea provided a profitable means of making a living. Before Nathaniel could marry his high school sweetheart, he had to be able to earn enough money to support a family. This provided the motivation for Nathaniel to sign on board the *Henry*, a ship captained by an old school pal, Henry Price.

After a few days at sea, Nathaniel felt certain that he could improve upon the methods of navigation that the sailors were

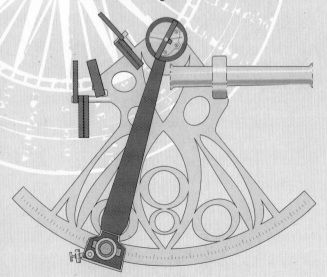

using. At the time, sailors navigated their ships mainly by intuition and experience. Nathaniel proposed using mathematical formulas to calculate the ship's longitude and latitude. This would allow sea captains to pinpoint their exact location on any given day.

The veteran sailors on board the *Henry* scoffed at Nathaniel's proposal. However, Captain Price agreed to allow him to try out his theory once they reached the open seas. Using Bowditch's new methods of navigation, the *Henry* reached its destination in the Indian Ocean and returned to Salem in record time. Nathaniel had piloted the vessel across the ocean in a straight line!

Impressed, Captain Price asked Nathaniel to accompany him on voyages to the Philippines and to Spain. Just before the ship left for Spain, Edmund M. Blunt, a publisher, asked Nathaniel to correct a set of navigational figures devised by the English mathematician John Hamilton Moore. Although the tables were the most advanced navigational aid of their time, sailors insisted that they were full of miscalculations. While at sea, Nathaniel discovered that Moore's unreliable formula for determining longitude had resulted in more than 8,000 errors in his calculations!

Upon returning home, Nathaniel discovered that his wife had died. Heartbroken, he agreed to sail again to Manila with his friend Captain Price. On this voyage, he began work on a book that would contain his own navigational calculations and formulas. As he wrote, Nathaniel realized that his book would be used by sailors who had little formal education. Wondering if they would be able to grasp the mathematical principles necessary for navigation, he

1773 - 1838

began to teach the crew both mathematical and navigational skills. When he was finished, the age of mathematical navigation had dawned.

Nathaniel's book, *The New American Practical Navigator,* was published in England and the United States in 1802. The book, more than just a navigational aid, was a valuable reference tool for sailors. It contained chapters on a variety of topics such as marine terminology, currents, and geography. The book also instructed the reader in the principles of mathematics, ranging from basic decimals to advanced trigonometry and calculus.

This book soon became required reading for sailors throughout the world. It continued to be used by the United States Navy until technological advances made it obsolete just prior to the start of World War II. However, to this day *The New American Practical Navigator* is still considered a basic reference textbook on mathematical navigation.

11.1 Finding a Percent of a Number

Gary earned $320 last month. He gave 15% of that amount to a special missionary project in China. How much did Gary give to the project?

You can write and solve an equation to find this amount.

Let n = the amount that Gary gave.

Equation:
$15\% \times 320 = n$
$0.15 \times 320 = n$
$48 = n$

You can also write and solve a proportion to find this amount.

Let n = the amount that Gary gave.

Proportion:
Think: "15 is to 100 as n is to 320."

$$\frac{15}{100} = \frac{n}{320} \begin{array}{l} \blacktriangleleft \text{part} \\ \blacktriangleleft \text{whole} \end{array}$$

$320 \cdot 15 = 100 \cdot n$

$$\frac{4{,}800}{100} = \frac{100 \cdot n}{100}$$

$48 = n$

Gary gave $48 to the missionary project.

Additional Examples

Solve.

a. 50% of 78 is what number?

$$\frac{1}{2} \times 78 = n$$

$$39 = n$$

b. $9\frac{1}{2}\%$ of 500 is what number?

$$0.095 \times 500 = n$$

$$47.5 = n$$

CHAPTER 11

c. 120% of 90 is what number?

$$1.20 \times 90 = n$$
$$108 = n$$

d. 62.5% of 140 is what number?

$$\frac{62.5}{100} = \frac{n}{140}$$

$$140 \cdot 62.5 = 100 \cdot n$$

$$\frac{8,750}{100} = \frac{100 \cdot n}{100}$$

$$87.5 = n$$

☑SKILL CHECK

Find the percent of each number. Use a lowest-term fraction for the percent.

1. 30% of 70 **2.** 8% of 300 **3.** 75% of 96

Find the percent of each number. Use a decimal for the percent.

4. 45% of 120 **5.** 7% of 48 **6.** 160% of 95

Solve.

7. 2.5% of 180 is what number? **8.** 115% of 65 is what number?

Using Percent

Exercises

Find the percent of each number. Use a lowest-term fraction for the percent.

1. 30% of 90

2. 80% of 125

3. 6% of 200

4. 25% of 64

5. 90% of 500

6. 50% of 240

7. 85% of 160

8. 10% of 350

9. 4% of 3,200

Find the percent of each number. Use a decimal for the percent.

10. 35% of 240

11. 40% of 9

12. 5% of 26

13. 100% of 94

14. 62% of 85

15. 75% of 280

16. 12.5% of 500

17. 150% of 96

18. 7.5% of 2,900

Solve.

19. 60% of 70 is what number?

20. 35% of 26 is what number?

21. 8% of 95 is what number?

22. 120% of 9 is what number?

23. 42% of 170 is what number?

24. 16% of 580 is what number?

25. 7.5% of 400 is what number?

26. 200% of 215 is what number?

27. 3% of 148 is what number?

28. 12% of 198 is what number?

29. 37.5% of 420 is what number?

30. 125% of 89 is what number?

Application

31. Mr. Mason earns $769 a week. He wants to give a tithe (10%) to his local church. What is 10% of his weekly earnings?

32. There are 225 students enrolled in Grace Christian School. Forty-eight percent of the students bring their lunches from home. How many students do *not* bring their lunches?

11.2 Sales Tax

Todd bought a 35 mm camera to take pictures on a summer mission trip. The camera cost $119.95. The state sales tax was 6%. What was the amount of tax on the camera? What was Todd's total cost for the camera?

STEP 1	**STEP 2**
To find the amount of sales tax, multiply the selling price by the sales tax rate.	To find the total cost, find the sum of the selling price and the sales tax.

sales tax = $119.95 × 6%
= $119.95 × 0.06
= $7.197, or $7.20 ◄ Round to the nearest cent.

total cost = $119.95 + $7.20
= $127.15

The total cost of the camera was $127.15.

In addition to a state sales tax, some cities also levy local sales taxes. Consider the following example.

Additional Example

What is the total cost of the following purchase?

Stereo: $475
State tax: 5%
City tax: 1.5%

STEP 1	STEP 2	STEP 3
Find the total sales tax rate.	Find the sales tax.	Find the total cost.

$$5\% + 1.5\% = 6.5\%$$

$$s = \$475 \times 6.5\%$$
$$= \$475 \times 0.065$$
$$= \$30.875, \text{ or } \$30.88$$

$$c = \$475 + \$30.88$$
$$= \$505.88$$

The total cost of the stereo is $505.88.

☑SKILL CHECK

Find the sales tax. Round to the nearest cent.

1. selling price: $19.75;
   sales tax rate: 5%

2. selling price: $850;
   state tax rate: 4.5%;
   city tax rate: 1.5%

Find the total cost of each purchase.

3. tie: $14.97;
   sales tax: 6%

4. CD player: $135;
   state tax: 5%;
   city tax: 1.5%

Exercises

Find the sales tax. Round to the nearest cent.

1. selling price: $19.35;
sales tax rate: 6%

2. selling price: $24.50;
sales tax rate: 5%

3. selling price: $38.52;
sales tax rate: 4%

4. selling price: $62.95;
sales tax rate: 3%

5. selling price: $126;
sales tax rate: 6.5%

6. selling price: $280.50;
sales tax rate: 7%

7. selling price: $427;
sales tax rate: 5%;
city tax: 1.5%

8. selling price: $96;
sales tax rate: 3%;
city tax: 1.75%

An entry in Bowditch's journal from his voyage on the Henry reads, "Thursday thought of a method for making a lunar observation." He had devised a method for determining a ship's position in longitude (east or west) by sighting on the moon and a fixed star or the sun. Others had been trying without success for over two hundred years to come up with a reliable method for determining position.

Find the total cost of each purchase.

9. watch: $87.50;
   sales tax rate: 6%

10. shoes: $39;
    sales tax rate: 4%

11. sweater: $24.98;
    sales tax rate: 5%

12. car: $6,500;
    sales tax rate: 4.5%

13. bicycle: $287.50;
    sales tax rate: 3%

14. tent: $129.90;
    sales tax rate: 4%

15. computer: $679;
    sales tax rate: 6.5%;
    city tax: 1%

16. basketball: $18.75;
    sales tax rate: 4.5%;
    city tax: 1.5%

Application

17. Todd bought a zoom lens for $87.50. The sales tax rate was 7%. What was the total cost for the zoom lens?

18. Dom purchased a $119 suit and a $57 pair of shoes. The sales tax rate was 6.5%. What was the total cost for these purchases?

19. Mr. Hill bought 4 new tires for his van. Each tire cost $67. The state sales tax was 5.5%, and the city sales tax was 1.5%. What was the total cost for the tires?

20. David bought a propane lantern for $26.50. The sales tax rate was 5%. He gave the clerk $30 to pay for this purchase. How much change did he receive?

11.3 Discount and Sale Price

The Outdoor Store reduced the price of their mountain bikes by 20%.
Hal bought a mountain bike with a regular price of $480. What was
the amount of discount? What was the sale price of the mountain bike?

STEP 1

To find the discount, you multiply the
regular price by the percent of
discount.

discount amount = $480 × 20%
= $480 × 0.20
= $96

STEP 2

To find the sale price, you subtract
the discount amount from the
regular price.

sale price = $480 − $96
= $384

The sale price of the bike was $384.

Additional Example

Find the discount and the sale price.

regular price: $198.60

discount = $198.60 × 35%
= $198.60 × 0.35
= $69.51
The discount is $69.51

percent of discount: 35%

sale price = $198.60 − $69.51
= $129.09

The sale price is $129.09.

☑ SKILL CHECK

Find the discount and sale price for each.

1. regular price: $75
   rate of discount: 30%

2. regular price: $186.95
   rate of discount: 40%

Using Percent

3. regular price: $9.20
   rate of discount: 15%

4. regular price: $1,275
   rate of discount: 5%

Exercises

Complete the chart.

	Regular Price	Rate of Discount	Discount	Sale Price
1-2.	$94	25%		
3-4.	$56.80	5%		
5-6.	$127.45	40%		
7-8.	$96	8%		

Find the sale price.

9. regular price: $90

   rate of discount: 20%

10. regular price: $150

   rate of discount: 15%

The U.S.S Constitution is a ship from Bowditch's time. She is the oldest commissioned naval vessel in the United States. Today she is moored in Boston harbor as a historical exhibit, and is still manned by U.S. Navy sailors.

Modern ships use electronic navigational aids, such as satellite navigation, loran, inertial navigation, and radar (the T-shaped antennas above the ship's cabin). These systems allow mariners to determine their position even when they cannot see the stars.

11. regular price: $39.90
    rate of discount: 10%

12. regular price: $7.60
    rate of discount: 25%

13. regular price: $1,695
    rate of discount: 5%

14. regular price: $4,500
    rate of discount: 9%

15. regular price: $27.95
    rate of discount: 40%

16. regular price: $695
    rate of discount: 22%

Which store has the lower price on the same item? How much lower?

17. Value Place
    original price: $95
    rate of discount: 20%

    Bargain Center
    original price: $105
    rate of discount: 30%

18. Shoe Barn
    original price: $65
    rate of discount: 10%

    Whose Shoes
    original price: $69
    rate of discount: 15%

Application

19. Ron wants to buy a backpack. The regular price is $129.50. All backpacks are 40% off. What is the sale price of the backpack?

20. Sleeping bags are on sale at a discount of 35%. What is the sale price of a sleeping bag that has a regular price of $89?

Using Percent

11.4 Finding the Percent

On a math test, Melody answered 34 of the 40 problems correctly. What percent of the problems did she answer correctly?

You can write and solve an equation to find this percent.

Let n = the percent correct

Equation:

What percent of 40 is 34?

$$\downarrow \qquad \downarrow \downarrow \downarrow$$
$$n \qquad \cdot \ 40 = 34$$

$$\frac{n \cdot 40}{40} = \frac{34}{40}$$

$$n = 0.85$$

So, $0.85 = 85\%$

You can also write and solve a proportion to find this percent.

Let n = the percent correct

Proportion:

Think: "n is to 100 as 34 is to 40."

$$\frac{n}{100} = \frac{34}{40} \ \blacktriangleleft \text{ part}$$
$$\blacktriangleleft \text{ whole}$$

$$40 \cdot n = 100 \cdot 34$$

$$\frac{40 \cdot n}{40} = \frac{3,400}{40}$$

$$n = 85$$

So, $\frac{85}{100} = 85\%$

Melody answered 85% of the problems correctly.

Some percents are greater than 100 or less than 1. Consider the following examples.

Additional Examples

a. 45 is what percent of 30?

$$45 = n \times 30$$

$$\frac{45}{30} = \frac{n \cdot 30}{30}$$

$$1.5 = n$$

So, $1.5 = 150\%$

b. What percent of 500 is 4?

$$\frac{n}{100} = \frac{4}{500}$$

$$500 \cdot n = 4 \cdot 100$$

$$\frac{500n}{500} = \frac{400}{500}$$

$$n = 0.8$$

So, $\frac{0.8}{100} = 0.8\%$

☑ SKILL CHECK

Find each percent.

1. What percent of 20 is 7?
2. What percent of 50 is 4?
3. 75 is what percent of 50?
4. What percent of 600 is 3?

Exercises

Solve.

1. $n\% \times 20 = 14$
2. $n\% \times 180 = 9$
3. $17 = n\% \times 50$
4. $n\% \times 8 = 12$
5. $28 = n\% \times 14$
6. $n\% \times 300 = 87$

Find each percent.

7. What percent of 10 is 3?
8. What percent of 40 is 2?
9. 16 is what percent of 64?
10. What percent of $55 is $22?
11. What percent of 150 is 3?
12. 2 is what percent of 500?
13. What percent of $45 is $5.40?
14. What percent of 900 is 432?

Find each percent. Write the remainder as a fraction.

Example: What percent of 3 is 2? $\rightarrow n \times 3 = 2$

$$\frac{n \times 3}{3} = \frac{2}{3}$$

$$n = 0.66\tfrac{2}{3}, \text{ or } 66\tfrac{2}{3}\%$$

15. What percent of 8 is 3?
16. What percent of 6 is 5?
17. What percent of 12 is 1?
18. What percent of 21 is 2?
19. What percent of 16 is 14?
20. What percent of 18 is 17?
21. What percent of 9 is 12?
22. What percent of 12 is 20?

Application

23. In a class of 25 students, 4 were absent. What percent of the class were absent?

24. Wayne batted 40 times during the baseball season. He made 12 hits. What percent of the times at bat did he make a hit?

25. A classical guitar class is limited to 20 people. A total of 28 people have signed up. What percent of the limited class size is the number of people who signed up?

11.5 Percent of Change

The Greenwood Christian Academy had an enrollment of 200 students last year. This year there are 240 students enrolled. What is the amount of change in the enrollment? What is the percent of change in the enrollment?

STEP 1	STEP 2
Subtract to find the amount of change.	Compare the amount of change to the original amount to find the percent of change.

$$\text{amount of change} = 240 - 200$$
$$= 40$$

$$\text{percent of change} = \frac{\text{amount of change}}{\text{original amount}}$$

$$= \frac{40}{200}$$

$$= 0.2 \text{ or } 20\%$$

The percent of change is a 20 percent increase.

The percent of change can also be a decrease. Consider the following example.

Additional Example

Find the percent of change. Specify increase or decrease.

original amount: 40   new amount: 34

$$\text{amount of change} = 40 - 34 \qquad \text{percent of change} = \frac{6}{40}$$

$$= 6 \qquad\qquad\qquad\qquad = 0.15 \text{ or } 15\%$$

The amount of change is a decrease of 6.   The percent of change is a 15% decrease.

☑SKILL CHECK

Find the percent of change. Specify increase or decrease.

1. original amount: 24

   amount of increase: 12

2. original price: $60

   amount of decrease: $45

3. original amount: 50

   new amount: 115

4. original price: $35.00

   new price: $28.70

5. from 25 to 19

6. from $8.00 to $9.20

Exercises

Find the percent of change. Specify increase or decrease.

1. original amount: 25

   amount of increase: 4

2. original amount: 40

   amount of decrease: 10

3. original amount: 200

   new amount: 120

4. original amount: 150

   new amount: 198

5. original price: $1.75

   new price: $2.24

6. original price: $45.00

   new price: $34.20

7. from 30 to 45

8. from 60 to 45

9. from $5.00 to $5.20

10. from 75 to 27

11. from $28.00 to $23.80

12. from 40 to 90

13. from $1.80 to $3.15

14. from 350 to 245

15. from 410 to 492

16. from 380 to 247

Application

17. The temperature in the morning was 40 degrees. By midafternoon the temperature had gone up to 66 degrees. What was the percent of increase in the temperature?

18. Mr. Cook's heating bill last month was $120. This month the bill dropped to $102. What was the percent of decrease in Mr. Cook's bill?

19. Gordon bought a can of tennis balls for $2.50. Later he bought another can of balls for $2.80. What was the percent of increase in the price?

20. The city zoo had 5 gorillas. The manager traded one of the gorillas for a baby rhinoceros. What was the percent of decrease in the gorilla population at the zoo?

Using Percent

11.6 Simple Interest

David put $400 into a savings account. The account earns interest at an annual rate of 6%. If he plans to keep the money in the account for 3 years, how much interest will David earn?

To calculate simple interest, you find the product of the principal (P), the rate (r), and the time (t). In the above problem: $P = \$400$, $r = 6\%$, and $t = 3$ years.

$$I = P \cdot r \cdot t$$

interest (I): payment for the use of money

$$= \$400 \cdot 6\% \cdot 3$$

principal (P): amount deposited or borrowed

$$= \$400 \cdot 0.06 \cdot 3$$

rate (r): percent earned or charged

$$= \$72$$

time (t): length of time the principal is deposited or borrowed

David will earn $72 in interest.

The **balance (B)** of an account is the sum of the principal (P) and the interest (I). Calculate the balance of David's account using the following formula.

$$B = P + I \qquad \blacktriangleleft balance = principal + interest$$
$$= \$400 + \$72$$
$$= \$472$$

The balance of David's savings account is $472.

When using the simple interest formula, you always express the time as part of a year. Consider the following example.

Example

Calculate the interest on the following loan.

loan: $1,000

rate: 8.5%

time: 6 months

$I = P \cdot r \cdot t$

$= \$1,000 \cdot 0.085 \cdot 0.5$ ◄ 6 months = 0.5 year

$= \$42.50$

The interest is $42.50.

☑ SKILL CHECK

Find the interest earned or paid for each.

1. bank deposit: $450

   rate: 6%

   time: 2 years

2. loan: $5,000

   rate: 10.5%

   time: 3 years

3. principal: $1,400

   rate: 9%

   time: 6 months

Exercises

Find the interest.

1. bank deposit: $700

   rate: 5%

   time: 1 year

2. loan: $2,000

   rate: 12%

   time: 3 years

3. principal: $5,600

   rate: 8%

   time: 2 years

4. loan: $10,000

   rate: 16.5%

   time: 4 years

5. bank deposit: $300

   rate: 7%

   time: $\frac{1}{2}$ year

6. principal: $950

   rate: 10%

   time: 3 years

Using Percent

7. bank deposit: $2,800

rate: 4.5%

time: 5 years

8. loan: $15,000

rate: 13%

time: $2\frac{1}{2}$ years

9. principal: $3,450

rate: 8%

time: 6 months

Find the balance of the savings account.

10. bank deposit: $5,200

rate: 9%

time: 2 years

11. bank deposit: $1,750

rate: 6.5%

time: 1 year

12. bank deposit: $490

rate: 5%

time: 18 months

Application

13. Rhonda deposited $600 in a bank account that pays 4.5% interest. How much interest will she earn in $1\frac{1}{2}$ years?

14. Dan borrowed $7,000 for college tuition. The interest rate was 8.75%. He paid back the loan after 3 years. How much interest did he pay?

15. Jasmine put $900 in a savings account. The interest rate was 12%. After 9 months, she decided to withdraw all her money, including the interest. What was the total amount?

11.7 Finding the Total Number

Miss Robbins announced that 7 students from her homeroom were listed on the honor roll. They represent 25% of her total class. How many students are in Miss Robbins's class?

You can write and solve an equation to find the number of students.

Equation:

Let n = the number of students

25% of what number is 7?

$$25\% \cdot n = 7$$
$$0.25 \cdot n = 7$$
$$\frac{0.25 \cdot n}{0.25} = \frac{7}{0.25}$$
$$n = 28$$

You can also write and solve a proportion to find the number of students.

Proportion:

Let n = the number of students

Think: "25 is to 100 as 7 is to n."

$$\frac{25}{100} = \frac{7}{n} \quad \blacktriangleleft \text{ part} \atop \blacktriangleleft \text{ whole}$$

$$25 \cdot n = 100 \cdot 7$$

$$\frac{25n}{25} = \frac{700}{25}$$

$$n = 28$$

There are 28 students in Miss Robbins's class.

Additional Examples

Solve.

a. 6% of what amount is $4.20?

$$6\% \times n = \$4.20$$
$$0.06 \times n = \$4.20$$
$$\frac{0.06 \times n}{0.06} = \frac{\$4.20}{0.06}$$
$$n = \$70$$

b. 49 is 140% of what?

$$49 = 140\% \times n$$
$$49 = 1.40 \times n$$
$$\frac{49}{1.40} = \frac{1.40n}{1.40}$$
$$35 = n$$

Using Percent

☑SKILL CHECK

Solve.

1. $75\% \times n = 45$ 2. $150\% \times n = 120$ 3. $7.5\% \times n = 3$

Write and solve an equation or a proportion.

4. 30% of 250 is what number?   5. 2 is 8% of what number?

Exercises

Solve.

1. $30\% \times n = 6$ 2. $50\% \times n = 19$ 3. $80\% \times n = 72$

4. $25\% \times n = 24$ 5. $60\% \times n = 32.4$ 6. $2.5\% \times n = 36$

Write and solve an equation or proportion.

7. 40% of what number is 6?   8. 7% of what number is 5.6?

9. 45 is 15% of what number?   10. 100% of what number is 163?

11. 56% of what number is 42?   12. 20% of what amount is $1.80?

13. 150% of what number is 120?   14. 98% of what number is 343?

15. $21 is 75% of what amount?   16. 8.5% of what number is 17?

Find the percent of each number.

17. 6% of 175 is what?   18. 80% of 320 is what?

19. 140% of 65 is what?   20. What percent of 75 is 30?

21. What percent of 250 is 15?   22. What percent of $96 is $72?

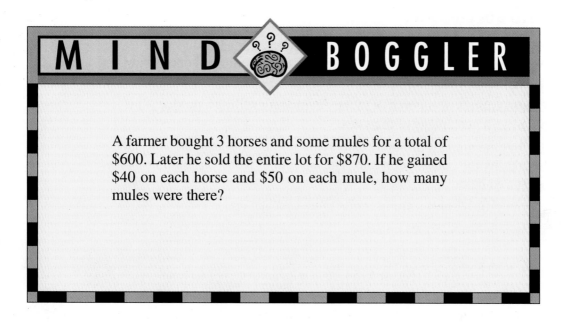

MIND ?? BOGGLER

A farmer bought 3 horses and some mules for a total of $600. Later he sold the entire lot for $870. If he gained $40 on each horse and $50 on each mule, how many mules were there?

Application

23. There are 15 boys on the school's baseball team. They represent 5% of the boys in Grace Christian School. In all, how many boys are there in the school?

24. Angie spent 15% of her allowance to buy a school pencil. The pencil cost $0.45. How much money does Angie receive for her allowance?

25. The price for a school jacket is 125% of last year's price. If the current price is $28, what was last year's price?

Using Percent

11.8 Commission

Robert sold $856.45 worth of Christian books. He earned a commission rate of 18% on his sales. What was the amount of commission that Robert earned?

Commission is an amount of money earned for selling a product. It is based on a percentage of the sales.

To find the amount of commission earned, you multiply the amount of sales by the commission rate. The amount of Robert's commission is figured below.

$$\text{commission} = \text{sales} \times \text{commission rate}$$
$$= \$856.45 \times 18\%$$
$$= \$856.45 \times 0.18$$
$$= \$154.161, \text{ or } \$154.16 \quad \blacktriangleleft \text{Round to the nearest tenth.}$$

Robert earned $154.16 in commission.

You can also find the amount of sales or the commission rate. Consider the following examples.

Additional Examples

a. Find the amount of sales.

commission: $189

commission rate: 25%

$$\text{sales} = \frac{\text{commission}}{\text{rate}}$$
$$= \frac{\$189}{25\%}$$
$$= \frac{\$189}{0.25}$$
$$= \$756$$

b. Find the commission rate.

commission: $210

sales: $3,500

$$\text{rate} = \frac{\text{commission}}{\text{sales}}$$
$$= \frac{\$210}{\$3,500}$$
$$= 0.06, \text{ or } 6\%$$

☑SKILL CHECK

Find the commission. Round to the nearest cent if necessary.

1. total sales: $752.90

   commission rate: 30%

2. total sales: $1,295

   commission rate: 8.5%

Find the amount of sales.

3. commission: $243

   commission rate: 15%

Find the commission rate.

4. sales: $1,900

   commission: $152

Exercises

Find the commission. Round to the nearest cent.

1. sales: $490

   commission rate: 7%

2. sales: $984

   commission rate: 10%

3. sales: $320.60

   commission rate: 15%

4. sales: $1,253.70

   commission rate: 25%

5. sales: $789

   commission rate: 3.5%

6. sales: $1,048

   commission rate: 18.6%

Find the amount of sales.

7. commission: $150

   commission rate: 20%

8. commission: $250

   commission rate: 4%

9. commission: $1,260

   commission rate: 35%

10. commission: $100

    commission rate: 12.5%

11. commission: $280

    commission rate: 16%

12. commission: $1,700

    commission rate: 40%

Find the commission rate.

13. sales: $600

    commission: $72

14. sales: $3,000

    commission: $270

Using Percent

15. sales: $8,250

commission: $2,475

16. sales: $2,800

commission: $210

Application

Solve. Round to the nearest cent.

17. Valene sells office supplies. Her commission rate is 25%. Last week her sales totaled $475. How much commission did she receive?

18. Anthony earns 9% commission on the appliances he sells. One day he sold a refrigerator for $519.75, a stove for $324.95, and a dishwasher for $280.50. What was his total commission?

19. Mr. Valdez receives 18% commission on everything he sells. He received $152.37 in commission one day. What was the total amount of his sales?

20. Luisa receives a regular salary plus 5% commission on her total sales. Last week her sales total was $843. Her total pay was $337.15. What is her regular salary?

Problem Solving: Make a Table

To solve word problems in which you must organize and then examine important information, you can use the strategy "Make a Table."

Study the following example.

In 1995, Nathan began working at a job with a starting salary of $28,000 and a raise of $1,200 each year. In the same year, Mark started a job with a beginning salary of $26,000 and a raise of $1,500 each year. In what year will Mark be earning $500 less than Nathan?

> ### ✓ Four-Point Check List
>
> **1** **READ** to understand the question and identify the needed data.
>
> **2** **PLAN** what to do to solve the problem.
>
> **3** **SOLVE** the problem by carrying out the plan.
>
> **4** **CHECK** to make sure the solution is reasonable.

1. READ: Understand the question.
   - In what year will Mark earn $500 less than Nathan?
   Identify the needed data.
   - Nathan's salary: $28,000 and a $1,200 annual raise
   - Mark's salary: $26,000 and a $1,500 annual raise

2. PLAN: Use the strategy "Make a Table."

3. SOLVE: Organize the data in a table.

Year	1995	1996	1997	1998	1999	2000
Nathan	$28,000	$29,200	$30,400	$31,600	$32,800	$34,000
Mark	$26,000	$27,500	$29,000	$30,500	$32,000	$33,500

Mark will earn $500 less than Nathan in the year 2000.

4. CHECK: Is the solution reasonable?
   The difference of $34,000 and $33,500 is $500, so the solution is reasonable.

Using Percent

✓SKILL CHECK

Make a table. Solve.

1. At the end of the fifth inning, the Patriots were leading the Crusaders 8 to 3 in a baseball game. During the last 4 innings, the Patriots scored 1 run per inning, and the Crusaders scored 2 runs per inning. What was the final score?

2. In January, Mike and Ron started part-time jobs. Mike's starting wage was $5 per hour with a $0.50 raise each month. Ron's starting wage was $4 per hour with a $0.75 raise each month. In what month will Mike and Ron earn the same salary?

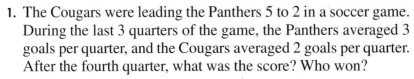

Exercises

Make a table. Solve.

1. The Cougars were leading the Panthers 5 to 2 in a soccer game. During the last 3 quarters of the game, the Panthers averaged 3 goals per quarter, and the Cougars averaged 2 goals per quarter. After the fourth quarter, what was the score? Who won?

CHAPTER 11

2. In 1990, Mr. Davis began working at a job that had a starting salary of $25,000 and a raise of $900 each year. In the same year, Mr. Clark started a job with a beginning salary of $24,000 and a raise of $1,300 each year. In 1995, who will be earning more money? How much more?

Mixed Review

Solve.

3. The ratio of boys to girls in the youth group is 3 to 5. If there are 12 boys in the group, how many girls are there?

4. Larissa has 2 more dimes than nickels. If the total value of the coins is $0.65, how many nickels does Larissa have? How many dimes?

5. Andrew made 4 out of every 5 free throws that he attempted. What percent of his free throws did he make?

6. Horace spent $12.03 on a quart of oil and gasoline at a service station. If a quart of oil cost $1.95 and gasoline sold for $1.20 per gallon, how many gallons of gasoline did Horace purchase?

Using Percent

7. Tim bought a used car for $9,200. He made a down payment of $2,500 and paid the balance in monthly installments of $336 for 2 years. How much more than the cost of the car did Tim pay?

8. Dr. Anderson spent $38.50 for tickets to a concert. He bought 3 adult tickets and 2 child tickets. If each adult ticket cost $8.50, what was the cost of a child ticket?

9. There are 8 teams in a soccer tournament. When a team loses, it is out of the tournament. How many games must be played to determine the champion?

10. Mrs. Koontz determined the following costs for making her daughter a dress: $3.95 for the pattern, $4.50 per yard for the material, and $2.25 for the buttons. If the pattern calls for $2\frac{1}{2}$ yards of material, how much will it cost to make the dress?

Chapter 11 Review

11.1 Find the percent of each number.

1. 9% of 300

2. 64% of 125

Solve.

3. 32% of 70 is what number?

4. 200% of 145 is what number?

11.2 Find the sales tax. Round to the nearest cent if necessary.

5. selling price: $36.42

   sales tax rate: 6%

6. selling price: $948

   state tax: 4.5%

   city tax: 1%

Find the total cost of each purchase.

7. football: $17.80

   sales tax rate: 5%

8. stove: $374

   sales tax: 5.5%

   city tax: 1%

11.3 Find the sale price.

9. regular price: $190

   rate of discount: 15%

10. regular price: $48.95

    rate of discount: 20%

11.4 Find each percent.

11. $n\% \times 50 = 2$

12. $n\% \times \$95 = \$76$

Solve.

13. 3 is what percent of 600?

14. What percent of 48 is 18?

11.5 Find the percent of change. Specify increase or decrease.

15. original amount: 60

    amount of decrease: 12

16. original price: $2.40

    new price: $2.76

17. from 75 to 30

18. from 80 to 180

Using Percent

11.6 Find the interest.

19. principal: $6,500

rate: 8%

time: 3 years

20. loan: $13,000

rate: 12%

time: $2\frac{1}{2}$ years

Find the balance of the savings account.

21. bank deposit: $6,400

rate: 7%

time: 2 years

22. bank deposit: $580

rate: 6%

time: 6 months

11.7 Solve.

23. $70\% \times n = 63$

24. $2.5\% \times n = 21$

Write and solve an equation for each.

25. 120% of what number is 72?

26. 48% of what number is 120?

11.8 Find the commission. Round to the nearest cent if necessary.

27. sales: $976

commission rate: 8%

28. sales: $2,537.40

commission rate: 4%

29. Find the amount of sales.

commission: $274

commission rate: 4%

30. Find the commission rate.

sales: $500

commission: $120

Chapter 11 Cumulative Review

1. Multiply. $3 \times 2\frac{1}{3}$
   a. $6\frac{1}{3}$ **b.** $4\frac{2}{3}$
   c. $5\frac{1}{3}$ **d.** not given

2. Divide. $\frac{7}{12} \div \frac{7}{9}$
   a. $\frac{3}{4}$ **b.** $1\frac{1}{3}$
   c. $\frac{9}{12}$ **d.** not given

3. Divide. $3\frac{1}{4} \div 3$
   a. $\frac{12}{13}$ **b.** $1\frac{1}{12}$
   c. $9\frac{3}{4}$ **d.** not given

4. Divide. $\left(\frac{5}{7} \div \frac{1}{3}\right) \div \frac{3}{4}$
   a. $\frac{30}{3}$ **b.** $\frac{5}{28}$
   c. 10   **d.** not given

5. Write 18.750 as a fraction in lowest terms.
   a. $18\frac{750}{1000}$ **b.** $18\frac{75}{100}$
   c. $18\frac{3}{4}$ **d.** not given

6. Write as an algebraic expression. "9 less than 2 times a number n"
   a. $9 - 2n$ **b.** $9n - 2$
   c. $2n - 9$ **d.** not given

7. Solve. $126 + r = 183$
   a. 57   **b.** 167
   c. 309   **d.** not given

8. Solve. $5x + 18 = 63$
   a. 40   **b.** 8
   c. 9   **d.** not given

9. Perform the operations.
   $18 - 2 \times (3 + 5) \div 4$
   a. 32   **b.** 14
   c. 18   **d.** not given

10. Evaluate $y + 3x$ for $x = 4$ and $y = 11$.
   a. 23   **b.** 37
   c. 56   **d.** not given

11. Choose the lowest-term fraction for $90:150$.
   a. $\frac{30}{50}$ **b.** $\frac{45}{75}$
   c. $\frac{18}{30}$ **d.** not given

12. Is $\frac{8}{12} = \frac{11}{15}$ a proportion?
   a. yes   **b.** no

13. Solve. $\frac{6}{8} = \frac{n}{12}$
   a. 8   **b.** 9
   c. 10   **d.** not given

14. Choose the decimal for 9%.
   a. 0.9   **b.** 0.09
   c. 9.0   **d.** not given

15. Choose the percent for $\frac{17}{20}$.
   a. 17%   **b.** 68%
   c. 85%   **d.** not given

S. JOSEPHINE BAKER
PREVENTIVE MEDICINE

Sara Josephine Baker, or Jo as she preferred to be called, was born in 1873. She grew up in a home that placed a high premium on education. As Josephine was making preparations to enter Vassar College, her younger brother died from typhoid fever. A few weeks later, her father was stricken by the deadly disease. These untimely deaths placed the responsibility of providing for her mother and sister on Josephine's shoulders.

With this in mind, Josephine decided to become a doctor—an almost unheard-of ambition for women during her day. She later recalled that her decision left "both sides of the family aghast at the idea of spending so much money in such an unconventional way." However, Josephine was determined to proceed with her plans. The deaths of her beloved father and brother only served to emphasize in her mind the need for skilled doctors.

After studying biology and chemistry on her own for a year, Josephine was accepted as a student at the Women's Medical College of the New York Infirmary for Women and Children in New York City. This college was founded by Dr. Elizabeth Blackwell, the first woman to earn a doctorate in medicine. Although her classes were difficult, Josephine worked hard and graduated second in her class.

Upon graduation in 1898, Josephine soon discovered that none of the hospitals at which she applied would hire her. Hospital after hospital told her that no one would want to be treated by a woman doctor. Finally, she secured a position as a medical intern at Boston's New England Hospital for Women and Children. There she learned first-hand about the sickness and squalor that existed in the city's slums.

In 1900 Josephine returned to New York City with her friend, Dr. Florence Laighton. After setting up an office, the two women waited for patients to come. By year's end, Josephine had earned only $185. Refusing to abandon her dream, she set out to find a way to supplement her income. Josephine was soon offered a position as a medical inspector for the city's health department. Unlike many inspectors, Josephine personally visited the slum apartments and schools to examine the children.

At the turn of the century, thousands of children were dying each year because of poor health conditions. During the summer of 1908, Josephine instituted a program in one of the East Side slums to teach mothers

1873-1945

INTEGERS

of newborn infants how to care properly for their children. At summer's end, there were 1,200 fewer deaths than the previous summer.

The city officials were shocked. They decided to form a Division of Child Hygiene. This was the first tax-supported agency in the world dedicated solely to children's health care. After Josephine was appointed director of the bureau, she vowed not to retire until similar agencies were established in all fifty states. True to her word, she faithfully served in that capacity for fifteen years until her conditions were met.

BACK

FRONT

RON

12.1 Integers

A thermometer may indicate temperatures above zero or below zero. Consider the record temperatures for South Carolina in the chart below.

South Carolina: Record Temperatures Through 1992			
Lowest	Date	Highest	Date
⁻19° F	January 21, 1985	111° F	June 28, 1954

Numbers less than 0 are called *negative* numbers.

Numbers greater than 0 are called *positive* numbers.

Zero itself is neither negative nor positive.

⁻19 is read as "negative nineteen."

111 is read as "positive one hundred eleven."

The negative numbers (⁻1, ⁻2, ⁻3, . . .); the positive numbers (1, 2, 3, . . .); and zero make up the set of numbers called the *integers*.

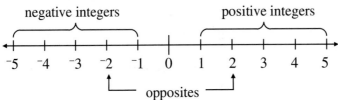

Numbers that are the same distance from zero on a number line are called *opposites.* On the above number line, observe that ⁻2 and 2 are opposites. Zero is its own opposite.

You can compare integers using the signs > and <. On the number line, the smaller of two integers is the one farther to the left.

In the examples below, observe that the inequality sign points toward the smaller number.

$5 > {}^{-}7$ ◀ 5 is greater than ⁻7 ${}^{-}8 < 3$ ◀ ⁻8 is less than 3

Additional Examples

Compare. Write > or <.

a. $10 \square {}^{-}1$

b. ${}^{-}15 \square 2$

$10 > {}^{-}1$ ◀ 10 is greater than ⁻1 ${}^{-}15 < 2$ ◀ ⁻15 is less than 2

☑ SKILL CHECK

Compare. Write > or <.

1. ${}^{-}5 \square {}^{-}9$ **2.** ${}^{-}4 \square 1$ **3.** ${}^{-}20 \square {}^{-}10$

Write the integers in order from least to greatest.

4. ${}^{-}8, 4, {}^{-}2, 0$ **5.** ${}^{-}6, 5, {}^{-}9, 2, {}^{-}1$

Exercises

Write an integer for each.

1. positive twenty-five   **2.** negative eighteen

3. 12 below zero   **4.** 67 above zero

Write the opposite of each integer.

5. 2   **6.** 9   **7.** ⁻5

8. ⁻30   **9.** 57   **10.** ⁻100

Compare. Write > or <.

11. ⁻4 ☐ 2   12. ⁻1 ☐ ⁻5   13. ⁻3 ☐ 6

14. 0 ☐ ⁻5   15. ⁻7 ☐ 7   16. 8 ☐ ⁻11

17. 2 ☐ ⁻4   18. ⁻30 ☐ ⁻20   19. ⁻17 ☐ 15

Write the integers in order from least to greatest.

20. ⁻3, ⁻5, 0, ⁻2   21. ⁻8, ⁻10, 3, 1

22. 2, ⁻5, 5, 0, ⁻2   23. 3, ⁻4, 1, ⁻1, 2

24. ⁻6, ⁻2, 3, ⁻9, 2, ⁻4   25. 2, 0, ⁻3, ⁻8, 5, ⁻4

Application

Write a positive or negative integer to describe each situation.

26. a loss of 3 yards
27. 80 m above sea level
28. a profit of $10
29. a gain of 2 pounds
30. a debt of $50

Josephine Baker was a pioneer for preventive childcare. She saved thousands of lives through programs that taught mothers to care properly for their children.

12.2 Adding Integers

Ashley went on a diet to lose weight. Consider her monthly weight change in the table below.

Month	Jan.	Feb.	Mar.	Apr.
Weight change (lb.)	-2	-3	+1	+2

How much weight did Ashley lose in the first two months?

Find $^-2 + ^-3$. You can use a number line to add integers.

1. Start at 0.
2. Move 2 units to the left.
3. Move 3 more units to the left.

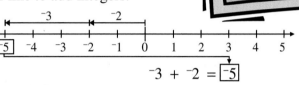

$$^-3 + ^-2 = \boxed{^-5}$$

Ashley lost 5 pounds in the first two months.

How much weight did Ashley gain back in March and April?

Find $1 + 2$. Use a number line.

1. Start at 0.
2. Move 1 unit to the right.
3. Move 2 more units to the right.

$$1 + 2 = \boxed{3}$$

Ashley gained back 3 pounds in March and April.

The rules for adding integers with like signs are summarized in the box below.

Adding Integers: Like Signs
■ The sum of 2 negative integers is a negative integer. ■ The sum of 2 positive integers is a positive integer.

Additional Example

Add. $^-2 + {}^-1 + {}^-3$

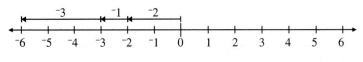

So, $^-2 + {}^-1 + {}^-3 = {}^-6$

☑SKILL CHECK

Add.

1. $^-6 + {}^-7$ 2. $15 + 8$ 3. $^-4 + {}^-13 + {}^-5$

Compare. Write >, <, or =.

4. $^-8 + {}^-3 \square {}^-6 + {}^-4$ 5. $16 + 0 \square 5 + 11$

Exercises

Write an addition equation for each number line.

1. 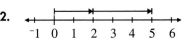   2.

Add.

3. $^-4 + {}^-4$ 4. $7 + 9$ 5. $^-8 + {}^-3$

6. $2 + 6$ 7. $^-4 + {}^-9$ 8. $^-8 + {}^-1$

9. $^-9 + {}^-7$ 10. $5 + 19$ 11. $^-13 + {}^-8$

12. $17 + 6$ 13. $^-17 + {}^-18$ 14. $24 + 19$

15. $9 + 3 + 15$ 16. $^-10 + {}^-6 + {}^-9$ 17. $^-12 + 0 + {}^-19$

18. $26 + 14 + 35$ 19. $^-24 + {}^-18 + {}^-12$ 20. $^-14 + {}^-42 + {}^-36$

Compare. Write >, < or =.

21. $2 + 5 \square {}^-3 + {}^-7$ 22. $^-3 + {}^-8 \square {}^-5 + {}^-6$

23. $^-9 + {}^-1 \square 2 + 3$ 24. $^-6 + {}^-2 \square {}^-7 + {}^-3$

25. ⁻6 + 0 ☐ ⁻4 + ⁻2   **26.** ⁻16 + ⁻9 ☐ ⁻12 + ⁻12

27. ⁻9 + ⁻8 ☐ ⁻11 + ⁻7   **28.** 5 + 13 ☐ 11 + 7

Application

29. Terri owed George $7. If she borrowed $2 more from him, how much does Terri owe George now?

30. Gary got on an elevator on the first floor and went up 3 floors. If he then went up 8 more floors, what floor is Gary now on?

12.3 Adding Positive and Negative Integers

The ***absolute value*** (| |) of an integer is its distance from zero on the number line. Regardless of direction, absolute value is always positive.

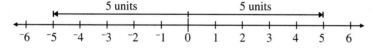

What is |5|?

The absolute value of 5 is 5 because the integer is located 5 units from 0.

What is |⁻5|?

The absolute value of ⁻5 is also 5 because the integer is located 5 units from 0.

Study the number line below, which illustrates the sum ⁻6 + 4.

Find ⁻6 + 4.

1. Start at 0.

2. Move 6 units to the left.

3. Then move 4 units to the right.

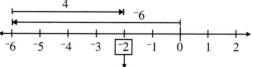

⁻6 + 4 = ⁻2   ◄ The sum is negative.

Notice that the sum of a positive integer and a negative integer has the sign of the integer with the greater absolute value.

Integers

To add integers with unlike signs, follow the steps in the example below.

Find $^-9 + 3$.

STEP 1	**STEP 2**
Find the difference of the two absolute values.	Use the sign of the integer that has the larger absolute value.

$$|^-9| - |3| = 9 - 3$$
$$= 6$$

$$^-9 + 3 = ^-6$$

The sum is negative because $|^-9| > |3|$.

Additional Examples

a. Find $5 + ^-2$.

$$|5| - |^-2| = 5 - 2$$
$$= 3$$

So, $5 + ^-2 = 3$ ◄ $|5| > |^-2|$

b. Find $^-7 + 7$.

$$|^-7| - |7| = 7 - 7$$
$$= 0$$

So, $^-7 + 7 = 0$

☑SKILL CHECK

Perform the indicated operations.

1. $^-9 + 4$ 2. $^-5 + ^-8$ 3. $21 + ^-8$ 4. $22 + ^-31$

5. $(^-1 + ^-9) + 6$ 6. $8 + ^-11 + 6$ 7. $(^-22 + 17) + ^-5$

Exercises

Tell whether each of these sums is positive or negative.

1. $^-8 + 13$ 2. $^-4 + ^-12$ 3. $9 + ^-15$ 4. $^-11 + 7$

Add.

5. $8 + ^-3$ 6. $^-9 + 2$ 7. $^-4 + ^-7$ 8. $^-15 + 8$

9. $7 + ^-12$ 10. $14 + 8$ 11. $^-23 + 6$ 12. $18 + ^-9$

13. $^-16 + 16$ 14. $29 + ^-18$ 15. $35 + ^-7$ 16. $^-11 + ^-9$

17. $33 + ^-18$ 18. $^-22 + ^-27$ 19. $41 + ^-32$ 20. $^-28 + 59$

Find the sums.

21. $(5 + {}^-8) + 7$

22. $({}^-2 + {}^-6) + 3$

23. ${}^-7 + {}^-2 + {}^-8$

24. $(18 + {}^-4) + {}^-7$

25. ${}^-9 + 12 + {}^-7$

26. ${}^-13 + (16 + 2)$

27. ${}^-23 + ({}^-16 + 7)$

28. $17 + 18 + 15$

29. $({}^-21 + 34) + {}^-19$

Application

30. The Patriot football team lost 7 yards on the first play, gained 11 yards on the second play, and lost 9 yards on the third play. What was the team's net gain or loss on these plays?

Integers

12.4 Subtracting Integers

Study the number patterns below to find the missing numbers.

Subtract.	Add the Opposite.	Subtract.	Add the Opposite.
$4 - 3 = 1$	$4 + {}^-3 = 1$	$4 - 1 = 3$	$4 + {}^-1 = 3$
$4 - 2 = 2$	$4 + {}^-2 = 2$	$4 - 2 = 2$	$4 + {}^-2 = 2$
$4 - 1 = 3$	$4 + {}^-1 = 3$	$4 - 3 = 1$	$4 + {}^-3 = 1$
$4 - 0 = 4$	$4 + 0 = 4$	$4 - 4 = 0$	$4 + {}^-4 = 0$
$4 - {}^-1 = 5$	$4 + 1 = 5$	$4 - 5 = {}^-1$	$4 + {}^-5 = {}^-1$
$4 - {}^-2 = ?$	$4 + 2 = ?$	$4 - 6 = ?$	$4 + {}^-6 = ?$

same
answer

same
answer

From the above patterns, you can see that subtracting an integer gives the same result as adding its opposite.

The general procedure for subtracting integers is summarized in the box below.

Subtracting Integers
For any integers a and b, $a - b = a +$ (the opposite of b)

Study the following examples, which illustrate how to apply the general procedure.

Examples

a. $^-7 - 4 = {}^-7 + {}^-4$ ◄ To subtract 4, add the opposite of 4.
$= {}^-11$

b. $^-9 - {}^-13 = {}^-9 + 13$ ◄ To subtract $^-13$, add the opposite of $^-13$.
$= 4$

c. $4 - 16 = 4 + {}^-16$ ◄ To subtract 16, add the opposite of 16.
$= {}^-12$

d. $11 - {}^-3 = 11 + 3$ ◄ To subtract $^-3$, add the opposite of $^-3$.
$= 14$

☑ SKILL CHECK

Complete.

1. $^-2 - 8 = {}^-2 + \square$ 2. $3 - {}^-6 = 3 + \square$

Subtract.

3. $6 - 8$ 4. $1 - {}^-9$ 5. $^-8 - 3$

6. $^-1 - {}^-1$ 7. $7 - {}^-4$ 8. $^-13 - {}^-3$

Exercises

Complete.

1. $5 - 7 = 5 + \square = \square$ 2. $^-8 - {}^-3 = {}^-8 + \square = \square$

Subtract.

3. $6 - 9$ 4. $^-3 - 5$ 5. $^-4 - {}^-7$ 6. $2 - {}^-9$

7. $7 - {}^-7$ 8. $^-9 - 2$ 9. $6 - {}^-4$ 10. $^-3 - {}^-8$

11. $0 - {}^-6$ 12. $12 - 20$ 13. $^-4 - {}^-4$ 14. $^-18 - {}^-7$

15. $^-13 - 14$ 16. $18 - {}^-12$ 17. $^-11 - 16$ 18. $15 - 19$

Add or subtract. Perform the operations inside the parentheses first.

19. $(4 - 7) + {}^-2$ 20. $5 + ({}^-2 - 1)$ 21. $(10 - {}^-2) + {}^-7$

22. $({}^-9 + {}^-6) - {}^-3$ 23. $(2 - 8) - 3$ 24. $(4 + {}^-10) - 2$

Integers

Solve.

25. If negative 4 is subtracted from positive 9, what is the difference?

26. If positive 4 is subtracted from negative 9, what is the difference?

Application

27. During the month of December, the low temperature was ⁻23° F, and the high temperature was ⁻2° F. What is the difference between these temperatures?

28. In a single day, the temperature dropped from 8° F to ⁻19° F. What is the difference between these temperatures?

12.5 Multiplying Integers

The number of inches of snow on a mountaintop is decreasing at a rate of 3 inches per day. If this rate continues, how much less snow will there be on the mountain after 4 days?

To find $4 \cdot {}^-3$, you can write the product as repeated addition.
$${}^-3 + {}^-3 + {}^-3 + {}^-3$$
On the number line below, ${}^-3$ represents the melting of 3 inches of snow.

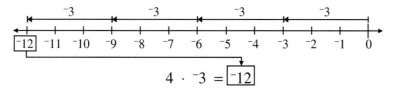

$$4 \cdot {}^-3 = \boxed{{}^-12}$$

After 4 days, there will be 12 inches less snow.

To multiply two integers, you multiply the absolute values of the integers; then, you determine the correct sign of the product.

Study the following patterns to discover the rules for determining the correct sign.

a. $2 \times 3 = 6$
$1 \times 3 = 3$
$0 \times 3 = 0$
${}^-1 \times 3 = {}^-3$ ◀ To continue the pattern,
${}^-2 \times 3 = {}^-6$ these products must be negative.

b. ${}^-3 \times 2 = {}^-6$
${}^-3 \times 1 = {}^-3$
${}^-3 \times 0 = 0$
${}^-3 \times {}^-1 = 3$ ◀ To continue the pattern,
${}^-3 \times {}^-2 = 6$ these products must be positive.

Multiplying Integers
■ The product of two positive integers is a positive integer.   ■ The product of two negative integers is a positive integer.   ■ The product of one positive integer and one negative integer is a negative integer.

Integers

Examples

Multiply.

a. $^-4 \cdot 6 = {}^-24$ **b.** $^-8 \cdot {}^-9 = 72$ **c.** $7 \cdot 5 = 35$ **d.** $3 \cdot {}^-12 = {}^-36$

☑ SKILL CHECK

Multiply.

1. $5 \cdot {}^-7$ **2.** $^-6 \cdot {}^-1$ **3.** $0 \cdot {}^-2$ **4.** $^-9 \cdot {}^-8$

5. $(^-2 \cdot {}^-3) \cdot 4$ **6.** $^-2 \cdot (2 \cdot {}^-2)$ **7.** $^-5 \cdot (3 \cdot {}^-1)$ **8.** $(7 \cdot 2) \cdot {}^-3$

Exercises

Multiply.

1. $3 \times {}^-2$ **2.** $^-5 \times {}^-4$ **3.** 6×9

4. $^-7 \times 8$ **5.** $^-3 \times 0$ **6.** $8 \times {}^-2$

7. $^-6 \times {}^-11$ **8.** $2 \times {}^-14$ **9.** $5 \times {}^-15$

10. 14×4 **11.** $^-12 \times 13$ **12.** $^-7 \times {}^-25$

Find the products.

13. $(3 \cdot {}^-2) \cdot {}^-4$ **14.** $^-5 \cdot ({}^-1 \cdot {}^-7)$ **15.** $(6 \cdot 2) \cdot {}^-5$

16. $9 \cdot ({}^-4 \cdot {}^-2)$ **17.** $(^-7 \cdot {}^-3) \cdot {}^-1$ **18.** $(^-3 \cdot {}^-3) \cdot {}^-3$

19. $(^-6 \cdot 3) \times 5$ **20.** $4 \cdot (5 \cdot {}^-5)$ **21.** $^-6 \times ({}^-2 \cdot {}^-6)$

Perform the indicated operations.

22. $4 \cdot (3 + {}^-5)$ **23.** $(^-5 \cdot 2) + ({}^-3 \cdot {}^-4)$ **24.** $^-7 + (2 \cdot {}^-6)$

25. $(3 \cdot {}^-5) - {}^-4$ **26.** $^-7 \cdot ({}^-9 + 6)$ **27.** $10 - ({}^-7 \cdot {}^-2)$

Application

28. On New Year's Day the temperature in northern Indiana was $^-3$ degrees. At the same time, the temperature in northern Minnesota measured 12 degrees colder than in Indiana. What was the temperature in Minnesota?

29. Jim had an average weight change of ⁻2 pounds a week for a period of 14 weeks. What was his total weight change?

30. An iceberg is 3,109 meters from top to bottom. If 813 meters of the iceberg is above sea level, how far below sea level is the bottom of the iceberg?

12.6 Dividing Integers

Division is the inverse operation of multiplication. The relationship between multiplication and division is illustrated in the example below.

$$3 \times 4 = 12 \quad \text{— therefore} \rightarrow \quad 12 \div 4 = 3$$

To divide two integers, you divide the absolute values of the integers; then you can use a related multiplication problem to determine the sign of the quotient.

$$3 \times {}^-4 = {}^-12 \text{ — therefore} \rightarrow \quad {}^-12 \div {}^-4 = 3$$

$$^-3 \times 4 = {}^-12 \text{ — therefore} \rightarrow \quad {}^-12 \div 4 = {}^-3$$

$$^-3 \times {}^-4 = 12 \text{ — therefore} \rightarrow \quad 12 \div {}^-4 = {}^-3$$

According to the above patterns, the rules for determining the sign of a quotient are the same as those for determining the sign of a product.

Dividing Integers

■ The quotient of two positive integers is a positive integer.
■ The quotient of two negative integers is a positive integer.
■ The quotient of one positive integer and one negative integer is a negative integer.

The quotient of zero and any integer is zero. For example, $0 \div 7 = 0$ and $0 \div {}^-4 = 0$.

Examples

Divide.

a. ${}^-27 \div {}^-9 = 3$ **b.** ${}^-96 \div 12 = {}^-8$ **c.** $\dfrac{18}{{}^-3} = {}^-6$

☑ SKILL CHECK

Complete.

1. $3 \times 5 = 15$ **2.** $3 \times {}^-5 = {}^-15$ **3.** ${}^-3 \times 5 = {}^-15$ **4.** ${}^-3 \times {}^-5 = 15$
    $15 \div 5 = \square$ ${}^-15 \div {}^-5 = \square$ ${}^-15 \div 5 = \square$ $15 \div {}^-5 = \square$

Divide.

5. $16 \div {}^-2$ **6.** ${}^-54 \div {}^-6$ **7.** $\dfrac{75}{15}$ **8.** $\dfrac{0}{{}^-13}$

Perform the indicated operations.

9. $({}^-4 \cdot 6) \div (2 \cdot {}^-3)$ **10.** $({}^-18 \div 2) \cdot ({}^-12 \div {}^-3)$

Exercises

Find each quotient.

1. ${}^-24 \div {}^-3$ **2.** ${}^-36 \div 4$ **3.** $18 \div {}^-9$

4. ${}^-72 \div 8$ **5.** $48 \div 6$ **6.** ${}^-63 \div {}^-7$

7. $45 \div 9$ **8.** $56 \div {}^-7$ **9.** ${}^-72 \div 12$

Divide.

10. $\dfrac{{}^-21}{{}^-7}$ **11.** $\dfrac{40}{{}^-5}$ **12.** $\dfrac{{}^-54}{6}$

13. $\dfrac{90}{9}$ **14.** $\dfrac{0}{{}^-11}$ **15.** $\dfrac{{}^-28}{{}^-4}$

16. $\dfrac{{}^-9}{{}^-9}$ **17.** $\dfrac{96}{{}^-6}$ **18.** $\dfrac{{}^-68}{17}$

Perform the indicated operations.

19. $(^-28 \div 4) \div ^-7$

20. $(^-3 \cdot 8) \div (^-3 \cdot 2)$

21. $(^-3 \cdot 15) \div 9$

22. $(^-16 + 4) \div (2 \cdot 3)$

23. $(^-15 \div 5) + (^-24 \div 4)$

24. $(^-16 \div 2) \cdot (^-20 \div 4)$

Perform the indicated operations. Use the rules for Order of Operations.

25. $^-6 + 3 \cdot ^-5 - 4$

26. $7 + ^-18 \div 2 \cdot 3$

27. $^-8 \div 4 - ^-2 \cdot ^-3$

28. $4 + ^-6 \cdot 2 - 15 \div 3$

Application

29. From 12:00 A.M. to 4:00 A.M. the temperature dropped from 4° to $^-8°$ F. What was the average temperature change per hour?

30. A landscaping business had a loss of $60 in April, a profit of $100 in May, and a loss of $70 in June. What was the average profit or loss per month?

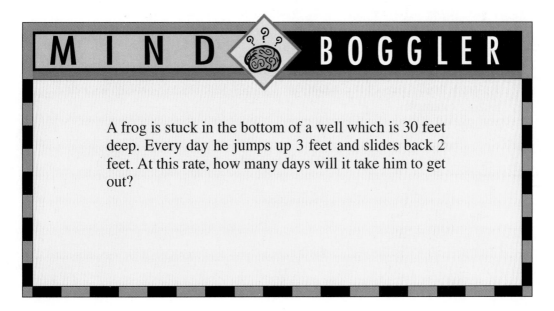

MIND BOGGLER

A frog is stuck in the bottom of a well which is 30 feet deep. Every day he jumps up 3 feet and slides back 2 feet. At this rate, how many days will it take him to get out?

Integers

12.7 Solving Equations with Integers

You solve equations with integers the same way that you solve equations with whole numbers.

To solve addition or subtraction equations, subtract or add the same integer on both sides of the equation. Study the following examples.

Examples

a. $x + 7 = {}^-2$

$x + 7 - 7 = {}^-2 - 7$ ◄ Subtract 7 from both sides.

$x = {}^-2 + {}^-7$

$x = {}^-9$

Check: $x + 7 = {}^-2$

$({}^-9) + 7 \stackrel{?}{=} {}^-2$ ◄ Substitute $^-9$ for x.

$^-2 = {}^-2$ ◄ true

b. $y - {}^-13 = 19$

$y - {}^-13 + {}^-13 = 19 + {}^-13$ ◄ Add $^-13$ to both sides.

$y = 6$

Check: $y - {}^-13 = 19$

$(6) - {}^-13 \stackrel{?}{=} 19$ ◄ Substitute 6 for x.

$6 + 13 \stackrel{?}{=} 19$

$19 = 19$ ◄ true

To solve multiplication or division equations with integers, divide or multiply both sides of the equations by the same integer. Study the following examples.

c. $^-4z = {}^-36$

$\dfrac{^-4z}{^-4} = \dfrac{^-36}{^-4}$ ◄ Divide both sides by $^-4$.

$z = 9$

Check: $^-4z = {}^-36$

$^-4(9) \stackrel{?}{=} {}^-36$

$^-36 = {}^-36$ ◄ true

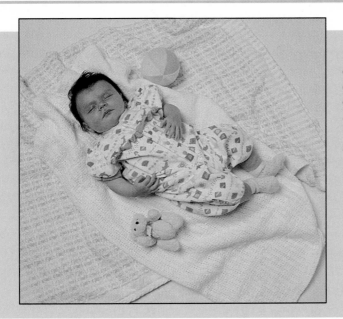

To prevent suffocation from tight clothing, Josephine Baker designed a pattern for baby clothes that opened down the front. This pattern was so popular that it was later purchased by the McCall's pattern company.

d. $\dfrac{w}{-9} = 15$

$\dfrac{w}{-9} \cdot {}^-9 = 15 \cdot {}^-9$ ◄ Multiply both sides by ⁻9.

$w = {}^-135$

Check: $\dfrac{w}{-9} = 15$

$\dfrac{({}^-135)}{-9} \stackrel{?}{=} 15$

$15 = 15$ ◄ true

Additional Examples

e. Write an equation for "7 less than a number n is ⁻18."
    equation: $n - 7 = {}^-18$

f. Write and solve an equation for "The quotient of an integer and ⁻6 is 14."

equation: $n \div {}^-6 = 14$ solution: $n \div {}^-6 = 14$
$n \div {}^-6 \cdot {}^-6 = 14 \cdot {}^-6$
$n = {}^-84$

Integers

☑SKILL CHECK

Solve and check.

1. $n + {}^-4 = 5$ 2. $a - {}^-6 = {}^-8$ 3. $s + 9 = {}^-4$ 4. $w - {}^-7 = 12$

5. $8r = {}^-48$ 6. $f \div {}^-3 = {}^-15$ 7. ${}^-7w = {}^-56$ 8. $\dfrac{h}{{}^-3} = 13$

Exercises

Solve the equation.

1. $n + 5 = {}^-3$ 2. $x + {}^-6 = 9$ 3. ${}^-8 = r + {}^-12$

4. $b - {}^-4 = 9$ 5. ${}^-17 = r - 26$ 6. ${}^-15 = x - 3$

7. ${}^-8a = {}^-48$ 8. ${}^-144 = 12x$ 9. $17y = 51$

10. $\dfrac{x}{14} = {}^-3$ 11. $r \div 5 = {}^-13$ 12. $\dfrac{w}{{}^-8} = {}^-17$

13. $20 = n + {}^-13$ 14. ${}^-15m = {}^-225$ 15. $53 = r - 27$

16. $r + 25 = 0$ 17. ${}^-x = {}^-36$ 18. $\dfrac{x}{{}^-24} = 4$

Write the correct equation.

19. A number n decreased by 7 is ${}^-12$.
20. ${}^-14$ equals a number n plus 3.
21. The product of a number n and ${}^-3$ is ${}^-27$.
22. A number n divided by ${}^-4$ is 12.
23. A number n increased by ${}^-8$ is 13.
24. 9 less than a number n is ${}^-23$.
25. 7 times a number n is ${}^-84$.
26. The quotient of a number n and ${}^-6$ is ${}^-13$.

Write an equation. Solve.

27. What integer increased by 3 is ${}^-9$?
28. What integer divided by ${}^-9$ is ${}^-12$?
29. What integer minus 25 is ${}^-15$?
30. The product of what integer and ${}^-8$ is 32?

Dr. Baker discovered the importance of holdir. orphan babies. Deprived of cuddling and love orphan hospitals, babies were dying of lonelir.

12.8 The Coordinate Plane

The ***coordinate plane*** on the right is formed by two intersecting perpendicular number lines.

In the coordinate plane, the horizontal axis is called the ***x-axis,*** and the vertical axis is called the ***y-axis.*** The axes intersect at a point called the ***origin.***

To locate a point on the coordinate plane, you use a pair of numbers called an ***ordered pair (x, y).***

In an ordered pair, the first coordinate tells the distance to the right or left of the origin. The second coordinate tells the distance above or below the origin.

Coordinate Plane

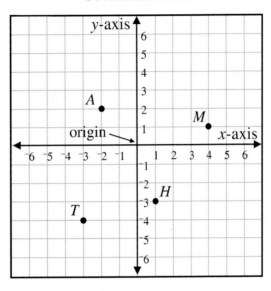

The ordered pair (0, 0) describes the location of the origin. Consider the location of points *M, A, T,* and *H* in the table below.

Point	Ordered Pair	Position
M	(4, 1)	4 units to the right of the origin 1 unit up from the origin
A	(⁻2, 2)	2 units to the left of the origin 2 units up from the origin
T	(⁻3, ⁻4)	3 units to the left of the origin 4 units down from the origin
H	(1, ⁻3)	1 unit to the right of the origin 3 units down from the origin

Integers

☑SKILL CHECK

Write the ordered pair for each point.

1. *A*   2. *B*

3. *C*   4. *D*

Write the letter of the point named by each ordered pair.

5. (0, 3)   6. (5, 2)

7. (⁻3, ⁻5)   8. (3, ⁻4)

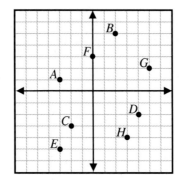

Exercises

Write the ordered pair for each point.

1. *A*   2. *B*

3. *C*   4. *D*

5. *E*   6. *F*

7. *G*   8. *H*

9. *I*   10. *J*

11. *K*   12. *L*

Write the letter of the point named by each ordered pair.

13. (⁻5, 3)   14. (3, 1)

15. (2, ⁻5)   16. (0, 2)

17. (⁻4, ⁻2)   18. (⁻5, 0)

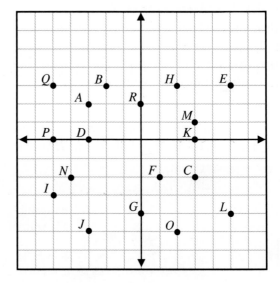

Graph and label each of the following points.

19. *S* (2, 5)   20. *T* (⁻3, ⁻2)   21. *V* (0, ⁻3)

22. *V* (⁻5, ⁻5)   23. *W* (⁻1, 4)   24. *X* (4, ⁻1)

25. *Y* (⁻4, 0)   26. *Z* (⁻5, 3)

Application

Graph each ordered pair. Connect the points in order. What type of quadrilateral is formed?

27. $(1, ^-2), (5, ^-2), (5, ^-5), (1, ^-5)$

28. $(0, 0), (2, 2), (5, 2), (3, 0)$

29. $(^-1, 0), (^-5, 0), (^-5, 3), (^-3, 3)$

30. $(^-6, ^-4), (^-6, 4), (2, ^-4), (2, 4)$

Problem Solving: Find a Pattern

In some word problems there is a pattern present. To solve problems like these, you can use the strategy "Find a Pattern."

Study the following example.

On his fortieth birthday, Mr. Cropsey opened a savings account and deposited $500. On each succeeding birthday, he deposits $200 more than he deposited the previous year. At this rate, what will be the total in his account when he is 46 years old?

1. READ: Understand the question.
   - What will be the total in Mr. Cropsey's account when he is 46 years old?

   Identify the needed data.
   - The initial deposit was $500.
   - In each succeeding year, Mr. Cropsey deposited $200 more than the previous year.

2. PLAN: Use the strategy "Find a Pattern."

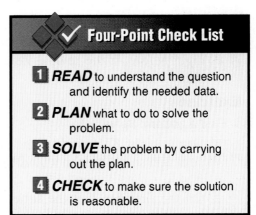

✓ Four-Point Check List

1. **READ** to understand the question and identify the needed data.

2. **PLAN** what to do to solve the problem.

3. **SOLVE** the problem by carrying out the plan.

4. **CHECK** to make sure the solution is reasonable.

Integers

3. SOLVE: Organize the information to show the pattern.

Birthday	40	41	42	43	44	45	46
Deposit	$500	$700	$900	$1,100	$1,300	$1,500	$1,700
Total	$500	$1,200	$2,100	$3,200	$4,500	$6,000	$7,700

Mr. Cropsey will have $7,700 in his account when he is 46 years old.

4. CHECK: Is the solution reasonable?
   Estimate the solution by rounding the deposits to the nearest $1,000.

Birthday	40	41	42	43	44	45	46
Deposit	$1,000	$1,000	$1,000	$1,000	$1,000	$2,000	$2,000
Total	$1,000	$2,000	$3,000	$4,000	$5,000	$7,000	$9,000

The estimate is in line with the actual answer, so the solution is reasonable.

☑ SKILL CHECK

Find a pattern. Solve.

1. A fast-growing tree is 1 ft. high after the first year, 2 ft. high after the second year, 4 ft. high after the third year, and so on. How high will the tree be at the end of six years?

2. On the first night of a revival, 2 people were saved. On each succeeding night, there was 1 more person saved than on the night before. If the revival lasted for 5 nights, a total of how many people were saved?

Exercises

Find a pattern. Solve.

1. Gary weighs 87 pounds. If he gains 5 lb. this year, 6 lb. next year, and so on, how much will he weigh in 5 years?

2. On the first day that the fitness center opened, there were 4 people in attendance. On each succeeding day, there were twice the number of people in attendance as the day before. At the end of the fifth day, how many total people had attended?

Mixed Review

Solve.

3. The home economics class made muffins to sell at the soccer game. They expected that 2 out of every 5 people would buy a muffin. If they made a total of 54 muffins, how many people did they expect at the soccer game?

4. Hal has 5 days in which to complete a 215-mile bicycle tour of Vermont. On the first and second days, he covered 31 and 58 miles respectively. In order to complete the trip, what distance must he average per day on the last 3 days of the tour?

5. The Lions football team lost 7 yards on the first play of the game and gained 11 yards on the second play. What was the total loss or gain for the two plays?

6. The library charges $0.25 for the first day that a book is overdue. For each day after that, the charge is $0.15. How much is the total fine on the fourth day that a book is overdue?

7. The Green Thumb Nursery gives a 15% discount on orders over $100. Mr. Cochran placed orders for $176, $225, and $190. What was the amount of discount that Mr. Cochran received?

8. John drove 625 miles in two days. On the second day, he drove 75 miles more than the first day. How many miles did he drive each day?

9. Randy purchased a home gym from Fitness Quest for $895. If the sales tax rate is 6%, what was the total cost of the gym?

10. David called his sister in Pennsylvania. The rate was $1.95 for the first three minutes and $0.26 for each additional minute. If David talked for 12 minutes, what was the cost of the call?

Integers

Chapter 12 Review

12.1 Compare. Use > or < for each box.

1. $^-7 \square 2$

2. $^-5 \square ^-13$

3. $3 \square ^-15$

Write in order from least to greatest.

4. $^-6, 5, ^-1, 2, ^-4$

5. $3, 0, ^-4, ^-9, 5, ^-7$

12.2 - 12.4 Add or Subtract.

6. $^-8 + ^-6$

7. $5 + 17$

8. $^-11 + ^-5 + ^-9$

9. $9 + ^-5$

10. $^-16 + 3$

11. $^-24 + 24$

12. $5 - 9$

13. $^-7 - 11$

14. $^-3 - ^-15$

15. $(5 - 8) + ^-6$

16. $(^-8 + ^-7) - 4$

17. $(^-13 + 22) + ^-19$

12.5 - 12.6 Multiply or divide.

18. $^-6 \times 9$

19. $3 \times ^-16$

20. $8 \times ^-25$

21. $63 \div 9$

22. $40 \div 8$

23. $\dfrac{^-91}{^-7}$

24. $(^-36 \div ^-3) \div ^-2$

25. $(^-24 \div 4) \cdot (18 \div ^-3)$

26. $(^-7 \cdot 2) + (^-4 \cdot ^-5)$

12.7 Solve.

27. $a + 7 = ^-8$

28. $^-14 = r - 9$

29. $13y = ^-52$

30. $\dfrac{x}{^-8} = ^-15$

12.8 Write the ordered pair of each point.

31. A

32. B

33. C

34. D

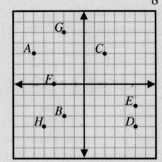

Write the letter of the point named by each ordered pair.

35. $(5, ^-2)$

36. $(^-2, 5)$

37. $(^-3, 0)$

38. $(^-4, ^-4)$

Chapter 12 Cumulative Review

1. Perform the operations.

$24 - 3 \cdot 2 + 12 \div 3$

a. 14   **b.** 22

c. 18   **d.** not given

2. Evaluate $\frac{z}{3} - y$ for $y = 4$ and $z = 18$.

a. 1   **b.** 2

c. 5   **d.** not given

3. Write an equation for "25 decreased by the product of 2 and a number b equals 7."

a. $2b - 7 = 25$ **b.** $2b - 25 = 7$

c. $25 - 2b = 7$ **d.** not given

4. 17 more than a number is equal to 43. What is the number?

a. 60   **b.** 36

c. 26   **d.** not given

5. Solve. $\frac{n}{24} = 13$

a. 37   **b.** 302

c. 312   **d.** not given

6. Choose the mixed number in lowest terms for 185%.

a. $1\frac{85}{100}$ **b.** $\frac{37}{20}$

c. $1\frac{17}{20}$ **d.** not given

7. Choose the unit price: $52 for 13 piano lessons.

a. $4/lesson   **b.** $5/lesson

c. $52/lesson   **d.** not given

8. Write = or ≠ for $\square$. $\frac{7}{4}$ $\square$ $\frac{28}{20}$

a. =   **b.** ≠

9. Solve. $\frac{10}{12} = \frac{15}{n}$

a. 16   **b.** 17

c. 18   **d.** not given

10. Choose the percent for 34 out of 50.

a. 34%   **b.** 68%

c. 102%   **d.** not given

11. Find the percent. Use a lowest-term fraction. 40% of 90

a. 3.6   **b.** 36

c. 360   **d.** not given

12. Find the sales tax. Selling price: $29.50; Sales tax rate: 6%.

a. $1.77   **b.** $31.27

c. $17.70   **d.** not given

13. Find the amount of discount. Regular price: $65.80; rate of discount: 5%.

a. $62.51   **b.** $32.90

c. $3.29   **d.** not given

14. Solve. $n\% \times 80 = 28$

a. 25%   **b.** 35%

c. 45%   **d.** not given

15. Find the percent of change. Original amount: 60; increase: 9.

a. 10%   **b.** 15%

c. 85%   **d.** not given

M. C. ESCHER
ART

Maurits Cornelis Escher, or Mauk as he liked to be called, was not a very good student. In 1918 he barely passed "hogere burgerschool," the Dutch version of high school. The following year he was forced to withdraw from technical school. Although he struggled academically, Mauk excelled in art.

After dropping out of technical school, Mauk devoted his time to art. He was accepted as a student at the School for Architecture and Decorative Arts in the Dutch city of Haarlem. Upon seeing Mauk's drawings, Samuel Jessum de Mesquita, the professor of graphic arts, suggested that Escher continue as a graphic arts student.

The art professor soon became Mauk's mentor. The two artists continued to stay in touch until the Germans sent Professor de Mesquita, a Jew, to a Nazi concentration camp. Although Escher never saw his friend after that, he kept one of the professor's paintings, imprinted with a German soldier's boot, tacked to a cupboard in his studio.

As a teenager Mauk had learned to carve scenes out of a piece of linoleum. He would then ink them and print them on sheets of paper. Over the years, he had perfected this technique until he could produce highly detailed black-and-white prints of people, landscapes, and animals. These cuttings won him recognition in art shows throughout the Netherlands. He soon became interested in transferring this technique to wood.

In 1936 Mauk took a trip through several Mediterranean countries. While in Spain he became interested in the geometrical mosaics created by Moorish artists. Fascinated with the mosaics, Mauk decided to create the same effect in his woodcuts.

1898-1972

PERIMETER
·
AREA
·
VOLUME

To accomplish this end, Escher turned to mathematics. Although he had barely passed his math courses in school, Mauk later remarked, "I seem to have more in common with mathematicians than with my fellow artists." Mauk used mathematical principles to design a motif. He would then duplicate the motif many times over and fit the pieces together like a jigsaw puzzle.

Escher liked to create visual riddles which played tricks on the eye. One of his most famous prints, *Waterfall,* looks at first glance like a normal scene of a waterfall and a waterwheel. However, a closer look reveals that the path taken by the water to the pool underneath the waterwheel is on the same level as the waterfall. Since the water does not go either uphill or downhill, it would be impossible for the water to fall. As with many of his prints, one could sit for hours trying to figure out how the scene could be visually logical and yet impossible.

Escher's prints became enormously popular throughout the world. They have been used in posters, book covers, wrapping paper, and even neckties. Mathematicians, scientists, and artists have all applauded his whimsical ability to depict the world around him in artistic and mathematical ways.

13.1 Perimeter

Each morning Stephanie jogs around the outside edge of the park in the diagram on the right. How far does she jog?

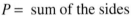

To find how far Stephanie jogs, you must find the perimeter of the park. The distance around a geometric figure is called its *perimeter.* The perimeter of a polygon is equal to the sum of its sides.

The general formula for perimeter (P) is given below.

$$P = \text{sum of the sides}$$

You can use this formula to find the perimeter of the park in the introductory problem.

$$P = 500 + 1,000 + 600 + 350$$
$$= 2,450$$

The perimeter of the park is 2,450 m.

Squares and rectangles have specific formulas that you can use to find their perimeters. Study the examples below.

Square:
The perimeter of a square is 4 times the length of a side (s).

$$P = 4s$$
$$= 4 \cdot 4$$
$$= 16$$

4 cm

4 cm

Rectangle:
The perimeter of a rectangle is twice the length (l) plus twice the width (w).

$$P = 2l + 2w$$
$$= 2 \cdot 5 + 2 \cdot 3$$
$$= 10 + 6$$
$$= 16$$

3 m

5 m

The perimeter of the square is 16 cm.

The perimeter of the rectangle is 16 m.

☑ SKILL CHECK

Find the perimeter of each polygon.

1.
8 cm
18 cm

2.
6.8 m
12.7 m
11.3 m

3.
29 m
15 m
18 m
14 m
30 m

Find the perimeter of the square.

4. $s = 7.3$ cm

Find the perimeter of the rectangle.

5. $l = 15$ m
$w = 4.9$ m

Exercises

Find the perimeter of each figure.

1.
5 m
6 m
4 m
9 m

2.
7 cm
7 cm

3.
5.3 m
3.8 m
7.6 m

4.
10 cm
9 cm
8 cm
8 cm
11.3 cm

5.
2.9 m
6 m
2.9 m
2.9 m
6 m
2.9 m

6.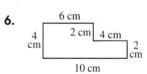
6 cm
4 cm
2 cm
4 cm
2 cm
10 cm

Find the perimeter of each square.

7. $s = 4$ m

8. $s = 8.7$ cm

9. $s = 17$ cm

Find the perimeter of each rectangle.

10. $l = 14$ cm
$w = 9$ cm

11. $l = 18.5$ m
$w = 12$ m

12. $l = 21.8$ mm
$w = 9.6$ mm

To find the perimeter of a regular polygon, you multiply the number of sides by the length of each side.

Find the perimeter of each regular polygon.

13. triangle; $s = 5$ m

14. pentagon; $s = 18.4$ cm

15. quadrilateral; $s = 27$ mm

16. octagon; $s = 0.9$ m

Solve.

17. A regular hexagon has a perimeter of 84 centimeters. Find the length of each side.

18. The perimeter of a rectangle is 42 meters. The length is 13 meters. Find the width.

Application

19. Anthony is building a fence around a rectangular backyard. The yard measures 32 feet by 48 feet. How many feet of fence does he need?

20. Anthony is starting at one corner and placing a wooden fence post every 4 feet. How many fence posts does he need?

In Escher's woodcut, Day and Night, *the central square plots of farmland are cleverly transformed into a pattern of flying ducks over a mirrored hamlet.*

13.2 Area of Rectangles and Squares

The floor in a living room is 6 m long and 4 m wide. What is the area of the floor?

The ***area*** of a region is the number of square units needed to cover the region.

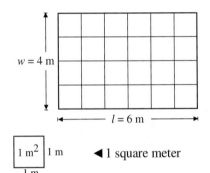

A ***square meter*** (1 m^2) is the area enclosed by a square having sides that measure 1 m each.

To find the area of the above floor, you can simply count the number of square meters in the diagram. There are 24 m^2 in the living room.

Since the floor is a rectangle, you can also find its area by multiplying the length by the width. The example below illustrates the use of the formula for finding the area of a rectangle.

Area of rectangle = length × width

$$A = l \cdot w$$
$$= 6 \text{ m} \times 4 \text{ m}$$
$$= 24 \text{ m}^2$$

The area of the floor is 24 m^2.

Perimeter • Area • Volume

Since the length and width of a square are the same, you can find the area of a square by multiplying the length of a side by itself.

Area of a square = side × side.

$$A = s \times s, \text{ or } A = s^2$$

Additional Example

Find the area of a square whose sides measure 9 cm.

$$A = s^2$$
$$= 9 \cdot 9$$
$$= 81$$

The area of the square is 81 cm^2.

☑ SKILL CHECK

Find the area of each figure.

1. 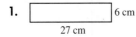 6 cm
27 cm

2.
11 cm
11 cm

3. 18 m
7 m

Find the area of each rectangle or square.

4. $l = 14$ cm, $w = 8$ cm

5. $s = 13$ m

Exercises

Find the area of each figure.

1. 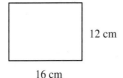 3 m
8 m

2. 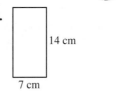 14 cm
7 cm

3. 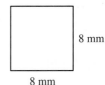 8 mm
8 mm

4. 12 cm
16 cm

5. 24 m
24 m

6. 15 mm
13 mm

Find the area of each rectangle or square.

7. $l = 9$ cm
$w = 4$ cm

8. $l = 17$ m
$w = 6$ m

9. $s = 7$ mm

10. $l = 18$ m
$w = 4.5$ m

11. $s = 8.4$ mm

12. $l = 23.4$ cm
$w = 9.6$ cm

Find the area of each shaded region.

13.
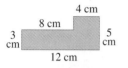

14.
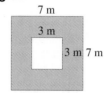

15.
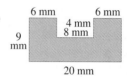

16.
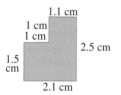

17.
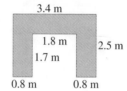

18.
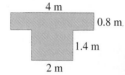

Application

19. Carpeting costs $1.75 per square foot. How much will it cost to carpet a floor that measures 16 feet by 28 feet?

20. A rectangular wall is 8 feet high and has an area of 152 square feet. What is the length of the wall?

Perimeter ● Area ● Volume

13.3 Area of Parallelograms and Triangles

If you cut a parallelogram into parts and rearrange the parts to form a rectangle, the rectangle formed will have the same area as the parallelogram. Study the example below.

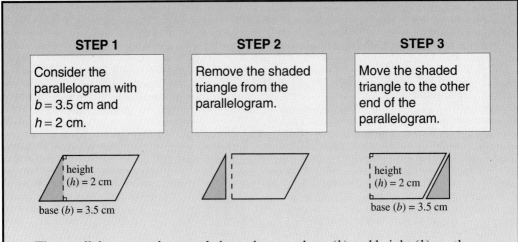

STEP 1	**STEP 2**	**STEP 3**
Consider the parallelogram with $b = 3.5$ cm and $h = 2$ cm.	Remove the shaded triangle from the parallelogram.	Move the shaded triangle to the other end of the parallelogram.

height $(h) = 2$ cm
base $(b) = 3.5$ cm

height $(h) = 2$ cm
base $(b) = 3.5$ cm

The parallelogram and rectangle have the same base (b) and height (h), so the area of both polygons is the same. Therefore, you can find the area of a parallelogram by multiplying the base by the height: $A = b \cdot h$.

What is the area of the parallelogram on the right?

area of parallelogram = base × height

$$A = b \cdot h$$
$$= 3.5 \text{ cm} \cdot 2 \text{ cm}$$
$$= 7 \text{ cm}^2$$

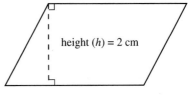

height (h) = 2 cm

The area of the parallelogram is 7 cm².

base (b) = 3.5 cm

By drawing a diagonal, you can divide a parallelogram into 2 congruent triangles. The area of each triangle is equal to $\frac{1}{2}$ of the area of the parallelogram.

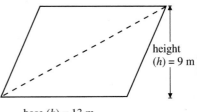

height (h) = 9 m

base (b) = 13 m

area of triangle = $\frac{1}{2}$ × area of parallelogram

To find the area of a triangle, you multiply $\frac{1}{2}$ times the base times the height. What is the area of the triangle below?

area of triangle = $\frac{1}{2}$ × base × height

$$A = \frac{1}{2} bh$$
$$= \frac{1}{2} \times 13 \text{ m} \times 9 \text{ m}$$
$$= 58.5 \text{ m}^2$$

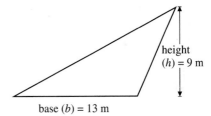

height (h) = 9 m

base (b) = 13 m

The area of the triangle is 58.5 m².

☑SKILL CHECK

Find the area of each figure.

1.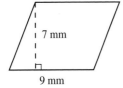
$h = 2.8$ cm
$b = 4.6$ cm

2.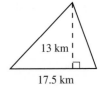
$h = 2.5$ m
$b = 3.2$ m

Exercises

Find the area of each parallelogram.

1.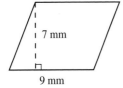
7 mm
9 mm

2.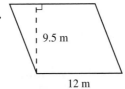
9.5 m
12 m

3.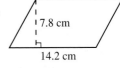
7.8 cm
14.2 cm

4. $b = 15$ cm
$h = 5$ cm

5. $b = 32$ m
$h = 14$ m

6. $b = 9$ km
$h = 7.2$ km

7. $b = 4.5$ m
$h = 2.6$ m

8. $b = 15.8$ cm
$h = 3.6$ cm

9. $b = 19.7$ km
$h = 12.5$ km

Find the area of each triangle.

10.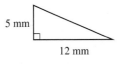
5 mm
12 mm

11.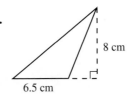
8 cm
6.5 cm

12.
13 km
17.5 km

13. $b = 15$ cm
$h = 5$ m

14. $b = 32$ cm
$h = 14$ cm

15. $b = 9$ km
$h = 7.2$ km

16. $b = 4.5$ cm
$h = 2.6$ cm

17. $b = 15.2$ m
$h = 3.8$ m

18. $b = 20.7$ mm
$h = 12.5$ mm

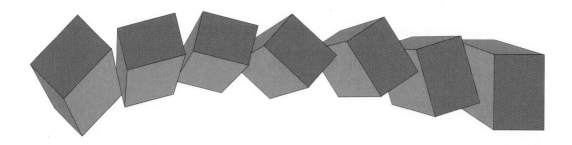

Application

19. Rudy is cutting a triangle from a piece of plywood. The triangle has a base of 45 cm and a height of 16 cm. What is the area of the triangle?

20. Sally is cutting 4 parallelograms from poster board as part of a tangram puzzle. Each parallelogram has a base of 13 cm and a height of 8 cm. What is the combined area of the parallelograms?

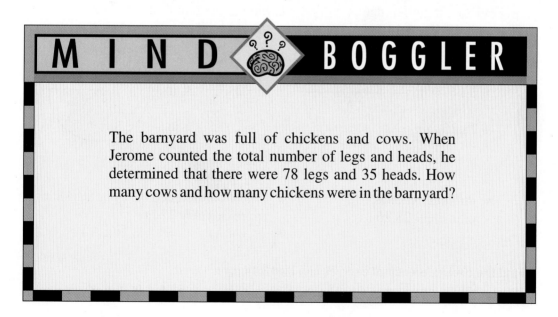

M I N D B O G G L E R

The barnyard was full of chickens and cows. When Jerome counted the total number of legs and heads, he determined that there were 78 legs and 35 heads. How many cows and how many chickens were in the barnyard?

13.4 Circumference

The distance around a circle is called its ***circumference.*** For every circle, the ratio of the circumference (C) to the diameter (d) is the same. This ratio, $\frac{C}{d}$, is represented by the Greek letter π.

$$\pi = \frac{C}{d} = 3.14159265\ldots \quad \blacktriangleleft \pi \text{ is a nonterminating, nonrepeating decimal.}$$

The symbol $\approx$ means "is approximately equal to." Two common approximations for π are given below.

$$\pi \approx 3.14 \qquad\qquad \pi \approx \frac{22}{7}$$

From the equation $\pi = \frac{C}{d}$, you can derive two formulas for finding the circumference of a circle.

To find the circumference of a circle with diameter d, use the formula $C = \pi d$.

To find the circumference of a circle with radius r, use the formula $C = 2\pi r$.

Examples

a. Find the circumference of the circle. Use 3.14 for π.

$C = \pi d$

$\approx 3.14 \cdot 9$ m

≈ 28.26 m

9 m

The circumference is approximately 28.26 m.

b. Find the circumference of the circle. Use $\frac{22}{7}$ for π.

$C = 2\pi r$

$\approx 2 \cdot \dfrac{22}{7} \cdot 3\frac{1}{2}$ in.

$\approx \dfrac{2}{1} \cdot \dfrac{22}{7} \cdot \dfrac{7}{2}$ in.

≈ 22 in.

$3\frac{1}{2}$ in.

The circumference is approximately 22 in.

☑ SKILL CHECK

Find the circumference of each circle. Use 3.14 for π.

1. $d = 7$ cm

2. $r = 2$ m

3. $d = 16.5$ mm

Building on a method of representing the illusion of infinity that he discovered through an earlier work entitled Circle Limit 1, *M. C. Escher masterfully creates this pattern of interlocking animals, appropriately entitled* Smaller and Smaller.

Find the circumference of each circle. Use $\frac{22}{7}$ for π.

4. $d = 14$ m **5.** $r = 3\frac{1}{2}$ in. **6.** $d = 17\frac{1}{2}$ ft.

Exercises

Find the circumference of each circle. Use 3.14 for π.

1.
5 m

2.
12 cm

3.
8 mm

4.
20 cm

5. $d = 9$ cm **6.** $r = 5$ km **7.** $d = 14$ m **8.** $r = 11$ mm

9. $r = 2.5$ m **10.** $d = 3.7$ cm **11.** $r = 6.1$ m **12.** $d = 14.8$ in.

Find the circumference of each circle. Use $\frac{22}{7}$ for π.

13. $d = 7$ cm **14.** $r = 17\frac{1}{2}$ in. **15.** $r = 28$ m **16.** $d = 10\frac{1}{2}$ ft.

Perimeter • Area • Volume

Find the distance around each of the figures. Use 3.14 for π.

17.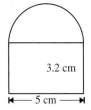

3.2 cm

5 cm

18.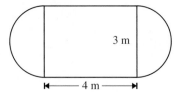

3 m

4 m

Application

Solve. Use 3.14 for π.

19. The glass mirror of the great Hale telescope on Mount Palomar in California is 200 inches in diameter. What is the circumference of this mirror?

20. A wheel has a radius of 35 cm. How many centimeters does the bicycle travel when the wheel revolves five times?

13.5 Area of Circles

Dottie is making a circular flower bed. If the circle has a radius of 5 feet, how much area will the flower bed cover?

To discover the formula for finding the area of a circle, you can use your knowledge about the circumference of a circle and the area of a parallelogram.

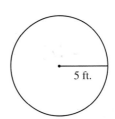

5 ft.

STEP 1	**STEP 2**
Divide a circle with radius r into 8 equal parts.	Rearrange the parts to form a curved "parallelogram."

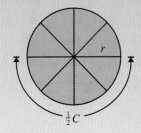

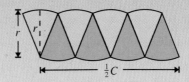

The base is $\frac{1}{2}$ the circumference (C).

The height is the length of the radius (r).

Observe that the area of the circle is equal to the area of the curved "parallelogram."

area of circle $= b \cdot h$

$$= \left(\frac{1}{2} C\right) \cdot r \qquad \blacktriangleleft b = \frac{1}{2}C$$

$$= \frac{1}{2}(2\pi\, r) \cdot r \qquad \blacktriangleleft C = 2\pi\, r$$

$$= \pi \cdot r \cdot r$$
$$= \pi\, r^2$$

So, the formula for the area of a circle is $A = \pi\, r^2$.

Examples

a. Find the area of the circular flower bed. Use 3.14 for π.

$A = \pi\, r^2$
$\quad = 3.14 \times 5^2$
$\quad = 3.14 \times 25$
$\quad = 78.5$
The area is 78.5 ft.^{2}

5 ft.

b. Find the area of a circle with a diameter of 28 cm. Use $\frac{22}{7}$ for π.

$A = \pi\, r^2$

$\quad = \dfrac{22}{7} \times 14^2$

$\quad = \dfrac{22}{7} \times 196$

$\quad = 616$
The area is 616 cm^2.

28 cm

☑ SKILL CHECK

Complete.

1. $A = 3.14 \times \square^2$

3 cm

2. $A = 3.14 \times \square^2$

10 m

Find the area of each circle. Use 3.14 for π.

3. $r = 6$ cm

4. $d = 20$ mm

5. $r = 2.5$ m

Exercises

Find the area of each circle. Use 3.14 for π.

1.

2 in.

2.

5 m

3.

1.5 m

4.

8 mm

5.

1.2 cm

6.

3.4 m

7. $r = 9$ mm

8. $d = 12$ in.

9. $r = 0.5$ km

10. $d = 30$ m

11. $r = 3.1$ cm

12. $d = 0.8$ m

Find the area of each circle. Use $\frac{22}{7}$ for π.

13. $r = 7$ ft.

14. $d = 28$ m

15. $r = 21$ cm

Find the area of each shaded region. Use 3.14 for π.

16.
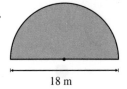
18 m

17.
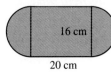
16 cm
20 cm

18.

3 in.
5 in.

Application

19. What is the area of a circular skating rink with a radius of 30 feet?

20. Larry brought a 16-inch pizza to the party. Mike brought two 10-inch pizzas. Who brought more pizza? How much more?

M.C. Escher is probably best known for his lithographs of physical impossibilities. Waterfall *is fun to study as a two-dimensional drawing; however, this scene would be impossible to build as a three-dimensional model.*

13.6 Three-Dimensional Figures

A geometric figure whose points do not all lie in the same plane is called a ***three-dimensional figure.*** A three-dimensional figure has length, width, and height.

Three dimensional figures that have flat faces shaped like polygons are called ***polyhedrons.*** The intersection of two faces of a polyhedron is called an ***edge.*** Three or more edges intersect at points called ***vertices.***

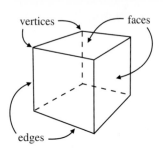

A ***prism*** is a polyhedron with at least two congruent and parallel faces called ***bases.*** The other faces are parallelograms. Prisms are named according to the shapes of their bases. Consider the following prisms.

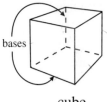

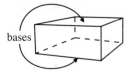

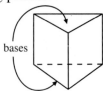

cube   rectangular prism   triangular prism

A *pyramid* is a polyhedron with only one base. The base can be any polygon. The faces of a pyramid are triangles. Pyramids are also named according to the shapes of their bases. Consider the following pyramids.

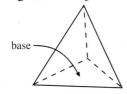

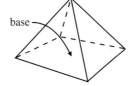

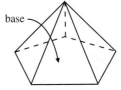

triangular pyramid   rectangular pyramid   pentagonal pyramid

Other three-dimensional figures have curved surfaces. These are not polyhedrons. Consider the following examples.

cylinder   cone   sphere

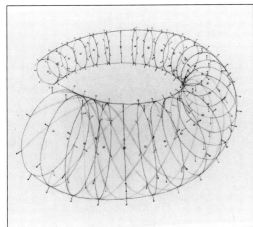

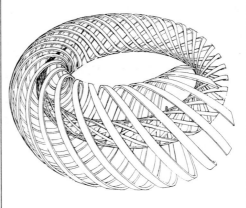

Two preliminary sketches Escher did for studies of spirals. He set himself a particularly difficult task by making the spirals form a spiral tube that turns in upon itself.

Perimeter • Area • Volume

☑SKILL CHECK

Name each figure. Write the number of faces, edges, and vertices.

1.

2.

3.

Exercises

Write the name for each three-dimensional figure.

1.

2.

3.

4.

5.

6.

7.

8.

9.

Complete the table below.

	Polygon	Number of Faces	Number of Edges	Number of Vertices
10.	cube			
11.	rectangular prism			
12.	rectangular pyramid			
13.	triangular prism			
14.	triangular pyramid			

Write true or false.

15. A cube is a prism.

16. A triangular prism has 6 faces.

17. All the faces of a pyramid are triangles.

18. The two bases of a cylinder may be different sizes.

19. A rectangular prism has three pairs of congruent faces.

Application

20. Randy is making models of geometric solids out of poster board. Choose the pattern below that he can fold to make a triangular prism.

a.
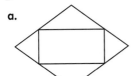

b.

c.
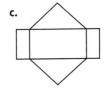

Perimeter ● Area ● Volume

13.7 Surface Area of Prisms and Pyramids

Robin is wrapping a birthday present for her brother. How much paper will it take to cover the surface of the box?

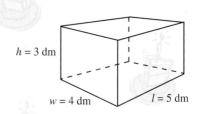

To determine the amount of paper that she needs, Robin must find the *surface area* of the box (a rectangular prism).

The *surface area* of the geometric solid is the sum of the areas of the faces that make up the figure.

To find the surface area of a rectangular prism, you find the sum of the areas of its rectangular faces.

$$\text{Surface Area } (S) = \begin{array}{c}\text{area of top}\\\text{and bottom}\end{array} + \begin{array}{c}\text{area of front}\\\text{and back}\end{array} + \begin{array}{c}\text{area of}\\\text{sides}\end{array}$$

$$= \quad 2(l \cdot w) \quad + \quad 2(l \cdot h) \quad + \quad 2(w \cdot h)$$

You can use this formula to find the surface area in the introductory problem.

$$\begin{aligned}S &= 2(l \cdot w) + 2(l \cdot h) + 2(w \cdot h)\\ &= 2(5 \cdot 4) + 2(5 \cdot 3) + 2(4 \cdot 3)\\ &= 2 \times (20) + 2 \times (15) + 2 \times (12)\\ &= 40 + 30 + 24\\ &= 94\end{aligned}$$

Robin will need 94 dm^2 of paper to cover the box.

To find the surface area of a square pyramid, you find the sum of the area of the square base and four times the area of a triangular face. Study the following example.

Surface area $(S) = s^2 + 4\left(\dfrac{1}{2}bh\right)$

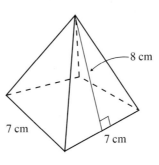

$\qquad = 7^2 + 4\left(\dfrac{1}{2} \cdot 7 \cdot 8\right)$

$\qquad = 49 + 4(28)$

$\qquad = 49 + 112$

$\qquad = 161$

The surface area of the square pyramid is 161 cm^2.

☑ **SKILL CHECK**

Find the surface area of each.

1.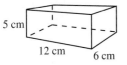

2.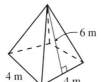

3.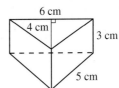

Exercises

Find the surface area of each.

1.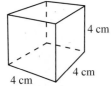

2.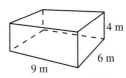

3.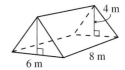

Perimeter • Area • Volume

4.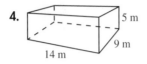
5 m
9 m
14 m

5.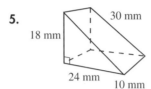
30 mm
18 mm
24 mm
10 mm

6.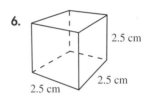
2.5 cm
2.5 cm
2.5 cm

7.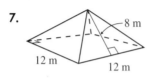
8 m
12 m
12 m

8.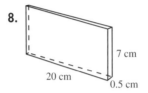
7 cm
20 cm
0.5 cm

9.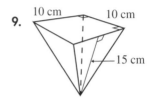
10 cm
10 cm
15 cm

Application

10. Mr. Stephens is building a dollhouse out of plywood. The dimensions are given in the drawing on the right. Including the floor, how much plywood will he use?

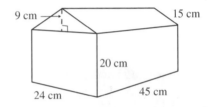
9 cm
15 cm
20 cm
24 cm
45 cm

13.8 Volume of Prisms

The amount of space contained in a three-dimensional figure is called its *volume.*

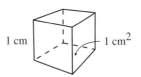

The volume of a cube which has a base with an area of 1 cm^2 and a height of 1 cm is 1 *cubic centimeter* (1 cm^3).

Volume is always measured in cubic units.

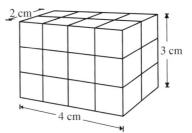

What is the volume of the rectangular prism on the right?

Each layer of the rectangular prism contains 4×2, or 8 cm^3. The volume of the prism is 8 cm$^3 \times 3$ (layers) or 24 cm^3.

You can also find the volume of a rectangular prism by using the following general formula.

Volume (V) = area of base (B) $\times$ height of prism (h).

Consider the following example, which applies this formula to find the volume of the rectangular prism above.

$$V = Bh$$
$$= (4 \times 2) \times 3 \blacktriangleleft B = l \times w$$
$$= 24$$

The volume of the rectangular prism is 24 cm^3.

You can use the formula $V = Bh$ to find the volume of any prism. What is the volume of the triangular prism below?

$$V = Bh \qquad \blacktriangleleft B = \text{area of triangular base; } h = \text{height of prism.}$$

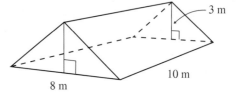

$$= \left(\frac{1}{2} \cdot 8 \cdot 3 \right) \times 10$$
$$= 12 \times 10$$
$$= 120$$

The area of the rectangular prism is 120 m^3.

☑ SKILL CHECK

Find the volume of each prism.

1.
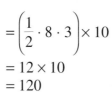
3 cm
3 cm 3 cm

2.
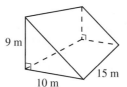
9 m
10 m 15 m

3.
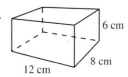
6 cm
12 cm 8 cm

Exercises

Find the volume of each prism.

1.
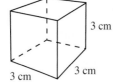

8 cm
8 cm 8 cm

2.
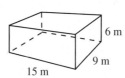
6 m
15 m 9 m

3.
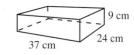
9 cm
37 cm 24 cm

4.
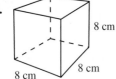

7 m
9 m 12 m

5.
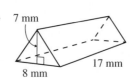
7 mm
8 mm 17 mm

6.
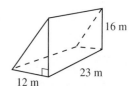
16 m
12 m 23 m

7. triangular prism

$B = 42 \text{ cm}^2$

$h = 18 \text{ cm}$

8. triangular prism

$B = 120 \text{ m}^2$

$h = 13.6 \text{ m}$

9. rectangular prism

$l = 12 \text{ cm}$

$w = 8 \text{ cm}$

$h = 6 \text{ cm}$

10. rectangular prism

$l = 19 \text{ m}$

$w = 16.7 \text{ m}$

$h = 5 \text{ m}$

Solve.

11. A triangular prism has a height of 2 m and a volume of 24 m^3. What is the area of its base?

12. A rectangular prism has a base that measures 4 cm by 7 cm. The volume of the prism is 308 cm^3. What is its height?

13. The volume of a rectangular prism is 312 cm^3. If its length is 8 cm and its height is 13 cm, what is its width?

Application

14. A swimming pool is 5 m wide, 10 m long, and 3 m deep. What is the volume of the pool?

15. Steven sold an aquarium that was 30 cm long, 20 cm wide, and 25 cm high. He bought another tank that was twice as long, wide, and high. What was the volume of his new aquarium?

Perimeter • Area • Volume

Problem Solving: Divide and Conquer

To solve complex word problems, you can use the strategy "Divide and Conquer." With this strategy, you divide the problem into parts, complete each part, and then combine the results to find the solution.

Study the following example.

A department store had 98 coats with a price tag of $89.95. A total of 27 coats were sold at this regular price. The remaining coats were reduced in price by $22.49 and then sold. How much money did the department store receive from the sale of all these coats?

Four-Point Check List

1 READ to understand the question and identify the needed data.

2 PLAN what to do to solve the problem.

3 SOLVE the problem by carrying out the plan.

4 CHECK to make sure the solution is reasonable.

1. READ: Understand the question.
   - What was the total amount of money received from the sale of all 98 coats?

   Identify the needed data.
   - 27 coats were sold at $89.95.
   - The remaining coats were reduced in price by $22.49 and then sold.

2. PLAN: Use the strategy "Divide and Conquer."

3. SOLVE: Divide the problem into parts, solve the parts, and then combine the results.
    A. Find the amount received from the coats sold at the original price.
        $89.95 × 27 = $2,428.65
    B. Find the amount received from the coats sold at the reduced price.

    1. 98 − 27 = 71   **2.** $89.95 − $22.49 = $67.46   **3.** $67.46 × 71 = $4,789.66

    C. Find the total by adding the amounts.
        $2,428.65 + $4,789.66 = $7,218.31

    The department store received $7,218.31 from the coats.

4. CHECK: Is the solution reasonable?
            Estimate the answer.

    1. 30 × $90 = $2,700   **2.** 70 × $70 = $4,900   **3.** $2,700 + $4,900 = $7,600

    The estimate is in line with the answer; so the solution is reasonable.

☑SKILL CHECK

Divide and Conquer. Solve.

1. Jane purchased 3 rolls of film for $4.59 per roll. She paid $5.75 to have each roll of film developed. What was her total cost for these pictures?

2. Randy purchased a bicycle for $485. He could have bought it on the installment plan for $48.50 down and $39 per month for 12 months. How much did Randy save by paying cash for the bicycle?

Exercises

Divide and Conquer. Solve.

1. A bicycle shop had 72 bicycles with a price tag of $149.95. Before Christmas, they reduced the price by $22.49 and sold 49 of the bicycles. The rest of the bicycles were sold at the original price. How much money did the bicycle shop receive from the sale of these bicycles?

2. The train ride from Miami to Sun Beach is 482 miles. A train traveled for 2 hours at a speed of 55 mph and for 3 hours at 60 mph. If the train could go 64 mph, how long would it take to complete the remainder of the trip?

Mixed Review

Solve.

3. Jenny wants to triple a recipe for muffins. If the recipe calls for $1\frac{2}{3}$ cups of flour, how much flour should Jenny use?

4. In the school cafeteria, there are small square tables that seat 4 people. When two tables are placed end to end, 6 people can be seated. If 6 tables are placed end to end, how many people can be seated?

5. At Calvary Christian school, 91 of the 140 students ride to school in a car pool. What percent of the students is this?

6. A certain number is added to 8. When the sum is multiplied by 3, the result is 39. What is the number?

7. A circular rug has a diameter of 3 m. What is the area of the rug? Use $\pi = 3.14$.

Perimeter • Area • Volume

8. Debbie spent $126 on a shopping spree. She bought a coat for $89.75 and a skirt for $23.88. The rest of the money was spent on a blouse. How much did Debbie pay for the blouse?

9. Dan is building a fence around his rectangular backyard. The yard is 30 feet long and 18 feet wide. If the fence cost $22.95 for an 8-foot section, how much will it cost Dan to purchase the fence?

10. The admission price for an adult to a home and garden show is $4.50. Mr. Pedrosa paid $12.50 to get into the show with his wife and 2 children. What was the admission price for a child?

Chapter 13 Review

13.1 Find the perimeter of each figure.

1.

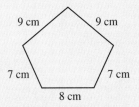

9 cm 9 cm 7 cm 7 cm 8 cm

2.

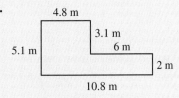

4.8 m 3.1 m 6 m 5.1 m 2 m 10.8 m

3. Find the perimeter of a rectangle with $l = 13.8$ cm and $w = 7.4$ cm.

4. A regular pentagon has a perimeter of 65 cm. Find the length of each side.

13.2 Find the area of each rectangle or square.

5. $l = 17$ m
   $w = 8$ m

6. $s = 9.2$ cm

Find the area of each shaded region.

7.

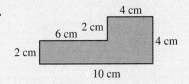

4 cm 2 cm 6 cm 4 cm 2 cm 2 cm 10 cm

8.

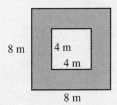

8 m 4 m 4 m 8 m

13.3 Find the area of each figure.

9.

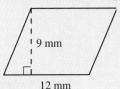

9 mm 12 mm

10.

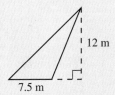

12 m 7.5 m

11.

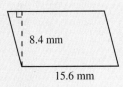

8.4 mm 15.6 mm

12. A parallelogram has a base of 18 cm and an area of 126 cm^2. What is the height of the parallelogram?

13.4 Find the circumference of each circle. Use 3.14 for π.

13. $d = 4$ m

14. $r = 9$ cm

Perimeter • Area • Volume

15. Find the circumference of a circle with a diameter of 14 ft. Use $\frac{22}{7}$ for π.

13.5 Find the area of each circle. Use 3.14 for π.

16. $r = 4$ cm **17.** $d = 11$ m

18. Find the area of a circle with a radius of 7 cm. Use $\frac{22}{7}$ for π.

13.6 Name each three-dimensional figure.

19. **20.** 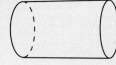 **21.**

22. Write the number of faces, edges, and vertices of a rectangular pyramid.

13.7 Find the surface area of each figure.

23. 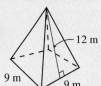 **24.** 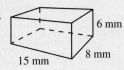 **25.**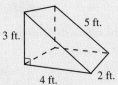

13.8 Find the volume of each prism.

26. 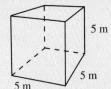 **27.** 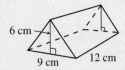 **28.**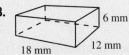

Chapter 13 Cumulative Review

1. Find the ratio equal to "7:5."
   - **a.** 14:10
   - **b.** 21:16
   - **c.** 10:14
   - **d.** not given

2. Solve. 5 is to 9 as 15 is to n.
   - **a.** 18
   - **b.** 27
   - **c.** 36
   - **d.** not given

3. Find the lowest-term fraction for 84%.
   - **a.** $\frac{42}{50}$
   - **b.** $\frac{21}{25}$
   - **c.** $\frac{7}{8}$
   - **d.** not given

4. Choose the percent for 1.25.
   - **a.** $1\frac{1}{4}\%$
   - **b.** 25%
   - **c.** 125%
   - **d.** not given

5. Write $\frac{3}{8}$ as a percent.
   - **a.** $\frac{3}{8}\%$
   - **b.** 37.5%
   - **c.** 38%
   - **d.** not given

6. Find 75% of 96.
   - **a.** 24
   - **b.** 72
   - **c.** 48
   - **d.** not given

7. Find the total cost.
   CD player: $125
   sales tax: 5%
   - **a.** $6.25
   - **b.** $130
   - **c.** $131.25
   - **d.** not given

8. Find the interest.
   bank deposit: $900
   interest rate: 4%; time: 2 years
   - **a.** $7.20
   - **b.** $72
   - **c.** $720
   - **d.** not given

9. Solve. $70\% \times n = 140$
   - **a.** 2
   - **b.** 20
   - **c.** 200
   - **d.** not given

10. Find the commission.
    total sales: $960
    commission rate: 8%
    - **a.** $76.80
    - **b.** $7.68
    - **c.** $768
    - **d.** not given

11. Find the integers written in order from least to greatest.
    - **a.** $^-2, 0, 3, ^-4$
    - **b.** $^-2, ^-4, 0, 3$
    - **c.** $^-4, ^-2, 0, 3$
    - **d.** not given

12. Add. $^-5 + ^-9$
    - **a.** $^-14$
    - **b.** 14
    - **c.** $^-4$
    - **d.** not given

13. Add. $^-17 + 9$
    - **a.** 8
    - **b.** $^-8$
    - **c.** $^-26$
    - **d.** not given

14. Subtract. $3 - ^-8$
    - **a.** $^-5$
    - **b.** 11
    - **c.** $^-11$
    - **d.** not given

15. Multiply. $^-5 \times ^-12$
    - **a.** $^-60$
    - **b.** $^-17$
    - **c.** 60
    - **d.** not given

Perimeter • Area • Volume

CHARLES DREW
BLOOD TRANSFUSIONS

1904-1950

Charles Drew was an outstanding athlete at Amherst College in the mid-1920s. In fact, he was much more interested in athletics than in his studies. This was true until he enrolled in a biology class. Inspired by his love of biology, Charles decided to become a doctor.

After saving enough money to pay for his medical education, Charles moved to Montreal, Canada, and enrolled in McGill University's medical college. While at McGill, Charles was an excellent student. He earned his doctorate in medicine and a Master of Surgery degree as well. Upon graduation, he accepted a position as a pathology instructor at Howard University's medical college.

While completing research for a second doctorate, Charles developed an interest in the area of blood transfusions. Curious about the ability to store blood over a period of time, he learned that plasma, the clear liquid in which red and white blood cells are suspended, could be stored longer than whole blood. It was this discovery that encouraged doctors to use plasma in blood transfusions. Charles later developed a "bank" in which to store large amounts of plasma.

With the start of World War II, Charles was able to devote himself full-time to plasma research. It was his idea to send dried plasma overseas to British and French military doctors for use in battlefield hospitals. Charles also helped to establish blood banks in the United States and England. These banks provided the blood which was badly needed to save the lives of thousands of servicemen.

When the American Red Cross asked Charles to direct its plasma bank for U.S. soldiers, he readily accepted the invitation. However, Charles later resigned the position as a result of a dispute over the way that they labeled the blood. At that time, the Red Cross had a policy of differentiating between blood drawn from whites and blacks.

Charles bitterly objected to this policy. He firmly believed that blood should be separated according to type, A, B, or O, and not according to skin color. Red Cross officials openly admitted that Charles's position was scientifically correct, and that their policy was actually a reflection of the prejudice which permeated American society at that time.

In 1949 Charles became a consultant for the surgeon general. The following year, while traveling to give a speech at Alabama's Tuskegee Institute, Charles fell asleep at the wheel and wrecked his car just outside of Burlington, North Carolina. Contrary to popular opinion that Charles was denied treatment at an all-white hospital and died

MEASUREMENT

while on the way to the black hospital across town, the white hospital he was taken to did all that it could to save him; but his injuries were too severe.

Throughout his life, Charles was known for his charming personality. He possessed a sense of humor which did much to endear him to his patients. However, he is best remembered for his research with plasma and blood transfusions. This work has saved millions of lives throughout the years, both in war and in peacetime.

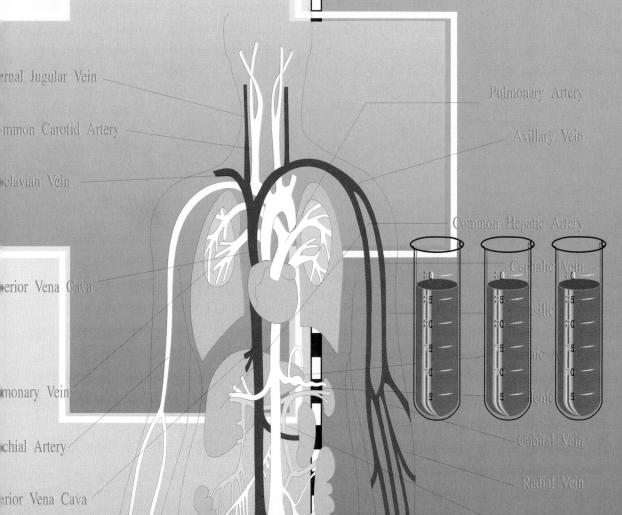

rnal Jugular Vein

mmon Carotid Artery

clavian Vein

Pulmonary Artery

Axillary Vein

Common Hepatic Artery

Cephalic Vein

erior Vena Cava

monary Vein

chial Artery

rior Vena Cava

silic

nic

enic

Cubital Vein

Radial Vein

14.1 Metric Units of Length

In the metric system, the basic unit of length is the **meter (m).** A baseball bat is about 1 m long.

The other metric units of length are related to the meter. The relationships between the units are based on powers of 10. Study the table below.

Unit	Symbol	Relation to the meter
kilometer	km	1000 m
hectometer	hm	100 m
dekameter	dkm	10 m
meter	m	1 m
decimeter	dm	0.1 m
centimeter	cm	0.01 m
millimeter	mm	0.001 m

The kilometer (km) is used to measure long distances.

One **kilometer:** about the length of five city blocks

The centimeter (cm) and millimeter (mm) are used to measure shorter lengths.

One **centimeter:** about the width of a paper clip

One **millimeter:** about the thickness of a dime

☑SKILL CHECK

Choose km, m, cm, or mm as the most likely unit of measure.

1. the distance across Indiana

2. the length of a soccer field

3. the diameter of a penny

4. the width of a sheet of paper

Write the missing unit.

5. 1000 m = 1 ___

Write the missing number.

6. 1 dkm = ___ m

Exercises

Choose km, m, cm, or mm as the most likely unit of measure.

1. length of your index finger

2. height of a door

3. thickness of a quarter

4. distance from Los Angeles to Chicago

Choose the best estimate.

5. length of a shoe   **a.** 24 mm   **b.** 24 cm   **c.** 0.24 dm

6. height of a bedroom ceiling   **a.** 3 mm   **b.** 3 cm   **c.** 3 m

7. distance of a cross-country race   **a.** 5 km   **b.** 5 hm   **c.** 5 dkm

Measurement

8. width of a   **a.** 9 mm   **b.** 9 cm   **c.** 9 dm
    post card

9. length of a   **a.** 13 mm   **b.** 13 cm   **c.** 13 m
    calculator

10. width of a   **a.** 7 mm   **b.** 7 cm   **c.** 7 dm
    pencil

11. length of a   **a.** 1 dkm   **b.** 1 hm   **c.** 1 km
    soccer field

Write the missing units.

12. 10 dm = 1 ____   **13.** 1000 ____ = 1 m

14. 0.01 m = 1 ____   **15.** 0.001 ____ = 1 mm

Write the missing numbers.

16. 1 hm = ____ m   **17.** ____ cm = 0.01 m

18. 1000 m = ____ km   **19.** ____ m = 1 hm

Use the ruler below for exercises 20-25.

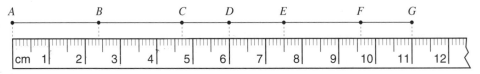

Write the measure of each line segment to the nearest millimeter (mm).

20. $\overline{AG}$ **21.** $\overline{AC}$ **22.** $\overline{AE}$

Write the measure of each line segment to the nearest centimeter (cm).

23. $\overline{AB}$ **24.** $\overline{AD}$ **25.** $\overline{AF}$

Application

26. Benjamin ran 1.5 km in an event at a track meet. How many meters did he run?

14.2 Renaming Metric Units of Length

Study the metric units of length listed in the following table.

kilometer (km)	hectometer (hm)	dekameter (dkm)	meter (m)	decimeter (dm)	centimeter (cm)	millimeter (mm)
1 km = 1000 m	1 hm = 100 m	1 dkm = 10 m	1 m	1 dm = 0.1 m	1 cm = 0.01 m	1 mm = 0.001 m

To rename metric units of length in larger or smaller units, you multiply or divide by a power of 10. Study the diagram below.

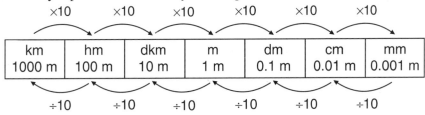

To rename a larger unit as a smaller unit, you multiply by a power of 10.

$7 \text{ m} = \underline{\hphantom{000}} \text{ cm}$

$7 \times 100 = 7\underline{00}$ ◄ Multiply by 10^2, or 100.

So, 7 m = 700 cm

To rename a smaller unit as a larger unit, you divide by a power of 10.

$360 \text{ mm} = \underline{\hphantom{000}} \text{ m}$

$360 \div 1{,}000 = 0.\underline{360}$ ◄ Divide by 10^3, or 1,000.

So, 360 mm = 0.36 m

Additional Examples

Complete.

a. $9.2 \text{ hm} = \underline{\hphantom{000}} \text{ dkm}$

$9.2 \times 10 = 9\underline{2}$

So, 9.2 hm = 92 dkm

b. $13.4 \text{ dm} = \underline{\hphantom{000}} \text{ hm}$

$13.4 \div 1{,}000 = 0.0\underline{134}$

So, 13.4 dm = 0.0134 hm

☑ SKILL CHECK

Complete.

1. $17 \text{ cm} = \underline{\hphantom{000}} \text{ m}$

2. $3.2 \text{ m} = \underline{\hphantom{000}} \text{ dm}$

3. $0.8 \text{ km} = \underline{\hphantom{000}} \text{ dkm}$

Measurement

Compare. Use >, <, or =.

4. 3 dm ☐ 3 dkm   **5.** 45 cm ☐ 0.45 m   **6.** 0.19 hm ☐ 1.9 m

Exercises

Rename each length in meters.

1. 178 cm   **2.** 2.4 km   **3.** 9.53 hm

Rename each length in centimeters.

4. 3.75 m   **5.** 8.6 dkm   **6.** 48 mm

Rename each length in kilometers.

7. 908 m   **8.** 200,000 mm   **9.** 83 hm

Rename each length in millimeters.

10. 2 dm   **11.** 4.7 cm   **12.** 0.09 m

Complete.

13. 0.416 km = ___ m   **14.** 5 cm = ___ m

15. 8.9 m = ___ dm   **16.** 73 mm = ___ cm

17. 1.4 hm = ___ m   **18.** 0.25 cm = ___ dkm

19. 3 dm = ___ mm   **20.** 50 m = ___ dkm

Complete. Use >, <, or =.

21. 2 m ☐ 2 hm   **22.** 300 cm ☐ 30 dm

23. 750 mm ☐ 7.5 cm   **24.** 0.37 hm ☐ 3.7 m

25. 9 cm ☐ 0.09 dkm   **26.** 275 mm ☐ 2.75 dm

Application

27. Mary lives a distance of 1.7 km from the church. Her friend Anneliese lives 1450 m from the church. Who lives closer to the church? How much closer?

In addition to the ABO system of blood grouping, Charles Drew also researched how to group blood according to its Rh factor. This process is very important in matching a blood donor and recipient, especially when the recipient is a pregnant woman.

14.3 Metric Units of Capacity and Mass

The amount of fluid that a container will hold is called its *capacity.* In the metric system, the basic unit of capacity is the *liter (L).* Smaller capacities are measured in *milliliters (ml),* and larger capacities are measured in *kiloliters (kl).*

Study the relationships between the units of capacity in the table below.

Unit	Relationship	Example
Milliliter (ml)—a thousandth of a liter	1 ml = 0.001 L 1000 ml = 1 L	A few drops of water are about 1 ml.
Liter (L)—a thousand milliliters	1 L = 1000 ml 0.001 L = 1 ml	A pitcher of milk that fills about 4 drinking glasses holds about 1 L.
Kiloliter (kl)—a thousand liters	1 kl = 1000 L 0.001 kl = 1 L	A hot tub that measures 1 m long, 1 m wide, and 1 m high holds 1 kl.

The amount of matter in an object is called its *mass.* In the metric system, the *kilogram (kg)* is the unit of mass used to weigh heavy objects. Lighter objects are weighed in *grams (g)* and *milligrams (mg).* The *metric ton (t)* is used to weigh very heavy objects.

Measurement

Study the relationships between the units of capacity in the table below.

Unit	Relationship	Example
Milligram (mg)—a thousandth of a gram	1 mg = 0.001 g 1000 mg = 1 g	A few grains of sand weigh about 1 mg.
gram (g)—a thousand milligrams	0.001 g = 1 mg 1 g = 1000 mg	A paper clip weighs about 1 g.
kilogram (kg)—a thousand grams	1 kg = 1000 g 0.001 kg = 1g	Two textbooks weigh about 1 kg.
metric ton (t)—a thousand kilograms	1 t = 1000 kg 0.001 t = 1 kg	A small car weighs about 1 t.

☑**SKILL CHECK**

Complete.

1. 2 L = ___ ml

2. ___ L = 5 kl

3. 7000 ml = ___ L

4. 3 g = ___ mg

5. 15000 mg = ___ g

6. ___ t = 6000 kg

Exercises

Choose the best estimate for the capacity of each.

1. a teaspoon	a. 5 ml	b. 0.5 ml	c. 50 ml
2. a bottle of medicine	a. 1.5 ml	b. 15 ml	c. 150 ml
3. a car's gas tank	a. 40 L	b. 400 ml	c. 4 kl
4. a glass of milk	a. 25 L	b. 250 ml	c. 2.5 kl
5. a pot of coffee	a. 9.5 L	b. 950 ml	c. 95 kl
6. water in a swimming pool	a. 100 L	b. 1000 ml	c. 100,000 kl

Complete.

7. $12000 \text{ ml} = \underline{\hspace{1cm}} \text{ L}$ 8. $8 \text{ L} = \underline{\hspace{1cm}} \text{ ml}$ 9. $7000 \text{ L} = \underline{\hspace{1cm}} \text{ kl}$

10. $\underline{\hspace{1cm}} \text{ L} = 19000 \text{ ml}$ 11. $2 \text{ kl} = \underline{\hspace{1cm}} \text{ L}$ 12. $\underline{\hspace{1cm}} \text{ kl} = 6200 \text{ L}$

Choose the best estimate for the mass of each.

13. an aspirin	**a.** 150 mg	**b.** 50 g	**c.** 5 kg
14. a football	**a.** 5000 mg	**b.** 500 g	**c.** 5 kg
15. an apple	**a.** 28 mg	**b.** 280 g	**c.** 2.8 kg
16. a hardback book	**a.** 1 kg	**b.** 10 g	**c.** 100 mg
17. a straight pin	**a.** 300 mg	**b.** 30 g	**c.** 3 kg
18. a bowling ball	**a.** 800 mg	**b.** 80 g	**c.** 8 kg

Complete.

19. $13000 \text{ mg} = \underline{\hspace{1cm}} \text{ g}$ 20. $7 \text{ t} = \underline{\hspace{1cm}} \text{ kg}$ 21. $4 \text{ g} = \underline{\hspace{1cm}} \text{ mg}$

22. $9 \text{ kg} = \underline{\hspace{1cm}} \text{ g}$ 23. $\underline{\hspace{1cm}} \text{ mg} = 17 \text{ g}$ 24. $\underline{\hspace{1cm}} \text{ t} = 9000 \text{ kg}$

Application

Choose liter (L) or milliliter (ml) to measure each.

25. the juice from a lemon   26. a large pitcher of lemonade

Measurement

Choose milligram (mg), gram (g), kilogram (kg), or metric ton (t) to measure each.

27. a few grains of salt

28. a hot dog bun

29. ten soccer players

30. a pumpkin

14.4 Customary Units of Length

On a baseball diamond, the distance between first and second base is 30 yards. How many feet are there in 30 yards?

You use the relationships between the units to rename customary units of length. Study the following table of commonly used units of length.

Unit	Symbol	Relationship Between Units
inch	in.	12 in. = 1 ft.
foot	ft.	3 ft. = 1 yd.
yard	yd.	1,760 yd. = 1 mi.
mile	mi.	5,280 ft. = 1 mi.

To rename a larger unit as a smaller unit, multiply.

$$30 \text{ yd.} = \underline{\quad} \text{ ft.} \qquad\qquad 30 \text{ yards} = 30 \times 1 \text{ yard}$$
$$= 90 \text{ ft.} \qquad\qquad\qquad\qquad = 30 \times 3 \text{ ft.} \blacktriangleleft 1 \text{ yd.} = 3 \text{ ft.}$$
$$= 90 \text{ ft.}$$

The distance between first and second base is 90 ft.

To rename a smaller unit as a larger unit, divide.

45 in. = ___ ft.   45 inches = $45 \div 1$ ft.

$\quad = 3\frac{3}{4}$ ft. $= 45 \div 12$ in. ◀ 1 ft. = 12 in.

$\qquad\qquad\qquad\qquad\qquad = 3\frac{9}{12}$ ft.   ◀ Simplify.

$\qquad\qquad\qquad\qquad\qquad = 3\frac{3}{4}$ ft.

You can add or subtract customary units of length. Study the following examples.

Additional Examples

a. Add.   **b.** Subtract.

7 ft. 5 in.   14 yd. 1 ft. =   13 yd. 4 ft.
+ 2 ft. 11 in.   − 8 yd. 2 ft.   − 8 yd. 2 ft.
9 ft. 16 in. ◀ 16 in. = 1 ft. 4 in.   5 yd. 2 ft.
9 ft. + 1 ft. 4 in. = 10 ft. 4 in.

☑ **SKILL CHECK**

Complete.

1. 5 ft. = ___ in.   **2.** 7 ft. = ___ yd.   **3.** $\frac{1}{4}$ mi. = ___ ft.

Add or subtract.

4.   4 ft. 9 in.   **5.**   8 ft. 6 in.   **6.**   2 yd. 1 ft. 7 in.
      + 3 ft. 7 in.   − 3 ft. 9 in.   + 1 yd. 1 ft. 8 in.

Exercises

Choose the most likely customary measurement.

1. the width of   **a.** 28 in.   **b.** 28 mi.   **c.** 28 ft.
      a house

2. the height of   **a.** 1 yd.   **b.** 10 ft.   **c.** 100 in.
      a desk

3. the length of   **a.** 1 yd.   **b.** 6 in.   **c.** 3 ft.
      a pencil

Measurement

Complete.

4. 7 ft. = ___ in.

5. 5 yd. = ___ ft.

6. 72 in. = ___ yd.

7. 3 mi. = ___ ft.

8. 6 ft. 7 in. = ___ in.

9. 96 in. = ___ ft.

10. $5\frac{3}{4}$ ft. = ___ in.

11. 16 in. = ___ ft.

12. $\frac{3}{8}$ mi. = ___ ft.

13. 11 ft. = ___ yd.

14. 3,520 yd. = ___ mi.

15. 32 ft. = ___ yd. ___ ft.

Add or subtract.

16.   3 ft. 8 in.
    + 5 ft. 3 in.

17.   4 yd.
    − 1 yd. 2 ft.

18.   5 ft. 10 in.
    + 2 ft.   8 in.

19.   9 yd. 1 ft.
    − 4 yd. 2 ft.

20.   4 ft. 8 in.
    + 3 ft. 9 in.

21.   1 yd. 1 ft. 5 in.
    + 3 yd. 2 ft. 9 in.

22.   7 yd. 1 ft. 3 in.
    − 5 yd. 2 ft. 4 in.

23.   5 yd. 1 ft. 10 in.
    + 3 yd. 1 ft.   3 in.

24.   4 yd. 2 ft. 7 in.
    − 1 yd. 2 ft. 9 in.

Application

25. A football field is 100 yards long. Each end zone is 10 yards long. If you include the playing field and the end zones, how many feet long is a football field?

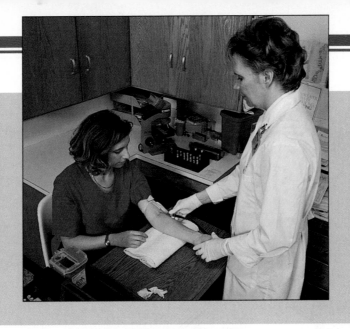

Blood accounts for about 8% of a person's body weight. An average-sized male has a blood volume of 5 to 6 liters (5 to 6 quarts), and an average-sized female has a blood volume of 4 to 5 liters.

14.5 Customary Units of Capacity and Weight

Recall that the amount of fluid a container will hold is called its capacity. Study the customary units of capacity listed in the table below.

Unit	Symbol	Relationship Between Units
fluid ounce	fl. oz.	8 fl. oz. = 1 cup (c.)
cup	c.	2 c. = 1 pint (pt.)
pint	pt.	2 pt. = 1 quart (qt.)
quart	qt.	4 qt. = 1 gallon (gal.)

You use the relationship between the units to rename customary units of capacity.

To rename a larger unit as a smaller unit, multiply.

3 qt. = ___ pt.

$3 \times 2 = 6$ ◄ 1 qt. = 2 pt.

So, 3 qt. = 6 pt.

To rename a smaller unit as a larger unit, divide.

18 fl. oz. = ___ c.

$18 \div 8 = 2\frac{2}{8}$, or $2\frac{1}{4}$ ◄ 1 cup = 8 fl. oz.

So, 18 fl. oz. = $2\frac{1}{4}$ c.

Measurement

Study the customary units of weight in the table below.

Unit	Symbol	Relationship Between Units
ounce	oz.	16 oz. = 1 pound (lb.)
pound	lb.	2,000 lb. = 1 ton (tn.)
ton	tn.	1 tn. = 2,000 lb.

You use the relationships between the units to rename customary units of weight.

Additional Examples

Complete.

a. $2\frac{1}{2}$ lb. = ___ oz.

$2\frac{1}{2} \times 16 = 40$ ◀ 1 lb. = 16 oz.

So, $2\frac{1}{2}$ lb. = 40 oz.

b. 100 oz. = ___ lb.

$100 \div 16 = 6\frac{4}{16}$, or $6\frac{1}{4}$ ◀ 1 lb. = 16 oz.

So, 100 oz. = $6\frac{1}{4}$ lb.

☑SKILL CHECK

Complete.

1. 6 gal. = ___ qt.

2. 3 qt. = ___ fl. oz.

3. 6 c. = ___ qt.

4. $2\frac{1}{2}$ qt. = ___ pt.

5. 4 tn. = ___ lb.

6. $1\frac{1}{2}$ lb. = ___ oz.

Exercises

Choose the most likely customary measurement.

1. a bottle of apple juice
    a. 2 fl. oz.
    b. 2 gal.
    c. 2 qt.

2. a single serving carton of milk
    a. 8 fl. oz.
    b. 8 pt.
    c. 8 qt.

3. a plastic container of fabric softener
    a. 128 pt.
    b. 128 c.
    c. 128 fl. oz.

Complete.

4. 16 fl. oz. = ___ pt.

5. 2 qt. = ___ fl. oz.

6. 10 gal. = ___ qt.

7. 96 fl. oz. = ___ qt.

8. 4 pt. = ___ c.

9. 1 qt. = ___ c.

10. 3 gal. = ___ pt.

11. 3 pt. = ___ qt.

12. 4 gal. = ___ fl. oz.

13. 14 c. = ___ qt.

14. 28 fl. oz. = ___ pt.

15. $5\frac{1}{4}$ c. = ___ fl. oz.

16. 12 pt. = ___ gal.

17. 4 gal. 3 qt. = ___ qt.

Choose the most likely customary measurement.

18. a dictionary   **a.** 2 oz.   **b.** 2 lb.   **c.** 2 tn.

19. an elephant   **a.** 3 tn.   **b.** 30 lb.   **c.** 300 oz.

20. an apple   **a.** 8 oz.   **b.** 8 lb.   **c.** 80 oz.

Measurement

Complete.

21. 3 lb. = ___ oz.

22. 64 oz. = ___ lb.

23. 3 tn. = ___ lb.

24. $1\frac{3}{4}$ lb. = ___ oz.

25. 40 oz. = ___ lb.

26. 1500 lb. = ___ tn.

Application

27. Roger needs 2 quarts of orange juice to make punch for a party. How many fluid ounces is this?

28. Christiana is helping with the laundry. She uses 4 fl. oz. of fabric softener in each load. If she has $1\frac{1}{2}$ pints of fabric softener, how many loads can she do?

29. One package of hamburger weighs 3 lb. 5 oz. Another package weighs 1 lb. 13 oz. How many more ounces are in the first package?

14.6 Time Zones

The world is divided into twenty-four time zones. The time difference from one zone to the next is one hour. Study the map below, which shows five of the time zones in the United States.

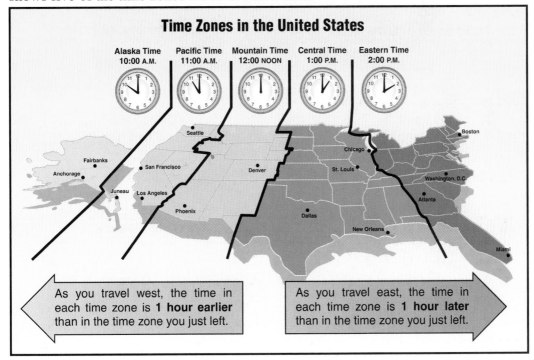

Time Zones in the United States

You can use this map to find the time in any place in the continental United States.

If it is 11:00 A.M. (central time) in Chicago, what time is it in each of the following cities?

San Francisco, California:
9:00 A.M.
It is 2 hours earlier, since San Francisco is 2 time zones west of Chicago.

Washington, D.C.:
12:00 noon.
It is 1 hour later, since Washington is 1 time zone east of Chicago.

Measurement

Denver!

☑**SKILL CHECK**

It is 7:00 P.M. (mountain time) in Denver. What time is it in each of the following cities?

   1. Phoenix   **2.** Miami   **3.** St. Louis

Solve.

   4. It is 1:00 P.M. (central time) in Dallas. What time (Pacific time) is it in Los Angeles?

   5. What time (eastern time) is it in Atlanta when it is 12:00 noon (Pacific time) in Seattle?

Exercises

Name the time zone for each city.

   1. Santa Fe   **2.** Miami   **3.** New Orleans

It is 12:00 noon (eastern time) in Atlanta. What time is it in each of the following cities?

   4. Dallas   **5.** Cheyenne

   6. Los Angeles   **7.** Anchorage

It is 3:30 P.M. (mountain time) in Denver. What time is it in each of the following cities?

   8. San Francisco   **9.** Anchorage

10. Dallas

11. Atlanta

It is 7:05 A.M. (Pacific time) in San Francisco. What time is it in each of the following cities?

12. Boston

13. Boise

14. Seattle

15. St. Louis

It is 11:55 P.M. (central time) in Chicago. What time is it in each of the following cities?

16. New York

17. San Francisco

18. Phoenix

19. Anchorage

Solve.

20. It is 7:00 A.M. (mountain time) in Cheyenne. What time (Pacific time) is it in Los Angeles?

21. What time (eastern time) is it in Boston, when it is 5:00 P.M. (Alaska time) in Fairbanks?

22. Randy lives in Miami. He called a friend in Chicago at 9:45 P.M. (eastern time). What was the time in Chicago?

23. Denise lives in Seattle. At 9:10 A.M. (Pacific time), she called a friend in St. Louis. What was the time in St. Louis?

Measurement

Application

24. A nonstop flight from Boston to Denver left Boston at 8:10 A.M. (eastern time). It arrived in Denver at 9:50 A.M. (mountain time). How long was the flying time?

25. The flying time of a nonstop flight from Los Angeles to New York is 5 h. 35 min. If a flight from Los Angeles arrived in New York at 2:40 P.M. (eastern time), what time did the plane leave Los Angeles?

14.7 Temperature

In the metric system, temperature is measured in degrees Celsius (C). On the Celsius scale, water freezes at 0° C and boils at 100° C.

The scale on the thermometer at right is like a vertical number line. Note that there are 10° between heavy marks on the scale.

Study the common Celsius temperatures in the table below.

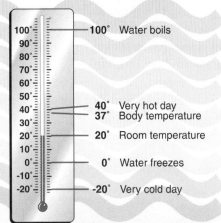

Celsius Thermometer

100°	Water boils
40°	Very hot day
37°	Body temperature
20°	Room temperature
0°	Water freezes
-20°	Very cold day

Common Celsius Temperatures		
Water freezes: 0° C	Room temperature: 20° C	Very cold day: ⁻20° C
Water boils: 100° C	Body temperature: 37° C	Very hot day: 40° C

Temperature can also be measured in degrees Fahrenheit (F). On the Fahrenheit scale, water freezes at 32° F and boils at 212° F.

Study the common Fahrenheit temperatures in the table below.

Common Fahrenheit Temperatures		
Water freezes: 32° F	Room temperature: 68° F	Very cold day: ⁻4° F
Water boils: 212° F	Body temperature: 98.6° F	Very hot day: 104° F

You can convert Fahrenheit temperatures to Celsius temperatures, and vice versa.

Converting Temperatures from Fahrenheit to Celsius

Example: 50° F = ? C

STEP 1	STEP 2	STEP 3
Subtract 32.	Multiply by 5.	Divide by 9.
$50 - 32 = 18$	$18 \times 5 = 90$	$90 \div 9 = 10$
		So, 50° F = 10° C

Converting Temperatures from Celsius to Fahrenheit

Example: 12° C = ? F

STEP 1	STEP 2	STEP 3
Multiply by 9.	Divide by 5.	Add 32.
$12 \times 9 = 108$	$108 \div 5 = 21.6$	$21.6 + 32 = 53.6$
		So, 12° C = 53.6° F

Measurement

☑SKILL CHECK

Choose the most likely temperature for each.

1. ice-skating	**a.** $^{-}5°$ C	**b.** $10°$ C	**c.** $30°$ C
2. water-skiing	**a.** $28°$ F	**b.** $58°$ F	**c.** $88°$ F

Complete.

3. $75°$ F = ___ C   **4.** $60°$ C = ___ F

Exercises

Write the letter that shows the Celsius temperature on the thermometer scale below.

1. cool breeze: $10°$ C   **2.** hot dishwater: $60°$ C

3. normal body temperature: $37°$ C   **4.** ice cube: $^{-}15°$ C

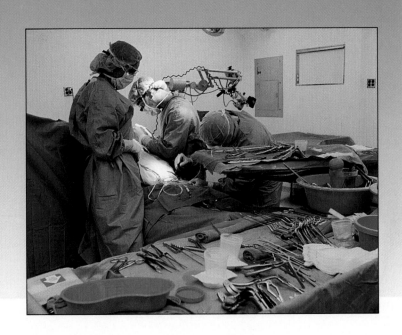

In order to eliminate the risk of receiving contaminated donor blood, many people who know that they will be having surgery choose to undergo autologous transfusions. An autologous transfusion occurs when a person donates his own blood to be stored for use in his upcoming surgery.

CHAPTER 14

Choose the most likely Celsius temperature for each.

5. ice cream   a. ⁻1° C   b. 10° C   c. 20° C

6. swimming at   a. 0° C   b. 15° C   c. 30° C
   the beach

7. ice fishing   a. ⁻30° C   b. ⁻10° C   c. 20° C

8. boiling water   a. 150° C   b. 125° C   c. 100° C

9. planting flowers   a. 20° C   b. 0° C   c. ⁻20° C

10. hot radiator   a. 7° C   b. 17° C   c. 70° C

Choose the most likely Fahrenheit temperature for each.

11. oven for bak-   a. 50° F   b. 100° F   c. 350° F
   ing cookies

12. a cold soda   a. 35° F   b. 55° F   c. 75° F

13. room tem-   a. 58° F   b. 68° F   c. 78° F
   perature

14. snow skiing   a. 22° F   b. 42° F   c. 62° F

15. a rainy   a. 25° F   b. 55° F   c. 95° F
   spring day

16. a hot cup of tea   a. 80° F   b. 210° F   c. 150° F

Complete each conversion.

17. 41° F = ___ ° C   18. 59° F = ___ ° C   19. 80° F = ___ ° C

20. 0° C = ___ ° F   21. 10° C = ___ ° F   22. 35° C = ___ ° F

Application

23. A child has a temperature that is 2.7° F above the normal body temperature. What is the child's temperature?

24. The temperature is 32° C. Are you more likely to play ice hockey or water polo on an outing at the lake?

25. The temperature in Sault Sainte Marie varies from ⁻17° F to 86° F. What is the range of these temperatures?

Measurement

14.8 Precision in Measurement

Stan recorded the length of the pencil below as 12 cm. Sharon measured the same pencil and recorded its length as 123 mm. Whose measurement is more precise?

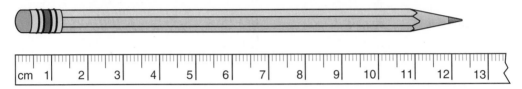

A smaller unit of measure results in a more precise measurement. Since a millimeter is a smaller unit than a centimeter, 123 mm is more precise than 12 cm. Therefore, Sharon's measurement is more precise.

Which measurement, 8 m or 800 cm, is more precise?

If two measures, like 8 m and 800 cm, express the same length, the one with the smaller unit of measure is more precise. Since a centimeter is smaller than a meter, 800 cm is more precise than 8 m.

The number used to record a measurement also determines the degree of precision reflected by the measurement. For example, a measurement of 8.0 km is more precise than a measurement of 8 km, because 8.0 km is precise to the nearest tenth of a kilometer.

All measurements are approximations. In any measurement, the greatest possible error (GPE) is $\frac{1}{2}$, or 0.5 of the unit used in the measurement. For example, if a piece of wire measures 24 cm, the GPE of the measurement is 0.5 cm. This means that the actual length of the wire is 24 ± 0.5 cm; so it is between 23.5 and 24.5 cm long.

☑SKILL CHECK

Which measurement is more precise?

1. 3 kg or 2895 g   **2.** 500 cm or 5 m   **3.** 78° F or 78.4° F

What is the GPE of each measurement?

4. 305 ml   **5.** 19 m   **6.** 175 kg

Exercises

State which measurement is more precise.

1. 1 yd. or 3 ft.   **2.** 32 m or 31.9 m   **3.** 16 oz. or 1 lb.

4. 3 m or 300 cm   **5.** 40° C or 40.7° C   **6.** 4100 m or 4 km

7. 57 cm or 570 mm   **8.** 6.4 cm or 6.42 cm   **9.** 2 h. or 120 min.

Write the letter of the most precise measurement.

10. height of a table   **a.** 1 m   **b.** 10 dm   **c.** 100 cm

11. temperature of hot soup   **a.** 180.00° F   **b.** 180.0° F   **c.** 180° F

12. capacity of a juice glass   **a.** 0.1 L   **b.** 0.125 L   **c.** 0.12 L

13. mass of an elephant   **a.** 2 t   **b.** 2.2 t   **c.** 2250 kg

Measurement

Write the GPE of each measurement.

14. 293 ml

15. 36 cm

16. 75 g

17. 6 L

18. 842 mg

19. 54 mm

The length of a hammer is recorded as 28 cm.

20. What is the length of the hammer to the nearest cm?

21. What is the GPE of the measurement?

22. What is the greatest actual length of the measurement?

23. What is the least actual length of the measurement?

Application

24. Randy measured the length of a screw. He said it was 3 cm long. David measured the screw and said it was 32 mm long. Which measurement was more precise?

25. The actual length of a screwdriver is between 17.5 and 18.5 cm. What is the length of the screwdriver to the nearest cm?

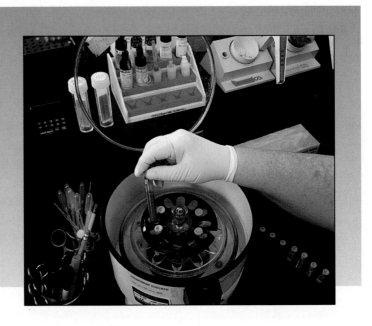

Centrifugal force is used in a separator to separate blood into its component parts: 45% formed elements (red blood cells, white blood cells, and platelets) and 55% plasma (water, proteins, and solutes).

Problem Solving: Use Logical Reasoning

To solve word problems in which it is difficult to organize the data, you can apply the strategy "Use Logical Reasoning." A Venn diagram is very helpful when using this strategy.

Study the following example.

A total of 27 students participated in the drama club and the computer club. There are 14 students who are in the drama club only and 4 students who participate in both drama and computer clubs. How many students are members of the computer club only?

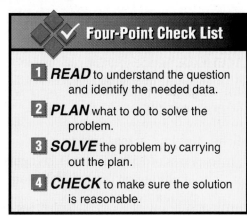

Four-Point Check List

1 **READ** to understand the question and identify the needed data.

2 **PLAN** what to do to solve the problem.

3 **SOLVE** the problem by carrying out the plan.

4 **CHECK** to make sure the solution is reasonable.

1. READ: Understand the question.
    - How many students are members of the computer club only?
    Identify the needed data.
    - 27 students participate in the drama club and the computer club.
    - 14 students are members of the drama club only.
    - 4 students are members of both clubs.

2. PLAN: Apply the strategy "Use Logical Reasoning."

3. SOLVE: Draw a Venn diagram to organize the information.

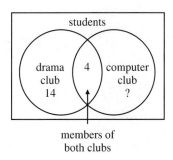

members of
both clubs

To find the number in the computer club, subtract the sum of 14 and 4 from 27.

Measurement

$$27 - (14 + 4) = 27 - 18$$
$$= 9$$

There are 9 students who are members of the computer club only.

4.   CHECK: Is the solution reasonable?
The sum of $14 + 4 + 9$ is 27, so the solution is reasonable.

☑ **SKILL CHECK**

Solve. Use logical reasoning.

1. In a class of 15 students, 11 students are on the football team and 8 students are on the baseball team. How many students belong to both teams?

2. Everyone at a youth activity was wearing either navy or red. There were a total of 10 people wearing navy, 8 people wearing red, and 3 people wearing both navy and red. How many people were at the youth activity?

Exercises

Solve. Use logical reasoning.

1. Miss Tipton surveyed the 26 students in her music class. She determined that 5 students liked both Bach and Vivaldi, while 12 students liked only Bach. The remaining students liked only Vivaldi. How many of her students liked only Vivaldi?

2. There are 27 students in Mr. Smith's homeroom. Of his students, 7 are in the orchestra and 16 are in the band. If 8 of the students are in neither orchestra nor band, how many students are in both orchestra and band?

Mixed Review

Solve.

3. Jill bought 3 notebooks for $1.95 each, and 2 mechanical pencils for $1.79 each. The sales tax rate was 5%. How much was her total purchase including sales tax?

4. An eccentric math teacher told his class that he would assign 1 problem on the first day of school, 2 problems on the second day, 4 problems on the third day, 8 problems on the fourth day, and so on. At this rate, how many problems would he assign on the tenth day?

5. David has 15 coins. The coins are only nickels and dimes. Their total value is $1.20. How many of each coin does he have?

6. The Lehmans need 21 square yards of carpet for their living room. Regular carpet costs $11.95 per square yard, and commercial carpet costs $16.50 per square yard. If the Lehmans purchase the commercial carpet, how much more will it cost?

7. The Tigers baseball team plays 3 out of every 5 games on their home field. Last month the team played 20 games. How many home games did they play?

Measurement

8. Janet cannot remember the 3-digit street address of her grandmother's home. She does recall that the digits in the address are 3, 4, and 9. How many different addresses are possible with these digits?

9. There are 29 students in Mr. Tompkins's class. The number of girls in his class is 7 less than 2 times the number of boys. How many of the students in his class are boys? How many are girls?

10. Mr. Johnson bought 9 gallons of paint for his house. He used $1\frac{3}{4}$ gallons of white paint, $5\frac{3}{8}$ gallons of beige paint, and $\frac{5}{6}$ gallons of blue paint. How many gallons of paint were left?

Chapter 14 Review

14.1 Choose the most likely estimate.

1. width of your hand
   a. 9 mm
   b. 9 cm
   c. 9 dm

2. height of a flagpole
   a. 10 m
   b. 10 dkm
   c. 10 hm

Complete.

3. 10 mm = 1 ___

4. 1 dkm = ___ m

5. 10 ___ = 1 m

14.2 Complete.

6. 7.5 cm = ___ mm

7. 400 dm = ___ dkm

8. 2300 m = ___ km

9. 3.25 hm = ___ cm

Compare. Use >, <, or =.

10. 520 cm ___ 5.2 m

11. 9 dm ___ 90 mm

14.3 Choose the best estimate for the capacity or mass of each.

12. a glass of orange juice
    a. 15 L
    b. 150 ml
    c. 1.5 kl

13. a baseball
    a. 2 kg
    b. 20 mg
    c. 200 g

Complete.

14. 3000 ml = ___ L

15. 5 kl = ___ L

16. 7 g = ___ mg

17. 2 t = ___ kg

14.4 Complete.

18. 4 ft. = ___ in.

19. 13 ft. = ___ yd.

20. $\frac{3}{4}$ mi. = ___ yd.

Add or subtract.

21.   4 ft. 11 in.
    + 3 ft. 7 in.
    _____

22.   9 yd.
    − 6 yd. 2 ft.
    _____

Measurement

14.5 Choose the most likely unit of customary measure.

    23. an orange   **a.** 6 oz.   **b.** 6 lb.   **c.** 6 tn.

    24. a can of soda   **a.** 1 qt.   **b.** 6 pt.   **c.** 12 fl. oz.

Complete.

    25. 3 qt. = ___ fl. oz.   **26.** 56 oz. = ___ lb.   **27.** 4 tn. = ___ lb.

14.6 Solve.

    28. It is 5:30 A.M. (mountain time) in Boise. What time (eastern time) is it in Miami?

    29. Gary lives in Atlanta. At 2:05 P.M. (eastern time), he called a friend in San Francisco. What time (Pacific time) was it in San Francisco?

14.7 Choose the most likely temperature for each.

    30. a hot cup of soup   **a.** 72° F   **b.** 142° F   **c.** 212° F

    31. oven temperature for baking pizza   **a.** 25° C   **b.** 100° C   **c.** 175° C

Complete.

    32. 60° C = ___° F   **33.** 59° F = ___° C

14.8 Write the letter of the most precise measurement.

    34. length of a desk   **a.** 2 m   **b.** 20 dm   **c.** 200 cm

    35. temperature of a cool drink   **a.** 35° F   **b.** 35.00° F   **c.** 35.0° F

What is the greatest possible error (GPE)?

    36. 175 cm

Chapter 14 Cumulative Review

1. Find the sale price of an item with a regular price of $1,895 and a 5% rate of discount.
   a. $94.75   **b.** $1,800.25
   c. $1,989.75   **d.** not given

2. What % of 250 is 5?
   a. 2%   **b.** 5%
   c. 20%   **d.** not given

3. Find the new balance.
   bank deposit: $3,700
   interest rate: 5%; time: 3 years
   a. $555   **b.** $3,145
   c. $4,255   **d.** not given

4. 7% of 85 is what number?
   a. 0.595   **b.** 5.95
   c. 59.5   **d.** not given

5. Find the commission rate.
   sales: $600
   commission: $90
   a. 1.5%   **b.** 15%
   c. 150%   **d.** not given

6. Add. $^-5 + {}^-13 + {}^-9$
   a. 27   **b.** $^-17$
   c. $^-27$ **d.** not given

7. Add. $(17 + {}^-3) + {}^-6$
   a. 8   **b.** 14
   c. 20   **d.** not given

8. Divide. $^-36 \div 4$
   a. $^-32$ **b.** $^-40$
   c. 9   **d.** not given

9. Solve. $n + 8 = {}^-4$
   a. 4   **b.** $^-4$
   c. $^-12$ **d.** not given

10. Write the ordered pair for point A.

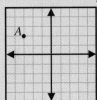

   a. (3, 2)   **b.** ($^-3$, 2)
   c. (3, $^-2$)   **d.** ($^-3$, $^-2$)

11. Find the perimeter of a rectangle with a length of 13 cm and a width of 8 cm.
   a. 21 cm   **b.** 42 cm
   c. 104 cm   **d.** not given

12. Find the area of a rectangle with a length of 19 m and a width of 7.5 m.
   a. 26.5 cm^2 **b.** 53 cm^2
   c. 142.5 cm^2 **d.** not given

13. Find the area of a triangle with a base of 12.6 m and a height of 3.4 m.
   a. 16 m^2 **b.** 21.42 m^2
   c. 42.84 m^2 **d.** not given

14. Find the circumference of a circle with a diameter of 12 cm. Use 3.14 for π.
   a. 18.84 cm   **b.** 37.68 cm
   c. 65.94 cm   **d.** not given

15. Find the area of a circle with a radius of 7 mm. Use $\frac{22}{7}$ for π.
   a. 22 m^2 **b.** 154 mm^2
   c. 164 mm^2 **d.** not given

Measurement

ELISHA OTIS
ELEVATOR

While working as a master mechanic at the Bedstead Manufacturing Company in Yonkers, New York, Elisha Otis designed a machine that would one day make him famous—the safety elevator.

In 1852, Elisha's employer asked him to design a freight elevator to be used in the factory. Although elevators had been in use since the time of the Pharaohs, they all possessed the same serious defect. If the rope used to hoist the platform upward broke, the elevator and its contents would plummet rapidly to the bottom of the shaft. This design flaw was responsible for untold deaths over the years, and Elisha was determined to do something about it.

For several months, Elisha experimented with different types of safety systems. His final version consisted of a wagon spring attached to the top of the elevator car, coupled with a ratchet bar joined to the rails which lined the shaft. If the elevator cable broke, the sudden absence of the car's weight would cause the spring to release. The spring would then activate the ratchet bars, stopping the elevator from plunging down the shaft.

Before Elisha's company could make much use of his new design, it went bankrupt. Unemployed, he considered seeking his fortune in the gold fields of California. However, before he could make his travel plans, Elisha received an order for two safety elevators from a furniture company in New York. Grasping the potential of his new invention, Elisha decided to start his own company.

At this time, elevators were considered extremely dangerous contraptions. Since people did not trust them, Elisha realized that he had to do something to promote the safety of his invention. In 1854 at the Crystal Palace Exposition in New York City, Elisha climbed aboard a working model of his elevator and signaled for his assistant to raise the platform. As the crowd watched in horror, his assistant calmly cut the elevator cable. Immediately the spring mechanism activated and stopped the platform before it could fall an inch. Above the thundering applause, Elisha shouted, "All safe, gentlemen, all safe."

This event marked the beginning of the E.G. Otis Elevator Company. Three years later, Elisha Otis supervised as his company installed the first passenger elevator in the E.V. Haughwout & Company Store of New York City. This five-story building was one of the tallest of its day. The elevator that the Otis company installed was powered by a central steam source which enabled it to lift 1,000 pounds at a rate of 40 feet per minute.

1811-
1861

The elevators of today are not considered to be the least bit dangerous. They are widely used in department stores, hospitals, and office buildings. Some are simple, functional devices used to transport people or equipment from floor to floor. Others are glass-enclosed mechanical pieces of art used to whisk riders up the neon-lighted walls of skyscrapers. Regardless of these differences, all elevators are safe—thanks to the mechanical genius of Elisha Otis.

15 CHAPTER

SETS
•
STATISTICS

15.1 Sets

A group or collection of objects is called a *set.*

A set is named with a capital letter and enclosed in set braces. The set brace symbols, { }, mean "the set whose members are."

You can describe or list the members of a set. Consider the example of set G below.

description: G = {the four gospels in the New Testament}

list: G = {Matthew, Mark, Luke, John}

The objects in a set are called *members* or *elements.* The symbol $\in$ means "is an element of," and $\notin$ means "is not an element of."

Study the examples below which demonstrate the use of these symbols.

Mark $\in G$ ◀ "Mark is an element of set G."

James $\notin G$ ◀ "James is not an element of set G."

A set with no members is called the *empty set.* The symbols $\varnothing$ or { } mean "the empty set." Consider set B below.

description: B = {the set of biblical characters living on earth today}

How many members are in this set?

list: B = { } or $\varnothing$ ◀ There are no members in this set.

If the members of a set can be readily determined, the set is *well defined.* Consider the following examples.

D = {days of the week} ◀ Set D is well defined.

E = {all pretty days} ◀ Set E is not well defined.

☑SKILL CHECK

Describe the members of set M.

1. M = {January, February, March}

List the members of set D.

2. D = {the days of the week}

Use the sets in 1 and 2. Tell whether the following statements are true or false.

3. January $\notin M$

4. Monday $\in D$

Tell whether the following sets are well defined. Write yes or no.

5. G = {girls in your classroom}

6. T = {tall boys in your school}

Exercises

Describe the following sets. Use proper set notation.

1. S = {s, a, v, e, d}

2. T = {Father, Son, Holy Spirit}

3. E = {2, 4, 6, 8}

4. H = {Saturday, Sunday}

List the members of the following sets. Use proper set notation.

5. A = {the days of the week that begin with T}

6. B = {the last three months of the year}

7. $C = \{$all dogs that are cats$\}$

8. $D = \{$the letters in the word *math*$\}$

Write true or false. Use the sets from exercises 1-8.

9. $v \in S$

10. Sunday $\in H$

11. $10 \in E$

12. Tuesday $\in A$

13. Monday $\notin H$

14. January $\in A$

15. $3 \in E$

16. m $\in D$

17. Friday $\in A$

18. Saturday $\notin H$

19. October $\notin B$

20. collie $\in C$

Determine whether the following sets are well defined. Write yes or no.

21. $B = \{$boys in your classroom$\}$

22. $V = \{$good music$\}$

23. $L = \{$the three largest cities in the United States$\}$

24. $T = \{$the teachers in your school$\}$

25. $S = \{$the best singers in your class$\}$

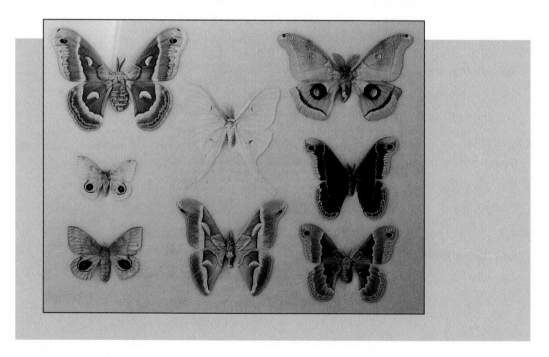

15.2 Subsets

Consider the following sets.

$$B = \{\text{the books in the Bible}\}$$
$$N = \{\text{the books in the New Testament}\}$$

Is every book in the New Testament also a book in the Bible?

Set N is a ***subset*** of set B since all the members of set N are also members of set B.

You can write this as $N \subseteq B$. The symbol $\subseteq$ means "is a subset of."

Every set is a subset of itself. The empty set is a subset of every set. So, $N \subseteq N$ and $\emptyset \subseteq N$.

Is every book in the Bible a book of the New Testament?

Set B is not a subset of set N since not all the members of set B are also members of set N.

You can write this as $B \not\subseteq N$. The symbol $\not\subseteq$ means "is not a subset of."

To show the relationships between two or more sets, you can use a ***Venn diagram.*** Consider the diagram below which illustrates the relationship between the people living in Indiana and the people living in the United States.

$S = \{\text{the people living in the United States}\}$

$I = \{\text{the people living in Indiana}\}$

To express the relationship between S and I, you write $I \subseteq S$.

☑SKILL CHECK

Are the following sets subsets of {1, 3, 5}? Write yes or no.

1. $\{3, 5\}$ 2. $\emptyset$ 3. $\{1, 3, 5\}$ 4. $\{0\}$

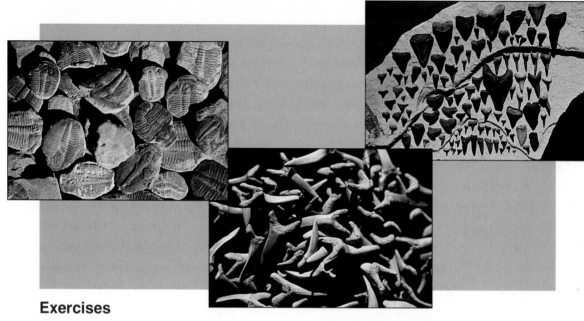

Exercises

For each set on the left, state the letter naming the set of which it is a subset.

1. {2, 4, 6, 8}

2. {Indiana}

3. {r, s}

4. {Joseph}

5. {fall, winter}

6. {peaches, pears}

7. {o, s}

8. {math, English}

9. {trees, flowers}

10. {Peter}

A = {the seasons of the year}

B = {the subjects I am taking in school}

C = {the plants}

D = {the disciples of Jesus}

E = {the letters in the word *girls*}

F = {the even numbers between 0 and 10}

G = {the fruit we eat}

H = {the states in the United States}

I = {the sons of Jacob}

J = {the letters in the word *so*}

Use sets A, B, C, D, E, and F below. Indicate whether statements 11-19 are true.

$A = \{2, 4, 6, 8, 10\}$ $D = \{b, e, d\}$

$B = \{a, b, c, d, e\}$ $E = \{4, 10\}$

$C = \{2, 4, 6\}$ $F = \{e, d\}$

11. $F \subseteq D$ **12.** $C \subseteq E$ **13.** $D \not\subseteq B$

14. $\varnothing \subseteq D$ **15.** $A \subseteq F$ **16.** $E \not\subseteq C$

17. $F \subseteq E$ **18.** $E \subseteq A$ **19.** $\varnothing \not\subseteq B$

Are the following sets subsets of {2, 4, 6}? Write yes or no.

20. $\{2, 4, 6\}$ **21.** $\{0\}$ **22.** $\varnothing$

Use the Venn diagram on the right to answer exercises 23-25.

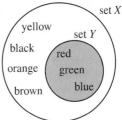

23. List all the members of X.

24. List all the members of Y.

25. State a relationship between the two sets using $\subseteq$.

15.3 Union and Intersection of Sets

Juan, Luisa, Bob, Sue, Ann, and Chen sing in the junior high choir ensemble. Consider set C below.

Set $C = \{$Juan, Luisa, Bob, Sue, Ann, Chen$\}$

Jim, Luisa, Juan, Mary, Chen, Felicia, Ann, and Elihu play in the junior high band ensemble. Consider set B below.

Set $B = \{$Jim, Luisa, Juan, Mary, Chen, Felicia, Ann, Elihu$\}$

What is the union of set C and set B?

To find the **_union_** of two sets, you combine the members of both sets. The symbol "$\cup$" means union.

Study the union of set C and set B illustrated by the following Venn diagram.

The union of set C and set B

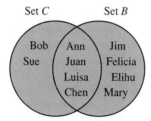

$C \cup B$ = shaded area

Description:

$C \cup B = \{$the students who are in either the choir or band ensemble$\}$

List:

$C \cup B = \{$Bob, Sue, Ann, Juan, Luisa, Chen, Jim, Felicia, Elihu, Mary$\}$

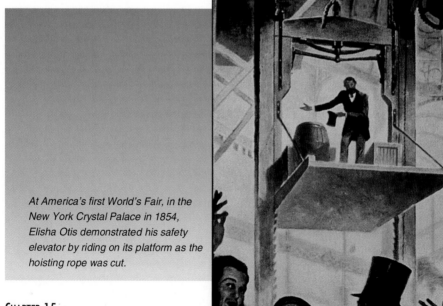

At America's first World's Fair, in the New York Crystal Palace in 1854, Elisha Otis demonstrated his safety elevator by riding on its platform as the hoisting rope was cut.

CHAPTER 15

What is the intersection of set C and set B?

To find the *intersection* of two sets, you identify the elements which are members of both sets. The symbol ∩ means intersection.

Study the intersection of set *C* and set *B* illustrated by the following Venn diagram.

The intersection of set *C* and set *B*

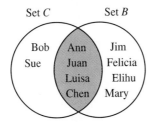

$C \cap B$ = shaded area

Description:

$C \cap B$ = {the students who are in both the choir and band ensembles}

List:

$C \cap B$ = {Ann, Juan, Luisa, Chen}

☑**SKILL CHECK**

Describe the following unions and intersections.

1. B = {the boys who play on the basketball team}
   G = {the girls who are cheerleaders}
   $B \cup G$ = ?

2. M = {the students in your class who are girls}
N = {the students in your class who have blond hair}
$M \cap N$ = ?

Use set notation to write the union and intersection for the following sets: C = {1, 2, 3, 4, 5, 6} D = {3, 6, 9, 12, 15}.

3. $C \cup D$ 4. $C \cap D$

Exercises

Describe the following unions and intersections.

1. O = {the books of the Old Testament}
N = {the books of the New Testament}
$O \cup N$ = ?
2. G = {the students in your class who wear glasses}
M = {the students in your class who are male}
$G \cap M$ = ?
3. X = {the authors of the books in the New Testament}
Y = {the disciples of Jesus}
$X \cap Y$ = ?
4. B = {the male students in your class}
G = {the female students in your class}
$B \cup G$ = ?
5. J = {the months of the year that start with J}
S = {the summer months of the year}
$J \cap S$ = ?
6. V = {the men mentioned in the Old Testament}
M = {the men mentioned in the New Testament}
$V \cup M$ = ?
7. A = {the teachers in your school}
B = {the students in your class}
$A \cap B$ = ?
8. C = {the students in your school with a C average or above}
D = {the students in your school with an A average}
$C \cup D$ = ?

Using set notation, list the unions or intersections of sets *A, B, C, D,* *E,* and *F* below for exercises 9-15.

$A = \{1, 3, 5, 7, 9\}$

$B = \{1, 2, 3, 4, 5\}$

$C = \varnothing$

$D = \{2, 4, 6, 8\}$

$E = \{4, 8, 12\}$

$F = \{10, 20, 30\}$

9. $A \cup F$

10. $B \cap A$

11. $C \cup E$

12. $D \cap F$

13. $D \cap E$

14. $E \cup F$

15. $(B \cup D) \cap A$

16. $F \cap (A \cup E)$

An early Otis elevator. Note the drive system of ropes and pulleys that work together with a hydraulic cylinder to lift the car.

15.4 Finite and Infinite Sets

A set in which all of the elements can be counted or listed is called a *finite* set. Consider set *X* below.

$$X = \{5, 1, 7, 3, 2, 8, 10\}$$

You can count seven elements in set *X*, so it is finite.

A set that is not finite is called an ***infinite set.*** Consider set *Y* below.

$$Y = \{2, 4, 6, 8, 10, \ldots\}$$

The 3 dots . . . indicate that the elements continue in the same pattern. You cannot count all of the elements in set *Y*, so it is an infinite set.

In a finite set, you can use three dots . . . to shorten a long list of numbers. Consider set Z below.

$$Z = \{\text{the whole numbers less than 100}\}$$

You can abbreviate this set as $Z = \{0, 1, 2, \ldots 98, 99\}$

The number line and Venn diagram below illustrate the relationships between the following infinite sets: natural numbers, whole numbers, and integers.

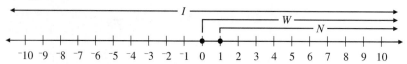

The set of numbers used for counting is called the set of **natural numbers, N.**

$$N = \{1, 2, 3, 4, 5, \ldots\}$$

The union of N and the set $\{0\}$ is called the set of **whole numbers, W.**

$$W = \{0, 1, 2, 3, 4, \ldots\}$$

The union of W and the set $\{^-1, ^-2, ^-3, \ldots\}$ is called the set of **integers, I.**

$$I = \{\ldots, ^-3, ^-2, ^-1, 0, 1, 2, 3, \ldots\}$$

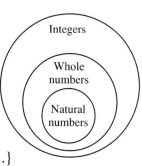

☑**SKILL CHECK**

Tell whether the following sets are finite or infinite.

1. {the grains of sand on the earth}

2. {the whole numbers multiplied by 2}

Write true or false.

3. Every natural number is a whole number.

4. Every integer is a whole number.

Exercises

Tell whether the following sets are infinite or finite.

1. {the students named Jim}

2. {the whole numbers greater than 20}

3. {the whole numbers less than 11}

4. {the days God has lived}

5. {the hairs on your head}

6. {the days in your earthly life}

7. Write a description of a finite set.

8. Write a description of an infinite set.

Use ∈ or ∉ to indicate whether the following numbers are members of the designated set.

Integers:

9. 21   **10.** 2.47

Whole numbers:

11. ⁻7   **12.** 1

Natural numbers:

13. 100,000   **14.** 0

Write true or false.

15. Every whole number is a natural number.

16. Every natural number is an integer.

Write the set (*N, W,* or *I*) that is the union or intersection of each of the following.

17. $N \cup W$ **18.** $I \cap W$

19. $N \cap W$ **20.** $I \cup N$

15.5 Range and Mode

Statistics is the branch of mathematics that deals with collecting, organizing, and analyzing sets of numerical data.

Consider the set of numerical data displayed in the table below.

Math Test Scores				
85	81	85	86	88
	90	90	85	81

To organize a set of data, you can make a *frequency table.* In the frequency table below, the frequency column indicates the number of times that each score occurs.

Frequency Table		
Score	Tally	Frequency
81	II	2
85	III	3
86	I	1
88	I	1
90	II	2

In a set of data, the difference between the greatest score and the least score is called the *range.* What is the range of the scores in the above table?

range = greatest score − least score
= 90 − 81
= 9

The range is 9.

The *mode* is the score that occurs most often in a set of data. In the above table, there are 3 scores of 85; so the mode is 85.

A collection of data may have more than one mode. However, if no number appears more than once, there is no mode.

☑SKILL CHECK

Make a frequency table for the set of data. Find the range and the mode.

Hours Worked Per Day									
7	4	3	2	5	3	1	2	5	3

1.

Find the range and the mode for the set of data.

2. 12, 16, 10, 12, 13, 10, 19, 14

Exercises

The frequency table below lists the ages of youth group members. Use the table to answer exercises 1-5.

1. How many members are age 15?

2. What age has a frequency of 1?

3. What is the range?

4. What is the mode?

5. How many members are in the youth group?

Age	Tally	Frequency
12	III	3
13	II	2
14	I	1
15	IIII	4
17	III	3

Make a frequency table for each collection of data. Find the range and the mode(s) for each.

6.

Math Test Scores			
95	90	94	92
100	97	89	98

7.

Earnings per week				
$240	$300	$270	$210	$240
$330	$210	$240	$300	$230

8.

Ages of Grandchildren					
3	7	9	4	11	3
9	5	3	9	7	10

9.

Daily Low Temperature (°F)						
57°	60°	63°	60°	61°	59°	65°
63°	57°	60°	61°	59°	60°	63°

Find the range and the mode(s) for each set of data.

10. 4, 9, 5, 12, 6, 9

11. 24, 28, 26, 29, 26, 24, 21

12. 12, 16, 10, 0, 15, 8, 13, 6

13. 283, 294, 275, 261, 365, 319, 238, 216, 257, 294

Application

Use the table below to answer exercises 14 and 15.

14. What is the mode for the players' free throw percentages?

15. What is the range for the players' free throw percentages?

Free Throw Percentages			
Barry	89.1%	Davis	86.2%
Bradley	88.3%	Greer	88.5%
Brown	86.2%	Jones	84.8%
Chambers	88.5%	Maravich	87.8%
Cousy	85.8%	Smith	86.2%

15.6 Mean and Median

Consider the table on the right which lists the number of stories for the nine tallest buildings in a city.

To analyze the numbers in a set, you can use statistical measures, such as the *mean, median,* and *mode.*

Find the mean, median, and mode for the numbers in the table.

To find the *mean* of a set of data, you add the numbers in the set; then divide the sum by the number of elements.

Tall Buildings	
Name	Stories
Carew Tower	49
Central Trust Tower	33
Dubois Tower	32
Netherland Plaza	31
Central Trust Center	27
Atrium Two	30
Star Bank Center	26
Clarion North Tower	33
Commerce Center	29

$$\frac{49 + 33 + 32 + 31 + 27 + 30 + 26 + 33 + 29}{9} = \frac{290}{9} \quad \begin{array}{l} \blacktriangleleft \text{ sum of the numbers} \\ \blacktriangleleft \text{ number of elements} \end{array}$$

$$\approx 32.\overline{2} \quad \blacktriangleleft \text{Round to the nearest whole number.}$$

$$\approx 32$$

The mean is about 32 stories.

To find the *median* of a set of data, you order the numbers in the set from smallest to largest. The median is the middle number in the ordered set.

$$26, 27, 29, 30, \mathbf{31}, 32, 33, 33, 49$$
$$\uparrow$$
median

The median is 31 stories.

Recall that the mode of a set of data is the number that occurs most frequently.

$$26, 27, 29, 30, 31, 32, \mathbf{33, 33,} 49$$

↑ ↑

mode

The mode is 33 stories.

Additional Example

Find the median: 43, 38, 33, 35, 32, 47

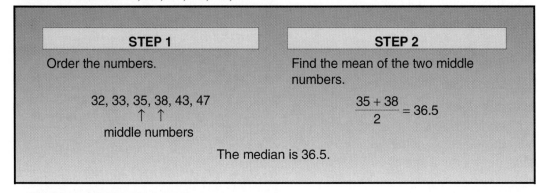

STEP 1	STEP 2
Order the numbers.	Find the mean of the two middle numbers.
32, 33, 35, 38, 43, 47 ↑ ↑ middle numbers	$\dfrac{35 + 38}{2} = 36.5$

The median is 36.5.

☑SKILL CHECK

Find the mean, median, and mode for each set of data.

1. Number of people baptized each month for the first six months:
   5, 3, 1, 6, 0, 9
2. Number of students enrolled in each of seven evening classes:
   22, 24, 17, 16, 22, 20, 12

Exercises

Find the mean and median for each set of data.

1. 1,260; 1,490; 1,070; 1,320; 1,280

2. 83, 90, 81, 91, 86, 97

3. 31, 34, 28, 33, 17, 25, 21

Complete the chart for each set of data.

	Set of Data	Range	Mean	Median	Mode(s)
Sit-ups per day	9, 12, 15, 19, 14, 21, 15	4. ☐	5. ☐	6. ☐	7. ☐
Bowling scores	137, 110, 116, 124, 185, 132	8. ☐	9. ☐	10. ☐	11. ☐
Meal expenses	$6.75, $7.80, $9.40, $8.90, $6.75, $7.80	12. ☐	13. ☐	14. ☐	15. ☐

Application

Use the table on the right to answer exercises 16-20.

16. How many people are employed at the camp?

17. What is the mode of the salaries?

18. What is the total amount paid in salaries?

19. What is the mean salary? Hint: Use the answer from exercise 18. Round to the nearest dollar.

20. What is the median salary?

Wildwood Camp Salaries		
Job	Number	Salary
Camp Director	1	$32,000
Program Directors	2	$30,000
Cook	1	$28,000
Full-time staff	4	$25,000
Part-time staff	7	$10,000

Sets • Statistics

15.7 Bar Graphs

In a survey at Calvary Christian School, students were asked to indicate their favorite subjects. The results of the survey are displayed in the table on the right.

To present the above data in pictorial form, you can use a **bar graph.** It is easy to compare data when it is displayed in a bar graph.

To make a bar graph, follow these steps.

Students' Favorite Subjects	
Math	20
Science	30
English	10
Bible	40
Heritage Studies	30

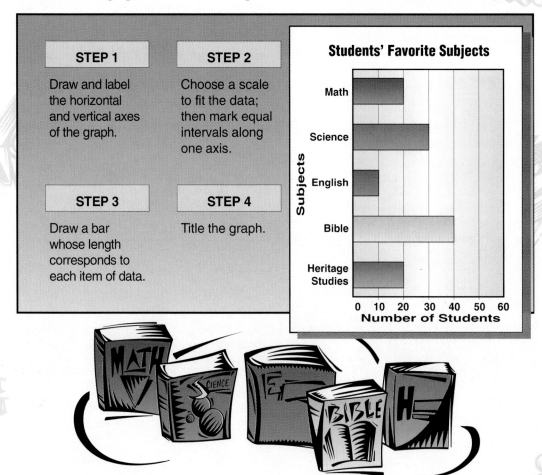

STEP 1

Draw and label the horizontal and vertical axes of the graph.

STEP 2

Choose a scale to fit the data; then mark equal intervals along one axis.

STEP 3

Draw a bar whose length corresponds to each item of data.

STEP 4

Title the graph.

A *double bar graph* is used to compare related data. The double bar graph below compares the survey responses of boys to those of girls.

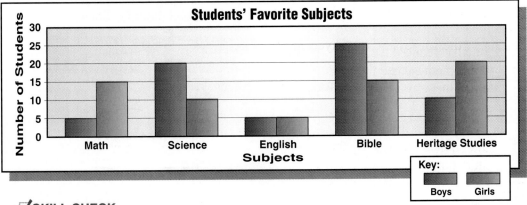

Students' Favorite Subjects

☑SKILL CHECK

Use the above bar graphs to answer the following questions.

1. What subjects were preferred by more than 20 students?
2. What subject was the overall favorite of the students?
3. What subject was the overall favorite of the girls?
4. What subjects were the favorites of less than 10 boys?
5. What subjects were the favorites of more boys than girls?

Exercises

Use the bar graph to answer exercises 1-4.

1. Which class donated the greatest amount?

2. Which class donated the least amount?

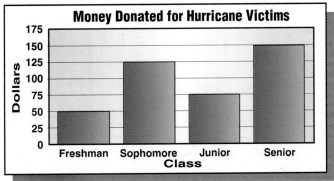

Money Donated for Hurricane Victims

3. Order the classes from least to greatest according to the amount donated.

4. What was the total dollar amount donated?

Use the double bar graph to answer exercises 5-8.

5. In what year was the total attendance 45?

6. In what year did the girls' enrollment exceed the boys' enrollment by 15 students?

7. In what year did the total attendance increase by 35 students?

8. For the years 1980-1995, what was the mean of the girl student enrollment to the nearest whole number?

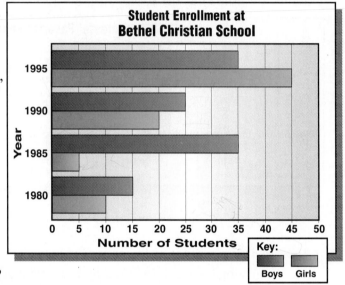

Student Enrollment at Bethel Christian School

Number of Students

Year

Key: Boys Girls

Application

Construct a bar graph from the following data.

9. Number of goals scored during soccer season: Roger, 8; Kevin, 5; John, 10; Andrew, 13.

Construct a double bar graph from the following data.

10. Hobbies of junior high students:
   7th grade: tennis, 15; cycling, 20; piano, 25; photography, 5
   8th grade: tennis, 10; cycling, 5; piano, 20; photography, 15

15.8 Line Graphs

After starting a fitness program, Ashley kept a monthly record of the number of sit-ups that she could do at one time. Consider her data displayed in the table on the right.

Ashley's Sit-Ups				
Jan.	Feb.	Mar.	Apr.	May
12	16	14	20	24

To show Ashley's improvement in pictorial form, you can use a *line graph.* Line graphs are best used to show changes over a period of time.

To make a line graph, follow these steps:

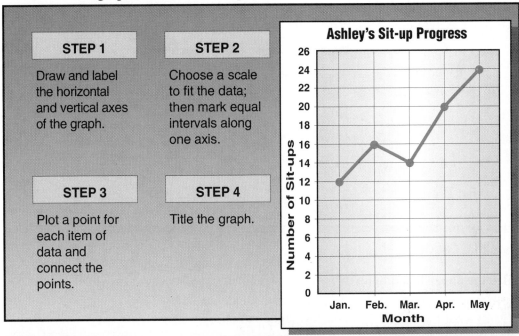

STEP 1

Draw and label the horizontal and vertical axes of the graph.

STEP 2

Choose a scale to fit the data; then mark equal intervals along one axis.

STEP 3

Plot a point for each item of data and connect the points.

STEP 4

Title the graph.

Ashley's Sit-up Progress

Number of Sit-ups vs *Month* (Jan., Feb., Mar., Apr., May)

Elevators in the atrium of a modern hotel. The next time you are in an elevator, look for an "Otis" nameplate.

Sets • Statistics

A *double line graph* is used to show changes over time for two sets of data. Consider the double line graph below which depicts the numbers of sit-ups for Ashley and her sister Jill.

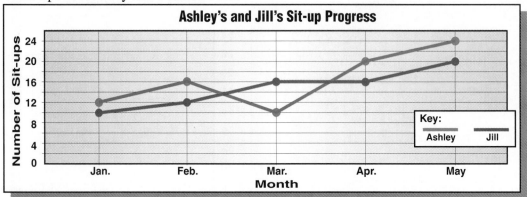

☑SKILL CHECK

Use the above line graphs to answer the following questions.

1. In what month did Ashley's performance decrease by 2?
2. In what month did Jill's performance increase by 2?
3. In which month did Jill do more sit-ups than Ashley?
4. In which month was Ashley's largest increase?

Exercises

Use the line graphs to answer exercises 1-13.

1. In which month did Eureka receive the most rainfall?

2. In which month did Eureka receive the least rainfall?

3. In which month did Eureka receive 3 inches of rainfall?

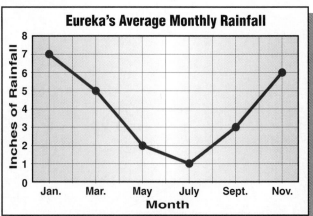

4. Between what months did the average monthly rainfall decrease?

5. How much did the average monthly rainfall increase between July and November?

6. In what years did the Crusaders win the same number of games?

7. Between what two years did their number of wins decrease by 6?

8. Between what two years did the Crusaders' number of wins increase by 2?

9. Between what two years did the Crusaders' number of wins increase the most?

10. In what year did the Crusaders win twice as many games as they won in 1993?

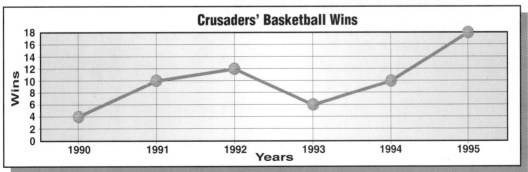

Crusaders' Basketball Wins

Wins

Years

11. During what month is the temperature difference between the two cities the least?

12. Which city has the greater increase in temperature from March to May?

13. Which city has no change in temperature from July to September?

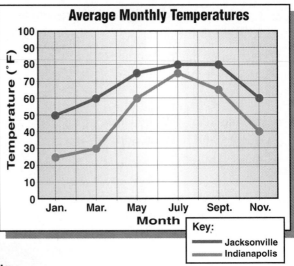

Average Monthly Temperatures

Key:
— Jacksonville
— Indianapolis

Make a line graph for the set of data.

14. Points scored by Hal in five basketball games: game 1, 10 points; game 2, 18 points; game 3, 22 points; game 4, 14 points; game 5, 20 points.

Make a double line graph for the set of data in the table.

15.

Mortgage Loans					
Month	Jul.	Aug.	Sept.	Oct.	Nov.
Fixed rate	10	25	15	20	5
Variable rate	5	20	10	15	25

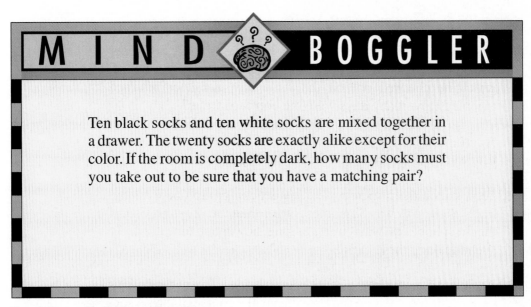

M I N D ❖ B O G G L E R

Ten black socks and ten white socks are mixed together in a drawer. The twenty socks are exactly alike except for their color. If the room is completely dark, how many socks must you take out to be sure that you have a matching pair?

Problem Solving Review

Solve, using the strategies presented in chapters 1-14.

1. The school library has some tables that seat 4 students, and other tables that seat 6 students. The seating capacity for the 9 tables in the library is 42 students. How many tables that seat 4 students are available?

2. Melba installed a fence 20 feet long and 12 feet wide around her rectangular garden plot. She put one post at each corner and one post every 4 feet in between. How many posts did Melba use?

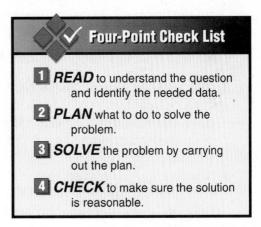

Four-Point Check List

1 **READ** to understand the question and identify the needed data.

2 **PLAN** what to do to solve the problem.

3 **SOLVE** the problem by carrying out the plan.

4 **CHECK** to make sure the solution is reasonable.

3. The public library charges $0.35 per book on the first day that a book is overdue. For each day after that, they charge $0.20 per book. Randy paid a total of $2.30 in fines for the two books, which he checked out on the same day and later returned together. How many days were the books overdue?

4. A certain number is divided by 4. When 3 is subtracted from the result, the difference is 5. What is the original number?

5. Terry called the 5 members of his deacon group one evening. Each phone call was 3 minutes longer than the previous call. If the first phone call was 4 minutes long, how much time did Terry spend making these calls?

6. There are 6 teams in the youth soccer league. Every team plays each of the other teams one time during the course of the season. How many total games will be played?

7. For mowing the lawn, Mr. Leedy agreed to pay his son Ben $0.20 for the first week, $0.40 for the second week, $0.80 for the third week, and so on. At this rate, how much would Ben get paid on the tenth week?

8. Phil buys and sells old books. He bought a Greek New Testament for $275 and then sold it for $350. Later, he bought it back for $375 and resold it for $425. How much did Phil gain or lose from these transactions?

9. The five starting players on the Patriots basketball team scored the following points: 9, 14, 8, 19, 15. What was the mean number of points scored for these players?

10. Ashley is required to practice the clarinet 5 hours each week. She practiced $\frac{7}{8}$ hour daily Monday through Thursday. If she practiced $\frac{3}{8}$ hour on Friday, how long must she practice on Saturday?

CHAPTER 15

Chapter 15 Review

15.1 Describe the following set. Use proper set notation.

1. $X = \{1, 2, 3, 4\}$

List the members of the following set. Use proper set notation.

2. $Y = \{\text{months of the year that begin with } M\}$

Write true or false. Use the sets from questions 1 and 2.

3. $0 \in X$

4. $\text{November} \in Y$

Is the following set well defined? Write yes or no.

5. $\{\text{the students in your class wearing glasses}\}$

15.2 Write true or false. Use sets *X, Y*, and *Z* below.

$$X = \{1, 3, 5\} \qquad Y = \{1, 2, 3, 4, 5, 6\} \qquad Z = \{2, 4\}$$

6. $Y \subseteq X$

7. $Z \nsubseteq Y$

8. $\varnothing \subseteq Z$

Are the following sets subsets of {9, 8, 7}? Write yes or no.

9. $\{7, 8\}$

10. $\{10, 9, 8\}$

15.3 Describe the following union.

11. $A = \{\text{baseball teams in the American League}\}$
$N = \{\text{baseball teams in the National League}\}$
$A \cup N = ?$

Describe the following intersection.

12. $P = \{\text{piano students in your school}\}$
$G = \{\text{girl students in your school}\}$
$P \cap N = ?$

Use set notation to list the unions and intersections for 18-20. Use sets *A, B*, and *C* below.

$$A = \{3, 6, 9\} \qquad B = \{1, 2, 3, 4\} \qquad C = \{5, 10, 15\}$$

13. $A \cap B$

14. $B \cup C$

15. $C \cap A$

15.4 Indicate whether the following sets are infinite or finite.

16. $\{\text{the whole numbers greater than 7}\}$
17. $\{\text{the people in the United States}\}$

Sets • Statistics

Write true or false.

18. $^-9 \in W$

19. $5 \in I$

15.5 Find the range and the mode(s) for each collection of data.

20. 13, 17, 9, 1, 14, 9

21. 18, 29, 36, 13, 32, 21, 24

15.6 Find the mean and median for each collection of data.

22. 7.5, 2.3, 5.9, 8.1, 4.2

23. 71, 90, 82, 94, 88, 97

15.7 Use the bar graph for exercises 24-27.

24. Which class collected the greatest amount of food?

25. Which class collected the least amount of food?

26. What was the total amount of food collected?

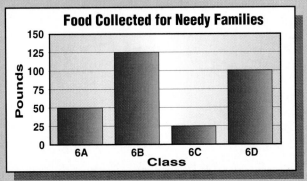

15.8 Use the line graph for exercises 27-30.

27. In what year did the Patriots win the same number of games?

28. Between what two years did the Patriots' number of wins decrease by 2?

29. Between what two years did the Patriots' number of wins increase the most?

30. Between what two years did the Patriots' number of wins decrease the most?

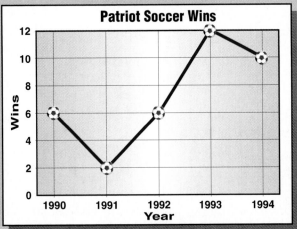

Chapter 15 Cumulative Review

1. Simplify. $(4 - 9) + {}^-5$
   a. 0
   b. ⁻10
   c. 10
   d. not given

2. Simplify. $(8 \cdot {}^-3) \cdot {}^-2$
   a. ⁻48
   b. ⁻10
   c. 48
   d. not given

3. Simplify. $({}^-12 \div 4) + (18 \div {}^-9)$
   a. ⁻5
   b. ⁻1
   c. 5
   d. not given

4. Solve. $^-12x = {}^-156$
   a. 13
   b. 144
   c. ⁻13
   d. not given

5. Write the ordered pair that identifies point *D*.
   a. (3, 2)
   b. (⁻3, 2)
   c. (3, ⁻2)
   d. (⁻3, ⁻2)

6. Find the circumference of a circle with a radius of 14 m. Use $\frac{22}{7}$ for π.
   a. 44 m
   b. 66 m
   c. 88 m
   d. not given

7. Find the area of a circle with a diameter of 0.6 m. Use 3.14 for π.
   a. 0.2826
   b. 1.1304
   c. 1.884
   d. not given

8. Name the geometric solid.
   a. triangular prism
   b. cone
   c. triangular pyramid
   d. not given

   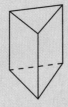

9. Find the surface area of the cube.
   a. 32 cm²
   b. 48 cm²
   c. 64 cm²
   d. not given

   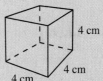

10. Find the volume of a rectangular prism with a length of 12 cm, a width of 7 cm, and a height of 5 cm.
    a. 420 cm³
    b. 210 cm³
    c. 105 cm³
    d. not given

11. Complete. 73 mm = ___ cm
    a. 7.3
    b. 0.73
    c. 0.073
    d. not given

12. Complete. 13,000 ml = ___ L
    a. 1300
    b. 130
    c. 13
    d. not given

13. Subtract.   6 yd. 1 ft. 5 in.
                 − 2 yd. 2 ft. 9 in.

    a. 4 yd. 1 ft. 4 in.
    b. 3 yd. 1 ft. 8 in.
    c. 4 yd. 3 ft. 8 in.
    d. not given

14. It is 10:00 A.M. (Pacific time) in San Francisco. What time (eastern time) is it in Detroit?
    a. 11 A.M.
    b. 12 noon
    c. 1 P.M.
    d. not given

15. Choose the most likely Fahrenheit temperature of an oven for baking cookies.
    a. 4° F
    b. 40° F
    c. 400° F
    d. not given

Sets • Statistics

Table 1: Geometric Formulas

Area of a Rectangle:

$A = l \cdot w$

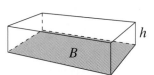

Area of a Square:

$A = s^2$

Area of a Parallelogram:

$A = b \cdot h$

Area of a Trapezoid:

$A = \frac{1}{2}(b_1 + b_2)h$

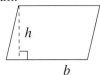

Area of a Circle:

$A = \pi r^2$

Area of a Triangle:

$A = \frac{1}{2}b \cdot h$

Volume of a Prism:

$V = B \cdot h$

B = base area

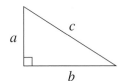

Volume of a Cylinder:

$V = \pi r^2 \cdot h$

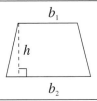

Volume of a Cone:

$V = \frac{1}{3}B \cdot h$

B = base area

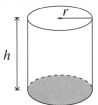

Volume of a Pyramid:

$V = \frac{1}{3}B \cdot h$

B = base area

Pythagorean Theorem:

$c^2 = a^2 + b^2$

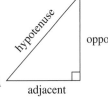

Trigonometric Ratios:

$\sin A = \dfrac{\text{opposite}}{\text{hypotenuse}}$

$\cos A = \dfrac{\text{adjacent}}{\text{hypotenuse}}$

$\tan A = \dfrac{\text{opposite}}{\text{adjacent}}$

Table 2: Measures		
	Metric Units	Customary Units
Length	1 millimeter (mm) = 0.001 meter (m) 1 centimeter (cm) = 0.01 meter decimeter (dm) = 0.1 meter 1 dekameter (dkm) = 10 meters 1 hectometer (hm) = 100 meters 1 kilometer (km) = 1000 meters	1 foot (ft.) = 12 inches (in.) 1 yard (yd.) = 36 inches 1 yard = 3 feet 1 mile (mi.) = 5,280 feet 1 mile = 1,760 yards
Mass/ Weight	1 milligram (mg) = 0.001 gram (g) 1 centigram (cg) = 0.01 gram decigram (dg) = 0.1 gram 1 dekagram (dkg) = 10 grams 1 hectogram (hg) = 100 grams 1 kilogram (kg) = 1000 grams 1 metric ton (t) = 1000 kilograms	1 pound (lb.) = 16 ounces (oz.) 1 ton (tn.) = 2,000 pounds
Capacity	1 milliliter (ml) = 0.001 liter (L) 1 centiliter (cl) = 0.01 liter deciliter (dl) = 0.1 liter 1 dekaliter (dkl) = 10 liters 1 hectoliter (hl) = 100 liters 1 kiloliter (kl) = 1000 liters	1 cup (c.) = 8 fluid ounces (fl. oz.) 1 pint (pt.) = 2 cups 1 quart (qt.) = 2 pints 1 quart = 4 cups 1 gallon (gal.) = 4 quarts
Temperature	0° Celsius . . . . . . Water freezes 100° Celsius . . . . . . Water boils	32° Fahrenheit . . . . . . Water freezes 212° Fahrenheit . . . . . . Water boils

absolute value   The distance an integer is from 0 on a number line, regardless of direction. For example, |5| = 5, and |¯5| = 5.

acute angle   An angle that measures less than 90°.

acute triangle   A triangle with three acute angles.

algebraic expression   A mathematical phrase that contains at least one variable.

angle   Two rays that share a common endpoint called the vertex.

arc   A part of a circle.

area   A measure of the amount of surface in a closed region; measured in square units.

associative property   The sum (or product) of three or more numbers is the same regardless of grouping: $a + (b + c) = (a + b) + c$, or $a \cdot (b \cdot c) = (a \cdot b) \cdot c$.

base   The number that is used as a factor in exponential form. In 3^4, 3 is the base.

capacity   The amount of fluid that a container will hold, given in terms of liquid measure.

central angle   An angle with its vertex at the center of the circle.

chord   A line segment whose endpoints are on a circle.

circle   The set of all points in a plane that are equidistant from a given point.

circumference   The distance around a circle.

commission   An amount of money earned for selling a product, based on a percentage of total sales.

commutative property   The sum (or product) of any two numbers is the same regardless of the order in which they are added (or multiplied): $a + b = b + a$, or $a \cdot b = b \cdot a$.

complementary angles   Two angles whose measures have a sum of 90°.

composite number   A number greater than 1 that has more than two factors.

congruent angles   Angles having the same measure.

congruent polygons   Polygons whose corresponding sides and corresponding angles have the same measure.

coordinate plane   A plane containing two intersecting perpendicular number lines used to graph ordered pairs of numbers.

diagonal   A line segment that joins two vertices of a polygon and is not a side of the polygon.

distributive property of multiplication   The product of a factor and a sum is equal to the sum of the products: $a \times (b + c) = (a \times b) + (a \times c)$.

divisible   A whole number is divisible by another whole number if the remainder is 0 when the first number is divided by the second number.

elements   The objects that are members of a set.

equation   A mathematical sentence that contains an equal sign, =.

equilateral triangle   A triangle with three sides of the same length.

equivalent decimals   Decimals that name the same number. For example, 0.5 = 0.50 = 0.500 are equivalent decimals.

exponent   The number that indicates how many times a base is used as a factor. In 3^4, 4 is the exponent.

exponential form   A method of writing a number using a base and an exponent. For example, 3^4 is in exponential form.

factor   A number that is multiplied by another number to give a product.

finite set   A set in which the elements can be counted or listed.

geometry   The study of points and the shapes that they form.

greatest common factor (GCF)   The greatest number that is a factor of each of two or more given numbers.

identity property of addition   The sum of any number and zero is that number: $a + 0 = a$ and $0 + a = a$.

identity property of multiplication   The product of any number and one is that number: $a \times 1 = a$ and $1 \times a = a$.

infinite set   A set that is not finite.

integers   The set of whole numbers and their opposites: $I = \{\ldots {}^-2, {}^-1, 0, 1, 2 \ldots\}$.

interest   Payment for the use of money, paid by the borrower to the lender.

intersection ($\cap$)   The set found by identifying the elements that are members of both of two sets being considered.

isosceles triangle   A triangle with at least two sides of the same length.

least common multiple (LCM)   The smallest nonzero number that is a multiple of two or more given numbers.

line   A set of points along a straight path with no endpoints.

line segment   A part of a line that has two endpoints.

mass   The amount of matter in an object.

mean   The sum of the numbers in a set divided by the number of members in the set.

median   The number that is the middle number in an ordered set of data.

mixed number   A number, such as $2\frac{1}{3}$, that is composed of a whole number and a fraction.

mode   The number that appears most frequently in a set of data.

numerical expression   A mathematical phrase made up of numbers and operations that names a number.

obtuse angle   An angle that measures greater than 90° and less than 180°.

obtuse triangle   A triangle with one obtuse angle.

opposites   Two numbers that are located the same distance from zero on the number line but in opposite directions. For example, 2 and ⁻2 are opposites.

ordered pair   A pair of numbers that gives the location of a point in a coordinate plane.

parallel lines   Lines in the same plane that never intersect.

parallelogram   A quadrilateral with both pairs of opposite sides parallel.

percent   A ratio that compares a number to 100. For example, 6% means 6 per hundred, $\frac{6}{100}$, or 0.06.

perimeter   The distance around a geometric figure.

perpendicular lines   Lines that intersect to form right angles.

place value   The value of a digit based upon its position in the numeral.

plane   A flat surface that extends endlessly in all directions.

point   An exact location in space having no length, width, or thickness.

polygon   A closed geometric figure whose sides are segments.

polyhedron   A three-dimensional figure whose faces are shaped like polygons.

prime factorization   The expression of a composite number as the product of prime numbers. For example, $60 = 2 \cdot 2 \cdot 3 \cdot 5$.

prime number   A whole number greater than 1 that has exactly two factors, 1 and itself.

principal   An amount of money that is deposited or borrowed.

prism   A polyhedron that has at least two congruent and parallel faces called bases. The other faces are parallelograms.

proportion   An equation that states that two ratios are equal.

protractor   An instrument used to measure angles.

pyramid   A three-dimensional figure with a polygon for a base and triangle faces.

radius   A line segment from the center of the circle to a point on the circle.

range   The difference between the smallest number and the largest number in a set.

rate   A ratio that compares different kinds of units, like miles and hours.

ratio   A pair of numbers used to compare one quantity to another. The ratio 10 to 6 can be written as 10:6, or $\frac{10}{6}$.

ray   A part of a line that has one endpoint and extends endlessly in one direction.

reciprocal   Two numbers whose product is 1. For example, $\frac{3}{4}$ and $\frac{4}{3}$ are reciprocals, because $\frac{3}{4} \times \frac{4}{3} = 1$.

rectangle   A parallelogram with four right angles.

relatively prime   Two numbers are relatively prime if their greatest common factor is 1.

repeating decimal   A decimal with a digit or a group of digits that repeats endlessly. For example, $0.\overline{5}$ and $0.8\overline{3}$ are repeating decimals.

rhombus   A parallelogram with all sides of the same length.

right angle   An angle that measures 90°.

right triangle   A triangle that has one right angle.

scalene triangle   A triangle with no two sides of the same length.

scientific notation   A method of expressing a number as the product of a number from 1 to 10 and a power of 10. For example, in scientific notation, 5,400 is written as 5.4×10^3.

set   A group or collection of objects.

solution   A value of the variable that makes an equation true.

square   A rectangle with all sides of the same length.

statistics   The branch of mathematics that deals with collecting, organizing, and analyzing sets of numerical data.

straight angle   An angle that measures 180°.

subset ($\subseteq$)   A set is a subset of another set if all the members of the first set are also members of the second set.

supplementary angles   Two angles whose measures have a sum of 180°.

surface area   The sum of the areas of all the faces of a geometric solid.

terminating decimal   A decimal that ends or terminates. For example, 0.5 and 0.125 are terminating decimals.

three-dimensional figure   A geometric shape whose points do not all lie in the same plane.

transversal   A line that intersects two or more lines.

trapezoid   A quadrilateral with at least one pair of opposite sides parallel.

unit rate   A ratio in which the second term is 1. For example, 18 miles per 1 hour, or 18 miles/hour is a unit rate.

variable   A letter used to represent a number in an algebraic expression.

vertex   The common endpoint shared by two rays of an angle.

volume   The amount of space contained in a three-dimensional figure; measured in cubic units.

well defined   A set having members that can be readily defined.

***x*-axis**   The horizontal number line in the coordinate plane.

***y*-axis**   The vertical number line in the coordinate plane.

The following agencies and individuals have furnished materials to meet the photographic needs of this textbook. We wish to express our gratitude to them for their important contribution.

Association of American Railroads • Astronomy Chartered, David Batchelor • British Airways • George R. Collins • Cordon Art B.V. • Corning Glass Works • Richard Frear • International Business Machines (IBM) • Brian D. Johnson • Dr. Tim Keesee • Grant H. Kessler • Library of Congress • Missouri Historical Society, St. Louis • National Aeronautics and Space Administration (NASA) • National Archives • National Cancer Institute • National Institute of Health (NIH) • National Library of Medicine • New York Academy of Medicine Library • Otis Elevator Corporation • Purdue University Bands • Sky Publishing Corporation; Dennis di Cicco • Smithsonian Institution • Solomon R. Guggenheim Foundation, New York • United States Air Force (USAF) • United States Marine Corps (USMC) • United States Navy (USN) • Unusual Films • Warner-Lambert Company

Chapter 1
Tim Keesee 7; USAF 14, 15; Missouri Historical Society, St. Louis 16; Library of Congress 23 (both); Smithsonian Institution, National Air and Space Museum 24; National Archives 25 (left); British Airways 25 (right)

Chapter 2
Unusual Films 35, 36, 50, 54, 56, 59, 64, 65; Library of Congress 55

Chapter 3
USN 71; Grant H. Kessler 76

Chapter 4
Smithsonian Institution 100; David Batchelor 101; NASA 104, 109, 121; Dennis di Cicco 105; Unusual Films 112

Chapter 5
Brian D. Johnson 128 (all); Unusual Films 130; Solomon R. Guggenheim Foundation, New York 139

Chapter 6
Unusual Films 169, 180; Library of Congress 171, 174

Chapter 7
Courtesy of the New York Academy Library of Medicine 196; Unusual Films 204; National Cancer Institute 216 (both); Warner-Lambert Company 217

Chapter 8
IBM 235; Unusual Films 236, 237, 243

Chapter 9
NASA 256, 257, 259, 263, 269; Unusual Films 265, 266, 267

Chapter 10
Purdue University Bands 291; USMC 296, 300

Chapter 11
Unusual Films 309; Richard Frear 314; George R. Collins 315

Chapter 12
Unusual Films 342, 357, 358

Chapter 13
© 1995 M. C. Escher, Cordon Art, Baarn, Holland 371, 379, 384, 385; Corning Glass Works 380; Unusual Films 396; Association of American Railroads 397

Chapter 14
Unusual Films 405, 415, 420, 421, 428; National Library of Medicine 409; NIH 424

Chapter 15
Unusual Films 440; Brian D. Johnson 442 (all); Otis Elevator Corporation 444; George R. Collins 459